W9-AQL-587

Paul Ramsey is currently Professor and Chairman of the Department of Religion at Princeton University. He is a member of the American Philosophical Association, the American Theological Society, and the National Council on Religion in Higher Education.

OTHER BOOKS BY *PAUL RAMSEY*

Basic Christian Ethics
Jonathan Edwards' Freedom of the Will (editor)
Faith and Ethics: The Theology of H. Richard Niebuhr (editor)
Christian Ethics and the Sit-In
War and the Christian Conscience

NINE MODERN MORALISTS

". . . The tendency of general benevolence to produce justice, also the tendency of justice to produce effects agreeable to general benevolence, both render justice pleasing to the virtuous mind."

Jonathan Edwards,
A Dissertation on the Nature of True Virtue

NINE MODERN MORALISTS

Paul Ramsey

A SPECTRUM BOOK
Prentice-Hall, Inc.
Englewood Cliffs, N.J.

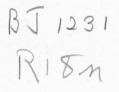

Acknowledgments

The author is grateful for permission to reprint the following material:

"Religious Aspects of Marxism," by Paul Ramsey. From *The Canadian Journal of Theology*, Vol. V. © 1959 by *The Canadian Journal of Theology*. Reprinted by permission of the publishers.

"God's Grace and Man's Guilt," by Paul Ramsey. From *The Journal of Religion*, Vol. XXXI (January 1951). Reprinted by permission of The University of Chicago Press.

"On Living Atheism: No Morality without Immortality," by Paul Ramsey. From *The Journal of Religion*, Vol. XXXVI (April 1956). © 1956 by The University of Chicago. Reprinted by permission of the publishers.

Selections from *Being and Nothingness*, by Jean-Paul Sartre, translated by Hazel Barnes. © 1956 by The Philosophical Library, Inc. Original title L'Être et le néant; © 1949 by Librairie Gallimard. Reprinted by permission of the Philosophical Library.

"Christ Transforming Relativism," by Paul Ramsey. From *Faith and Ethics: The Theology of H. Richard Niebuhr*, Paul Ramsey, ed. © 1957 by Harper & Brothers. Reprinted by permission of the publishers.

"Christian Love and Natural Law," by Paul Ramsey. From *Reinhold Niebuhr: His Religious, Social and Political Thought*, Charles W. Kegley and Robert W. Bretall, eds. © 1956 by The Macmillan Co. Reprinted by permission of the publishers.

Dedicated to my twin daughters
JENIFER and JANET RAMSEY
Individual pearls of equal price

TABLE OF CONTENTS

Introduction

Something about Christian Social Ethics

The greatness of the men whose insight and reflections are the subject of the following chapters is obviously a sufficient justification for this volume. The reader who simply wants to learn what was felt and thought and believed by some of the outstanding minds of the immediate past and of the present can, it is hoped, do so by reading the chapters of this book as expository essays. Here he will find their thought anatomized; and, in relatively brief compass, it may be possible for him to become seriously engaged in thinking their thoughts after them. Certainly, no one can come to an understanding of the latest and best of contemporary ideas and ideals by going around these men; only by going through them can one gain a deeper understanding of himself and of our epoch. That is the first purpose of this book: to provide an introduction to nine selected modern moralists.

The second purpose is constructive and critical. Exposition and explanation by themselves are not the aim of these chapters. The highest tribute one can pay any thinker, or any body of writing, is to wrestle with it; and this may well be the best way to bring out the innermost and most vital meaning of what any man has said. I trust that in this wrestling I have nowhere simply commanded an issue to be gone, or have ignored the real meaning or the strength of an idea or point of view in rejecting or reformulating it. The procedure employed in "criticism" is always an internal one. This is to say that it always seems best to go as far as one can with another man's thought, developing it up to the point where some criticism or objection or revision unfolds itself, as it were, from within the system or structure of thought under examination. In this way the most constructive results may be expected from criticism; and, in this way also, constructive and critical essays may fairly aim to be explanatory ones.

As expository essays the chapters that follow may be taken one at a time and in any order, or one or more without the others. Their constructive and critical purpose, however, connects them all together. The author has been somewhat surprised at the extent to which this is true, when preparing for publication these papers which were written in some cases years apart.

Upon this connecting theme, or constructive viewpoint, that emerges in the several chapters, some introductory comment may be helpful.

There is a growing need today for some fresh turning of the earth in the field of Christian social philosophy, or theory of society. This may seem to be the statement of an unduly ambitious undertaking. Certainly it is, for a volume of essays on some modern moralists, Christian and otherwise, even if, independent or dependent on one another, these thinkers have had wide influence in ethical and social thought. Certainly it is the statement of an unduly ambitious undertaking for an author who has been diverted from this task of urgent and central theoretical and theological importance for ethics by a need felt to write on *special problems* in Christian ethics, and who must needs continue to be so diverted for the years to come (as may *posthumous* publications show!). But this simply means that the task of Christian social ethics— basically so theological, basically so oriented toward concrete action in every sphere—is a well nigh impossible one. Still it would be to pass over in silence the *ultimate* intention even of this volume if I did not express my deepening conviction about what most sorely needs to be done in Christian social ethics at the present hour.

We can no longer spin in the spot where we have stood; the exhilaration and stimulation offered by the recent decades of theological revival will not bear simple repetition. This may be only because a rapidly changing society teaches us to inquire anew into how we are to understand our duties. You cannot step into the same river twice, or if you do you will find your feet in rather stagnant and tepid waters. Yet fresh thought is also needed because, at the level of theory itself, any formulation of Christian social ethics is always in need of reformulation, and our statements of the Christian view of political society—if the light it mediates is not to grow dim—in some ages need to be relit, and in all ages need to be kept trim. We should not hastily assume that wisdom will die with our immediate predecessors who have given us great statements of Christian social ethics, and modestly go on repeating their categories and their analysis. It may turn out to have been the case that we are less perceptive than they; yet the task of theological ethics in providing the guidelines for human action is a continuing one. Standing upon the shoulders of the past—including more than our immediate past—we may be able to see visions of lands they did not fully glimpse, or see them in a new focus made possible by their work and by our own changing times.

Each of the following chapters attempts to send down a drill into deeply buried strata beneath some perennial and therefore contemporary issue of Christian ethical reflection. These, however, are not only separate essays upon a theme of chief importance for the moralist whose thought is the subject of each chapter. They are that, and what is attempted here is certainly not the complete construction of a Christian social ethic. Yet everywhere the thread of connection should be discernible. The unifying theme may be stated as "Christ transforming the Natural Law," itself framed with conscious reference to Professor H. Richard Niebuhr's formulation of one main type of Christian social outlook as "Christ transforming Culture" or converting the works of men, in his book *Christ and Culture.*

We have to grapple with the problem of justice, both in concrete cases of decision and action, and in theory: how this is arrived at in moral choices, in law, in social institutions, and in principle; and what bearing faith in Jesus Christ may have upon human decision about right and wrong action. The reader of this volume should therefore pay attention, in his own processes of making judgment and arriving at a practical conclusion, to the *why* as well as the *what* of Christian social action: to the reason and grounds for certain criticisms and recommendations he may himself make for the good of society.

There may be some who will say that I make too much of the ancient tradition of moral theology in the Christian past—which by an optical illusion and by Protestant refusal of it may seem to be Roman Catholic teaching alone. To this I can only reply that when we make a vice of the rigidity and inflexibility of moral theology in the Roman Church we may be in danger of making a virtue of the lack of rigor and substance in our own thinking about the moral life. There will also be those who say that I give too much credit to man's natural capacity for justice, and those who say I give too little. Some readers may say that so much direction is gained from the human sense of justice that justification by faith and the proper and saving work of divine grace are destroyed, while others will be of the opinion that so much is derived from the enlightenment of our path by supernatural charity that the back of natural reason is broken and natural justice put to flight. So be it. It is high time we ceased to use these and other sweeping generalities and attempt to say with exactness and rigor what we mean in the field of Christian ethics. When persons discussing these subjects know what each means they may discover that they mean much the same thing. "By natural law," Karl Barth writes in the course of rejecting this type of ethical analysis altogether, "we mean the embodiment of what man is alleged to regard as universally right or wrong, as necessary, permissible and forbidden 'by nature,' that is, on any conceivable premise." [1] This may be what was sometimes meant by the law of nature in continental ethics and jurisprudence; but it is not the meaning of natural law in Anglo-Saxon legal and moral theory. Let me say in advance that this book in no way defends a proper place for the exercise of man's sense of natural justice, if this means something that is regarded as universally right and wrong on any conceivable premise. That generality, like the opposite generality that we certainly know that man has no such power, should perhaps be put aside as we try to study the elements that compose moral choice and action, as surely as both are put aside when we are in the actual process of arriving at practical conclusions.

Christian ethics, especially in Protestant circles, is bedeviled by the fact that, whether we come to praise or to bury them, we always have in mind continental theories of the natural law. We have in mind a whole realm populated by universal principles. This has to be corrected in the direction in which M. Jacques Maritain, the distinguished Roman Catholic philosopher, has pointed. The excessive rationalism of some strands in this tradition of ethics has to be replaced by an assertion of man's capacity to make moral decisions in the face of concrete, particular circumstance and cases, by his knowledge of the human essence through its basic inclination in him and the choices he is impelled to make, leaving in the wake of his acts of judgment a deposit of "natural" law that first becomes visible, not to abstract reason, but in *jus gentium*.

Logically joined with continental notions of the so-called law of nature, Christians whose minds have been shaped by the Reformers have most often supposed that "sin" or the sinfulness which they assert to be now characteristic of human nature also means a whole realm, a great field of corrupt forces, a distorted kingdom in which men dwell; and this affords them additional reason for denying that the natural law comprises any part of the furniture of the world in which men dwell. Or if a moralist happens to be a moderate humanist and a moderate Reformer all in one, these two realms—the realm of the light of nature and the realm of darkness—contest or divide the ground in his view of man and of morals.

In the following pages I affirm that there is some virtue in man's ordinary moral decisions, and, as it were, challenge the reader, who may have an ingrained prejudice against a wrong conception of the natural law, to say whether he means to deny this. I also affirm that no moral judgment is sufficient by nature alone, without in one way or another the saving and transforming power of the *agape* of Christ. The position I try to work out by no means forces us to a denial of a radical doctrine of sinfulness but only to reject, if I may so express it, *continental* doctrines of sin as a realm of *clear darkness* along with that false doctrine of natural justice as a realm of clear light. Along with inclinations of the human essence toward the just and good in specific decisions there may well be, too, inclinations toward evil corrupting the competence there is in us to see and to do the right. But to deny that a foundation for natural justice is laid in us would be to derive from radical doctrines of sin in the Reformation tradition the inference that sin has completely dehumanized mankind, and *that* the Reformers never meant nor said.

The co-presence of good and evil tendencies in every moral decision suggests only that our account of ethics cannot be wholly confined to an examination of decision and action within reason alone, or be based on

natural justice alone. We must also go on to speak of "Christ transforming, renewing, reshaping, and redirecting the natural law." This
point of view may be most succinctly expressed as follows: Prudence, or
practical wisdom in actual exercise, is always in the service of prior insight, conviction, or principle. Its function is the application in living
action of something prior which governs our choices. There is a prudence
which lives within reason and finds the fit embodiment for a man's sense
of justice or injustice. There is also a prudence which lives beyond
natural justice and through which divine charity finds fitting embodiment. Both these prudences become one in the Christian life; and here
is the point of fruitful Christian ethical analysis. At the point of the
exercise of prudence, of decision and action in the face of situations that
challenge us to the best resolution of them, charity leads, but a sense
of justice is there also showing us the way to the action that should be
done or not done. Only if we still are thinking in terms of realms would
this lead us to suppose a realm of justice below and a realm above,
where charity holds sway, or to locate the sense of natural justice at one
level and the elevation of men by grace and by supervening virtues at
another. Instead, love interpenetrates and invigorates justice at every
point, and often refashions it. This book undertakes to show that this is
the case in correct Christian ethical theory, as it should also be exhibited
in any adequately Christian analysis of any of the problems of practical
social ethics.

Divine *agape* or "charity" provides the supreme and controlling determination of what the Christian should do, or of what he thinks in
ethics. This is the supreme light in which we walk, and we need to seek
and to find, and then say forthrightly, what illumination a full and
realistic Christian love may throw upon the issues of action in matters
in which, we also know, the human sense of justice also speaks. The
view should be rejected which holds that the order of nature, the orders
of creation, or the structures in human relationships or human nature as
such, always supply by themselves a certain and a sufficient indication
of right and wrong action in any area, or an exhaustive account of the
"natural law means" that are licit and those that are illicit for a Christian to use in order for him to do *rightly* what love requires. This is
not to say that it is right to do "wrong" that good may come of it, or
that the end justifies the means. We should affirm rather that right and
wrong actions, justice or injustice, have not yet been adequately defined
so long as love has not also entered to reshape, enlarge, sensitize, and
sovereignly direct our apprehensions (based on nature alone) of the meaning of right and wrong action or of the just and the unjust. Where
Christ reigns, *agape* enters into a fresh determination of what it is right
to do; yet Christ does not reign over a structureless world or over men
who are bereft of any sense of natural injustice.

Perhaps a word inserted here about the relation between these chapters and the author's other writings may prove for someone a helpful introduction. In my *Basic Christian Ethics*,[2] I tried to work out, first in my own mind and then in dialogue with some solitary reader, an understanding of the *distinctive* contribution of Christian ethics to moral theory and to moral action. The way I took need not be traversed again here, except to say that I refused to locate natural law as belonging to the new that had come with Christ. I then attempted to show that, beside the dimension of Christian love, as love goes into action and in search of a social policy it is not so much a prisoner of its own unique nature as to be unable to make full use of ethical wisdom that may come from whatsoever source, nor so fully equipped as yet by its own self-imposed directives alone as not to need any helpful insight that may be found. I did not deny that natural law, in some sense, might form an important part of the completed edifice of Christian ethics, but only that it was not to be found in that which is *distinctive* and also *primary* in Christian ethics.

It is true that if philosophical ethics and worldly wisdom generally prove unable to discover an essential human nature or permanently valid norms or a competent sense of justice in men, Christian love would not thereby be blinded. It would remain dominant in its directive for our lives, and we would still understand ourselves to be required to do whatever love requires, that our lives still are judged in these terms, while we proceed to turn to social case studies—to what is lately called the science of decision-making or the study of policy—for the sort of enlightenment that is needed in framing any action, even if this is not the same as the wisdom to which the Holy Spirit leads us. This left entirely open the question whether, in fact, Christian love does not, in going in search of a social policy, find that there are within nature suggestions deeper than empirical studies would yield as to right conduct, which in turn it strengthens and renews for the sake of our companions in Christ, and constantly also refashions and transforms.

Nowhere in the following pages do I intend to affirm that natural justice or the law of nature is basic Christian ethics. Nor, of course, do I concede that Christian love would be halted, lamed, or blinded, or Jesus Christ any less the lord of life, if there are more ethical principles to be found in the land of the living than is allowed by certain contextual or situational ethics. From the fact that my earlier book on ethics was criticized from both sides, I conclude that the point of it was made clear to at least any two reviewers combined. Certain Lutheran and Calvinist commentators objected to the emphasis placed on the need of neighbor-regarding love for enlightenment, for an *"enlightened* unselfishness," and they declared that while this was ethics it was not a Christian ethic. These correctly discerned that I did not mean to assert that the Scriptures are the only and a *sufficient* rule for practice, nor that the Holy Spirit releases us altogether from seeking worldly wisdom. On the other hand, rationalists and Boston personalists declared they found certain hidden and unacknowledged "value judgments" in the volume, and they criticized from this point of view any attempt to rest Christian ethics primarily (though not exclusively) on revelation. These correctly discerned the significant role allowed for moral reason.

If, instead of the foregoing, I ought rather to make full confession of how my mind has changed in the past ten years, this could mean at most that my intention may have come to greater clarity because of something my former teacher, Professor H. Richard Niebuhr, chanced to remark about my first book, which was published the year before his *Christ and Culture*. He once commented to me, "The position you have elaborated is 'Christ transforming Natural Law'; while the point of view I sought to express was 'Christ transforming Relativism.' " In subsequent essays (here reprinted) I have tried to show, at considerable length, that this motif ("Christ transforming Natural Law") is, despite appearances, profoundly at work in the thought of both Reinhold Niebuhr and H. Richard Niebuhr, and that, if their reflections were acknowledged or consciously shaped in this direction, the result would be a more adequate statement of Christian ethics, on or off their own premises.

The present volume carries forward this same effort to lift this motif into fuller view as the real groundwork of Christian ethics in the thought of many of its greatest contemporary exponents, e.g., in the chapter where the writings of Paul Tillich and Emil Brunner are examined in some detail. It also carries forward the effort to gain a sound understanding of natural law, law, and jurisprudential reason and decision-making, e.g, in the chapters on Jacques Maritain and Edmond Cahn. The reader may be either dismayed or happily surprised to discover the extent to which it can be demonstrated that the Roman Catholic social philosopher Jacques Maritain, this country's most renowned Protestant theologian and social analyst Reinhold Niebuhr, and the professor of jurisprudence Edmond Cahn, are each *radical revisionists* among natural law theorists. Consequently, their views are not so far apart as is often supposed.

Ethical reflection could easily go too far in that direction, with the result that the *agape* of Christ might seem to be only a vague religious term for the best human moral insight which certifies him as one of our great teachers. To be *in* the world with transforming power, the *agape* of Christ must clearly be understood as not *of* this world. Lest *agape* be naturalized or become identified as only an immanent principle of righteousness, this volume also carries forward an analysis of the primary dimension in Christian ethics which stems from revelation. This is the ultimate purpose, for example, of the first two chapters on Dostoevski, and of the final chapter on man's Exodus from the natural law; but, more importantly, the unique perspectives of Christian ethics are also sought to be clarified and strengthened throughout every chapter that also carries forward the analysis of the natural bases of morality and the relation between the two.

The possible constructive contribution of Sartre's existentialism is not in the area of this main concern, but in connection with the special ethical problem indicated by the chapter title. However, the challenge of Sartre to ethics natural or revealed cannot be ignored. His position needs fair and full exposition, and then to be wrestled with. It is particularly fruitful to view him not, as ordinarily is the case, as one who strongly objects to objective standards in morality; but as one who throws down the gauntlet to every form of I-Thou sentimentalism. Today there exists a whole school of Christian thought that seems to believe that I-Thou "meeting" is so readily possible in interpersonal relations that Jesus Christ need not have died or have been raised by God's mighty hand to restore and enact covenant among men; or that it is somehow more credible to affirm that in a man's present experience of authentic existence or authentic border or crisis situations the Word of God is made flesh than to affirm that in the past event of Jesus Christ that Word dwelt among us. It may be of importance for the Christian reader to face up to what I call Sartre's phenomenology of fallen humanity if he is to think without sentimentality about Christian love and its possibility or impossibility. I have some reason also to hope that any reader will find this chapter an aid to understanding this important contemporary philosopher.

Permission to republish articles or chapters has been granted me by the following journals or publishers: *The Journal of Religion*, for the chapters on Dostoevski, from their issues XXXI, 1 (Jan. 1951) and XXXVI, 2 (April, 1956); the *Canadian Journal of Theology*, for the chapter on Marx which appeared in V (1959), 3; The Macmillan Company, for the chapter on Reinhold Niebuhr, from Charles W. Kegley and Robert W. Bretall, ed.: *Reinhold Niebuhr: His Religious, Social and Political Thought* (New York: 1956); and Harper and Bros., for the chapter on H. Richard Niebuhr, from Paul Ramsey, ed.: *Faith and Ethics: The Theology of H. Richard Niebuhr* (New York: 1957). Thus, five of the following chapters have been published before in separate places, while four are entirely new; and of the nine moralists treated, my presentation and analysis of four of them has appeared before, while in the case of five of these subjects (Sartre, Tillich, Brunner, Maritain, Cahn) this volume offers hitherto unpublished exposition. The author hopes, if he does not exactly expect, that these essays on nine modern moralists, brought together in one volume, will prove to be of use to the general reading public, to philosophers and theologians, to Christian readers generally, and to students in colleges and in seminaries.

THE CLARENCE D. ASHLEY LECTURES ON LAW AND THEOLOGY

Finally it should be noted that the final two chapters are based on two of three lectures given at the New York University School of Law in 1958 as the Clarence D. Ashley Lectures on Law and Theology. Since the Second World War there has been increasing consideration within the legal profession of the role of ethics and theology. Many legal educators and practicing attorneys have realized that theological ideas have a direct effect in the shaping of legal norms and in the operation of these norms. It was out of this interest, among some members in the community of the New York University Law Center, in the issues of religion and law that the School of Law joined with Judson Memorial Church and the Episcopal Diocese of New York to establish the Clarence D. Ashley Memorial Lectures on Law and Theology. The lecture series was named for a prominent churchman and former Dean of the New York University School of Law, Dr. Clarence De Grande Ashley. Dr. Ashley was Dean of the Law School from 1896 until his death in 1916. The 1957-58 Committee for The Clarence D. Ashley Memorial Lectures on Law and Theology was composed of the following persons: Professors Elmer M. Million, Sheldon D. Elliot, Robert B. McKay, and Bertel M. Sparks; Assistant Professor Richard W. Duesenberg; Marcus E. Powers, Instructor and Assistant to the Dean, New York University School of Law; and Rev. Howard R. Moody, Pastor, Judson Memorial Church, New York City, Rev. Norman O. Keim, Eastern Regional Director, Department of Campus Christian Life, Board of Education and Publications of the American Baptist Convention, William Stringfellow, Esq., Counsel, East Harlem Protestant Parish, New York City.

I am grateful to Dean Russell Niles of the New York University School of Law, to Professor Elmer Million and the members of the Ashley Lecture Committee, for having afforded me this opportunity to speak and for having come and stayed to listen. The latter was but one more expression of the friendly hospitality I received at the Law School from faculty and students alike. Finally, I would be negligent to one to whom I owe much of the challenge and stimulation—first from his writings and then from a number of long conversations—to which in great measure these lectures were a response, if I did not mention with gratitude the name of Professor Edmond Cahn.

Princeton University   Paul Ramsey
Princeton, N.J.
1962

One

Fyodor Dostoevski
On Living Atheism: No Morality without Immortality

It is certain that the mortality or immortality of the soul must make an entire difference to morality. And yet philosophers have constructed their ethics independently of this: they discuss to pass an hour.—Pascal, *Pensées*, No. 219.

[handwritten: Camus]

I

"The fool says in his heart, 'There is no God.'" This verse from the Psalms (14:1 and 53:1) draws our attention to the fool saying such a thing not in his head but in his heart. Therefore, the most illuminating commentary upon this verse will be one which draws out the existential consequence and not, as did Anselm, the theoretical inconsistency of atheism. What does it mean for a human being, possessed as he is of human or "finite freedom," to attempt from his heart to live by and live out the thought that for him there is no God?

First of all, let us avoid the mistake of supposing that man has need of God only for the sense that "underneath are the Everlasting Arms." Religious people do believe that God upholds and strengthens them, and without much doubt theism provides a world view which upholds human being and human value. Still there is another primary meaning of God in human experience: He is one who, on account of the dynamic upthrust of human freedom, alone can put a limit upon man and set boundaries that may not be removed. Both the atheist Nietzsche and the theist Kierkegaard knew this; and as the former exclaimed, "If there were a god, I could not endure not being he," so the latter wrote, "Without God, man is [not too weak, but] too strong for himself." [1]

This is the mode of free personal existence in this world when one actually lives by the thought that there is no God: without God, there is no limit fixed to the ever renewed and restless *deployment* of human freedom. A limitless exercise of freedom is the meaning of atheism when one actually lives by the thought that there is no God. Peerless are the writings of Dostoevski in portraying this consequence of the foolish thoughts of men's hearts. He poured scorn upon the parlor atheists of his day, who, under what they believed to be French influence, were

11

setting about to remake the world more nearly to their hearts' desire. He alone among them, Dostoevski believed, really understood the meaning of a *vital* atheism, for his hosanna of faith had burst forth from a huge furnace of doubt, doubt lived to the hilt in his passionate thought. Those atheists were simply not alive enough to the unavoidable meaning of the idea of God's non-existence.

This is the genesis of human action *de profundis* that Dostoevski probes in the analysis of Raskolnikov's crime. One by one, the explanations that only explain away the reality fall to the ground; Raskolnikov sheds external layers of self-understanding until finally he sees himself for what he is and is loved by Sonia even as what he is. He did not do the deed because of poverty or just to get money ("If I'd simply killed her because I was hungry . . . I should be *happy* now"), or because the roof of his garret was too low and cramping for the soul, or to provide for his widowed mother and save his sister, or to benefit mankind by building parks for the children of the poor to play in. He was not impelled by a mother-fixation, according to critics who have noted that he was unable to return Sonia's love until after his mother was dead. (Perhaps Dostoevski does not explicitly dismiss this latter-day explanation because he was not so stupid as to think of it!) He did not commit the murder simply as an act rationally required by his own theory that there are "exceptional men" for whom the ordinary laws of morality have no bearing—though this comes as close as any *theory* can to the existential truth. Yet even this is "almost all talk!"

> I wanted *to have the daring.* . . . I only wanted to have the daring, Sonia! That was the whole cause of it! . . . I wanted to murder without casuistry, to murder for my own sake, for myself alone! . . . It wasn't to help my mother I did the murder—that's nonsense—I didn't do the murder to gain wealth and power and to become a benefactor of mankind. Nonsense! I simply did it; I did the murder for myself alone. . . . I wanted to find out then and quickly whether I was a louse like everybody else or a man. Whether I can step over barriers or not, whether I dare stoop to pick up or not, whether I am a trembling creature or whether I have the *right*.[2]

The reason is that the deed was for no reason; the explanation is that it was on account of no casuistry; the cause is that it was for no apprehendable *cause*—but only out of freedom for freedom's sake. The human spirit, like God in the beginning, broods over chaos with a will to shape itself and its world. Freedom acts out of nothing to create a deed which before was not. Bound to the moorings of finitude, man's finite freedom nevertheless transcends any particular force or power that would shape him and it also transcends any particular inner cosmos.

Imaging God, man creates *ex nihilo* an act and a self which before were not. Raskolnikov's criminal act was not the offspring of any rational immaculate conception but the product of meonic freedom. *Opto, ergo sum.* In order to protect and to portray this freedom, Dostoevski represents the action before the act as taking place almost in a trance, and shows Raskolnikov as never able to bring himself to *think out* clearly and in succession the steps and precautions he proposes to take:

> And, indeed, if it had ever happened that everything to the least point could have been considered and finally settled, and no uncertainty of any kind had remained, he would, it seems, have renounced it all as something absurd, monstrous and impossible. But a whole mass of unsettled points and uncertainties remained. . . . But those were all trifles which he had not even begun to consider, and indeed he had no time. He was thinking of the chief point, and putting off trifling details, until he *could believe in it all.*[3]

The chief point was whether he could act or not, whether he could be what he was to become or not, and, by becoming, *be.* The final verdict at the trial comes, then, as the height of irony, for the lawyers and jury "immediately drew the deduction that the crime could only have been committed through temporary mental derangement, through homicidal mania" because it was "*without object* or the pursuit of gain." [4] Clearly, a man must be *beside himself* if he is not determined by calculable motives, which is to say, if he *is himself* (albeit an as yet unredeemed self) and not a railway timetable!

Given the dynamic nature of human freedom, it follows—or so Dostoevski teaches in various characters and situations he portrays—that without God there is no limit upon the exercise of such freedom. We have now to examine the chief ways in which this boundless and boundary-transcending freedom of man deploys itself; and these are (1) individually, (2) socially, and (3) in general or universally. Freedom in the heart of a person attempting to live by the thought that there is no God cannot, in principle, stop short of deploying itself against the conditions of its own existence in the world, against every structure of social existence, and against every moral norm. Without God, there is *nothing* a man is *bound not to do*.

1. As an individual matter, or with reference to itself, finite freedom, which attempts to *live by* and *live out* the thought that there is no God, cannot, in principle, stop short of deploying itself against the conditions of its own existence in the world. This mode of human freedom saying in its heart that there is no God Dostoevski depicts in the person of Kirillov in *The Possessed.* Suicide is an inner logical consequence of *vital* atheism.

Kirillov is a man with more than a single idea. He plays gleefully with the child next door. He drinks tea and sleeps. He practices gymnastic exercises to keep himself in good physical health. "Yes, I'm fond of life!" says he. "What of it?" [5] Kirillov is going to commit suicide. There is no environing cause or compelling reason for his doing so: precisely *this* is the reason and the cause! There are lots of suicides "with good cause. But to do it without any cause at all, simply for self-will, I am the only one." [6] Kirillov's passion is the achievement of full human freedom. There will be full freedom only when there is *nothing* a man is *bound not to do*. With reference to the agent himself, "there will be full freedom when it will be just the same to live or not to live." As long as a man exists and feels bound to accept his own existence, he is not fully free; and when full freedom is, he is not. When finite freedom becomes god, that moment "this god will not be." [7]

Kirillov says in his heart there is no God, and he wants to live and to die by what this means:

> If there is no God, then I am God. . . . If God exists, all is His will and from His will I cannot escape. If not, it's all my will and I am bound to show self-will. . . . I want to manifest my self-will. . . . I am bound to shoot myself because the highest point of my self-will is to kill myself with my own hands . . . without any cause at all, simply from self-will. . . . I am bound to show my unbelief. . . . I have no higher idea than disbelief in God . . . to recognize that there is no God and not to recognize at the same instant that one is God oneself is an absurdity. . . . The attribute of my godhead is self-will! That's all I can do to prove in the highest point my independence and my new terrible freedom. For it is very terrible. I am killing myself to prove my independence and my new terrible freedom.[8]

In short, when God is dead, at the same instant one becomes God himself; and when one is like God, fully free, at the same instant he must die, since he is no longer bound to accept the conditions of his own existence. Of course, there is a still higher manifestation of freedom to come, namely, to recognize that one is *sovereign* and yet not deploy the terrible freedom which one has. This greater glory is reserved for future generations: whether they live or whether they die will be up to the Lord, freedom. But now one single individual (Kirillov) must provide crucial demonstration of the freedom of man and of the boundless nature of this freedom.

If all this sounds too extravagant or too peculiarly Russian, it may be in order to point out that so serene a mind and precisely French and clear a writer and so rationalistic a philosopher as the neo-Thomist Jacques Maritain accepts the complete validity of the foregoing analysis.

He writes: "Every absolute experience of atheism, if it is conscientiously and rigorously followed, ends by provoking its psychical dissolution, in suicide." Absolute humanism wills its own freedom; it must subordinate everything else to this absolute freedom; and the last thing which must be subordinated if one is to have no God is one's own being. To live atheism means subordinating one's own existence to one's own absolute independence.[9]

It would be more to the point, however, to compare Dostoevski's prophetic vision of what happens in freedom and by freedom when a person lives from the thought that there is no God with the substantial actualization of this expectation in one of the central teachings of *atheistic* existentialism today. *If* there were a God, there would be a fixed, given human nature; and if a fixed structure of human nature, no freedom. *Since* there is freedom, there is no fixed nature and no God. This is a basic belief of atheism in its existential form. So far, so good.

But now the philosopher notices, as any sober-minded person will, that man is actually not free in many respects—those precisely which may be classified under the heading of the physical and historical conditions of his existence. The bondage of man to forces other than his own freedom goes, indeed, to the root of his biological being. Here we are in the world without anyone asking us. We were simply thrown into existence by a natural act or event of cohabitation. Every person, as the saying goes, was once only a gleam in his father's eye. "What, without asking, hither hurried whence?/And, without asking, whither hurried hence?" There is something almost insulting about all this, or at least everyone knows that his *experienced freedom* is a reality quite *incommensurate* with this origin. The incommensurability between the dimension of freedom and the impingement of natural forces upon man presents a problem to the person determined to live in "transcendence" and not in "immanence." What shall he do?

The prescription is that he should *think through* the idea of his own suicide. He should allow the thought that he need not hold his hands back from self-slaughter to penetrate and pervade every moment of his personal subjective consciousness, and then not actually do the deed. As a "thought-experiment," suicide is to be taken quite seriously, perhaps more seriously than if the deed were done. To what purpose and with what result? So that ever after one may live with the exhilaration of perfect freedom. For now he has become the one who gives himself being and each moment continues to give himself being. He lives from freedom and not from any necessity. He is his own creator and sustainer and bows to no one and no thing. Freedom will then have encompassed within its grasp, if only in thought, what formerly came from beyond himself. Each moment he passes from death into life, from non-being into being, by his own choice and by the power of personal freedom. By the unlimited deployment of freedom into the furthest reaches of the thought that one might hurry himself hence, one becomes he who each moment hurries himself whence.

The contrast is complete: a religious man who says in his heart there is a God receives his life daily by divine appointment as a gift and a task set before him. The man who says in his heart there is no God, if he is free and not just a pawn, receives his life daily by self-appointment. Thus it is impossible to live by and live out the thought that there is no God except by exalting one's self beyond all measure. "The human being who denies his nature as a created being," Marcel writes, "ends up by claiming for himself attributes which are a sort of caricature of those that belong to the Uncreated." [10]

2. Socially, or with reference to others or to the social order, finite freedom, which attempts to *live by* and *live out* the thought that there is no God, cannot stop short of deploying itself against every existing condition of social existence. This mode of human freedom Dostoevski depicts in the revolutionaries in *The Possessed*, especially in their leader Pyotr Stepanovitch and his theoretician Shigalov. Without God, freedom is boundless; and boundless freedom inevitably demands boundless submission. This is the essence of revolution and, before that, of atheistic social liberalism.

Here, too, there is inward self-contradiction in the working-out of unlimited social freedom. Shigalov pronounces: "I am perplexed by my own data and my conclusion is a direct contradiction of the original idea with which I start. Starting from unlimited freedom, I arrive at unlimited despotism. I will add, however, that there can be no solution of the social problem but mine." And another member at the meeting explains: "He suggests as a final solution of the question the division of mankind into two unequal parts. One-tenth enjoys absolute liberty and unbounded power over the other nine-tenths. The others have to give up all individuality and become, so to speak, a herd . . . through boundless submission." [11] And elsewhere this solution is mockingly described as "the last new principle of general destruction for the sake of the ultimate good. He demands already more than a hundred million heads for the establishment of common sense in Europe; many more than they demanded at the last Peace Congress." [12]

Again, as freedom comes up against the conditions of individual existence, so now freedom is confronted by and must overcome the stolid contentment of the masses who, in their apathy, insist that the irrationalities of the world must be accepted. "Bridges are rarely on fire, and fires in towns occur only at regular intervals, in turn, at the proper season. In the law courts judgments are as wise as Solomon's, and the jury only take bribes through the struggle for existence, to escape starvation." [13] The techniques of the revolutionaries, described by Pyotr after his arrest, direct their efforts against just this complacency:

> When asked what was the object of so many murders and scandals and dastardly outrages, he answered with feverish haste, that "it was with the idea of systematically undermining the foundations, systematically destroying society and all principles; with the idea of nonplussing everyone and making hay of everything, and then, when society was tottering, sick and out of joint, cynical and sceptical though filled with an intense eagerness for self-preservation and for some guiding idea, suddenly to seize it in their hands." [14]

This, of course, is almost frenetic exaggeration, but it is exaggeration with a point.

Perhaps it would be appropriate to append here a more sober statement of the same issue, one made in a day which has seen Dostoevski's predictions abundantly fulfilled in "that crisis which bears the name of the totalitarian state":

> The state must know its limits. . . . Its realization of its subordination to a higher power is no mere political ornament but the foundation of political wisdom. . . . There is only one limit to the sovereignty of the state; it is the knowledge of the sovereignty of God. . . . Where this is lacking there is no limit to the *superbia* of the state, for there is only one remedy for *superbia*—fear of God. How else shall the power which claims for itself the title of "supreme" realize its limits save in that most supreme power? By the will of the people? As if the will of the people could not itself fall victim to that *superbia!* The unlimited sovereignty of the people and the unlimited sovereignty of the state are simply two forms of *superbia,* the one individualistic, the other totalitarian.[15]

Or, rather, both totalitarian!

3. We have examined the foolishness of the conviction of the heart that there is no God as it affects the self's freedom in relation to itself and in relation to the social order. These two meet in and arise from a general or universal principle which is the foundation of both. Without God, no moral obligation. Dostoevski saw clearly that "an immortal human soul" is the only ground for the truth of morality or for integrity of conscience. This will require somewhat more extended exposition.

II

One teaching of the philosophy of existentialism is likely to prove a permanent contribution to contemporary thought. This is the doctrine that in human affairs everything, or almost everything, depends upon man's understanding of himself. What man thinks of himself or believes himself to be, this he *becomes*. If he believes himself a thriving earthworm, unfit to meditate much upon God, the human mind, or the *summum bonum*, for him the depths of his being and the real world contract to these wormly limits. If he believes himself a child of God, this as surely he becomes. Thus, as Gabriel Marcel makes the point, "Man depends, to a very great degree, on the idea he has of himself and . . . this idea [this self-understanding] cannot be degraded without at the same time degrading man." [16]

In his book *Man against Mass Society*, Marcel employs this insight (which, after all, is a bit of wisdom at least as old as the words "As a man thinks in his heart, so is he") in an analysis of the death throes of humanity audible today and the striking degradation of human beings in modern times. A person sinks to the most pitiable and miserable level of human existence not when he is degraded in the eyes of another but when he is degraded in his own eyes, when he himself accepts the judgment that he is nothing and worth less than nothing. This was the technique of degradation used in the concentration camps. The aim was not simply to transform men and women little by little into human waste products but to transform them into beings who in the very depths of their own souls were conscious of themselves as mere waste. No person is completely victimized until he thus annuls himself. Therefore, Marcel writes:

> The persecutor . . . sets out to destroy in another human being that being's awareness, whether illusory or not, of having a value. He must become for himself what those who judge him, or claim to judge him, say he is in reality; the person who is worth nothing must recognize his own nothingness, and it is not enough that he should do so intellectually; it is necessary also that he should *sense* his nothingness, as we sense an odour of decay. . . . But why . . . is this necessary? . . . Because this is the sole means of having this other human being wholly at one's mercy; a being who retains even the smallest awareness of his own value remains capable of reacting against us in a way which, if not dangerous, is at least vexing.[17]

Such is the plight not only of some people at a few times and places in recent years. It is, quite literally, the predicament of every human being who lives in an environment calculated to degrade his understanding of himself and of the being of others. Environmental pressures and mechanical techniques more and more subordinate people to things. And, meantime, philosophers of various schools since the eighteenth century "have set themselves systematically to darken the human sky" and remove from our understanding of man any living link with the supernatural. Most of the materialists of the nineteenth century "were still men who went on behaving as if they held the religious beliefs which they declared they had lost. The fact was that they benefited, without being aware of it, from the Christian atmosphere around them. Today one may say that this is no longer the case and that, on the contrary [the mental climate of materialism having undergone a strange, yet not unexpected, modification], the materialist [today] tends to live more and more like a materialist; and we are beginning to know what that means." [18] The whole modern world may, without too great exaggeration, be described as a vast and ghastly concentration camp in which social forces and movements of thought combine to destroy for the individual the divine significance of his name. When we live by and live out the thought that "God is dead," our own self-understanding and our estimate of the being of others suffer radical alteration. Forsaking all recourse to the Transcendent, we thereby admit in our own hearts that we may, not improperly, be flattened out by earthly ends and means. We may think we still place high value upon human life, but the convictions on which this rests have already been abandoned by multitudes of people. If we still have the *feeling* that man is a thing of worth, that is only because the checks we draw daily have not yet cleared the bank, where it will be discovered that the account is exhausted—indeed, long overdrawn or, rather, *under-deposited*.

Today it has become extraordinarily easy to live by the "golden rule," which in these times may require only the reciprocal exchange of *dis*respect: "I'm no good, but neither is my neighbor," [19] I'm only an earthbound animal, and so is my neighbor. It is by no means evident that human beings have any transcendent value if the Transcendent does not value them or that the individual has any sacredness or infinite worth unless there is an Infinite God who values him. Loss of the sense of the Sacred or the attempt to understand one's self wholly in spatio-temporal terms leads inevitably to the debasing of man beyond all measure.

The modern period began with expectations other than these. The Enlightenment did not anticipate that deicide would end in suicide; or cutting man's living link with the Eternal, in conscientious murder. The anticipation was rather of a heavenly city or at least a friendly city upon the earth, a hope eloquently expressed by Versilov in Dostoevski's novel *A Raw Youth*:

> I suppose the struggle to be over. There is quiet again after the curses and the hissing and the mud; men are left alone as they desired, the great idea of the past is gone from them; the mighty disposer of power from whom they drew their food and warmth for so long has disappeared like the sun at evening in the pictures of Claude Lorrain: one would think that it is the last day of mankind. All of a sudden men realize that they are alone, they feel as though they were orphans. . . . When they are deserted

they will stand together more closely and more affectionately, they will hold each other's hands in the knowledge that henceforward they together represent the whole universe. For to fill the place of the lost great idea of immortality men will give to the world, to nature, to their neighbors, to every blade of grass, that overflowing love which they formerly consecrated to the vision of eternal life. So frenziedly will they cherish the earth and its life that gradually they will grow accustomed to seeing in it their beginning and end, and they will cherish it with a special affection, no longer the same as before. They will explore the phenomena of nature and discover unexpected secrets in her, for they will be looking at the world with new eyes. . . . They will come to themselves and hasten to embrace one another, knowing that their days are numbered and that there is nothing else. They will work for one another, each giving his earnings to all and being only too glad to do so. Every child will know that he can find a father or mother in any human creature—for every man and woman will think as he watches the setting sun: Tomorrow may be my last day; but what matter? —There will be others here when I am gone, and after them their children. So they will be supported, not by the hope of a meeting beyond the grave, but by the thought that others will replace them on earth who will always love and tremble for one another. They will turn quickly to love to stifle the sorrow that will be deep down in their hearts. They will be bold and fearless for themselves but nervous for others, each fearful for the safety and happiness of his neighbor. They will be mutually affectionate without embarrassment and as endearing together as children; when they meet they will regard each other with a searching and meaningful look, a look filled with both love and sadness.[20]

The great Russian novelist himself did not believe that this would be the outcome of mankind's outgrowing religion; his own view he expresses through one of the characters in *The Brothers Karamazov*, who declares roundly that, without belief in immortality, there would be no basis at all for morality. There is no law of nature, he affirms, that men should love mankind, and, if there has been any love on earth hitherto, it is not due to any laws of our human nature but simply because men have believed in immortality. This (to us) astonishing doctrine was no mere artistic creation among others within the structure of the novel. Dostoevski accepted this judgment in sober earnestness in real life, and this gave him his remarkable clairvoyance about what is happening in our world half a century later. In his *Diary of a Writer* he wrote:

> Neither a man nor a nation can live without a "higher idea," and there is only one such idea on earth, that of an immortal human soul; all the other "higher ideas" by which men live follow from that. . . . Following on the loss of the idea of immortality, suicide appears a complete and ineluctable necessity for every man who is in the slightest degree above the

level of the beasts of the field. . . . The idea of immortality is life itself, the definitive formulation and the first source of the truth and integrity of conscience.[21]

In attempting to understand how the idea of an immortal human soul is "the definitive formulation and the first source of the truth and integrity of conscience" or (shorthand for this) how there can be "no morality without immortality," it must be grasped as a purely Christian or a purely religious idea and not at all as a matter of prudential calculation. We must not make the mistake of attributing to the genius of Dostoevski the perhaps puerile and childish idea that, without supernatural sanctions threatening us with punishment in hell or promising rewards in heaven, there would be no reason for good behavior. I say this latter may be childish; yet even this was the firm conviction of many great thinkers of the past—including John Locke our more recent master—and it ill suits the present myth-making generation to dismiss it lightly.

In any case this was not what Dostoevski meant. Not what the agent calculates as *his own future* destiny deterring him from evil or impelling him to do the difficult good, but what he *now* feels about the significance of human life, in his own self-understanding and understanding of his neighbor—this gives basis for morality. It is not peril of eternal torment but a man's estimate of the *present* meaning of another man's life which ultimately holds his hand back from murder. To speak of the idea of an immortal human soul means, in the present context, the present significance of the life of an individual in relation to God which no action of ours should contradict. This same estimate we express with a whole cluster of other religious notions: man is a child of God, created by God, in God's image, and, if we are Christians, redeemed and renewed by God's prodigious grace in Christ. Without immortality, which in sum contains all God's estimate of human life, anything is permitted which the necessity of the historical situation seems to require of us for the good of the group or cause to which we belong.

In *Crime and Punishment* Raskolnikov's torment of conscience arose not from the fact that he violated long-standing social mores, nor from the conflict between his action and his "generalized other" internalized, nor from the contradiction between his individual action and his "social self." Instead, "an immortal human soul" was "the definitive formulation and the first source of the truth and integrity of [Raskolnikov's tortured] conscience." In killing the dirty old pawnbroker, he not only denied the divine significance of her name but his own as well, and slew himself.

Thinking which proceeds without this thought of God's hold on man is already murderous thinking and will soon prove so in the act. The word "murderous" is not too strong a word for conceptions of the world without God in which "everything is permitted." We easily understand how a person would be put on his good behavior in the presence of the Queen Mother, for the time being restraining passion and temper. How can we avoid understanding the same in the presence of God, in whose absence no one ever stands or possesses being? How else give grounds for morality which will not finally prove to be immoral grounds?

Tracing immorality home to man's inmost understanding of himself without God parallels the teaching of Jesus which traces murder home to its source in the inner motive of the heart. Anger which holds a lasting grudge against a brother, jealousy which stands in the way of reconciliation with him, and the attitude of despising him as an utter fool were condemned by Jesus as severely as the old law condemned actually killing him. To prohibit murder fixes our attention upon a symptom. In forbidding anger and envy, Jesus diagnosed the disease itself which needs to be cured. And in this stress on inward motive Jesus was a true spokesman for Israel, as can be seen in the Old Testament where many injunctions, such as not coveting, loving God and one's neighbor, and Job's reference to "adultery of the eye," can be obeyed only with the right inner intention. This does not mean, however, that actual murder is not an additional crime. It only means that the actual murder began long ago and deeper down in the hardness and anger of the heart. Such a state of mind is made of a piece with the act. The deed simply extends the thought in the direction in which thought has already moved.

It is important to distinguish between momentary thoughts and a steady or habitual frame of mind. John Wesley (and before him Martin Luther) commented on Jesus' teaching about lustful thoughts: "You can't prevent birds from flying over your head, but you can keep them from building nests in your hair." This applies also to what Jesus says about anger. Passing moods of irritation or even moments of impulsive anger may come and go like birds over our heads. Of course, in one of these heated moments a man may actually kill, and this shows that purely impulsive actions are not unimportant.

Nevertheless, Jesus was talking about hardened hatred, holding a grudge. He was speaking about wrath that persists as a permanent attitude. Paul approved of a certain sort of anger, but quite in the spirit of Jesus' teaching he said: "Be angry but do not sin; do not let the sun go down on your wrath" (Eph. 4:26). Jesus also had in mind wrath that continues after the sun goes down. Such a steady inner attitude means indeed that one has already committed murder in his heart. In thought he has already blotted out the image of the other person and consigned him to oblivion. Like a savage practicing magic, he has drawn a picture of his enemy in the sand and has already stuck a knife through it. He says in his heart, "You fool! You nonentity! The world would be better off, or at least no worse off, if you were no longer in it and if in your stead there were only empty space." Thus he lives absolutely unreconciled to the being of another man, unwilling to accept him alive. *Raca,* "Thou fool!" is an Aramaic word meaning "empty." It was an expression of utter contempt. Saying *"Raca"* to another person obliterates him and expresses thought which blots him out and thus is continuous with the murderous deed itself. Actually killing him adds nothing essential that the steadfastly angry mind has not already thought through implicitly. The enemy has therefore already been wiped out in thought before this happens in fact.

Is it true only of anger that people cut their actions from the same cloth that thoughts are made of? Are wrath and "Thou fool!" the only thoughts of the heart out of which come acts of great importance for man's estimate of his fellow man? Is not the same thing true most notably of man's self-understanding in any epoch? Is it not true of any fundamental "philosophy of life" that it never fails to operate, whatever else one may think or say he believes? What, then, is the importance for human life—and for preventing the murder of men in great groups—of the religious conviction that the individual should be evaluated in the light of God's estimate of him in creating man in His own image an immortal human soul? Surely the answer is scrawled in blood across our historical heaven: that without this conviction man will finally be regarded as a mere pawn to be moved around by those who hold the centers of power in society, for what they regard as the common good. The idea that man belongs only to the group and not to his Creator is one that already deals in death—if not today, then tomorrow! What people say in their hearts about man and God has a great deal to do with whether or not in their morality they have any real regard for human life—if not today, then tomorrow!

This is the meaning of Dostoevski's thesis that without immortality there is no morality. God has made us and not we ourselves. God created our neighbors, and we did not. God creates and sustains in existence every individual human being who has existence. He alone should place death's terminal point at the end of an individual's existence, for he alone can be beside us in death to see that we cannot drift beyond his love and care. This fixes God's canon against slaughter and against self-slaughter. The Law given on Sinai only revealed that this is true. The fact that we now are God's special creature raises us above physical nature and above bondage to the social group. God has made us for himself and not for mere inclusion within society. Man is a *theonomous* animal: this means that only God has final governance over him. Man is a *religious* animal: this means that he is built for worship and for fellowship with God, and not for the supremacy of earthly goals over his life.

Without the conviction that this is true, there is no basis for morality. *Why* this should be true is no less easy to see than *that* it is true. Without belief that our neighbor is an immortal soul made for his life with God and not merely for his life with us, nothing is left in our estimate of him to prevent our taking his life whenever some worldly reason seems to demand that we do so. We may not yet have done the deed, any more than we actually take the lives of everyone with whom we are angry. But an unreconciled spirit who would be happier were another person not alive has already blotted him out in thought. The same is true when we think about man from any other point of view than God's estimate of him.

The Declaration of Independence affirms that all men have been endowed by their Creator with certain inalienable rights. Only a few decades after its signing, men supposed a separation of nature from nature's God and began to say that men are endowed with such rights by nature. And today the Charter of Human Rights of the United Nations is content with the statement that these rights have simply been endowed upon man—presumably by nothing and no one at all! Derived from the fullness of nonentity, suspended from vacancy, grounded in the grandeur of nothing, it is no wonder that human rights are fast running out. As one humanist said to another the other day, "Well, thank God, we still have each other!" Thank whom?

When they do not view man in the light of his position under God, men need not immediately become cruel or unnecessarily bloodthirsty. They will not at once begin to use their power over another's life with special brutality. But this does not mean that they find in the being of the neighbor something that essentially limits their rightful *dominion* over him. We grant just as much to the value of the lower animals in not inflicting unnecessary pain on them. Yet they have no *rights* which we should not infringe. Since animals have feelings, no one approves of needless cruelty to them. Nevertheless we do not renounce our dominion over them, the dominion which, according to Genesis, God gave man over the brutes. We simply exercise our dominion with as little brutality as possible. Whenever necessary, we dispose of animals painlessly—or, as we say, grossly misusing language, "humanely."

Man's inhumanity to man in the present day is a consequence of the inner thoughts of thousands of people who find no more essential limit than this to man's dominion over man. Never forget that Nazi gas chambers and medical experimentation on human beings conform to everything the Society for the Prevention of Cruelty to Animals can tell us we are duty-bound to do in relation to other living creatures; but man's dominion over man here became quite limitless. We should view with alarm the steadily increasing disregard for human life in our time, but this ought not to surprise us. These murderous deeds by evil men were already contained in the thought, which too many good people share with them—the thought that man belongs not to God but wholly to the species, the nation, or the party, or "the cause."

Unless we think that man has greater worth than to subserve even the noblest historical cause, we have already accepted debasement in our own eyes. Unless we think of man's life in terms of his worth to God, we have already in principle justified his possible murder for the sake of the "greatest happiness of the greatest number" or some other quite reasonable earthly goal. This way of thinking about man has already pressed the button.

The new barbarism of the present day flows from precisely this sort of thinking. Man is regarded as no more than part of the social group. Only geography and a few more years separate such thinking from the use of gas chambers. Whenever the collective life demands it, the individual is reduced to "a key on the keyboard of a piano" or "the handle of a hurdy-gurdy," [22] on whom the latest tunes are played by those who have the power. When a man's life is regarded as worth no more than its contribution to the progress of the future, it is not unreasonable to use him, in another of Dostoevski's apt phrases, "to manure the soil for the future harmony." [23] Men and women are regarded as no more than the race they run here below. Specters more real than the ghost of Hamlet's father importunately demand that we "swear" oaths of final allegiance to them. Like the man in one of Dostoevski's short stories who was swallowed by a crocodile and became a great social prophet from within its belly, we have to take our precautions and be on the alert in order not to be digested. We can scarcely enjoy our "private vices" without justifying them even to ourselves in the secret of our own hearts as "public virtues." And so the individual is reduced to a key on the keyboard of a piano or the handle of a hurdy-gurdy, which is due soon to prove murderous, even if the hurdy-gurdy now plays a merry, sociable tune.

The idea that the chief end of man is to glorify God and enjoy him forever is now so strange as to be almost unintelligible even to our greatest scholars. It used to be the first response of a children's catechism. Here we have a breakdown of tradition that has few parallels. As a consequence, speakers approach the subject indirectly, as, for example, by showing that, but for this chief end, there can be no basis for morality, which never was man's final end! Do what we may, generation after generation of students continue to graduate from our colleges whose noblest creed is—and it is a noble creed, one of earth's best—that in their lives they should serve the greatest happiness of the greatest number, and whose song of praise is Psalm 151:

> Oh! come, let us sing unto Sociology; let us heartily rejoice in the strength of our group consciousness.
>
> Let us come before her presence with thanksgiving; and show ourselves glad in her with projects.
>
> For Sociology is a great Hope; and a great Light above all hopes.
>
> In her hand are all the varieties of the experimental method; and the strength of statistics is hers also.
>
> The Social Group is hers and she has made it; and her hands prepared the charts thereof.
>
> Oh! come, let us study and fall down; and let us do case studies before Sociology, our Guide.
>
> For she is the maker of all contacts, and we are the people of her Adjustments and the Sheep of her Complexes.
>
> Oh! worship Sociology in the beauty of the group spirit; let both the privileged and the underprivileged stand in awe of her.
>
> For she cometh, for she cometh, to evaluate the earth, and with statistical measurements to judge the world and the people with an intelligence test.
>
> Glory be to Sociology, to statistics, and to the Group!

I know that this is a caricature of social science, but it is not of the ideas and faiths that actually operate in people's lives today. On election night giant computers are set to work predicting the outcome, while the announcer plaintively warns that if this is in error, it can't be the machine's fault but must be due to some "human factor"—as if such resistance which human freedom still puts up to the total rationalization of life were quite deplorable! It is also always carefully explained that the machine, after all, can answer only the questions we put to it— as if the contrary supposition were more pleasant to contemplate.

A leading citizen addresses himself to the problem of juvenile delinquency, and the highest appeal he can think to make is to call upon us to remember that "our children are our greatest national resource." Koslow, a youthful killer in New York, is reported to have said, "Park bums are *no use to anybody* and are better off dead." And a few years ago when a brilliant young colleague of mine died suddenly of a heart attack, the remark most frequently uttered by the decent and high-minded—indeed, the religious—members of the Princeton faculty was: "What a great loss to the history department!" History-writing is a great good, but hardly the last end of man! If just once someone had voiced the suppressed feelings of us all upon the vanity of all human endeavors (including those we are engaged in) and how no man has his homeland here, it might have become evident that we knew our friend's name in the divine significance of it.

Modern men have talked so much about "social immortality" or about finding the meaning of life in identification with ongoing society; we have talked so much about people being runners in the relay race of civilization, that at last tyrants have caught on to the idea and given "social immortality" to millions of people who somehow stood in their way. Modern men began by denying the supernatural significance of a human life and trying to get along to utopia better by emphasizing what a man counts for in this world. From this beginning, it has taken only a century or two for us to come down to the Soviet labor camps and Chinese communes and, before that, to the most ghastly and wholesale murders under the guise of medical experiments on human beings. Such acts were contained in the original thought—that man *is only* for the good of the whole.

Arthur Koestler writes of the hardened young Communist Ivanov giving answer to an older comrade who had begun to feel scruples of conscience about what they were doing:

> Every year several million people are killed quite pointlessly by epidemics and other natural catastrophes. And we shrink from sacrificing a few hundred thousand for the most promising experiment in history? Not to mention the legions of those who die of undernourishment and tuberculosis in coal and quicksilver mines, rice fields, and cotton plantations. No one takes any notion of them; nobody asks why or what for; but if we shoot a few thousand objectively harmful people, the humanitarians all over the world foam at the mouth. Yes, we liquidated the parasitic part of the peasantry and let it die of starvation. It was a surgical operation which had to be done once and for all; but in the good old days before the Revolution just as many died in any dry year—only senselessly and pointlessly.[24]

Now, it must be acknowledged that there is very much we do not understand about the sovereign dominion of God over human life in a dry year—or any other year; but this we do know: that no man has such dominion over man. And the reason is each man's covenant-link with the Almighty.

It sometimes happens in college teaching that a student turns up who is just so stupid that his existence simply cannot be justified in terms of any of the goals of the university or in terms of the values we suppose make life worth living. What can human culture mean to him, or he to human culture? In such a situation the professor simply has to remember that at least his mother loves him! This is an image and a shadow of divine things: when we think through the problem of assigning dignity in many instances to the human blubber and forked animals we see on the streets of our cities, all too soon our attempts at justification fail which support morality in terms of some philosophy of immanence or which insert the individual wholly within the service of certain material *or spiritual* values. Why then we simply have to remember that at least God loves them and that the most significant thing about a human being is his reference to the Transcendent. What is true in these hard cases is also the marrow of the respect we should have for human personality in cases which more readily meet the standards by which we ordinarily measure out our regard. For this reason Marcel declares: "All philosophies of immanence have had their day." [25] The fundamental choice is not between materialism and philosophies of life which stress the importance of higher, spiritual values but between wholly immanental schemes of human values (be they material or spiritual) and some reference to that which transcends human value or human spirituality and upholds these. "Either everything in man can be traced as a development from below, or something must come from above," T. S. Eliot has written. "If you remove from the word 'human' all that belief in the supernatural has given to man, you can view him finally as no more than an extremely clever, adaptable and mischievous little animal." [26]

Our only hope lies in the conviction that at the very core something about each individual defies every sort of reduction to, or inclusion within, society. Every person is, of course, a part of the web of the common life, with requisite duties to the common good. But no person, writes Maritain, is a part of the web of life *to the whole extent of his being*. He transcends the community of men and stands alone before God his Maker. The only way to think about man is from the point of view of God's estimate of him; and this is the only conception of him that does not, in the final analysis, prove—for perfectly good worldly reasons—murderous.

To this it is no answer to point out that there are *two* norms combined in the utilitarian ideal—"greatest happiness" and "greatest number"—or to say that the latter reference to distribution among the greatest number means to include each and everyone individually. Why *should* the common good flow back upon each and every member of the group? No doubt there is still present here the waning shadow of theological ethics, with its witness to God's evaluation upon the human soul. Nevertheless, in principle the greatest good or happiness (however "good" and "happiness" be defined) of the greatest number must move backward, or onward, toward a theocentric ethic which *warrants* this emphasis upon just distribution and the inclusiveness of everyone who, simply by being, claims numbering; or else it must complete the movement toward a social monism which reduces everyone to mere parts of the whole. "The greatest happiness of the greatest number" slides imperceptibly into "the greatest happiness *regardless* of numbers"; and we are beginning to know what that means!

How not to despise even someone who by our standards seems of little account we learn from Jesus' parable of the lost sheep. The ninety-nine—the group—were not left safe in a sheepfold (as is frequently the representation in Christian art) but out on the hills, out in the wilderness, while the shepherd sought the single individual until he found him. Human shepherds quite rightly have more concern for the herd than that! God does not treat mankind as a herdsman cares for his herd. He cares for us one by one, even at cost to the herd as a whole. This should lift us forever above the herd-mind so prevalent today and show us what infinite value we should place on the life of every individual human being.

And upon the murderer also! Cain was the first man who killed his brother and thus based his own life, as ever since men have built their empires, on fratricide. He knew that, as a consequence, every man's hand would be against him. But God mercifully established conditions under which Cain might still live; just as when Adam and Eve were justly under the sentence of death from the day they ate the forbidden fruit, God mercifully suspended the sentence and restored conditions for life even for those who were, in principle, dead already.

The sevenfold vengeance God fixed upon anyone who killed Cain the killer needs today to be taken seriously, if not literally, if ever there is to be a stop to the bloodletting, the liquidation, the counterliquidation of people in great groups. Blood calls for blood. The party in power purges and liquidates its opposition; therefore, let them be purged and liquidated in their turn. That nation treats prisoners of war atrociously: therefore, let there be no regard for the lives of their nationals who fall into our hands. Yet God is mindful of the lost sheep who at the moment is contributing nothing to the warmth and welfare of the ninety-nine huddled together in the storm. God is mindful even of the one who has taken his brother's life. Happily, the extreme logical consequences of living by the thought that there is no God have not yet come to fruition everywhere. Men are often (if the reader will discern my meaning) better than they *think*. Still it is only God's concern to establish conditions for new life even for Cain that can halt the spiraling increase of the practice and approval of violence in our day and our steadily declining respect for the immortal soul who is every man.

The reader may ask: How, then, is the state ever justified in taking the life of a condemned criminal, and what justifies its asking the citizen to give up his life and to take the life of others in the common defense? Our first concern, however, should not be to deal with these practical questions but rather with a more fundamental issue, namely: Would we rather live in a society whose basic morality makes these serious practical questions for countless people in all stations of life, or in a society where the taking of human life for the sake of the group raises no issues at all? Only if we believe that men have been endowed by their Creator, by nature and by nature's God, with an inalienable core within their being which defies trespass or human dominion over them, is there basic assurance of human rights.

The brilliant and sensitive French novelist, Albert Camus, in his book, *The Rebel,* has written a historical study of the last three centuries of revolutionary upheavals in Western civilization, which remorselessly documents in retrospect the foolishness, pointed out in Dostoevski's prophetic foresight, of saying in one's heart there is no God —how by a steady, irreversible falling-off from deicide to regicide, humanocide, and suicide this leads to boundless slavery and immorality without limits. He roundly declares that "the philosophy of the age of enlightenment finally led to the Europe of the blackout." [27] As for his own position, Camus attempts to pass through all this to a reconstruction of humanistic moderation. This is all the more remarkable, since he sees so clearly the consequences of deicide. His humanism depends heavily upon his conception of the *self*-limitation involved in artistic creation. The artist is the true rebel, one who cannot accept the creation as it is or the Creator, and who in the process of artistic creation produces a more unified world of his own imagination. Yet, because this new unity must accept and affirm some part of real human experience while rejecting and rebelling against many aspects of it, artistic creation posits its own limits beyond which revolution cannot go. The artist, then, is at once the true humanist and the true rebel, the man of self-moderation; and thus he becomes an exemplar for humanism in ethical and political action. We should make an art out of life and, with no response to the Creator of life, draw from within the creative human thrust itself an affirmation of values-in-existence which puts a boundary around rejection.[28]

Apart from the aesthetic theory at issue here, the question is whether —human freedom being what it is and what Camus clearly sees it to be— the artistic analogy provides a viable solution of the problems posed by human freedom when it lives by the thought that there is no God in the actual arena of its life-and-death struggles or whether there is, after all, a real humanistic alternative to religious or theocentric humanism. On the last page Camus draws a picture of two humanists, which would be deserving of derision if it were not so tragic, each "disclaiming divinity" as together they prepare to take some historical action. "They shall understand how they correct one another, and that a limit, under the sun, shall curb them all. Each tells the other that he is not God." [29] Surely this is tragically inadequate in one who has shown, in the first and major part of his book, how impossible it is, without God, for men to say this and mean what they say.

III

Nevertheless, it is possible to press the analysis too far in the direction of "no morality without immortality" or without faith and love to God. This might be understood as a matter of the brain alone and not of the existing individual's mode of being in the world; and then religious ethics would wrongly be construed as a consequence of mere theoretical belief, and immorality of unbelief. Lest this happen, there stand in Scripture the warning words: "He who does not love his brother whom he has seen, cannot love God whom he has not seen" (I John 4:20). Although this verse has been the excuse for calling simple humanitarianism "Christian" and for moral theology which tries to erect the knowledge and love of God upon a supposed autonomous ethic, its meaning can be seen and its truth accepted without going to these extremes. As a matter of fact, there is in Dostoevski the same counterbalance. His portrayal of that enigmatic character, Ivan Karamazov, sets forth as one of the possible modes of human life that a person may have a rather deep love for his fellow man (even if without wholeness of heart) without any very explicit love for God whom he has not seen, whom, indeed, his mind denies.

This appears in the chapters entitled "The Brothers Make Friends" and "Rebellion" in *The Brothers Karamazov* (immediately preceding the famous legend of "The Grand Inquisitor" and to which the latter is some sort of answer), in which Ivan discloses to Alyosha "what the brother you love lives by." On one side of his complex personality Ivan is a man of Euclidean reason, who believes that human affairs will, or *should,* become wholly rationalized. Rejecting the idea of an immortal soul, he believes that "all things are permitted" the man who would subdue the irrational and remove such useless, stinking inconsistencies as his lecherous old father. This is the philosophy of life with which, in overheard table conversations, he feeds his bastard half brother and servant in their father's house, Smerdyakov. The other side of Ivan's personality—the fact that he dwells also in a realm of non-Euclidean human freedom—gains voice in the end through his "double," the midnight visitor, the devil or his poor relation, who declares that he hails from a world of "indeterminate, irrational equations" where there is always a "surd" left over and where he is appointed always to utter the "indispensable negative" or minus, without which there would be neither historical events nor newspapers (i.e., no freedom). When that fragment of the first aspect of his personality, Smerdyakov, has actually done the deed, Ivan admits to himself that he knew this would happen and wanted it to happen, and thus he acknowledges his own freedom and responsibility for the murder. Ivan is thrown into delirium by the rigid structuring and the tension in him between the ideals of Euclidean "order" and his deeper non-Euclidean sense of things.

This is what is at work in the conversation between the two brothers, in which Ivan gives a penetrating and sensitive account of the problem of evil unequaled elsewhere in the world's literature. In cases of the suffering of little children who "haven't eaten the apple," he refuses to apply his own Euclidean doctrine that everything is permitted for the sake of some more inclusive reign of good sense and happiness, on earth or in heaven. He confesses that, like a child, he believes in the exquisite joys of heaven:

> I believe like a child that suffering will be healed and made up for, that all the humiliating absurdity of human contradiction will vanish like a pitiful mirage, like the despicable fabrication of the impotent and infinitely small Euclidean mind of man, that in the world's finale, at the moment of the eternal harmony, something so precious will come to pass that it will suffice for all hearts, for the comforting of all resentments, for the atonements of all the crimes of humanity, of all the blood they've shed; that it will make it not only possible to forgive but to justify all that has happened with men—but though all that may come to pass I don't accept it. I won't accept it. Even if parallel lines do meet and I see it myself, I shall see it and say that they've met, but still I won't accept it. *That's what's at the root of me, Alyosha; that's my creed.*[30]

Yet he does not believe that any final harmony justifies the least present disharmonious use of one of the least of these innocent ones—the baby thrown into the air and bayoneted by soldiers in the sight of its mother, or the girl done to death by her own hand and her rape by another. Therefore, he "respectfully turns in his ticket" to the last great day and takes precautions against his own probable weakness *then*. *Respect* for the *transcendent* worth of the human beings he has seen prevents him. From love of humanity he doesn't want the final harmony:

> What pulls me up here is that I can't accept that harmony. And while I am on earth, I make haste to take my own measures. You see, Alyosha, perhaps it really may happen that if I live to that moment, or rise again to see it, I, too, perhaps, may cry aloud with the rest, looking at the mother embracing the child's torturer, "Thou art just, O Lord!" but I don't want to cry aloud then. While there is still time, I hasten to protect myself and so I renounce the higher harmony altogether. It's not worth the tears of that one tortured child who beat itself on the breast with its little fist and prayed in its stinking outhouse, with its unexpiated tears to "dear, kind God"! . . . I don't want the mother to embrace the oppressor who threw her son to the dogs! She dare not forgive him! Let her forgive him for herself, if she will, let her forgive the torturer for the immeasurable suffer-

ing of her mother's heart. But the sufferings of her tortured child she has
no right to forgive, she dare not forgive the torturer, even if the child were
to forgive him. And if that is so, if they dare not forgive, what becomes of
the harmony? . . . I don't want harmony. From love of humanity I don't
want it. . . . Too high a price is asked for harmony; it's beyond our means
to pay so much to enter on it. And so I hasten to give back my entrance
ticket, and if I am an honest man I am bound to give it back as soon as
possible. And that I am doing. It's not God that I don't accept, Alyosha,
only I most respectfully return Him the ticket.

Imagine that you are creating the fabric of human destiny with the object of making men happy in the end, giving them peace and rest at last,
but that it was essential and inevitable to torture to death only one tiny
creature—that baby beating its breast with its fist, for instance—and to
found that edifice on its unavenged tears, would you consent to be the
architect of those conditions? [31]

The legend of "The Grand Inquisitor" has been too often read out of
context and only for its attack upon the Roman Catholic and other
ways of improving Christ's work by substituting appeals to miracle,
mystery, and authority, or simply as an attack upon Western atheistic
social liberalism, which comes to the same thing. At its deepest level,
"The Grand Inquisitor" proposes a solution to the problem of suffering
in the terms in which it has been set forth. Christ is the one who suffers,
in all and for all, all the suffering there has been under the sun; and so
he alone is in a position—as the mother is not—to forgive the torturer,
not only for the immeasurable suffering of his own heart but also for
the suffering of the other innocents. Without believing this, Ivan cannot
really believe in God. This is precisely the point of offense over which
Camus stumbles, both in his own analysis of the problem of innocent
suffering in the spirit of Dostoevski in *The Plague* and in his more
recent study of rebellion. To believe in God without thus believing in
Christ is, no matter how we squirm on the point, to sanctify injustice.
There can therefore be no way of passing from "natural" theology to
confessional Christian theology, but only an elaboration of natural
grounds for believing in God without a parenthesis first drawn by faith
in Christ.

Yet it is significant that Ivan declares that "it's not that I don't accept
God, you must understand, it's the world created by Him I don't and
cannot accept." "I don't accept this world of God's," which would mean
directly sanctifying the injustice that now exists and justifying all the
injustice there has ever been by reference to an earthly or heavenly
utopia tacked on at the end of this world. What, then, are we to make
of Ivan's *present* belief in God? In Tillich's language, God is the ground
of being, and ground for the being of Ivan's love for "the sticky little

leaves as they open in the spring" [32] and of his love for humanity. This is the reason Alyosha says over Ivan in his delirium:

> "God, in whom he disbelieved, and his Truth were gaining mastery over his heart, which still refused to submit." . . . Alyosha smiled softly. "God will conquer!" he thought. "He will either rise up in the light of truth . . . or he'll perish in hate, revenging on himself and on everyone his having served the cause he does not believe in," Alyosha added bitterly, and again he prayed for Ivan.[33]

In short, in loving (even with half his heart) the brothers whom he has seen, Ivan loves in them what he has never seen. He respects their linkage with the Transcendent, and a near-religious awe prevents his pressing any rationale or scheme for improvement upon the life they keep between themselves and God. In this sense "an immortal human soul" is "the definitive formulation and the first source" of what truth and integrity there is in Ivan's divided conscience.

Two

Fyodor Dostoevski:
God's Grace and Man's Guilt

I

Forensic or judicial meanings have a remarkable way of clinging to Christian conceptions of God's relation to human sin. Everyone realizes, of course, that *dikaioun ton asebe* ought to be understood as "to justify the ungodly" (Cf. Rom. 4:5) and not in the stricter courthouse meaning, "to condemn the ungodly." But what does "justify" mean? In answering this question the alternatives have traditionally been: to *make* righteous, to impart or infuse righteousness, or to *declare* righteous, to impute righteousness. Both these interpretations suppose that in some sense righteousness is still prerequisite to salvation—the latter no less, though less obviously, than the former. Norman H. Snaith argues this point persuasively, and what he says is worth quoting at length:

> The only reason why such suggestions are made is that righteousness is conceived as being a necessary condition of Salvation. Since it is obvious that actual righteousness is out of the question, it is suggested that righteousness must be either imparted or imputed. That is, a man must have some sort of righteousness before he can be saved, even if it is either at the price of a fiction, or belonging to someone else.
>
> . . . We have not emancipated ourselves from that very doctrine which Paul spent most of his life in combatting—namely that salvation is by righteousness. . . . It cannot be maintained that a man can offer unto God any true righteousness of his own, so he is regarded as offering a fictional righteousness, or someone else's righteousness. The fact which is regarded as fixed is that God must have some sort of righteousness before He saves.
>
> We hold therefore most strongly that, according to both Old and New Testaments, God does not require righteousness as a condition of salvation, neither actual, nor imputed, nor imparted. He requires faith, and faith alone. Any other doctrine may be the orthodox doctrine of a part or parts of the Christian Church. In that case it ought to be recognized that it arises from the interpretation of the Greek *dikaiosune* and the Latin *justitia* in a non-Biblical way. It is non-Biblical theology.
>
> The order is Faith, Salvation, Righteousness. To assume that ethical righteousness, whether actual, imputed, or imparted (infused), is a necessary condition of salvation, is a travesty of Paul's teaching. . . . The reason the assumption is "imputed" to Paul is because the interpreters are still dominated by Greek ideas of *dikaiosune*.[1]

In a similar fashion, the judicial conception of guilt still is held in connection with the gospel of God's forgiveness. Such assertion of man's guilt may be regarded as an "independent anthropological statement" not yet expunged from Christian theology, or transformed by Christ. The fact of guilt is taken as "given" or presupposed instead of canceled by the Christian understanding of God and man. Such notions of guilt may be regarded as resulting from an insufficiently Christianized way of interpreting man's existence before God.

II

The phenomena of "guilt" need to be thoroughly reinterpreted from the point of view of forgiveness. Before making some suggestions in this direction, let us consider in general what sort of statements can be made by Christian theology about man, his sin and guilt or his goodness, his competence or his incompetence, his reason or his unreason.

It was Karl Barth who, years ago, protested against the presence of "independent anthropological statements" in Christian theology. This means that man must always be viewed in the light of Christ. It means that the doctrine of man is *Christocentric* doctrine no less than the doctrine of God. There can be no ground for objecting that in his use of this rule against *independent* anthropological statements Barth himself has been content with too few anthropological statements (of some sort!). Still there may be a danger that some who follow Barth's lead will fail to elaborate fully a doctrine of man or to articulate an ethic which results from the proclamation of the gospel and which may serve to clarify the church's proclamation. In short, it may be said there is peril in making too few *dependent* anthropological statements.

Nevertheless, the opposite state of affairs equally needs to be noted: American Christian thought, even where touched by the new theological winds, has remained primarily anthropological and, one suspects, utters words about man that stand in no dependent relation to the central truth of Christ. In any properly Christian theology it ought to be impossible to say, as sometimes one hears it said, that the peculiar emphases of "neo-orthodoxy" have taught us much about sinful man but that now we need to improve upon it by stressing again the more positive aspects of the Christian faith. Perhaps our American theology, composed in large part of independent anthropological and ethical statements, and some forms of European theology, content to be without a full-length doctrine of man or an ethic even in a dependent position, are both responsible for this sad misunderstanding. For theological anthropology proceeds the other way round: from knowledge of God in Christ we come to know ourselves. Precisely within this light we clearly see our own shadows.

Properly grasped, the doctrine of sin, for example, should always be understood as a *Christocentric* judgment concerning human nature. By any other measure men might not prove so sinful, or their defects prove to be *sin*. Only one illustration of this can be given here.[2] When Richard Hooker mediated medieval wisdom concerning rational, moral law to the English Reformation, he seems to have held the competence and goodness of human nature in higher regard than did the Continental Reformers. But this is largely an optical illusion due to the fact that man is judged in each instance by different standards of expectation. For Hooker it was "not easy to find men who are ignorant" of the natural, moral law. Examples of such universal, axiomatic moral principles are "that the greater good is to be chosen before the less," that God should be worshiped and parents honored, and that "others be used by us as we ourselves would be by them."

> The like natural inducement hath brought men to know that it is their duty no less to love others than themselves. For seeing those things which are equal must needs have one measure; . . . if I do harm, I must look to suffer; *there being no reason that others should show greater measure of love to me than they have by me showed unto them. My desire therefore to be loved of my equals in nature as much as possible* may be, imposeth upon me a natural duty of bearing to them-ward fully the like affection.[3]

Now it is certainly true to say that it is "not easy to find men who are ignorant" of these norms; but it is more significant to remark in the other direction that no wonder man appears as straight as the plumb line, or almost straight, when measured by this as the absolute moral norm.

Both Luther and Calvin also held a doctrine of natural law. We do not properly grasp the significance of this fact so long as we regard it merely as a holdover from scholasticism among their views. True, they were not centrally interested in natural law, and they did not make it the foundation on which Christian ethical theory rests. Nevertheless, they took natural law quite seriously as providing a valid morality and as uncontested evidence of the powers of natural reason. A pagan prince, for example, in his political decisions *should* and *can* conform to the standards of natural law. The Reformers' doctrine of the sinfulness or so-called total depravity of human nature was simply not set in juxtaposition to the requirements of natural morality but rather in contrast to the demand that a Christian man become a Christ to his neighbor. From this as the absolute norm—surely a more Christian norm—it follows as the night that all have sinned and sinned rather "totally." At least it is "not easy" to find men who have not fallen short, and repeatedly every moment continue to fall short, of the glory of God as

Christians understand him in Christ. Plainly, then, the doctrine of sin should never be set forth as an "independent anthropological statement" in Christian theology. No more should our understanding of "guilt."

Nevertheless, the present writer does not wholly agree with Barth's rule against independent anthropological and ethical statements. *Prima facie* this would exclude from Christian theology any illumination from the outside. What needs to be secured is that our knowledge of the nature of man drawn from philosophical and scientific sources be given a subordinate, and never a dominant, position when brought within the context of Christian theology. We must understand man and whatever elsewhere we learn about man from the perspective of the Christian faith. In the following reinterpretation of the meaning of "guilt" we shall therefore first make use of the understanding of man as self-transcending spirit—a viewpoint common to philosophical idealism, Dostoevski, present-day existentialism, and much contemporary theology. Then we shall attempt to subject the phenomena of guilt in man, so understood, to revision in light of the relation of guilt to Christ. In this way independent anthropological statements become dependent; and even our grasp of "guilt" may be converted and transformed by Christ into a proper understanding of it.

III

We ask, then, whether the phenomena to which the word "guilt" refers may perhaps be seen, when brought fully within the context of the Christian gospel, in a different light from the way guiltiness is ordinarily interpreted apart from Christ. Suppose, if only for the argument's sake, that the Christian message consists of the simple and unqualified announcement that our sins are forgiven. Forgiveness of sin is the "given"; only this need be presupposed. Statements about man, then, cannot be made independent of this announcement or be left unrevised in the light of it. As a consequence, what becomes of "guilt"? The idea of guilt shows as a vestigial remain of some former, sub-Christian way of thinking about God and man, like regarding as fixed the idea that God must secure some sort of righteousness from man (imparted or imputed, real or fictional) before saving him. Guilt is what the gospel lives by disabusing; where the word of God speaks, guilt can have no standing. "Where God speaks man must be present without considering his own merit" (Barth); where God speaks, man must be present without considering his own guilt or demerit. "In the strict sense there is no knowledge of sin except in the light of Christ's cross. For he alone understands what sin is, who knows that his sin is forgiven him." [4] In the strict sense there is also no knowledge of guilt except in the light of Christ's cross. For he alone understands what guilt is who knows that his guilt is forgiven him.

Yet in this light the nature and meaning of guilt become strangely transmuted. From the point of view of forgiveness, what, then, is guilt? The answer to this question may be stated in the following four propositions, which, in the last analysis, are simply four ways of affirming a single idea: (1) Guilt is a forensic term for the difficulty of repentance; (2) guilt is a forensic term for unwillingness to receive forgiveness; (3) guilt is a forensic term for continuation in sin in the teeth of proffered forgiveness; (4) guilt is a forensic term for despair over sin and for despairing of the forgiveness of sin. The whole phenomenon of guilt resolves itself into this single composite proposition; and this proposition about the nature of guilt, when seen in the light of forgiveness, is itself not capable of extension, variation, or more particular explication, and it affords no inference that affects human life in any other way than accomplishing the transmutation of guilt—which is indeed the goal of forgiveness. As often as God speaks or the gospel is spoken of, one can only give a plain assent to this understanding of what guilt means in the light of his Word.

Nevertheless, taking Dostoevski and Kierkegaard for our mentors, we may explore more fully the special difficulty of repentance, man's unwillingness even to be forgiven, the nature of continuation in sin in the teeth of forgiveness, and despairing of the forgiveness of sin. If what follows in this chapter appears to be like the case of the student who named the kings of Israel when asked on a Bible examination to compare the major and minor prophets, that is exactly as it should be. When asked about guilt or other conceptions appropriate only to a judicial viewpoint, a Christian should indeed speak of something else.

The difficulty of repentance can be fully understood only in connection with man's nature as a *self-transcending* spirit. "We not only know, but we know that we know, and can ponder in thought over the very fact that we are able thus to reflect in thought." [5] We not only have awareness but are aware that we are aware; we not only experience physical impulses but are aware that we have these impulses; we not only originate ideas but are conscious of having originated them; we not only pursue ideal ends but know we pursue them; and we can ponder in thought over the very fact that we are able thus to reflect in thought upon our sense perceptions and physical impulses or upon our original ideas and high ideals. As Pascal said, we not only die but also we know that we die; and this was his meaning in affirming that "our whole dignity consists in thought." [6] Thus every case of simple awareness is accompanied by its shadow, a not so simple instance of self-transcendence or awareness *of self*. We sense, and we are conscious not only of *sensing* but of *ourselves* sensing. We perceive, and are aware of ourselves perceiving. We feel the separate parts of our bodies, and are also aware of ourselves feeling and using them. We respond to the movements of impulse, and there is, in addition, the distinctly human experience of our*selves* as creatures of impulse. We think, and we know ourselves in the course of thinking.

Self-transcendence affects not only things internal to human nature but external relationships as well. We do good deeds, and, while we may be simply aware of that fact, we are also aware of ourselves as doers of such deeds. We sin, and, while we may be simply aware of that fact (which on encountering forgiveness would be tantamount to pure, thoroughgoing repentance), we are also aware of ourselves as sinners and objectify ourselves as such (which in defiance and despair makes the difficulty of repentance). We have relationships with other people, but, instead of simply being aware of them through friendship, we complicate matters by being aware of ourselves as friendly with varying degrees of virtuosity.

Self-centered self-transcendence sums up the endless and often puzzling convolutions of personal consciousness and the complications it introduces into human relationships in the great novels of Dostoevski. This was the "knife" in Grushenka's forgiveness of the officer who wronged her in her youth, as well as the "onion" given away, yet held onto, in every good deed done by Katerina Ivanovna in *The Brothers Karamazov*.

The latter character makes an especially interesting study. She it was who, having offered to sell herself to Dmitri for four thousand rubles, needed to save her father from ruin; while he, instead, gave the money to her; and ever thereafter she had her own virtue in mind, together with the additional, crowning virtue of resolving gratefully to sacrifice herself to her benefactor. Not only was she possessed by the noble idea of such self-sacrifice itself, but she was possessed by the idea of *herself* making this sacrifice. Dmitri, of course, in his own transcendence of the relationship, was aware of this. He transcended her transcendence, he was aware of her self-awareness: "She loves her own *virtue*, not me," he said. "She plays a role to herself." And Dmitri describes Katerina's attitude toward Grushenka, a later object of his passion: "She really was fascinated by Grushenka, that's to say, not by Grushenka, but by her own dream, her own delusion—because it was *her* dream, *her* delusion!" [7]

These moments of self-transcendence may be multiplied endlessly by the single individual alone; he first sees himself, then sees himself seeing himself, and so on. The ultimate subject of self-awareness is thus a receding limit. "I" never fully become an object to myself. In fact, it is "I" to whom, as subject, all things else are objects. It is "I" who know "myself"; how then can "I" be fully known, since in any case of self-knowledge "I" am also the ultimate subject of *this* knowledge and there-fore never quite entirely the me-object "I" know? The self is a hound that easily slips its leash.

The situation becomes more complicated when there is more than one self in intersubjective relationship with one other. Self-conscious selves intersecting, each indefinitely objectifying and spiritually removing itself from the situation between them, produce in one degree or another what Dostoevski called "laceration," or transcending the transcendence of another and employing this against him and against one of the selves a person might one's self become in relation to him. In *The Brothers Karamazov* Dostoevski portrays laceration as a universal human phe-nomenon and studies it among monks and among boys, in the monastery, in a drawing room, in a cottage, and in the open air. Katerina Ivanovna, the drawing-room figure, provides the most interesting example. When it seems inevitable that Dmitri will marry Grushenka, Katerina expresses her felt duty of gratitude thus:

> "I've already decided, even if he marries that—creature (she began solemnly), whom I never, never can forgive, *even then I will not abandon him*. Henceforward I will never, never abandon him!" she cried, breaking into a sort of pale, hysterical ecstasy. ". . . I will watch over him all my life unceasingly. When he becomes unhappy with that woman, and that is bound to happen quite soon, let him come to me and he will find a friend, a sister . . . only a sister, of course, and so for ever; *but he will learn at least* that that sister is really his sister, who loves him and has sacri-ficed all her life to him. *I will gain my point.* I will insist on his knowing me and confiding entirely in me, without reserve," she cried, in a sort of frenzy. *"I will be a god to whom he can pray—and that, at least, he owes me for his treachery and for what I suffered yesterday through him. . . .* I will become nothing but a means for his happiness, . . . an instrument, a machine for his happiness, and that for my whole life, my whole life, and *that he may see that all his life!"*

Her speech "betrayed that she was still smarting from yesterday's in-sult [Grushenka's refusal to kiss her hand in return], and that her pride craved satisfaction." Also present in Mme. Hohlakov's drawing room are Alyosha and Ivan. To the latter, it is suggested, Katerina was drawn by a more sincere admiration and affection, and he to her, even while she deceived herself for the purpose of playing her role. Ivan detects the true nature of her fancied duty of gratitude. He is aware of her aware-ness of herself posing as a martyr; yet he is not *simply* aware of this. At the same time he is aware of himself as being aware of her awareness of herself posing. He includes her consciousness of herself in a new mo-ment of consciousness which is at the same time *self*-conscious. He thereupon "lacerates" himself, her, and their relationship to each other by deliberately and self-consciously employing her manifest yearning for that role as a weapon against her and as a means of preserving himself. The following "was unmistakably said with some malice and obviously with intention; even perhaps with no desire to conceal that he spoke ironically and with intention":

> "In anyone else this moment would be only due to yesterday's impression and would be only a moment. But with Katerina Ivanovna's character, that moment will last her life. What for anyone else would be only a promise is for her an everlasting, burdensome, grim, perhaps, but unflagging duty. And she will be sustained by the feeling of this duty being fulfilled. Your life, Katerina Ivanovna, *will henceforth be spent in painful brooding over your own sufferings;* but in the end that suffering will be softened and will pass into *sweet contemplation of the fulfillment of a bold and proud design.* Yes, proud it certainly is, and desperate in any case, but *a triumph for you.*"

A moment later, when Katerina shows great self-possession and apparent gladness over the news that Ivan is going away, leaving her entirely free to sacrifice herself, Alyosha sees "the truth": "You're torturing Ivan, simply because you love him—and torturing him, because you love Dmitri through 'self-laceration'—with an unreal love—because you've persuaded yourself." But this seems "religious idiocy" to Ivan and Katerina, who, by virtue of self-transcendence, have *themselves* purposely put other "selves" forward into the business at hand. Ivan reassures Alyosha by giving an interpretation which is possibly also true (in these interlocking and pyramiding relationships, who knows who are the *true selves?*), and then again turns upon Katerina:

> "She kept me at her side as a means of revenge. She revenged with me and on me all the insults which she has been continually receiving from Dmitri ever since their first meeting. . . . I am going now; but, believe me, Katerina Ivanovna, you really love him. And the more he insults you, the more you love him—that's your 'laceration.' You love him just as he is; you love him for insulting you. If he reformed, you'd give him up at once and cease to love him. But *you need him so as to contemplate continually your heroic fidelity and to reproach him for infidelity.* And it all comes from your pride. Oh, there's a great deal of humiliation and self-abasement about it, but it all comes from pride. . . . I am too young and I've loved you too much. I know that I ought not to say this, . . . but I am going far away, and shall never come back. . . . It is for ever. I don't want to sit beside a 'laceration.' "

Self-consciousness splinters the self into many role-playing objectified selves—perhaps one for each of the relationships sustained with other persons—still, however, within the ultimate unity of the unknowable knowing subject or ground of all our acts of self-awareness. "I" splinter myself into many "me's," yet these, too, are "I," for I, their basal unity, say "I" in connection with every self and thus I identify myself with every self I project. It is I who protest too much or confess too much, I who repent too little, for that is the way "I" would have it. It is I who deceive and lacerate myself through some sort of pose, yet I am truly identical with that pose, it is a genuine "I," else I could not deceive myself so well. I who have a duty of gratitude fancy myself so.

These disaggregated splinter-selves within the self provide a better way of understanding the union of good and evil in the human breast than does "faculty psychology." By dividing man up into separate faculties, saying the will is corrupt and the mind only secondarily so, or the impulses are evil and the will only so thereafter, faculty psychology fails to grasp either the pervasiveness of evil throughout the spirit of man or the simultaneous presence of good and evil impulses in him, both equally identifiable as "himself." Instead of simply a number of faculties within a unitary self, the self's own name is legion. For this reason the self can truly identify *itself* (and not simply one or two faculties, more or less) with its love for both good and evil at the same time:

> "I can't endure the thought that a man of lofty mind and heart begins with the ideal of the Madonna and ends with the ideal of Sodom [says Dmitri]. What is still more awful is that a man with the ideal of Sodom in his soul does not renounce the ideal of the Madonna, and his heart may be on fire with that ideal, genuinely on fire, just as in his days of youth and innocence. Yes, man is broad, too broad, indeed. I'd have him narrower. . . . Is there beauty in Sodom? Believe me, that for the immense mass of mankind beauty is found in Sodom. Did you know that secret? The awful thing is that beauty is mysterious as well. God and the devil are fighting there and the battlefield is the heart of man."

But Dmitri cannot have him narrower. Man is broad; indeed, broad enough to include within a single self all the selves that self-awareness has time and occasion to produce, and then still another after that. This in itself is perfectly normal; only when one or another splinter-self becomes rigid is self-consciousness seriously "doubled" (as in the case of the visitor in Ivan's fever). But precisely the normal characteristics of self-consciousness make integrated selfhood and straightforward, unlacerating human relationships difficult. The myriad multiplication of selves in self-awareness also makes difficult an integral act of true repentance. Even in the face of proffered forgiveness, like Augustine we are always "willing and nilling" the same good at the same time; we will nothing wholly or entirely; we are in this sense unwilling to be forgiven. We will our sin and our forgiveness at one and the same moment; we nill the forgiveness we would and we will the sin we would not.

According to a recent book on existentialism, Jean-Paul Sartre's account of persons "existing-together" makes striking and unrestricted use of self-centered self-transcendence:

> It is the fact of another's looking at me, Sartre believes, that reveals the existence of another subject—not the mere physical presence of a pair of eyes directed my way but the whole transformation of my world that the look behind those eyes implies. For in that experience of being looked at by another I find myself to be but a mere object, a body appearing thus and thus in someone else's world.
>
> For the other person, whom I find looking at me, I become only a body, a thing within his horizon, as "objective" as the chair I am sitting in or the cup of coffee I am drinking.
>
> But the other existence which thus reveals itself is, at the same time, annihilation of myself as subject; and such an annihilation I am bound to try every means in my power to overcome. Therefore, between myself as subject and the other who sees me as object, between my freedom and its destruction in another's possession of me, there arises a circle of conflicts which constitutes, according to Sartre, the whole pattern of possible inter-subjective relationships. "Conflict is the original sense of being-for-another."

Sartre introduces this theory with two examples. Suppose that I am sitting in a park and see another person walking near me. Suppose the other person to be reading a book. He and his book are then as wholly "objects" as, say, the tree-on-the-grass or the fountain-in-the-square. Man-reading-book, like the other things in their places, is a self-contained unity, holding no obvious threat to me or my world. But suppose the stranger's eye, instead of being fastened attentively to his page, is wandering over the paths and borders, so that I may at any moment find he is looking at me. Such a shift in his attention would reveal *me* as an object in *his* world—and by this possibility the whole world of *my* consciousness, the world as *I* have ordered it, is threatened with disorganization and destruction. The awareness of such a possibility causes, Sartre says, an "internal hemorrhage" of my world: it bleeds in the direction of the stranger. Hence, for Sartre, the appearance of the other person in my world is the occasion for possible, if not actual, disruption of that world; and fear, the natural reaction on my part to such a possibility, would seem to be my original relation to him in such circumstances.

Or, Sartre continues, suppose I am listening at a keyhole, whether out of jealousy, spite, or whatnot—the motive is irrelevant. And suppose I suddenly feel myself, in turn, observed. All at once I feel the eyes of an observer on me and turn to find him looking at me. All at once, instead of being engaged as a free agent in a project of my own, I am revealed to myself, as to the unexpected observer, as an object in his view. My transcendence is, in turn, transcended by him as free agent; I am what *he* makes of me, not what I make myself. I recognize the indignity and absurdity of my position, stooping awkwardly at a keyhole; I am that laughable or despicable thing, an eavesdropper; and I am ashamed. But what makes my eavesdropping shameful is its discovery (see the innumerable scenes, in

Fielding, for example of servants discovered listening at doors). It is the transformation of a project into a posture that makes the posture ridiculous. And, in general, it is the transformation of myself from free agent shaping my own world to body seen by another that is the source of shame. Hence Sartre's explanation of original sin: it is the revelation of my body as a mere body that makes me ashamed; and that shame is at the root of the sense of sin.[8]

Like Dostoevski, Sartre *describes* very well the interlocking of self-transcendent spirituality. Significant, however, is the fact that for him the sense of shame is basic to the sense of sin, while the reverse is the case in the Christian story. Augustine, it will be remembered, traced home to original sin our sense of shame in having the sex act turned from a "project" to a "posture" by its being observed. The human situation can be understood very well in terms of awareness of how one's self appears in the awareness of another; but the primacy of sin in all that Sartre so aptly describes can be grasped only when such an interpretation is brought within the context of Christian faith.

To put the same point in more general terms: Because he is making an autonomous anthropological analysis, Sartre assumes that everything he observes about man's present personal existence is entirely natural and a state of affairs quite inevitable in relations between man and man. He makes no distinction between original nature and sinful nature. He makes no distinction between sinful consciousness and redeemed consciousness, or between the meeting of persons in conscious conflict and the meeting of reconciled persons who accept each other's existence and live for each other.* These distinctions are to be made quite decisively only by examining personal existence in relation to the new man in Christ. This will be our task in the following section, and we shall also see that in this light "guilt" may be forgiven. At the same time Christian understanding—the understanding afforded us by Dostoevski's Christian existentialism—penetrates to the heart of guilt's greatest intensity and obduracy.

IV

Dostoevski combines a deep understanding of sinful consciousness with redeemed consciousness as a real possibility. He speaks also of the significance of the look of the eyes. "All my life long," remarks the "author" in his *Letters from the Underworld,* "I have preferred to look people under the eyes rather than in them." Presumably *this* is the look which threatens to annihilate the other self by objectifying him, and a glance passing from eye to eye may serve as a vehicle for real interpersonal com-

---

* Chapter Four above gives a full length analysis of Jean-Paul Sartre.

munication in which one person lives for another rather than living by destroying him. After describing his own personal existence by use of the category of "freedom" in Part I of these notes from the underworld, in Part II the "author" presents an episode which can best be understood in terms of self-transcendence, transcending one's own former act of transcendence, transcending another person's transcendence of one's self and of himself, and his transcending that, and so on. I-Thou relationships are forever being annihilated and transformed into I-It relationships. This makes the difficulty in achieving straightforward relations among persons, which Dostoevski, unlike Sartre, regarded as at least possible. It also makes the difficulty, though not the impossibility, of repentance; for repentance and the possibility of redemption may be regarded as another factor entering my world, a relationship inserted into my world by Christ (or by one of Dostoevski's Christ-figures). And Christ speaks only to my freedom, he addresses my self-transcending spirit— which means that I may still regard forgiveness itself as some specially dire threat to encompass and alter my existence and may transcend and objectify it and hold out to the last as the center of my own little, spoiled world.

This can best be seen in Raskolnikov's relation to Sonia in *Crime and Punishment*. At first, and through long anguish, her "insatiable compassion" was met by resistance, hatred, and cruelty from Raskolnikov, cloaked by the explanation that "she is a religious maniac" and by his justifying the crime as only stupidity, clumsiness, and good riddance anyway. The presence of one of Dostoevski's Christ-figures always arouses the possibility that evil will simply become more demonic. It has sometimes been observed that, since the days of Jesus Christ in the flesh, along with the extension of his "church," evil within Christendom has also become more dynamic. It is a hard and difficult thing to encounter the Cross with any other result:

> "I have come for your cross, Sonia. It was you told me to go to the crossroads. . . ." His tone seemed strange to her; a cold shiver ran over her, but in a moment she guessed that the tone and the words were a mask. He spoke to her looking away, as though to avoid meeting her eyes.

At the crossroads he "clutched at the chance of this new unmixed, complete sensation" and "fell to the earth on the spot." Yet even in Siberia, "now in prison, *in freedom* [sic!], he thought over and criticized all his actions," which seemed to him blundering, but his theory no "stupider than others that have swarmed and clashed from the beginning of the world." Too late now, he felt he had only submitted to " 'the idiocy' of a sentence." His fellow convicts drew away from him; his own "dim consciousness of the fundamental falsity in himself" he attributed to the

dead weight of instinct. Then there happened another luminous moment with Sonia, and even the prisoners recognized a change in him.
Finally Dostoevski suggests that, beyond the pages of this novel (in a
world where sinful consciousness shall be entirely purged away), through
"great striving, great suffering," there may take place "the gradual renewal of a man," "his gradual regeneration," "his passing from one
world into another," his resurrection with Lazarus from the dead. It is
not so easy as Wordsworth supposed to join the days and ourselves "each
to each in natural piety."

Stavrogin's confession in the chapter entitled "At Tihon's" in Dostoevski's *The Possessed* gives another excellent illustration of a man's ob-
durate unwillingness to repent and receive forgiveness. After his injury
to the girl Matryosha, provoking her suicide, Stavrogin in excellent
spirits spends an evening with his friends. "For although at heart I felt
that I was a scoundrel," he says, "I was not ashamed of it and, in general, I was not much distressed." Yet a few days later

> "For no apparent reason at all I conceived the idea of somehow crippling
> my life, in the most repulsive manner possible.
> "One day as I was watching the lame Marya Timofeyevna Lebyadkin,
> who was more or less of a servant in my lodgings, I suddenly decided to
> marry her—at that time she was not yet insane, but simply a rapturous
> idiot, and secretly head over heels in love with me. . . . The thought of
> Stavrogin's marriage to a creature like that, the lowest of the low, tickled
> my nerves. It would be impossible to imagine anything more monstrous."

What was the meaning of this action, if it was "not solely 'for a bet,
after a drunken dinner' "? Part of Dostoevski's explanation, given earlier,
is that "the fundamental idea of the document is a terrible, undisguised
need of punishment, the need of a cross, of public chastisement. Mean-
while, this need of the cross in a man who doesn't believe in the cross—
why, 'that in itself is an idea.' " Yet more was at work in Stavrogin than
what is ordinarily called guilt seeking its due penalty. There was also,
and more fundamentally, sin in unacknowledged despair protecting itself from repentance by doing something more monstrous. Shatov pointed
this out to Stavrogin earlier:

> "Do you know why you made that base and shameful marriage? Simply
> because the shame and senselessness of it reached the pitch of genius! Oh,
> you are not one of those who linger on the brink. You fly head foremost.
> You married from a passion for martyrdom, from craving for remorse,
> through moral sensuality. It was a *laceration* of nerves. . . . Defiance of
> commonsense was too tempting. Stavrogin and a wretched, half-witted,
> crippled beggar! When you bit the governor's ear did you feel sensual
> pleasure? Did you?"

Stavrogin had not only broken with the good—which means also a breach with guilt, ethically defined—he also had broken with repentance —which covers a breach with the possibility of forgiveness. This Kierkegaard called "despair over sin," "which must constantly regard everything which is of the nature of repentance and everything which is of the nature of grace not only as empty and meaningless but as its foe. . . . Despair over sin is an attempt to maintain oneself by sinking still deeper." [9] This propulsion away from repentance by which sin would insure consistency with itself by plunging deeper into sin manifested itself in Stavrogin's desire to add bigamy to his marriage, and again at the conclusion of his interview with Tihon:

"I see . . . I see clearly," exclaimed Tihon in a penetrating voice and with an expression of most intense grief, "that never poor lost youth, have you stood nearer to a new and more terrible crime than at this moment."

"Calm yourself," Stavrogin begged him, positively alarmed for him. "Perhaps I will postpone. . . . You're right . . . I will not publish the sheets. Compose yourself."

"No, not after publication, but even before it, a day, an hour perhaps, before the great step, you will plunge into a new crime as a way out, and you will commit it solely to avoid the publication of these sheets, upon which you now insist."

The person who despairs over sin makes even confession and repentance itself an occasion for "sinking still deeper." He purposely exaggerates his crimes. Tihon's first remark after reading Stavrogin's confession was that its publication was "a lofty idea, and a Christian thought could not express itself more amply . . . if only. . . ."

"If only what?"

"If only it is really repentance and really a Christian thought. . . . It is as though you purposely wished to represent yourself as a coarser man than your heart would desire."

" 'Represent?' I repeat, I didn't represent myself, I did not pose. 'Coarser,' what is 'coarser'?" he grew flushed again and got enraged in consequence. "I know that what is described there—" he nodded in the direction of the sheets—"is vile, crawling and abominable, but let its very vileness serve to redouble. . . ."

Both Dostoevski and Kierkegaard observe the duplicity in such passionate proclamations as, "I can never forgive myself for it." Kierkegaard's words are an apt description of Stavrogin's despair over his own sin:

He can never forgive himself for it—but now in case God would forgive him for it, he might well have the kindness to forgive himself. No, his despair over sin, and all the more, the more it storms in the passion of expression, whereby without being aware of it in the least he informs against himself when he "never can forgive himself" that he could sin thus (for this sort of talk is pretty nearly the opposite of penitent contrition which prays God for forgiveness)—this despair is far from being a characteristic of the good, rather it is a more intensive characterization of sin, the intensity of which is a deeper sinking into sin.[10]

Along with employing confession as a device for "sinking still deeper," Stavrogin at the same time rises thereby to a higher pitch of defiance. Tihon observes this:

> "You have appealed to the judgment of the whole Church although you do not believe in the Church; am I not right? But it is as though you were already hating and despising in advance all those who will read what you have written, and challenging them to an encounter. . . . Since you are not ashamed to confess your crime, why are you ashamed of repentance? . . . 'Let them look at me,' you say; and you, how will you look at them? You are waiting for their malice, to respond with greater malice. Some of the passages in your account are couched in exaggerated language; it is as if you were admiring your own psychologizing, and you cling to each detail so as to amaze the reader by a callousness and a shamelessness which isn't really in you."

Undoubtedly the man who went to Canossa during all those three days and nights standing in the snow was thinking and planning how he would revenge himself on the pope for it. Because of the possibility of defiance at work, in despair over sin even in an instance of so-called "repentance," Dostoevski insists through the words of Sonia in *Crime and Punishment* that Raskolnikov can be redeemed only after going with sincere emotion to the crossroads, bowing down to the people, kissing the earth, and crying aloud to the whole world. Them Raskolnikov also despised—"running to and fro about the streets, every one of them a scoundrel and a criminal at heart and, worse still, an idiot"—but he came at last to "this new unmixed, complete sensation." The case of Stavrogin was different: on account of the degree of self-placarding challenge and malice in his very bowing down at the crossroads, he must sacrifice such "sacrifice" and impose a limit upon his self-imposed suffering. He must simply become a novice, Tihon advises; secretly, while living in the world, nobody knowing the difference. Only then can the humility of his act become sincere. Defiance, however, remained his mode of being:

> "Well, what if I have defied them by the crudeness of my confession, if you *did* notice the challenge? That's the right way. They deserve it. I will only force them to hate me more, that's all. It will only make it easier for me. . . . I am not in the habit of being frank, but since I have started

. . . with you . . . know that I despise them all, just as much as I do myself, as much if not more, infinitely more. No one can be my judge. . . . I wrote this nonsense," he nodded at the sheets, "just so, because the thought popped into my head, just to be shameless . . . perhaps I simply made up a story, I exaggerated in a fanatical moment," he broke off angrily.

Here indeed Dostoevski has portrayed a "whole life" comprised of plunging deeper into sin, even deeper into confession, and by confession deeper into sin, so that, as Luther remarked, "the whole life would be nothing else than confession, and . . . even this confession would have to be confessed in another confession." [11]

The interview between Stavrogin and Tihon passes in the end from "despair over sin" to what Kierkegaard designated as "despair of the forgiveness of sins." This all along was Stavrogin's primary mode of existence, not simply a final stage at which he arrived. "Despair of the forgiveness of sins is a definite position directly in the face of the offer of God's compassion." [12] Face to face with Christ, "the prodigious concession of God," [13] the *weakness* in a man like Stavrogin (or his *un*willingness simply to be himself the sinner he is and his *in*ability to repent with simple sincerity) becomes transmuted or potentiated into the *strength* of defiance. "When the sinner despairs of the forgiveness of sins it is almost as if he were directly picking a quarrel with God." [14] And what there was of *strong* defiance in Stavrogin's "despair over sin" (his resistance to repentance and grace as some foe or threat to him) becomes depotentiated into *weakness:* he simply is unable to receive forgiveness or to believe in the forgiveness of sins. This indeed is weakness, for he need acknowledge his sins only on ground where it has already been declared that they have already been forgiven him. This he cannot do, even on these reassuring conditions. Talk about "God never being able to forgive him for it" shows now as the blasphemy of a weak-defiance or a defiant-weakness which treads on God's toes by flying as far as possible from him. "To behave forwardly toward God one must retire backward far from him," [15] far from the forgiveness of sins. Thus Raskolnikov exclaimed to his sister, "If I am guilty forgive me (though I cannot be forgiven if I am guilty)." Such remains to the end Stavrogin's mood.

"Answer a question, but sincerely, speak to me alone, as you would to yourself in the darkness of night," Tihon began in a poignant voice. "If someone were to forgive you for this . . . , and not any one whom you have known, but a stranger, a man whom you will never know, who would forgive you mutely, in his own heart, while reading your terrible confession, would the thought of this make it easier for you, or would it be all the same to you? If it would injure your amour-propre to answer, do not speak, but only think to yourself."

"It would be easier," answered Stavrogin under his breath. "If you were to forgive me, it would make it much easier for me."

"I will forgive you, if you forgive me also," said Tihon.

But this reply arouses Stavrogin's irritation over "ancient monkish formulae" for bad humility, and gives occasion for his propelling himself backward from the forgiveness to which he had for a moment drawn close: "Listen, I will tell you the whole truth: I want to have you forgive me. And perhaps to have another man, or even a third, do so too, but by all means let everybody else hate me!" But such defiant courting of hatred, Tihon discerns, is only weakness protecting itself. Stavrogin could face people's rage more than he could endure their laughter, their sarcasm, their purposeful refusal to understand his document; more, indeed, than he could endure their forgiveness.

Here then we penetrate the soft underbelly and at the same time halt before the impregnable fortress of despairing of the forgiveness of sin. As Kierkegaard remarks, "The more conception of Christ, the more self. . . . But the more self, the more intense the sin." [16] This is the reason Dostoevski, in portraying his Christ-figures—Sonia of the "insatiable compassion"; Prince Myshkin, quite without guile; Alyosha, who never judges unrighteousness; and the "Christ," who, kissing the Inquisitor's lips, even in him appeals only to freedom—portrays also the increased demonic resistance to redemption which they also produce. Even in Raskolnikov there is *hatred* of Sonia, and for him also the possibility of offense which Stavrogin lives out, for Stavrogin should be regarded as to the end an unrepentant Raskolnikov.

When Stavrogin's despair over his sin becomes intensified into despairing of the forgiveness of sins, he "has lost every relation to grace—and to himself at the same time." [17] Unwillingness to receive forgiveness is the same thing as inability to forgive one's self. "Listen to me, Father Tihon: I want to forgive myself. That's my chief object, that's my whole aim! . . . That is why I seek measureless suffering, I seek it myself." Recognizing that one's sins are forgiven and forgiving one's self come, in fact, to the same thing, since only God's forgiveness gives ground for self-forgiveness:

"If you believe that you can forgive yourself, and if you seek to attain that forgiveness in this world by your suffering, then you have complete faith! . . . God will forgive your unfaith, for in truth even in ignorance of the Holy Ghost, you honour it."

"There is no forgiveness for me," Stavrogin said gloomily.

"As to that, I will give you joyous tidings," said Tihon with emotion; "Christ too will forgive you if you reach the point where you can forgive yourself. . . . Oh, no, no, do not believe that I am uttering blasphemy: even if you do not achieve reconciliation with yourself and self-forgiveness,

even then He will forgive you for your intention and your great suffering.
. . . Even if you don't [hold out], the Lord will take account of your
original sacrifice. Everything will be taken into account; not a word, not a
movement of the spirit, not a half-thought will be lost."

Here, plainly, relation to grace and relation to self may be gained at
the same time; and, in a different sense than before, "the more conception of Christ, the more self." Did not the conviction that a man
might declare sins forgiven, did not this in Jesus occasion some to be
offended at him? Humanly acknowledging forgiveness as well as forgiving another when truly only God can, traces home to the "joyous
tidings" that without exception our sins are already forgiven. This is
the gospel of God that all guilt has been removed.

V

At least two of the traditional interpretations of God's activity for
man's redemption manifestly rest upon the prior view that a man must
have some sort of righteousness (real or fictional, imparted or imputed)
before he can be saved. One of these is the substitutionary theory of the
Atonement, according to which the right Man must bear an infinite
penalty in man's stead before God can rightfully pardon him. Thus
guilty men stand before God clothed in the righteousness of Christ's
atoning act. Even contemporary writers will often be found asserting
that the modicum of truth contained in this forensic interpretation of
the Atonement is that it shows how serious a matter sin is and consequently how *hard* it is for God to forgive sins. As if the very glory of
God were not seen precisely in this: that He "thinks it not robbery to
be divine, that is, He does not hold on to the booty like a robber, but
God parts with himself," and "the depth of the Godhead, the greatness
of His glory . . . is revealed in the very fact that it can also completely
hide itself in its sheer opposite, in the profoundest rejection and the
greatest misery of the creature." [18]
The other great repository of pagan conceptions of man's righteousness before God has been the doctrine of infused grace, prevalent in
differing forms both in Roman Catholicism and in Protestantism. Substitutionary theories of the Atonement go along with the idea that certified
salvation can be gained only through the imputation of righteousness
or the transference of righteousness (or paid penalty) from one man to
another; while doctrines of infused grace are but another way of saying
that imparted or real righteousness is necessary to salvation.
Grace as a power or quality infused into and transforming human
moral character had its beginning with Augustine, and the meaning of
this doctrine can best be observed at its point of origin. The Pelagians

had objected that Augustine's views on sin and the inheritance of sin made of sin some real substance, and therefore called in question the goodness of the Creator of all substances. Pelagius contended that sin is "wholly a name without substance, whereby is expressed not a thing, not an existence, not some sort of body, but the doing of a wrongful deed," and he asked: "How could that which lacks all substance have possibly weakened or changed human nature?" [19] Augustine replied that sin indeed is not a substance but "the withdrawal from a substance," from God who is "the height of substance and the only true sustenance of the reasonable creature." [20] This withdrawal from substance has resulted in a substantial impairment of human nature such that only a disabled nature, or a nature lacking in substance, could be passed on by propagation from Adam to the rest of the race.

In the terms of their debate, without doubt Pelagius was effectively answered; but at the same time the stage was set so that thereafter nothing but a substantialist conception of grace could possibly get into the act or have any part to play in the drama of human redemption. If sin be not substance, but the lack of it, then grace which repairs human nature must necessarily be a substance. Redemption can take place only by a "transubstantiation" of human nature. By an infusion of real substance (grace) the individual gains for the first time the full or perfect manhood which is "connaturally" his own and which originally, of course, belonged by nature to the whole race. The Catholic notion of grace as substance came to full flower in the doctrine of the Sacraments and in Aquinas' views on infused theological virtues, infused moral virtues, infused "gifts," infused "fruits," and infused "beatitudes."

The idea of infusion gained currency in Protestant thought in the form of doctrines of prevenient grace and in answer to the question: What, then, is the source of faith, if faith be not an inner "work" that man himself performs? But it may be asked, What gain was there in supplanting an Augustinian notion of "infused love" by the Reformers' views on "infused faith," which contained within them in germ the whole doctrine of predestination? As Nicholas Berdyaev remarks, "Christ is not only the Truth, but *the truth about freedom,* unconstrained truth, . . . he is himself freedom and unconstrained love." [21] In the light of Jesus Christ, accounts of the grace of God may not even go so far as to render human freedom problematic, as is true when infused or prevenient grace divides the ground with freedom. "That truth [or love or faith or grace as infused substances] attracts to itself without the intervention of freedom is a dangerous illusion." [22] Christ *for us* means not Christ *in us* but Christ who kisses the Inquisitor's lips, who appeals only to freedom.

Against this background, what account can be given of the atoning work of Christ and of God's relation (as Christians understand him) to human sin and redemption? A first answer to this question is suggested by another aspect of the views of Augustine. It is impossible not to see vestiges of Platonism in Augustine's notion of sin as defect of substance, and this results in his view of grace as infused substance. There stands here in the shadows, keeping watch over its own, Augustine's "order of natures" or the great chain of being which was his heritage from Neo-Platonism. Yet at the same time, and mainly, Augustine analyzes the phenomena of sin in terms of positive self-contradiction within the will and disobedient spiritual pride, which it would scarcely occur to an unprejudiced mind to designate as "withdrawal from being" or a "decline from being into nonbeing." And another interpretation of the grace of God speaks especially to this understanding of sin, just as grace as infused substance is appropriate to sin understood as lack of substance. Augustine writes:

> Our conception is framed according to this notion, when we believe that God was made man for us as an example of humility, and to show the love of God towards us. For this it is which it is good for us to believe, and to retain firmly and unshakenly in our heart, that the humility by which God was born of a woman, and was led to death through contumelies so great by mortal men, is the chiefest remedy by which the swelling of our pride may be cured, and the profound mystery by which the bond of sin may be loosed.[23]

Substantial grace perhaps repairs any loss of substance that man has suffered; but only God's *humilitas* meets man's rather substantial pride. At the same time the humility of God appears objectively as Christ for us, kissing the lips and dwelling in the heart only through the decision of faith.

A second way of pointing out the atoning work of Christ is in terms of the suffering deity. A God who suffers establishes the only adequate ground upon which forgiveness of sins may be proffered and words of consolation be spoken to men who, out of sin, continue in sin and who cannot otherwise believe their sins are forgiven. Before Ivan read his "Legend of the Grand Inquisitor," he expounded to Alyosha his views on the problem of suffering, especially the suffering of children. He accepts God, but won't accept his world; he won't accept harmony, he finds the forgiveness of sins in this instance quite impossible, and so respectfully returns his ticket. He who himself suffers the consequences of some evil deed, and he alone, is in position to forgive sin. No one else has the right to forgive:

> "I don't want the mother to embrace the oppressor who threw her son to the dogs! She dare not forgive him! Let her forgive him for herself, if she will, let her forgive the torturer for the immeasurable suffering of her

mother's heart. But the suffering of her tortured child she has no right to forgive, she dare not forgive the torturer, even if the child were to forgive him! . . . Is there in the whole world a being who would have the right to forgive and could forgive?"

Alyosha sees that the answer to this question can be given only by One who has borne all our sufferings. *Therefore* he bears our sins and is in the position to forgive sin where men are not and when men do not. Only if it be true that Christ really suffers in all suffering, and if upon him as the God-Man all sin has actually fallen, can he have the right to forgive sin in the stead of those other sufferers who may not forgive us. He who feels that through Jesus Christ he has been forgiven must necessarily acknowledge that the evil he has done not only caused these little ones to suffer but at the same time crucified Christ afresh.

The humility of God, then, is "the chiefest remedy by which the swelling of our pride may be cured"; and the suffering of God is the remedy by which despair of the forgiveness of sins may be cured. These conditions God preveniently establishes, or so Christians believe, for the redemption of men, who were otherwise by sin plunging deeper into sin and guilt.

Three

Religious Aspects of Marxism

Karl Marx wrote that the criticism of religion is the beginning of all criticism. "Criticism of heaven is transformed into a criticism of the earth, criticism of religion into the criticism of the law, criticism of theology into the criticism of politics."

Marx's understanding of religion derives from the left-wing Hegelian Feuerbach, and it is what we commonly call today the theory of projection. In religion man alienates from himself something belonging properly to his own human essence, denies that this quality belongs to himself, and projects it upon the infinite. He dispossesses himself in order to have a god who has great possessions. Thus "the poor man possesses a rich God." Man finds himself "dispossessed of something essentially belonging to him for the benefit of an illusive reality." He "affirms in God what he denies in himself." He compensates for the fact that he is impoverished, or he impoverishes himself by enriching his God, in filling whom he empties himself. This has not been altogether a bad thing, Feuerbach says, since "strictly speaking, consciousness exists only in beings which can make their [own] essence and their species the object of thought." For a long time the religious contemplation of the essence of God has been the only manner in which man had self-consciousness or consciousness of his own essence "writ large" in the heavens. Tribute to the greatness of God has been a testimony to man's awareness of the greatness of man, since God is only the sum total of the attributes which make up the greatness of man. Perhaps this has been a necessary historical form of human self-consciousness. But the time has now come for man to "take back into his heart that nature which he has rejected," for him to recover what he has projected, for him to come into his own. The original title planned for Feuerbach's *Das Wesen des Christentums* was *Gnothi seauton* (know thyself).

Marx's only reproach of Feuerbach is for thus making religious self-alienation and projection some sort of strange metaphysical act or an isolated human act, instead of explaining it more positively and concretely in terms of sociological and economic facts. Otherwise he accepts and applies Feuerbach's analysis of religion. "Man makes religion" Marx writes; "it is not religion that makes man; religion is in reality man's own consciousness and feeling which has not yet found itself or has lost itself again." "The religion of the workers has no God, because it seeks to restore the divinity of man." Or his more famous statement: "This state and this society produce religion, a mistaken attitude to the world, because they themselves constitute a false world. . . . [Religion] is the imaginative realization of the human essence, because that essence has no reality. The misery of religion is at once the expression of real misery and also a protestation against actual misery. Religion is the sigh of the harassed creature (the sigh of a creature overwhelmed by unhappiness), the spirit of spiritless circumstances (the soul of a world that has no heart, as it is the mind of an era that has no mind). It is the opiate of the people. . . . Religion is only the illusory sun which moves around man so long as man does not move around himself."

With this view of religion it does not much matter to the orthodox Marxist whether the war is currently being prosecuted against organized religion or whether religious observances are momentarily tolerated while the war is being prosecuted against the social conditions which seem to make them necessary. The result will be the same, for as Marx wrote, "The demand that one reject illusions about one's situation is a demand that one reject a situation which has need for illusion." This may also be read in the other direction: The demand that one reject a situation which has need for illusion is a demand that one reject illusions about one's situation. Thus the criticism of religion is the beginning of all criticism in such a way that it does not much matter which end of the stick you first take hold of. To prosecute the war against economic exploitation may be the best way to attack religion, for it may equally well be said that the criticism of earth is transformed into a criticism of heaven, the criticism of the law into the criticism of religion, the criticism of politics into the criticism of theology.

Thus the Marxist movement in the mid-nineteenth century announced that the criticism of religion is the beginning of all criticism of politics and economics. It may be worthwhile for us in the mid-twentieth century to consider whether the beginning of all criticism of Marxism itself may not be the criticism of the religious aspects of Marxism. By "criticism," of course, I do not mean total or partial rejection, but the proper *understanding* of Marxism. Middleton Murry has said that "Communism is the one living religion in the world today." Rightly grasped, Marxism must be studied also as a religious movement, and not merely as a scientific or philosophical system. There are enough obscurities and inconsistencies in Marxism as a social science to prepare anyone for the conclusion that only a religion could have brought such errors to considerable triumph in the world. Perhaps we may even say that, as Marxism as an ideology endeavors to satisfy all the religious urges of men, its claim to be scientific is a necessary prerequisite in the modern age, for without pretending to be scientific, men in our day would not even be religious.

Of course, objectively viewed, Marxism is not a religion, since it has no place for belief in God, no point of reference to reality transcending the human and historical plane; and from this point of view it may seem foolish to speak of the religious aspects of Marxism. But, subjectively viewed, Marxism is but one more proof that Plato was right in describing man as "that most religious of animals." Even atheism, when it succeeds in becoming a vital movement, is informed by genuine religious components. To say that when subjectively viewed Marxism may be regarded as a religious movement, is to call attention first of all to the fact that men give to it their final loyalty, their absolute allegiance. They find in it their ground of ultimate concern, the resting place and warrant for their faith and hopes. They are engaged in it in such a way that all other concerns are either excluded or fall into subordinate place. Marxism may surely be said to have its fundamental religious aspect. If we are to credit Luther's words, "Trust and Faith of the heart alone make both God and the idol. Whatsoever thy heart clings to and relies upon, that is properly thy God."

Yet there is more analogy between Marxism and religion than this matter of the faith or commitment each evokes. The *faith* element cannot actually be separated from the *thought* element in either Marxism or religion. We may expect therefore to find many striking comparisons between the structures of thought and the world views of Marxism and of the biblical religions. How could this be otherwise, since it was the religious urges of specifically Western man which Marxism as an ideology endeavored to satisfy and redirect? It naturally sucks back into the human essence, and onto the plane of history, all that had been lost from humanity to the specifically *biblical* Deity. One ought not to forget that, when a grammar school boy, Karl Marx wrote a treatise entitled "The Union of the Faithful with Christ, according to John 15:1-14, in its Ground and its Essence, its Conditioned Necessity and its Effects." His mother is said once to have remarked that things would be better if only Karl didn't write so much about Capital and made some of it! She might have been sure that in writing about religion and about almost everything else, he had a good deal of it—not simply "religion in general" (which does not exist) but the particular religious convictions of men in the West, stemming from the Bible. Indeed, since the break-up of Calvinism, Marxism is almost the only biblical theology which has effectively molded the thought of ordinary men.

Consider first the religious source or the religious equivalent of some of the characteristics of life in the present age, as Marxism describes it.

"The history of all hitherto existing society is the history of class struggle." What can be more irreligious than this? Yet if we let the religious doctrine of the Fall of man have for a moment its proper place in our thinking, we shall find nothing inherently unlikely in the Marxist account of history as the history of class struggle. Assuming sinfulness, it may be quite plausible to argue that man's life now is conditioned by his greed and self-interest. Both Marxism and Christianity apparently affirm that man is alienated from himself, from his natural environment, from true community with his fellows. Granting this, the wonder is not that Marxism unfolds the story of mankind as a history of the struggle of man against man, but that it limits this struggle to classes.

St. Augustine was more realistic and thoroughgoing. For him the kingdoms of this earth are built up out of an uncertain order and an unjust peace imposed upon inveterate strife and dissension. Cain, the first murderer, was also the first builder of cities. He is the founder of the *civitas terrena*. This is a symbol for the fact that the kingdoms of men in this historical time are built upon fratricide. Of course, the transcendent reference in St. Augustine's view makes all the difference. There is for him a city—the city of God—in which men unite in love for an eternal good, in whom men need not fear to have colleagues. It is because men do not seek the *summum bonum et commune* that they are alienated from themselves and from one another. In inordinate love for earthly goods, in enjoying which men *must* fear to have colleagues, they base their lives on dissension and implicit fratricide. Their normal condition is war—within themselves and against others. But lopping off the religious reference to transcendent reality, as Marxism does, and viewing history, so to speak, from the underside, the resulting account of the primacy of strife is not so unlike that of the Augustinian tradition in Christianity—only St. Augustine was even more realistic.

Next, the role and function of the state. We ought not at once simply say that the state is an instrument of the dominant class. This it is in any epoch, but throughout them all the state has a more general function. In Engel's words: "in order to prevent these antagonisms—classes with conflicting interests—from consuming themselves and society in fruitless struggle, a power seemingly above society has become necessary which is to mitigate the conflict, to keep it within the bounds of 'order'; and this power, originating in society but placing itself above society and alienating itself more and more from it, is the state." Since the antagonisms which the state restrains have their source in the original alienation and dispossession of man, we may say that the state serves to restrain and remedy the original sin or disintegration of the human essence. This was precisely the function assigned to the state in Augustinian Christianity until St. Thomas gave it also a more positive purpose, and again this is the role of the state in Lutheranism: to build a dyke against sin and chaos. It is only because the state generally is an instrument to keep society going in its present form, that it thus becomes in any *given* age an instrument which serves to formalize and perpetuate the existing class structure and property relationships. Then it becomes automatically beneficial to the ruling classes. In this sense only does it turn into an "executive committee" of these classes.

Next, Marxist materialism and economic determinism. This is often wrongly supposed to be the polar opposite of religion, which in contrast, it is said, teaches the power of pious ideals and the ascendancy of spiritual over material things. It may be that in rejecting religion along with idealism, Marxism has misread religion, or at least biblical religion, with which it has close kinship. The material facts of life and the economic and political elements in history are of peculiar concern to the Bible. William Temple remarked that "Christianity is the most materialistic religion in the world." This language is perhaps too extreme, since it, too, omits to mention the transcendent point of reference in every religion. We might say, however, that biblical religion consists of a this-worldly other-worldliness—or if that is too paradoxical a phrase, that biblical religion is the most incarnational religion in the world, which places a stamp of approval or endorsement upon the concrete and the material facts of life. "It is no part of the Christian thesis," writes Alexander Miller, "that ideals have been more powerful in history than brute facts: as if God were able to manipulate ideas, but a bit helpless when it came to the sphere of the material and the economic, so that to acknowledge the power of hunger and class-interest and natural or biological causes would be to rob Him of His prerogatives" [1] to a greater extent than by acknowledging man's actions to be determined by ideas and ideals.

This is a difficult point for me to make, for it happens that I hold another philosophical view of human nature. Yet I have to admit that what the Bible affirms is not the primacy of the spiritual over the material, or the power of ideals in history, but the rule of God over all. It affirms that "God comes first, and not man," but it is not the least concerned to argue that thought precedes the act in man's individual and historical existence. It is not in the least concerned to prove that man is a thinking soul-substance. Where Genesis states that God breathed into man the breath of life and he became a "living soul," the word is *nephesh,* which should be translated "living being." It is also used of the animals: they too are living beings, and man is like them in his life. Where the New Testament asks, "What shall it profit a man if he gain the whole world and lose his own soul?" the word *psyche* is a translation of *nephesh* rather than one of the Greek meanings of *psyche.* The verse should read, "What shall it profit a man if he gain the whole world and lose his own life?" Do we feel that something of the inspiration and the spirituality has gone out of it when the verse is so read? Yes, indeed it has: the idealism has gone out of it, and religion as other-worldliness. While Marxism departs significantly from the Bible in denying the importance of the Divine appointment to which man is called, it carries on the biblical emphasis upon the historical and material setting in which human life is placed. Materialistic determination may be wrong, but to replace it by the power of ideas would not necessarily bring us a hair's breadth closer to the way the Bible understands God to rule in human affairs.

Next, the Marxist passion for social justice and for the humanization of dehumanized, exploited people. In the words of Karl Marx describing the misery of these present times, it is quite impossible not to hear ringing again the prophetic protest of an Amos of Tekoa: "There came a time when everything that men had considered inalienable became an object of exchange, of traffic, and could be alienated. This is the time when the very things which till then had been communicated but never exchanged, given but never sold, acquired but never bought—virtue, love, conviction, knowledge, conscience, etc.—when everything passed into commerce. It is the time of general corruption, of universal venality, or, to speak in terms of political economy, the time when everything, moral or physical, having become a marketable value, is brought to the market to be assessed at its truest value. . . ." Capitalism has "dissolved all natural-organic relationships into money relationships." "The bourgeoisie, wherever it has got the upper hand, has put an end to all feudal, patriarchal, idyllic relations. It has pitilessly torn asunder the motley feudal ties that bound man to his 'natural superiors,' and has left no other nexus between man and man than naked self-interest, and callous 'cash payment.' " Or as the college girl said after her boy friend had spent fifty dollars on her in one evening, "I think I *owe* him something." Thus the inalienable person herself became an object of exchange; and things formerly communicated but never exchanged, given but never sold, acquired but never bought, pass over into commerce. Marx stands squarely in the line of the prophets and the conscience of the West. His is one mighty protest against the bartering of people. Middleton Murry says rightly that Marxism alone does not explain Marx himself, his passion for social justice, his prophetic faith.

We can see Marx's concern for the *human relations* behind economic relations—in, with, and under them—more precisely and at particular points in his thought. This is true, I believe, even of that most abstract thought tracing all determination home to "the relations of production" in any society. What does the expression, "the relations of production," mean? Are the relations of production ever simply economic relations and not also human relations? Marx scathingly condemns what he calls "commodity fetishism," and calls up the wrath of an immanent deity against a world in which the social relations of production and all human relationships in general have turned into exchange relationships. Behind every commodity relation lurks a human relation.

Again, one cannot rightly grasp the "labor theory of value" in Marxist theory just by assessing its validity or invalidity as an economic theory. Rather, one must take into account the centuries-old justification of the right to appropriate personal property, that goes back through John Locke and Thomas Aquinas to Aristotle. Thus, the labor theory of value has its root both in classical humanism and in the Christian humanism of the Middle Ages; and for this reason Marx has been called the last of the schoolmen. Briefly the labor theory of property is that man gains a right of possession by the labor he puts forth into the state of nature. He extends his personality in mastering the earth and it becomes his. Whatever he puts his own person into belongs to him. To dispossess him of it is to dispossess him of a part of himself.

It is a striking and interesting fact that what is at the root of the positive moral justification of private property in Western thought is also at the root of the moral justification of communism—the labor theory of value—and that the argument used for communism against capitalism in the modern period is continuous with the argument Aristotle used for private property against Plato's communism. Market value and commodity fetishism under capitalism, according to the Marxist analysis, deprive the laborer of what belongs to him, and accomplish the final stage in the alienation of man from himself, just as theft or expropriation threatens human values in a private property system. Marxism says in effect that there needs to be less private monopoly-property in order that there can be more private property of the sort that really counts, in order that a man may not be deprived of what is his, the value of his labor and the product he puts himself into. For this reason "I think I could undertake to compile two columns of extracts about property, the one taken from Marxist text-books and the other exclusively from the various Papal Encyclicals on the Social Order, and defy anyone to tell from which source they respectively came. This is because the fundamental 'right to private property' which Catholic doctrine insists on has nothing to do with the bourgeois monopoly in property against which the Communist Manifesto—like the Encyclicals—was directed." [2] Something like this was done a few years ago by Rep. Brooks Hays, to the consternation of a witness before the Reece committee of the U.S. House of Representatives.

Next, consider the remarkable agreement between that great fulcrum of Marxist criticism—the concept of ideology—and the great fulcrum and critical perspective upon human affairs contained in the Christian notion of sin. Ideology means that self-interest and class-interest, or one's *locus* in the system of production, determines and corrupts what one *thinks* about ethics and politics and law, the arts and religion, and every other cultural activity created by man in every period. One might even say that these higher expressions of the human spirit are, for the Marxist, *totally* corrupt; and recall the story of the Calvinist who secured the advantage over an Anglican by declaring, "You are only a 'miserable offender,' while I'm totally depraved!"

The lack of any transcendent point of reference, however, deprives the Marxist of any capacity for *self*-criticism. He cannot, or does not, apply the concept of ideology to himself or to as radical a suspicion of the ideas and ideals and politics of the working-class movement as to other folk's ideology. By contrast, properly understood the fulcrum of the religious doctrine of the sinfulness or corruption of even (or especially) the highest reaches of the human spirit makes for confession of one's own sin before God and, as Luther said, throws the mantle of charity over the sin or the self-interested ideology of others. This provides ground both for seeking to see the truth and not only the error in the midst of the ideas and ideals of people who, because of their own special location in history or in the class structure, look out upon the world with different eyes than ours, and also for more self-criticism of the ideas and ideals, the philosophy and politics, of our own group. But, for all the difference, the religious point of view makes common cause with the probing concept of ideology, and similar criticism of the purity of reason put forward, e.g., by psychology, in the modern period; or rather, religion in the tradition of the Bible affirms that these discoveries are not so new and that all along this was known and summarized in the concept of the sinfulness of the whole man.

When we go beyond these comparisons of details, and consider the Marxist and the Christian philosophies of history as a whole, it is remarkable how alike they are. Consider, first, the Marxist unshakable belief in progress and how this functions in his thought as a surrogate for the belief in providence. This is so remarkable a feature of Communist faith that when, nearly a generation ago now, the Christian philosopher John Macmurray, of the University of London, first began to study Marxism sympathetically with a view toward effecting an intellectual *rapprochement* between it and Christianity, he suggested that perhaps only the Marxist really believes any longer in God's providential rule over human history.

> The Communist lives by a faith in a power, which he calls in his own jargon "the process of history". . . . This simply means that Communism, whatever its exponents may say, has recovered that essential core of a real belief in God, which organized Christianity has in our day largely lost.
>
> Anyone who concluded that the behaviour of the Christians showed that they did not really believe in God but only thought they believed, might then equally conclude that the Communists really believed in God and only thought they did not.

There would be nothing paradoxical in the discovery that a religion which had lost its faith in God must be overwhelmed by a faith which had rejected religion.[3]

Do we really believe in God, or—in the revised oath of allegiance to the United States, for example—do we only believe in believing in God?

Of course, the Marxian dialectical progress toward the new age which is the final goal of history removes the transcendent reference from the doctrine of providence, and places faith in a wholly immanent power. This is a significant difference, often too much overlooked by Marxist Christians. Nevertheless, Marxism does represent a continuation of the belief that linear, temporal history and all the events that happen upon this plane have basic significance—a belief which goes back as far as the ninth century B.C. to the earliest strand that found its way into the Pentateuch, the Yahwist writer's account of God's dealings with the generations of men. What happens here and now has a past and will have a future; the present arises out of memory of God's mighty acts in the past and leans forward in expectancy toward what God (or the process of history) is yet about to do; every event and each generation has a heritage and a destiny that falls within some overarching "purpose" being worked out in time, without which we have not properly understood "the time of our lives."

To grasp history as a meaningful field of activity—as event-full—it is necessary to speak of both the *terminus from which* every event comes and the *terminus toward which* it is tending. Plato, in the doctrine of creation and the creation of time as the relation between and measure of the motion of creatures, had a *terminus from which,* and to this extent spatio-temporal events had their meaning. But, lacking an eschatology or view of the *end toward which* temporal history is moving, events were not as meaningful for him as for the prophetic tradition in biblical religion. Consequently, Plato describes time as at best "a moving image of eternity." In it there takes place participation in the eternal or imitation of the heavenly essences. In their biographies individual men and societies may advance toward fuller comprehension and expression of these eternal verities, but each generation stands as close to them as any other. Time and history are not themselves moving toward any consummation. Marxism displays its true parentage when it comes into the world with the exuberant and frightening cry, "Now is our salvation nearer than the hour we first believed." In this the prophets still speak, with their conviction that the Eternal has moved purposefully into history, bending it, and the men who align themselves with its ultimate purpose, toward some appointed terminus in an age beyond the present.

Events in time are of more consequence than the passing shadows on the wall of Plato's cave. Instead they are the very plane upon which human destiny is being wrought out. This ingredient which Marxism shares with the Western tradition generally accounts for the fact that, until they are touched by the life and thought of the West, the depressed classes in other religious cultures are simply depressed, while among us they are depressed *into expectancy*. However fantastic be the forms of the expectation that something revolutionary and transforming is about to happen in history, Western man—and the Marxist no less than others—live by faith and are saved by hope. The worse the visible situation becomes, the harder the heel of the oppressor, the more evident is it that the powers of evil and injustice are being mustered for their last Armageddon. Or, as a line of the "Internationale" puts it: "Then, Comrades, come rally, and the *last* fight let us face."

Now, the biblical view of history and the Marxian belief in an immanent providence, which we have so far considered only in general terms, both break down into an articulate structure of successive periods. The analogy between their conception of these ages suggests still more strongly the prophetic and biblical component in Marxism. Biblical religion speaks of various "dispensations"—the garden of Paradise, the Fall of man into history as we know it, then the periods from Adam to Noah, from Noah to Moses, from Moses to Christ, and finally with quickening pace from Christ to the second coming of the Messiah. The word "dispensations" contains, of course, a reference to transcendent reality, to the free disposing purpose of the living God, which drops out in Marxism. But Marxism does have the structural equivalents of these ages in its view of history: primitive communism, the fall of man from this ideal state into slavery, then feudalism, then capitalism in which the Messianic class appears at first incognito among the common people, then revolutionary upheaval seizes the present age thrusting down the mighty from their seats, and the Kingdom of God or the final communism is ushered in through an intermediary period of socialism.

There is surely more to the Marxian conception of a golden age of primitive communism than was supplied by the researches of Lewis Morgan, the American anthropologist, among the Iroquois Indians. The more is Rousseau's *Discourse on the Origin of Inequality*. The more also is the Garden of Eden symbol. To this it might be objected that Marxism portrays primitive communism by no means as a paradise in which the first pair have only to tend the garden at leisure, but as a hard and perilous life in which mankind is slain all the day long by the forces of nature; and also that it pictures the Fall as increased mastery of nature.

However, in certain respects theology has always interpreted the Fall as a fall upward. And in any case, looking back upon it religious people have been inclined to "praise the sin" upon which precondition so great redemption has been wrought, much as Marxism pays tribute to the achievement of greater mastery over nature during historical ages since the Fall. Thus, the final communism is superior to primitive communism, as the Kingdom of God is to the original paradise, by virtue of what has gone between. And for all the hardship, in primitive communism man was still man, in full possession of his humanity, in spite of the fact that he—integral man—succumbed all the day long before the alien forces of nature. Though he died easily, nothing had yet alienated him from himself or dehumanized him. In primitive society, production was on the narrowest possible scale, but, to quote Engels, "it entailed the producers' mastery over their *processes* of production and its product. . . . As long as production is carried on on this basis it cannot grow over the producers' heads, cannot beget any monstrous foreign power facing them, as is regularly and inevitably the case in civilization." In short, while under primitive communism man was not much the master of physical nature, he was the master of his own productive processes. After the Fall he gains mastery over nature only at the expense of being enslaved to his own means of production. These "grow over his head," and become a "monstrous foreign power facing him."

This is the first great alienation of man which lies behind, or underneath, man's life in all later periods of history. Man is dispossessed of his full human stature, he is dehumanized, by the growth of the processes of production "over his head." This is, in Marxist mythology, the "original sin" of man in history as we know it. To grasp the parallel with biblical religion, we must not interpret "original sin" as an isolated action done, but also as a wounding of his human substance which man suffers. This wound, of course, he inflicts on himself. By sin comes slavery to sin, Christians say. And by putting forth himself into the processes of production there comes, say the Marxists, as a consequence man's own dispossession of himself when these grow over his head and face him as monstrous power. The original sin of man the historical animal means the distortion of the human essence under the conditions by which alone his freedom and economic power in the world were actualized. It is the alienation of man from his true nature, his self-alienation from himself. This, according to both Marxism and Christianity, has "always already" happened.

With Paradise and the Fall behind us, let us turn now and face toward the Kingdom of God to which the present age is rapidly drawing near. The Marxist analysis unfolds before us some remarkable expectations. This is an age of Messianic woes. The present age groaneth and travaileth waiting for the sons of God. A Messiah is expected who will bring division, setting father against son and son against father. Indeed, he may even now be present among us hidden among the common people.

Perhaps he is already laid in a manger in some stable among the sons of the poor; and thence about to take up his work and assume his rightful sovereignty over the kingdoms of this world. The Messiah, of course, is the working class come to self-consciousness as the proletariat. They will save Israel and usher in the Kingdom of God and wipe away all tears from our eyes.

Now what the Marxist says about this Messiah is quite paradoxical. He is not the Messiah you would have expected. We have already noticed that the Marxist confidence in the rationality and competence of working-class thoughts contradicts, or at least limits the application of, the concept of ideology. But notice the description of the qualifications of this Messiah emerging within the historical process. In the proletariat the self-alienation and dehumanization of man reaches its most extreme development. The working class is utterly alienated from essential humanity, hence able to overcome alienation; dehumanized, hence ready to carry the torch for humanity. The class-consciousness of the proletariat is actually the class-consciousness of man the *commodity*, the consciousness of men who have already been crucified, dead, and buried as men.

How can the manhood of the industrial worker, being so alienated from its own human nature, have power within itself to achieve its own emancipation, and at the same time the final salvation of mankind? By its position in history and in the processes of production, the proletariat constitutes a society all by itself, as it were, thrust outside of bourgeois society. It is a counter-society to the existing order, a universal class, a class to end all classes. Totally negated by the existing system, it becomes the total negation of that system, and therefore a total summation of human protest against partial humanity. It is a complete expression and veritable incarnation of humanity. Hence it has complete detachment from the ideology of class interest set against other classes within society. Thoroughly dehumanized, it thereby becomes the bearer of the new being, the new humanity, humanity for the first time since the Fall, essential humanity saved from the distortions that held sway during all former periods of history.

Must we not think in this connection of the crucified, suffering Messiah of another celebrated religion? He, too, was thrust altogether "outside the camp," was crucified, dead and buried; yet rises again to new life and obtains the renewal of all mankind. He grew up before us

> . . . Like a root out of dry ground;
> he had no form or comeliness that we should look at him,
>   and no beauty that we should desire him.
> He was despised and rejected by men;
>   a man of sorrows and acquainted with grief;

> and as one from whom men hid their faces.
>> he was despised, and we esteemed him not . . .
> yet we esteemed him stricken, smitten by God, and afflicted.

Yet he was the new being, the bearer of a new humanity, himself the new being and the new humanity, true man of true man, the savior of the world.

> But he was wounded for our transgressions,
>> he was bruised for our iniquities;
> upon him was the chastisement that made us whole,
>> And with his stripes we are healed   (Isaiah 53:2-5).

It has frequently been suggested that the final stage of perfect communism corresponds to the Kingdom of God. Let us see just how this is so, for Marxist terminology now shifts to accord with the nature of so great a consummation. We have not yet been speaking of history. History only now has its beginning. All that went before was prehistory. Likewise, the human being for the first time appears before our expectant eyes. All that went before was prehuman. As Engels wrote, "a truly human ethic, standing above class contradictions and above the memory of them, will be possible only on a stage of development in society which has not only overcome the antimony of class, but also has forgotten it for the practice of life." The lion shall lie down with the lamb and the infant shall play a flute before the hole of an asp, and a little child shall lead them. The state shall wither away, for there will be no more alienation of man from man or antagonism of class against class for it to restrain and remedy in order to preserve a just endurable peace among opposites. The church also—that is, the Communist party—shall wither away; and no longer shall one person say to another, "Let us go up to the house of the Lord"; but each shall dwell under his own vine and a fig tree and each for himself shall know and do what is for the general good.

Since Marxism takes *time* seriously and emphasizes the meaning of prehistory as it grinds violently from one stage of the dialectic to another, the final paradise cannot be regarded as a heaven static and at rest. The dialectic of thesis, antithesis, and synthesis continues, only now it works smoothly and by discussion and persuasion. Under communism there is *activity in* the goal, prehistory has been *activity toward* the goal. This is exactly what Christian theologians say about the vision of God in eternal life. Taking *time* seriously as a relation among creatures and the measure of the activity of creatures, and emphasizing the meaning of historical events, it then becomes quite impossible for the biblical religions to conceive of an altogether timeless eternity. As long as there are creatures whose individuality and actions have ultimate significance, it will take time to be their measure, only time redeemed from the agony of unfulfillment. There will be activity in the goal and a time beyond present history spent in adhering to God—eternal life in peace, peace in eternal life. We have the same thing in the attenuation of dialectical movement in the Marxist heaven, only there is no God there.

Jettisoning the religious reference to transcendent reality means that the Marxist attitude toward the components of prehistory must be one of total rejection and total revolution. Marxism does not accept, as Augustine said of the Manichees, "with good and simple faith this good and simple reason why the good God created" such a world as this—that for all the evil corrupting it, its basic nature still is good. Instead "everything," writes Engels, "that is real within the realm of the history of mankind is bound to become unreasonable after a while; hence it is already by definition unreasonable, is afflicted with unreasonableness from the very beginning. . . . Everything that exists deserves to perish." In other words, in the present stage of prehuman history, the unreasonable is the real and the real is the wholly unreasonable. On the other hand, in the final days the reasonable is destined to become real and all reality reasonable. "Everything," writes Engels, "that is reasonable within the heads of men is destined to become real, however much it may contradict the existing seeming reality."

Notice in this the Hegelian terminology of an immanent rational spirit in nature and history. Marx claimed he overturned Hegelianism and stood Hegel on his feet again, the feet of dialectical materialism. But Hegel was already bending over clutching his toes, the curvature of the body in that position being a symbol for his philosophy of immanent spirit or rationality. When Marx turned Hegel over, his posture was not much altered, since the system still manifests the structures of immanentism. There are the critical points of Marxism, for example, its failure to find firm moral grounds for *not* using individual men "to manure the soil for the future harmony," for the time to come when the reasonable shall become real. Today there is perhaps good ground for believing, with Gabriel Marcel, that "all philosophies of immanence have had their day." Yet point by point within the limits of a wholly immanent scheme, Marxism evidently provides a religion to end religion by offering viable substitutes for the specific articulated structures of biblical or prophetic religious faith on which it largely depends for its power.

Four

Jean-Paul Sartre:
Sex in Being

"These considerations do not exclude the possibility of an ethics of deliverance and salvation. But this can be achieved only after a radical conversion which we cannot discuss here." *

I

The Irish literary critic, Arland Ussher, in a book entitled *Journey through Dread*[1] minted three marvelous chapter titles for his treatment of the existentialist philosophers: "The Shudder before God" (Kierkegaard), "The Shudder before Death" (Heidegger), and "The Shudder before *The Other Person*" (Sartre). Jean-Paul Sartre's portrayal of man's mode of being in the world, which is primarily a being-before-the-other-person, will be the theme of this chapter, or (with no change of theme) the human significance of sexuality. Although Sartre has sometimes been thoughtlessly dismissed as a philosopher, those who have taken the trouble to study his works will not doubt that he is one of the most rigorous thinkers alive today. He never flinches before the conclusions to be drawn from his analysis (except in *Existentialism Is a Humanism*), and that is indeed a rare quality. Moreover, of the two movements of thought in the present day which restore sexuality to the full unity of human personality, Freudian psychology tends always to submit the psyche to the sway of dark, libidinous powers (against which other solitary ascetics through the ages have struggled in different fashion) while, to the contrary, Sartre's "existential psychoanalysis" views sexuality as belonging within the translucency of personal consciousness. The trial, at least, should be made to see whether a properly Christian and humane interpretation of the meaning of sexuality may not have a good deal to gain from Sartre, even by (in the end) specifically exposing where he is in error.

Sartre knows at least something of what human existence would be like if it were primarily determined by "the shudder before God." The

* An astounding footnote Sartre appends to his system: *Being and Nothingness* (Tr. Hazel E. Barnes). New York: Philosophical Library, 1956, p. 412, n. 14.

religious overtones of many of his basic categories, even their coinage apparently for the deliberate purpose of erecting an antireligious system that will finally "exclude God the Father," [2] has frequently been noted. And a character in one of his novels proclaims with infinite passion (if this is possible):

> But I know at last that I am. I adapt for my own use, and to your disgust, your prophet's foolish wicked words: "I think, therefore I am," which used to trouble me sorely, for the more I thought, the less I seemed to be; and I say: "I am seen, therefore I am." I need no longer bear the responsibility of my turbid and disintegrating self: he who sees me causes me to be; I am as he sees me. I turn my eternal shadowed face towards the night, I stand up like a challenge, and I say to God: Here I am. Here I am as you see me and I do not know myself. What can I do now?—You know me and I do not know myself. What can I do except support myself? And you whose look eternally creates me—do support me. Mathieu, what joy, what torment! At last I am transmuted into myself. Hated, despised, sustained, a presence supports me to continue thus forever. I am infinite and infinitely guilty. But I *am*. Mathieu, I am. Before God and before men I am. *Ecce homo*.[3]

Here we encounter a theme that is fundamental to Sartre's whole scheme: the meaning of *the look*, and of being looked at, as what alone obtains for man an essence (what joy!) and crowds out freedom (what torment!). Yet Sartre turns away from the possibility of existence in the divine presence. He does this, I think, for two reasons. The first may be termed his ontological argument for the nonexistence of God, or for the impossibility of God's existence, to which we shall return. The second, not so apparent, reason is that Sartre's realistic portrayal of human life fulfills what Nietzsche foretold in "The Ugliest Man" would finally murder God. This was man's implacable "revenge on the witness":

> Thou couldst not *endure* him who beheld *thee,*—who ever beheld thee through and through, thou ugliest man. Thou tookest revenge on this witness!

> But he—*had to die:* he looked with eyes which beheld *everything*—he beheld men's depths and dregs, all his hidden ignominy and ugliness.

> The God who beheld everything, *and also man:* that God had to die! Man *cannot* endure it that such a witness should live.[4]

Sartre also knows what human existence would be like if it were primarily determined by "the shudder before death." This he knew from Heidegger, and by opposing his views Sartre rejects the existential viewpoint familiar to us through Kierkegaard's (and Reinhold Niebuhr's) analysis of "anxiety," and he rejects as well the presence of person to person in Buber or Marcel. According to Heidegger, man is the place where being makes a "clearing" for the acknowledgment of the presence of being. In the midst of every particular thing-which-is, a man may recognize, revere, and "shelter" being itself. His mission is to realize the true proximity of being, "to live in the neighborhood of being," "to attend to being," to care for and preserve being.[5] This is the primary meaning of *Sorge* (care). Already profoundly implicit in this is the motive *Fürsorge* (solicitude), although care for the being of another is not yet explicitly distinguished. Care and solicitude are then accentuated by the realization that everything-which-is, including man, existence as a whole and in every part, is bound for death. Thus man lives constantly in anticipation of his own death. This means that he lives in *Sorge* in the other sense (sorrow, or even anxiety). He flees from his own grave toward it. Death means the "possibility of impossibility," and this is present as an inward event among all the possibilities which men consciously face.

Since death is there as an "anticipation," the trick is to turn it into a free "project." Authentic human existence, as distinct from the unauthentic lives of *Das Man* or the "crowd man," can be obtained only by living through the thought of one's own death and embracing it, accepting and appropriating it. By consciously flying so far (or perhaps not so far) into the future and then returning to the present moment, a state of, not exactly joy, but of sobriety and unanxious carefulness will be born in the souls of men. They will live every moment not in frenzy or like cattle, but to the full. There will even be an added zest to life that faces death; and a bracing sense of the menace of the "possibility of impossibility" will enhance and ennoble every particular possibility or project of men. The fact that "every man must do his own dying" will not necessarily lead to his own praying or his own faith, but to not unreasonable existentialist facsimiles of these spiritual acts. Moreover, when a man returns to the present moment from such a flight, he discovers that there are other, genuine persons with him. *Sorge* (care) becomes explicit *Fürsorge* (solicitude). Existence with others (*Mitsein*) means to have them in one's own care; this is solicitude for their being as being-toward-death (*Sein zum Tode*). It is to experience, as it were, on our own pulses the grief and grievances they bear. Love is respect for the shadow of death which falls across the face of Everyman. It is "pity for another doomed soul," although this expression of Unamuno's by no means fully conveys the bracing spiritual intent and the genuine active involvement of Heidegger's "solicitude."

With the refusal of "the shudder before death," Sartre's existentialism goes back in its own way to the Stoic and Epicurean maxim: when death is, we are not; and while we are, death is not. Death, Sartre says, is a totally "contingent fact which as such on principle escapes me and originally belongs to my facticity." [6] Death is a fact which descends upon conscious freedom to destroy it; it is a chance which is not as such one of my conscious possibilities or free projects, but the end of all such experiences. As "the nihilation of all my possibilities," death is "a nihilation which *itself is no longer a part of my possibilities.* Thus death is not *my* possibility of no longer realizing a presence in the world but rather an *always possible nihilation of my possibles which is outside my possibilities.*" [7] It is comprehensible that one can fearfully anticipate or even hopefully engage himself toward the possibility of a *particular* type of death, but Sartre denies that I can adopt "the project toward my death as the indetermined possibility of no longer realizing a presence in the world";[8] for this would be the destruction of all projects, including the one supposed. When death is, it is the annihilation of all my possibles; while possibilities remain open to me, death is not. It is forever "outside my possibilities and therefore I can not wait for it; that is, I can not thrust myself toward it as towards one of my possibilities. Death can not therefore belong to the ontological structure of the for-itself," i.e., the conscious self.[9]

With this, the existentialism we have known from the analysis of anxiety in Kierkegaard and Reinhold Niebuhr, and the concept of "generalized anxiety" in certain psychologists, are rejected. With this, also, is jettisoned the possibility of authentic being in relation to others or of genuine interpersonal or intersubjective relations which Kierkegaard secured by the grace of God and Heidegger by the immanent workings of natural solicitude. There can be no *Fürsorge*. There can be no *Mitsein* such as Heidegger describes. Therefore Sartre substitutes for the shudder before death "the shudder before *the Other person.*"

This is, for Sartre, all that "death" or the anxiety of finitude can mean for the conscious human being. My own death, so far as it is a possibility of which I am aware, means "the triumph of the point of view of the Other over the point of view which *I am* toward myself." [10] "*Mortal* represents the present being which I am for the Other; *dead* represents the future meaning of my actual for-itself for the Other." [11] My own death is a limit as inaccessible and as inapprehensible as the Other's conscious freedom; in fact, these are the same limit. What seizes me at the very heart of my conscious being in its upsurge into the world is the Other's gaze fixed upon me which steals my (dead) essences away from me. What the saints, and some others, have called this dying life or living death means rather that my life as I exist and live it is never what Others have in view and take away with their eyes.

Sartre can even write that "relation with the dead—with *all* the dead —is an essential structure of the fundamental relation which we have called 'being-for-others.'" [12] Thus, in the play *No Exit* which best epitomizes Sartre's whole philosophy, Garcin, the pacifist newspaper

editor who fled from the authorities and was apprehended at the border
and shot, wants Estelle to have a different image of himself than the
image of the coward left behind in the minds of all the people on earth
who "knew" him. "If there's someone, just one person," he says to this
Other who in death still constitutes the death of him, "to say quite
positively I did not run away, that I'm not the sort who runs away, that
I'm brave and decent and the rest of it—well, that one person's faith
would save me." [13] But this, as we shall see, is quite impossible. A man
cannot let himself be what he *has been*, or indeed whatever he *is*, in the
eyes of others; yet there is "no exit" from their embrace. In the famous
words at the end of this play (often misrepresented by the supposition
that a remedy might be found if only we or they were somehow different
people): "Hell is—other people!" And Hell is only a symbol for life in
interpersonal relations. *No Exit* is Sartre's play about the "communion
of the damned," which like the sometime communion of the saints includes together all the living and the dead. ("Living" means human life
as it is existed and experienced from within; the "dead" means this
same life as it is essentially viewed—by Others.)

II

Sartre's understanding of how man's mode of being in the world is
fundamentally affected by "the shudder before *The Other person*" may
be exhibited in full force, first, by probing still further the images and
dramatic action of *No Exit,* and then by a consideration of the analysis
of "being-for-others" in *Being and Nothingness.* All this will prove quite
indispensable to an adequate understanding of his interpretation of
human sexuality.

The fact that each of the three characters in the play is *without eyelids*
is a symbol far more important than the external and consequent
symbolism of the fact that the room where they are is without any
mirrors or windows or that it has a door which opens only if a porter,
who may not have heard, answers a bell that rarely, if ever, works. Each
is condemned "to live with one's eyes open all the time," which means
not so much the torment of never sleeping as of living forever under
the uninterrupted gaze of another. ". . . It's life without a break" they
have entered upon. There will be no more of those "four thousand little
rests per hour," no more of those "four thousand little respites—." The
"small black shutter" of the eyelid which, when we blink, clicks down and
provides the relief of an interruption in relationships, has been stripped
from them.

The diabolical scheme at once becomes clear to them. As Inez, older
than Estelle and a hardened woman of the world, puts the matter:
"Obviously there aren't any physical torments. . . . And yet we're in

hell. . . . In short, there's someone absent here, the official torturer.
. . . It's obvious what they're after—an economy of man-power—or devil-
power, if you prefer. The same idea as in a cafeteria, where customers
serve themselves. . . . I mean that each of us will act as torturer of the
two others." In vain they try, first, each to stay put in his or her corner
and take no notice of the others; and, then, each to make true confession frankly revealing who he actually is to the others. The former
procedure provides no escape, because if one of them makes even a little
movement, say, raises a hand to fan himself, the others will "feel a little
tug." Even if they remain completely motionless and no one looks at
another, each experiences a primary awareness *that* the others are aware
of him without being aware of *what* they are thinking about him. Each
knows *that* he is known, but not *as* he is known, much less as he exists
and knows himself to be. The absence of eyelids is only material image
for the fact that the consciousness of a consciousness of ourselves that
escapes us cannot be banished. The attempt at self-revelation, which tries
to have no longer anything secret to fear from the penetrating eyes of
others, fails because each is a freedom aiming at an "essence" he never
grasps* and can therefore never communicate who he really is to another;
and also because, even assuming he existed his essence, or that his existence and essence were one, he has no way of knowing that this has been
conveyed to another and actually determines the Other's view of him.†

In fact, there is a good deal of evidence that each is a distorting mirror
of the others. This is symbolized by the fact that there are no (impersonal)
mirrors in the room. Estelle, the young woman who drowned her child
and drove her lover to suicide, feels acutely the deprivation of a mirror.
"When I can't see myself I begin to wonder if I really and truly exist."
Whereupon Inez offers to provide her a glass in which she may be seen.
I can see you, she says. "Every inch of you. Now ask me questions. I'll
be as candid as any looking-glass." Estelle makes up her face following
Inez's promptings. This means only that Inez's look has begun to steal

---

* I take this to be one part of the meaning of the massive bronze ornament standing
on the mantelpiece, which Garcin seizes and attempts in vain to lift. This stand for
fixed, realized essence, which man never is. Cf. also Sartre's treatment of "bad
faith" (which with some gain and some loss of meaning Walter Kaufmann, *Existentialism from Dostoevsky to Sartre.* Meridian Books, 1956, pp. 241-70, translates
"self-deception"), with Sartre's extended illustration of the waiter in the café (*Being
and Nothingness*, pp. 255 f.) who plays the role of being the waiter he is not and is
not the waiter he is. Thus, consciousness never coincides with itself; sincerity is "an
attempt impossible to achieve" (*ibid.*, p. 260); and man is, because of the ontological
structure of self-consciousness, doomed to be insincerely sincere and sincerely insincere.

† The Bronze ornament stands also for a man's powerlessness before the fixed essences
others have in their views of him. At the end of the play, Garcin strokes the bronze
thoughtfully, and says, "I'm looking at this thing on the mantelpiece, and I understand that I'm in hell. . . . They knew I'd stand at the fireplace stroking this thing
of bronze, with all those eyes intent on me. Devouring me."

that face away. Though she says it is "far better," the result of such primping by proxy is: "Crueler. Your mouth looks quite diabolical that way." Estelle comments upon the peril she finds herself in: "I'm going to smile, and my smile will sink down into your pupils, and heaven knows what it will become." "Why, you've even stolen my face; you know it and I don't." ". . . All that's left of me is *the outside*—but it's not for you." And Garcin the journalist, after the collapse of his attempt to make love to Estelle, exclaims, "I won't let myself get bogged in your eyes. . . . Like an octopus. Like a quagmire." Such for Sartre is the meaning of "being-for-others."

The fact that there are three in the room complicates matters, and permits the momentary appearance of unities of person with person in varying combinations. When three are gathered together, the third by his gaze will make of the other two *one* (in *Being and Nothingness* Sartre calls this "the Us-Object"), or else two will combine against the third (Sartre calls this "the We-Subject"). Thus, when Garcin tries to make love to Estelle, Inez says to him, "Under my eyes. You couldn't do it. . . . I shan't take my eyes off you, Garcin; when you're kissing her, you'll feel them boring into you"; and to Estelle, "If you could see his big paw splayed out on your back, rucking up your skin . . ." Moreover, these momentary unities of us-objects and we-subjects are not only transient combinations. While they last they are also deeply infected by a singular relationship of one of the parties to the apparently excluded Other, which is bound to destroy them.* At one point Estelle, although Inez has drawn up close to her and addressed a question directly *in her ear*, gives her answer instead *to Garcin* who is watching. And when Estelle spits in Inez's face, the latter says *to Garcin*, "you'll pay for this"—not to Estelle.

When finally Garcin breaks down the door, opening the way to possible physical escape, and Inez says to him, "You're free to go," he cannot do it. "No, I couldn't leave you here, gloating over my defeat, with all those thoughts of me running in your head." Inez: "I'm watching you, everybody's watching, I'm a crowd all by myself." Garcin cannot break away from that embrace, even though the door is down. Forever the three will be there "with all those eyes intent on me. Devouring me." Each is a trap (whether he wishes to be or not) itself entrapped by the others (whether they wish it or not). Hell, i.e., existence in relations, is

---

* Cf.: ". . . If the Third looks at the Other who is looking at me. . . . the third transcendence transcends the transcendence which transcends me and thereby contributes to disarming it." This is a state of affairs "which will soon decompose depending upon whether I ally myself to the Third so as to look at the Other . . . or whether I look at the Third and thus transcend this third transcendence which transcends the Other" (*Being and Nothingness*, p. 416). This suffices for an account of the Us-object, and of the We-subject as a form of defense by counterattack. There is, however, more of substance in the nature of the We-subject; and to this we shall return at a later point in this chapter.

a party one is embarrassed to leave because of the gossipy *views* of himself he would leave behind fixed in the minds of others. A man cannot let himself be what he *has been,* or what he *is,* in the eyes of others. For in fact, as an exister, he was *not* and is *not* the man they grasp of him by their essences of him *in mente.*

III

The simplest approach to Sartre's philosophic work, and to existentialism generally, is to hyphenate the word "ex-istence." To be an "existing" human being means to have the power to stand consciously out (*ex*) of one's *istence,* one's "isness," and to have this capacity in uninterrupted exercise. "This newspaper does not deny concerning itself that it is the table on which it is lying." [14] The judgment that the paper *is not* the table and the table *is not* the paper requires the presence to them both of an outside witness, the conscious human mind. Yet this consciousness can say of itself, as those objects cannot, that it *is not* the table or the paper, and that they are not he. It can do this because human consciousness stands not only outside these physical objects but also outside itself, while yet bearing a peculiar presence to itself that it does not have to them. We say that creatures we call animals have, through sensation, a certain consciousness of the world. But consciousness in the only case we know—our own—requires also a *self*-consciousness. Every sensation or perception of objects out there in the world is also a consciousness of self along with these sensations or perceptions. Thus, "existence" means self-awareness, self-transcendence. Hence Sartre writes, "the necessary and sufficient condition for a knowing consciousness to be knowledge of its objects, is that it be consciousness of itself as being that knowledge." This is *necessary,* because otherwise, "if my consciousness were not consciousness of being conscious of the table, it would then be consciousness of that table without consciousness of being so"—which is impossible. It is a *sufficient* condition for knowledge of objects, because "my being conscious of being conscious of that table suffices in fact for me to be conscious of it." [15]

Now it is notorious that, contrary to J. S. Mill, in any comparison between Socrates and the pig, Socrates does not know both sides of the subject. Existentialism does not deny this when it affirms that, so far as we know, no other being in the world has "existence," in the sense explained, except man. If any creature, formerly called an animal, could be demonstrated to have consciousness of its consciousness of the world, it would be what is meant by an existing individual with the human mode of being. This is a matter of definition, and the use of terms. As a question of fact, it is only a question of where to draw the line in applying the term "man" or "existence" to living beings. A man is a self-reflecting mirror, whose mirroring of the world requires at the same time this astonishing act of mirroring himself mirroring the world, or reflecting upon his reflection of it. This being at a distance from self Sartre calls the "for-itself," and any being that simply coincides with itself, like newspapers, tables, the physical universe as such, and presumably an animal, he calls an "In-itself"; and we shall have to grow accustomed to this manner of speaking, as well as to the reservation of the term "existence" for human consciousness alone.

> The being of consciousness qua consciousness is to exist *at a distance from itself* as a presence to itself and this empty distance which being carries in its being is Nothingness. . . . The For-itself never . . . exist[s] except in the form of an elsewhere in relation to itself, as a being which perpetually effects in itself a break in being.[16]

By stressing the emptiness or nothingness in the relation of consciousness to itself, Sartre means to say not that consciousness is powerless but that it is a formal power which is under the necessity of obtaining from *the given,* from "facticity," all the matter which it reflects. Man's relation to facticity is *nausea,* which Sartre exhibited in an early book by that name. This means a man's sense of the sheer brute necessity of beginning with the specific particulars, the impulses, the sensations, those gnarled roots of the tree there, the time and place where his upsurge into the world has taken place; and his sense of the absolute incommensurability between all such facts that determine him and the freedom with which consciousness views such a world and by which he thrusts forward his own projects in it.

In order to bring the relationship between conscious subjects, or the meaning of being-for-others, into consideration, we have only to suppose there to be *two* mirrors, highly polished, empty of all content, and *facing each other.* Each is the reflection in the other, and each is in the act of reflecting the other. But what can be reflected in the one or the other is *only* its act of reflecting the other. We can apply to the case of interconscious relationships, indeed, some words of Sartre about the relation of consciousness to itself. The former is only the latter writ large, since so far and in both instances, only the formal power of consciousness is in question and we need take no account of the matter supplied by facticity. An individual reflects himself emptily; two individuals reflect one another emptily. In both cases there is an act of "nihilation" by which consciousness stands at a distance and declares that it is not this one with whom it is present. Both within and *between* subjects, i.e., as regards both intra- and interconscious relationships, there is a

> phantom dyad—the reflection-reflecting. The reflecting exists only in order to reflect the reflection, and the reflection is a reflection only in so far as it

refers to the reflecting. . . . But if the reflecting is nothing other than the reflecting of *this* reflection, and if the reflection can be characterized only by its "being-in-order-to-be-reflected in *this* reflection," then the two terms of this quasi-dyad support their two nothingnesses on each other, conjointly annihilating themselves. It is necessary that the reflecting reflect *something* [i.e., some given object] in order that the ensemble not dissolve into nothing.[17]

If it may be said that the presence of the Other alienates something from the self, this only accentuates the alienation from self that was already present within the self's presence to self invariably from a conscious distance. The emptiness of the power of consciousness, in itself and in relation to another, was expressed dramatically by Inez's comment upon her power over Garcin by a mere gaze: ". . . Just look at me, see how weak I am, a mere breath on the air, a gaze observing you, a formless thought that thinks you. . . . You can't throttle thoughts with hands. So you've no choice, you must convince me, and you're at my mercy."

Man is a Look-looking, and then by virtue of the Other he becomes a Look-looked-at, to escape which he can only look back and transform that other Look in turn into a Look-looked-at. He is a transcendence-transcending which becomes then a transcendence transcended and in return transcends that other transcendence. He is a surpassing-surpassed and then surpasses that surpassing; a pursuing-pursued which then, as a pursued-pursuing, momentarily overcomes that other pursuit.

Concrete being-for-others, or concrete relations to others, can be expressed, then, exclusively in terms of interlocking Looks, consciousnesses, transcendences, surpassings. They are locked in mortal combat; and therefore for Sartre any possible interpersonal relation has at its basis irremediable conflict. This he illustrates at length in the case of my taking a stroll in the park. As I look out upon the world, I unfold distances around me; and in this world of which I am the central subject there are various objects: the green grass, a tree, a dog, a park bench, and upon the bench a complex object, a "man-reading-a-book." All alike are objects *for me*. Then suppose the man turns and looks at me. This is the moment of earthquake at which I and my whole world shudder. Instead of grouping toward me, there enters an orientation at which everything flees from me. There takes place an "internal hemorrhage" and steady flow away from me. "Everything is traversed by an invisible flight towards a goal" which escapes me, a "permanent flight of things" toward that other consciousness beyond my reach. There is a "disintegration" of relations, a "decentralization," a "fixed sliding of the whole universe" a "bleeding" toward this "drainhold" that has opened up when I apprehend that I am apprehended, or that I am a Look-looked-at.[18] I discover that the "meaning of my being is outside of me, imprisoned in an absence." [19] I became a "spatializing-spatialized." [20]

Yet "I do not grasp the [Other's] actual surpassing; I grasp simply the death of my possibility. . . . The Other is the hidden death of my possibilities." [21] I cannot know that subject out of reach; I know that "I am stripped of my distanceless presence to my world, and I am provided with a distance from the Other." [22] A lived wrenching away of my world, "in fact my wrenching away from myself and the upsurge of the Other's freedom are one . . ." [23]

Or suppose I am stooping down peering through a keyhole. Under certain conditions this might even be a sensible project from my point of view. But suppose someone else rounds the corner of this hallway and catches me in that position. I now find myself at the end of his look, and instantly my free project is turned into a static and embarrassing posture. "I am *leaning over* the keyhole as this tree *is bent* by the wind"; I am for him an object just like any other.[24] "I grasp the Other's look at the very center of my act as the solidification and alienation of my own possibilities." [25] There takes place "a kind of violation by sight." [26]

Perhaps we may improve the illustration by supposing that, on peeping through the keyhole, I see looking at me from the other side *another eye*. That would be an "existential encounter" purified of any diverting details. I do not speculatively examine the color of the eye or the red lines in its whiteness. I do not even look at the other eyeball. I may *perceive* those things, but I *look* at the other *Look-looking*. The physical eyes are only the occasion, the means by which the subjects behind them meet and clash somewhere (which is no "where") out there in front of the eyes. He who looks into the abyss of another's look finds that the abyss has looked back into him. It is not that the Other's eyes are evil, nor even that they are careless; but that they are *eyes,* i.e., that there *are* Others who disintegrate even a very ordinary citizen in his daily rounds into a thousand fragments and solidify him into a thousand "essences" not of his freedom's making.

Sartre uses traditional religious terminology to express the fundamental character of being-for-others. "My *original fall* is the existence of the Other." [27] Perhaps we should say that the Fall happens primordially when any exister is thrown into the world where there are Others. Then the original fall, involved unavoidably in all being-for-others, may be read in either of two directions, as shame or as sin. *Original shame* registers the upsurge of the Other into my world. Shame is "an immediate shudder," [28] it is "the feeling of being finally what I am, but elsewhere, over there for the other." [29] It is the impact from being in the midst of being. "Shame is not a feeling of being this or that guilty object, but in general of being an object";[30] not a feeling of appearing as a specially shameful thing but of appearing at all, and as one must, to environing eyes.

Relation to others may also be read in the opposite direction; and then it is a question of the impact of my being upon others. *"Original sin* [Sartre does not hesitate to use the term] is my upsurge into a world where there are others; and whatever may be my further relations with others, these relations will be only variations on the original theme of my guilt. . . . Thus I am guilty toward the Other in my very being because the upsurge of my being, in spite of itself, bestows on the Other a new dimension of being; and on the other hand I am powerless either to profit from my fault or to rectify it." [31] Simply by being, I am guilty of alienating others from their being. Simply by their being, I am shamed. Guilty for their shame, shamed by their guilt, my being-for-others is, for Sartre, founded in a curious version of Dostoevski's sense of universal guilt and universal obligation: Each is responsible for all, and to all for everything—everything, in fact, except his very responsibility itself.[32] To be a man is to be wholly responsible yet wholly unjustifiable and without excuse in the world.

On the basis of this analysis of man's original situation in the midst of being, Sartre proposes an analysis of man's fundamental project in the world. "I am the project of the recovery of my being"—from the Other.[33] The measure of the difficulty of this undertaking needs to be fully understood, and this goes contrary to all the "I-Thou" thinking at present in vogue.

> The Other's soul [another word Sartre does not hesitate to use] is therefore separated from mine by all the distance which separates first my soul from my body, then my body from the Other's body, and finally the Other's body from his soul. . . . If the souls are separated by their bodies, they are distinct as this inkwell is distinct from this book; that is, we cannot conceive of the immediate presence of the one in the other. And even if we admit that my soul can be immediately present in the Other's body, I still have to overcome all the density of a body before I touch his soul.[34]

In the foregoing quotation Sartre seems to assume that it is the density of the Other's body, i.e., the distance that has to be traversed from it to his soul, which make genuine personal contact impossible. But the distances that have to be traversed (1) from my soul (my transcendence) to my body so as to coincide with it, (2) from Body to Body, and (3) from the Other's body to his soul (his transcendence) are equally wide (though of a different order); and, as we shall see, Sartre assumes that, in desire and in the caress, there can momentarily take place a mutual "enfleshment" of the souls each in its body, and that in this case the relationship fails at the instant an attempt is made to overcome the separation of bodies.

As the project of recovering my being

> What I constantly aim at across my experiences are the Other's feelings, the Other's ideas, the Other's volitions, the Other's character. This is because the Other is not only the one whom I see but the one *who sees me*. I aim at the Other in so far as he is a connected system of experiences out of reach in which I figure as one object among others.[35]

There are fundamentally *two ways* in which I can aim at the other "connected system of experiences." Both are doomed to failure; but the difference between the two attempts should be understood, since for Sartre these two attempts comprise the nature of sexuality as of all other human enterprises.

On the one hand, I can try to transcend the Other's transcendence and make it an object. I can "strive to determine as object the subject who denies my character as subject and who himself determines me as object." [36] "I am—at the very root of my being—the project of assimilating and making an object of the Other." [37] I seek to put him out of play, to imprison him as a Look-looked-at, as a transcendence-transcended. But in this case the only thing that was of any significance to me escapes me: the other as a Look-looking, as a free subjectivity, as a transcendence-transcending. Moreover, he has not been idle the while. "Everything which may be said of me in my relations with the Other applies to him as well. While I attempt to free myself from the hold of the Other, the Other is trying to free himself from mine. . . . Conflict is the original meaning of being-for-others." [38] Still it is the case that, in one part, my relations with the Other "are essentially made up of ruses designed to make him remain an object." [39]

The failure of this attempt motivates the other (and vice versa). In the second place, then, I strive "to incorporate that transcendence within me without removing from it its character as transcendence—such are the two primitive attitudes which I assume confronting the Other." [40] My relations to the Other are, in the second place, essentially made up of ruses designed to somehow get at him as a Look-looking, as a transcendence-transcending, as a free subjectivity. I aim directly at his feelings, ideas, etc., his experiences as such. But this is impossible, since it was his transcending looking which was originally apprehended in the act of abstracting those myriad essences which, I must insist, I am not. The second attempt founders upon the fact that only consciousness limits consciousness; the limit between the two is produced by the limiting consciousness and echoed in the heart of the one limited;[41] and each is a limiting-limited and a limited-limiting out of reach.

Thus, to sum up,

> . . . We can never hold a consistent attitude toward the Other unless he is simultaneously revealed to us as subject and as object, as transcendence-transcending and as transcendence-transcended—which is on principle impossible. Thus we are ceaselessly tossed from being-a-look to being-looked-at. . . . We pursue the impossible ideal of the simultaneous apprehension of his freedom and of his objectivity.[42]

> Thus I am referred from transfiguration to degradation and from degradation to transfiguration without ever being able to get a total view of the ensemble of these two modes of being on the part of the Other . . .[43]

Man, therefore, is a useless passion. We shall be forced to draw the same conclusion from a second (simultaneous) way of formulating, for Sartre, man's fundamental project in the world. But it is time now to apply Sartre's existential ontology to an understanding of the nature of sexual relations.

IV

The great merit of Sartre's work is to have articulated an understanding of human passions, and among them sexual desire, in *ontological* terms. That is to say, he regards no passion or fundamental desire as strictly biological or racial or societal (or otherwise objective) in its import. The passions of men, instead, are all ontological, i.e., the word (*logos*) of one being (*on*) going forth to another; they are voices of being crying unto being. An existing subject or being, and not an impulse or an organ, stands, so to speak, at the originating end of a passion; and his goal is, again not the state or activity of an organ or body, nor some racial or societal benefit, but the other being as such. Whatever else needs to be said about it, this unitary personal interpretation of sex-in-being is a great achievement of thought. It has rarely been approached before in the history of Western thought, perhaps least of all in the modern day by men who pay tribute to themselves for having overcome the "dualism" they attribute to the Christian thought of past ages.

The typology of sex relations which Sartre articulates in his philosophic work are subsumed under the two sorts of relations-with-others mentioned at the end of the previous section. Although there is alternation and intermixture of these ways of being-for-others, the types are clear enough; and they are decisive for concrete passions, sexual and other specific relations with others. (1) Along one line, the self tries to get hold of the Other as a transcendence-transcend*ing*, as a *subject* that is out of reach; the self seeks union with the other being-as-a-look-looking, attempting to fix that freedom upon the self without removing it as a transcendent freedom. In order to do this, the self risks affirming his object-status before the Other. Along this line, love—seduction—masochism are the principal projects. (2) Along the other line, the self tries to get hold of the Other as a transcendence-transcend*ed*, as an object, in his being-as-a-look-looked-at. In order to do this the self risks losing sight of the other as subject out of reach, by accentuating the self's own distance transcending him as object. Along this line, desire (by the caress enfleshing)—sadism—hate are the projects. At any moment, the failure of one may motivate the adoption of the other of these typical procedures.

In *love* there is always an explicit reference to the other consciousness or freedom as such. A man

> does not desire the enslavement of the beloved. He is not bent on becoming the object of passion which flows forth mechanically. He does not want to possess an automaton, and if we want to humiliate him, we need only try to persuade him that the beloved's passion is the result of a psychological determinism. . . . If the beloved is transformed into an automaton, the lover finds himself alone. Thus the lover does not desire to possess the beloved as one possesses a thing; he demands a special type of appropriation. He wants to possess a freedom as freedom. . . . He wishes that the Other's freedom should determine itself to become love . . . he wants this freedom to be captured *by itself.*[44]

Insofar, then, as love is a passion directed toward a body in the midst of the world, love desires to possess this body only because it is possessed by another consciousness that is a distanceless presence to it.

In *love,* therefore, and in order to accomplish the other freedom's self-determination to love, a man "consents to be an object." ". . . He wants to be the object in which the Other's freedom consents to lose itself." [45] To understand Sartre's thought at this point, it is necessary to digress a moment in order to grasp his analysis of "the Body." The Other and I have fundamentally different relations to my body. I "exist," I "live" my body, I have the taste of it; while only the Other "knows" my body. I do not know my body, any more than I know sight. It is through the sensory activity of sight that I know the inkwell, etc.; sight itself eludes my knowledge;[46] or rather, sight is surpassed in my act of knowing the inkwell, etc. So with the body generally. It is improper to say that in writing I "use" my hand. No, I *am* my hand *using* the pen. The body as lived "is perpetually the surpassed," [47] surpassed toward project goals that are comprised of objects in the world.* In living my body in acts of love, my body is always surpassed; and this time toward an "object" that is nowhere in the midst of the world, toward the other freedom. In any case, "my body as it is *for me* does not appear to me in the midst of the world" [48] as an object of knowledge.

However, my body in the midst of the world as it is for others is precisely what physicians and Others "know." ". . . The body symbolizes . . . our defenseless state as objects." [49] ". . . To be an object-for-others or to-be-a-body are two ontological modalities which are strictly equivalent expressions of the being-for-others on the part of the for-itself." [54] In the presence of others, "my body is there not only as the point of view which I am but again as a point of view on which are actually brought to bear points of view which I could never take; my body escapes me on all sides." [51] In the presence of others, the body which I live is "designated as a thing outside my subjectivity, in the midst of a world which is not mine. My body is designated as alienated." I cannot be embarrassed by my body as I live it; but I am nothing but embarrassed by my body-for-Others. My body-for-Others is strange to me, inapprehensible, alienated, foreign. [52] A good illustration of Sartre's meaning may be found in how strange and alien to us our voice sounds when it is played back by a tape-recorder. Even though we acknowledge the voice to be *our* voice-for-others, it is not our voice as we lived it, our voice-for-self. In fact, it is in many ways strange and alien, this voice as it is "known" to others.

Now, in love it is hoped that the beloved will bring back to me my body-for-others, restore to me my alienated self. This strange voice-for-others, the beloved consents to choose. My body as a whole which founds my existence in the midst of the world, even those of its parts most commonly hidden from any Look-looking, will perhaps no longer be experienced *as seen* and therefore no longer as alien from my body-as-lived, if that other point of view upon my body consents to become a Look-loving. This is what love promises:

> . . . My facticity is saved. It is no longer this unthinkable and insurmountable given which I am fleeing; it is that for which the Other freely

* On the meaning of "I *exist* my body," see Hazel E. Barnes's introduction to her translation of Sartre's *Being and Nothingness,* pp. xl-xli: In knowing or acting upon the world, consciousness or "the For-itself *is* its body. Without a body the For-itself could have no relation whatsoever with what we call the world. . . . The For-itself does not *have* senses. It is present to the world *through* the senses. . . . As for For-itself, although I can adopt the point of view of an Other by holding up a hand or foot and looking at it, I experience my body as mine only when I experience the world through it." In fact, it is by virtue of his notion of how "I *exist* my body" that Sartre can hold his view of the soul's transcendence without falling into the old soul-body dualism, and by virtue of this same notion he can assert the entire unity of transcendent spirit with bodily events without falling into a reductive naturalism.

makes himself exist; it is an end which he has given to himself. . . . By
means of this love I then have a different apprehension of my alienation
and of my own facticity. . . . These beloved veins on my hands exist—
beneficently. How good I am to have eyes, hair, eyebrows and to lavish
them away tirelessly in an overflow of generosity to this tireless desire which
the Other freely makes himself be. . . . Whereas we felt ourselves "*de
trop*," we now feel that our existence is taken up and willed even in its
tiniest details by an absolute freedom which at the same time our existence
conditions and which we ourselves will with our freedom. This is the basis
for the joy of love when there is joy: we feel that our existence is justified.[53]

Another's love would justify my bodily existence, encompassing it and
electing it by a free choice.

This love promises, but it is not what happens. "This project is going
to provoke a conflict" at the very moment the beloved consents to become my lover. For when she loves, she projects *being loved,* as I
did.[54] ". . . To love is in essence the project of making oneself be
loved." Each of the lovers projects being loved; "but at the same time
each one demands from the other a love which is not reducible to
the 'project of being loved.' . . . The lover . . . is captive of his very
demand since love is the demand to be loved."[55] Moreover, since love is
to wish to be loved and hence to wish the other to want to be loved in
turn, it is a deception in the form of a reference to infinity. "Each one
wants the other to love him but does not take into account the fact that
to love is to want to be loved and that thus by wanting the other to
love him, he only wants the other to want to be loved in turn."[56] Love,
therefore, like man himself, is a useless passion.

It should be said concerning Sartre's "shocking" view of love, as
simply the desire to be loved, that it may finally convince our theologians that "mutuality" is no definition of love at all.

Mutuality is only a predicate upon love itself; it is adjectival to whatever love is substantially. The injunction to let love be mutual only
suggests that love—whatever that means—should perhaps be returned;
but some love, it turns out, cannot be reciprocal. For it is precisely at
the moment Sartre's "love" is reciprocated that hell breaks loose; and
then it becomes apparent where such love all along was going, i.e., to
the self. To define love in terms of mutuality means, by preferring the
adjective to the thing itself, to refuse responsibility for stating to whom
love as such should be directed, and with what love he ought to be
loved. By contrast, to say that *agape* should be mutual, and indeed that
it creates mutuality, keeps the substantive and the predicate, cause and
consequent, intention and derivative result, in right relation. In any case,
Sartre's analysis makes it plain that, before saying a word about mutuality, it must first be shown whether it is at all possible for a person to
be present *to* and *for* the Other at all. Any other approach is rather

like Kierkegaard's seminary graduate who preached about seeking first the kingdom of God before the congregation where first he had sought a good living.

Upon the failure of love, I can still aim at the other's freedom while consenting to be an object before it; but this time the range of that freedom's subjective self-determination will be greatly narrowed. This project is *seduction*. ". . . I do not try to reveal my subjectivity to the Other," for that could be done only by looking at the Other as object, thus causing "the Other's subjectivity to disappear"—and that is exactly what I want to reach. Instead, retrospectively, my original attitude or act of "love can in no way be distinguished from the enterprise of seduction" which now becomes fully manifest.

> To seduce is to risk assuming my object-state completely for the Other; it is to put myself beneath his look and to make him look at me; it is to risk *being-seen* in order to effect a new departure and to appropriate the Other in and by the means of my object-ness. . . . I wish to engage in battle by making myself a *fascinating object*. . . . I propose myself as unsurpassable.

The Other must become nothing, must be fully captivated, in the face of my fascinating "plenitude" of being.[57]

In *masochism*, I do not simply aim at the Other's freedom by abdicating my transcendence (as in love-seduction); I now in addition *enjoy* this abdication. "Masochism is an attempt not to fascinate the Other by means of my objectivity [that is seduction] but to cause myself to be fascinated by my objectivity-for-others; that is, to cause myself to be constituted as an object by the Other in such a way that I . . . apprehend my subjectivity as a *nothing* in the presence of the in-itself which I represent in the Other's eyes."[58] By thus annihilating my subjectivity, I hope to gain the excruciating joy of so placing myself in the focus of the Other's attention that he cannot wrench his gaze away. His freedom will finally be reached and bound in relation to me. His gaze-gazing will actually be reached, at the heart of its alien point of view which my body bears in its wounds, when by my enjoyment of, by my "causing myself to be fascinated by," my own pain, I am laid bare before the bound freedom of his Look-looking. Then truly a relation between an "I" and a "Thou" might be established.

This project of the masochist fails precisely because it was such a tremendous effort of consciousness. It was by a conscious project that he sought to make himself an object in pain. A distance opens up between himself as the subject of that project and himself as the object. "It is in and through his transcendence that he disposes of himself as a being to be transcended. The more he tries to taste his objectivity [as a means of tasting the Other's fixed fascination], the more he will be submerged by the consciousness of his subjectivity."[59] He becomes a subject

self-removed from himself as object; the activity of transcendence-transcend*ing* comes again into play; and as a Look-looking he catches a
glimpse of the Other as a Look-looked-at and no longer as a transfixed
Look-looking. The other line of projects will now have to be espoused;
and, as we indicated, this means that our analysis must now turn from
love–seduction–masochism to desire–sadism–hate.

Sartre's treatment of *desire* (and of the caress) is perhaps the most
interesting and significant of all his analysis of human passions; and in
desire the voice of being crying unto being comes closest to attaining
its goal. When one abandons the attempt on the ground of one's object-
status to reach the Other's freedom, he can only attempt on the ground
of freedom, or transcendence, to confront the other freedom. But by
the sole fact that I affirm my transcendence-transcend*ing*, I make the
Other a transcendence-transcend*ed* and "perceive suddenly that I can act
upon the Other only insofar as this [his] freedom has collapsed beneath
my look." Every remaining attempt to confront his freedom must be
"across the total appropriation of the Other's body." I must now "build
my subjectivity upon the collapse of the subjectivity of the Other," first
perhaps by a studied indifference, but then by sexual desire.[60]

"My original attempt to get hold of the Other's free subjectivity
through his objectivity-for-me is sexual desire." [61] But Sartre rejects any
and all forms of the notion that the For-itself, i.e., human consciousness,
is sexual only "accidentally." "Can we admit," he asks rhetorically,
"that this tremendous matter of the sexual life comes as a kind of
addition to the human condition?" [62] Just as the pure existential encounter of Look-looking and Look-looked-at takes place by means of
physical eyes that are surpassed, so sexual desire is a basic modality of a
man's being-for-others to which sex as a biological mechanism is only
"accidental." * Sex in the latter sense is always designated as surpassed;
while sexuality as the utterance of a "word" of being to being inheres
in the surpassing consciousness itself. Sexual desire involves us more
deeply, and lasts longer, than sex organs desire (to speak quite improperly). ". . . The For-itself is sexual in its very upsurge in the face
of the Other . . . and through it sexuality comes into the world." [63]
For Sartre, sexuality is as "original" as sin or shame or any other primary
impact of being upon being in the world; it arises the moment consciousness finds itself limited as it only can be by another conscious-

---

* "Man, it is said, is a sexual being because he possesses a sex. And if the reverse
were true? If sex were only the instrument and, so to speak, the image of a fundamental sexuality? If man possessed a sex only because he is originally and fundamentally a sexual being as a being who exists in the world in relation with other
men? . . . Men who have become eunuchs do not thereby cease to feel desire. Nor
do old men. The fact of being able to make use of a sex organ fit to fertilize and
to procure enjoyment represents only one phase and one aspect of our sexual life."
Being and Nothingness, p. 383.

ness. Sexuality registers the presence of consciousness to consciousness. ". . . Everyone knows," writes Sartre, "that there is a great abyss
between sexual desire and the other appetites";[64] and "desire is by no
means a physiological accident, an itching of our flesh which may
fortuitously direct us on the Other's flesh." [65]

"I desire a human being, not an insect or a mollusk, and I desire
him (or her) as he is and as I am in the world and as he is an Other for
me and as I am an Other for him." [66] What then is sexual desire the
desire of? Not for any specific pleasure. Nor for any doing or bodily
action. Nor, indeed, for the other body as such, though sexual desire
traverses the body.[67] It seeks not "a sum of physiological elements," but
someone beyond all these things who constitutes himself or herself a
presence to them. The object to which desire is addressed is always
the other consciousness which "remains always at the horizon of the
desired body." [68] Moreover, the consciousness who is the subject of desire
has abolished its own distances and drawn as near as its own horizon to
the body. A desiring consciousness is "clogged" by sexual desire, "invaded
by facticity," "fallen wholly into complicity with the body";[69] and *for
this reason* it has possibly become accessible in this world to another
desiring consciousness.

This may perhaps be clarified by reference to what Sartre means by
"flesh," "the caress," and "incarnation." ". . . In desire," he writes, "I
make myself flesh *in the presence of the Other in order to appropriate the
Other's flesh.*" [70] "Flesh" means consciousness making itself body, it
means the "incarnation" of transcendence; and if desire is to draw near
to its goal, there must take place a reciprocal enfleshment by means of
the caress, which at once calls consciousness down from aloft and strips
the body of every orientation toward action.

> In caressing the Other I cause her to be born beneath my caress, under my
> fingers. The caress is the ensemble of those rituals which incarnate the
> Other.[71]

> I incarnate myself in order to realize the incarnation of the Other. The
> caress by realizing the Other's incarnation reveals to me my own incarnation;
> that is, I make myself flesh in order to impel the Other to realize *for-herself*
> and *for* me her own flesh, and my caresses cause my flesh to be born for me
> in so far as it is for the Other *flesh causing her to be born as flesh.* And so
> possession truly appears as a double reciprocal incarnation.[72]

By ensnaring the Other's freedom within his objective facticity (and my
own as well), I seem to have solved the problem posed by the fact that
I can grasp the Other only in this way, i.e., as an object in the world.
"So the Other's For-itself must come to play on the surface of his body,
and be extended all through his body; and by touching this body I

should finally touch the Other's free subjectivity. . . . It is certain I want to possess the Other's body, but I want to possess it in so far as it is itself a 'possessed'; that is, in so far as the Other's consciousness is identified with his body." [73] In order to taste the Other as a "simple presence," he and I must both be reduced to a simple embodied presence. I cease "every surpassing of my being-there," I cease from surpassing his being-there, in the hope of simply reaching his simply being-there. In order "to touch him in his flesh, his practical acts and functions and my own acts and functions are pushed aside and we become caressing, incarnate flesh. It would not be enough for the Other to become flesh to my eyes; he must become flesh in *his own eyes*;[74] or rather, on the part of each, desire must consist of a double reciprocal reaching forth toward the Other that is practically directionless and "eyeless in Gaza," an unspeakable utterance of being to being.

To let [my hand] run indifferently over the length of her body, to reduce my hand to a soft brushing almost stripped of meaning, to a pure existence, to a pure matter, slightly silky, slightly satiny, slightly rough—this is to give up for oneself being the one who establishes references and unfolds distances; it is to be made pure mucous membrane. At this moment the communion of desire is realized; each consciousness by incarnating itself has realized the incarnation of the other; each one's disturbance has caused disturbance to be born in the Other and is thereby so much enriched. By each caress I experience my own flesh and the Other's flesh through my flesh, and I am conscious that this flesh which I feel and appropriate through my flesh is flesh-realized-by-the-Other. It is not by chance that desire while aiming at the body as a whole attains it especially through masses of flesh which are very little differentiated, grossly nerveless, hardly capable of spontaneous movement, through breasts, buttocks, thighs, stomach. [Even] the caressing hand is too delicate, too much like a perfected instrument.[75] *

Nevertheless "the communion of desire" is an "impossible ideal" [76] "doomed to failure." [77] It is doomed, first, because the communion of flesh is soon traversed by an aim at specific pleasure; and "pleasure in fact—like too keen a pain—motivates the appearance of reflective consciousness which is 'attention to pleasure.'" "Desire misses its goal" when pleasure becomes the goal. This destroys desire's approximation to communion between incarnate beings-in-flesh by motivating the appearance of "a reflective consciousness *of* pleasure." This means that consciousness becomes discarnate, flesh falls back into body; the spirit transcends its body to take pleasure in it, and as the reflective enjoyment of pleasure "by the same token it is forgetful of the Other's incarnation." The almost

* Certainly, to Look would destroy incarnation and the caress: ". . . The Other's look fashions my body in its nakedness, causes it to be born, sculptures it, produces it as it is, sees it as I shall never see it." *Ibid.*, p. 364.

attained communion of being with being is irrevocably lost. Thus, for Sartre, "pleasure is the death and the failure of desire." [78] Indeed, it may be said that, according to Sartre, there has never been a satisfaction of desire in the whole history of mankind, only the death of desire— killed, not satisfied, by pleasure. This conclusion follows, in large part, from the fact that Sartre knows so well what was the goal of desire!

The communion of desire is doomed to failure for yet another reason, or rather the reason desire misses its goal may be expressed in a second way. The reciprocal incarnation of flesh, expressed by and effected in the caress, may be said to have crossed two of the three distances (mentioned earlier in this chapter) on the way to a real meeting of being with being: the distance from my soul to my body and the distance from the Other's soul to his or her body. There remains irremediable distance from body to body that must be traversed; and this would have to be accomplished without opening up those other distances again. This proves to be quite impossible.

> The caress has for its goal not only to impregnate the Other's body with con-sciousness and freedom. Now it is necessary to take this saturated body, to seize it, to enter into it. But by the very fact that I now attempt to seize the Other's body, to pull it toward me, to grab hold of it, to bite it, my own body ceases to be flesh and becomes again the synthetic instrument which I am. . . . Her consciousness, which played on the surface of her flesh and which I tried to taste with my flesh, disappears under my sight; she re-mains no more than an object with object images inside her. At the same time my disturbance disappears. This does not mean that I cease to desire but that desire has lost its matter; it has become *abstract;* it is a desire to handle and to take. I insist on taking the Other's body but my very in-sistence makes my incarnation disappear. . . . I surpass my body anew . . . and . . . the Other's body falls from the level of flesh to the level of pure object. This situation brings about the rupture of that reciprocity of in-carnation which was precisely the unique goal of desire.[79]

It is therefore altogether insufficient to say, as Sartre does, that "coitus remains a perfectly contingent modality of our sexual life." [80] The truth is that coitus, like attention to specific pleasure, is the death and the failure of sexual desire. No mere contingency, it kills desire and removes it. In the moment of desire the saturated bodies or incarnate beings-in-flesh seemed on the verge of touching the Other's touching. Now in the act of coitus there is an attempt to overcome the final separateness of bodies. For a consciousness to insist on traversing this last distance, it must awaken and in some measure discarnate itself, i.e., distance itself again from itself, and consequently from the Other by more than bodily separation. This means that the two will succeed only in establishing the relationship of a Touch-touching with a Touch-touched. They may even

—and this is an idea that could never occur to caressing flesh—find some advantage in deliberately entertaining the relation of Look-looking and Look-looked-at. Many are the ruses of transcendence in trying to confront another transcendence-transcended. Therefore, according to Sartre, once there has been brought about a rupture of the spirit's incarnation as flesh and a rupture of the communion of desire, coitus will tend always in the direction of either masochism (which we have already discussed) or sadism. "Thus sadism and masochism are the two reefs on which desire may founder—whether I suppress my troubled disturbance toward an appropriation of the Other's flesh or intoxicated with my own trouble, pay attention only to my flesh and ask nothing of the Other except that he should be the look which aids me in realizing my flesh." [81]

The *sadist* decides, as it were, to enjoy the discarnating distance from a body that was formerly impregnated with the presence of consciousness. Sadism "only enjoys the possession of the Other's flesh but at the same time in direct connection with this flesh, it enjoys its own non-incarnation. It wants the non-reciprocity of sexual relations, it enjoys being a free appropriating power confronting a freedom captured by flesh." [82] Yet even though the Other is primarily grasped as an object, what the sadist "wants to knead with his hands and bend under his wrists is the Other's freedom." He "does not seek to suppress the freedom of the one whom he tortures but to force this freedom freely to identify itself with the tortured flesh. This is why the moment of pleasure for the torturer is that in which the victim betrays or humiliates himself." [83]

But sadism too is "a blind alley." [84] ". . . When I have indeed before me a panting body, then I no longer know how to utilize this flesh. . . . It *is* there, and it is there for nothing." Sadism too is the failure of desire. As in coitus, "if pleasure enables us to get out of the circle, this is because it kills both the desire and the sadistic passion without satisfying them," because this like all passion was the desire for the simple presence to the self of the other person. Moreover, the victim has only to *look at* the sadist in order to escape his writhing flesh and his captor as well.[85]

Finally, *hate* is a generalized, destructive reference to the Other as object which I posit on the ground of my freedom. "What I hate is his existence in general as a transcendence-transcended." It is always "of all Others in one other." [86] As Garcin said of "all those eyes" intent on him: "What? Only two of you? I thought there were more; many more." The final victorious defeat of the self's project of recovering its being stands close at hand. Hates there a man the thing he would not kill? Yet if I suppress the Other's very existence in the world, I remove his views to an unbridgeable distance from me. The dead person becomes an eternal object, with object images of me inside him. The essences he has of me, my being-for-others, can now never be corrected; nor he be reached. John Brown's body may lie a-moulding in the grave, but his "truth" goes marching on; and it was the asserted truth about *me*. As Inez said, "You can't throttle thoughts with hands." He remains a formless thought that has thought me, and he is still, as before, beyond my reach. "He who has once been for-others is contaminated in his being for the rest of his days even if the Other should be entirely suppressed; he will never cease to apprehend his dimension of being-for-others as a permanent possibility of his being." [87] This is Sartre's last word on the subject of interpersonal relations. The symbol of Jonah (which had better be called the whale symbol) represents the impossibility of men's realizing their "dream of a non-destructive assimilation" of being.[88] Men are notorious liars in all their fish stories.

V

The whale symbol makes fully clear what the self, according to Sartre, wants in its project of recovering its being. This basic understanding of desire is in need of correction, while Sartre's contribution to our interpretation of the significance of the body and of sexuality for consciousness can as such be retained. The self projects the *assimilation* of the other being; thus Sartre accepts without question the "alimentary metaphors (absorption, digestion, assimilation)" with which Western epistemology "swarms." [89] There may be another way of "knowing" the Other than by assimilation which proves a failure; and yet sexual desire and the whole bodily life may be as intimately related to this "knowing" as it is to Sartre's. The self projects actual identification with the other being: "What I must attain is the Other not as I obtain knowledge of him, but as he obtains knowledge of himself—which is impossible. This would in fact suppose the internal identification of myself with the Other." [90] Such an account of what men want in relation to the Other should be replaced by "meeting" or covenant-relation of being with being; and yet an articulation of the central importance of sexuality can be given on this foundation which perhaps can successfully rival Sartre's. It is remarkable the number of great minds in the present day and researchers in various fields who have accepted, in varying degrees, some version of love as union-fusion-assimilation-identification: e.g., Sartre, Erich Fromm,[91] and Paul Tillich in his notion of love as reunion.[92] * Here is a break with the western tradition that is almost without parallel. Modern thought seems engaged in a great struggle to overcome Yahweh-god, and the biblical understanding of human existence on the foundation of covenant-meeting between mysterious presences that are ultimately out of reach.

* See Chapter Seven.

At the moment, however, the description so far given of man's fundamental project in the world needs to be related to another (simultaneous)
way in which Sartre describes this project, and man's consequent failure
and uselessness.

Vis-à-vis others, the goal of desire is complete union. In the ultimate
or "vertical" relation, however, "man is the being whose project is to
be God";[93] "human reality is the pure effort to become God . . ." [94] It
is quite incorrect to suppose that this language is chosen arbitrarily, or
at random, or that another expression for the thought might have
served as well.* Sartre does, of course, state the matter differently, and
in the technical terms of philosophy. The goal of desire is Hegel's *An-
und-für-sichselbstigkeit,* the In-itself-For-itself. Man wants to found himself as in-itself-as-self-cause. He is the perpetual project of becoming *ens
causa sui.* He seeks to attain the dignity of coinciding exactly with his
being, while still being conscious of doing so. He aims to be a being
who preserves within itself "the necessary translucency of consciousness
along with the coincidence with itself of being-in-itself . . . identity
with itself . . . exactly the self . . . as substantial being." [95] He wants
to be a Look-looking, but never Looked-at, not even looking at himself
from an unrealized distance; a Lack-lacking with nothing to lack, yet
with the excruciating awareness of lacking it—a Lack-having. "The
supreme value toward which consciousness at every instance surpasses
itself by its very being is the absolute being of the self with its characteristics of identity, of purity, of permanence, etc., and as its own
foundation." [96]

Sartre knows well enough that this by definition is God, and his
descriptions of human existence as the pure effort to become God are
not at all incidental. "My freedom," he writes, "is a choice of being God
and all my acts, all my projects translate this choice and reflect it in a
thousand and one ways. . . ." [97] Of course, God does not exist, for the
same reason that man cannot succeed: the ideal of man and the very
idea of God are both alike self-contradictory, and it is quite impossible
for the one to be realized or for the other to be real. Neither God nor
the Man-God can actually exist. Yet, it is exactly this "impossible vertical
surpassing which by its very non-existence conditions the flat movements
of consciousness," [98] i.e., which conditions the thousand and one "hori-
zontal" movements of consciousness in relation to Others. God is missing;
yet how can I endure not being He (cf. Nietzsche). "Everything happens
as if the world, man, and man-in-the-world succeeded in realizing only
a missing God," [99] i.e., as if he can never succeed in realizing an actual
God, which is the only fundamental trial men ever make in the world

---

* Such seems to be the view of Walter Kaufmann, *op. cit.,* p. 47: "This ideal, says
Sartre, one can call God. . . ." Hazel Barnes, *op. cit.,* p. xxxv, says quite correctly
that "Sartre's whole interpretation of existence postulates the pursuit of God. . . ."

and the Project present in the midst of all their projects. "Thus, the passion of man is the reverse of that of Christ, for man loses himself as man in order that God may be born. But the idea of God is contradictory and we lose ourselves in vain." And here—*not* in connection with the failure of every attempt at relation to others—Sartre delivers his celebrated verdict: "Man is a useless passion." [100]

The foregoing makes it clear that Sartre proposes an ontological argument for the nonexistence of God. He proposes to pass from the idea of God to his non-existence (with no disproofs drawn from the nature of the external world), as Anselm thought to conclude from the idea to the existence of God (with no proofs drawn from "natural theology"). Only the fool has said in his heart, There is a God; and in this saying the subject contradicts the predicate, and he contradicts himself. The answer to Sartre is, I suppose, the same as the one Aquinas gave to Anselm's argument. We must distinguish between that which perhaps may be "self-evident in itself, though not to us" and that which is "self-evident in itself, and to us"; and affirm that since we do not know the essence of God nor all Sartre thinks he knows about His mode of being, the proposition that God does not exist is "not self-evident to us, and needs to be demonstrated by things that are more known to us." [101] The missing God might know that it is impossible for God to exist, but hardly Sartre.

At the level of what Sartre thinks he knows about man's fundamental project to be God, quite another evaluation is in order. About this our author may know a great deal. The most obvious, and negative, criticism consists of pointing out that the two descriptions (of man's project of the recovery of his being in relation to others, and man's endeavor to be God) belong together; and that together they are the orientations of idolatrous spirit. The desire to assimilate the self to God, and the desire of the self to reach such identity with another as to absorb him, these belong together. If I am homeless until I can see the world as God sees it, I also am alienated unless I can look with the looking of another and touch his touching. This is the project of being alone in the world, with the promptings of no Other—no God and no neighbor—to evoke my response. This is the idolatry of a self who will consent to stand only in relation to self, even in all his religious aspirations and even in all his very real striving toward communion with others. It may be said that, just as the Christian man tries to realize in a *finite* way some likeness to the infinite perfections of God, striving for only a creaturely sharing in eternal life, so he seeks just a creaturely sharing in the life of the Other. If this is so, then, by contrast, Sartre's man is just as imperiously devoted to seeking an infinite understanding and a complete partaking of the Other as he is to attempting to become divine, or to constitute himself constituting a world. Perhaps, in relation both to God and to the Other,

Sartre was forced to conclude that man is a useless passion and an all round failure, because of what he says man fundamentally attempts.

Nowhere better than in Sartre's analysis of one particular passion can we see how internally related are a man's relation to the missing God and his relation to a thousand and one creaturely goods and projects. I refer to what Sartre has written about so seemingly simple a matter as *thirst*. "Thirst as an organic phenomenon," Sartre says, "as a 'physiological' need for water, does not exist." [102] What desire of the soul is always present, even when a man is thirsty? ". . . The aim is the thirst passed on to the plenitude of being, the thirst which grasps and incorporates repletion into itself." Man wants to be an eternal thirst-repletion. Thirst, sexual and every other desire that springs up in human consciousness are seeking "that coincidence with self which is satisfaction, where thirst knows itself as thirst at the same time that drinking satisfies it." [103] That toward which any lack is fled—any lack experienced by men in their finitude, and fed by whatever means, goods, others— is "to be a thirst which could be no longer a lack but a thirst-repletion." [104] Ever thirsty for being yet ever replete with it: such is the human goal. It may even be said that there has never been a satisfied thirst in the whole history of mankind, only thirsts that have been killed and removed by momentary pleasure. For what was lacked in every thirst was not what came to close its sluices.

On the one hand, then, Sartre's entire philosophy may be regarded as a not inaccurate phenomenological description of the fallen world, or of relations within a world in which the quest for communion with God and with others seems irremediably distorted by idolatry. To have probed so perceptively and unflinchingly into actual human relationships is a not inconsiderable achievement. Yet John Calvin's statement is relevant to Sartre: "It would be folly to seek for a definition of the soul from the heathen philosophers . . . because the philosophers, being ignorant of the corruption of nature proceeding from the punishment of the fall, improperly confound two very different states of mankind." [105] Sartre has no categories for distinguishing original being-in-relation (creation) from original sin, original shame, and original strife. There is only that ineffectual (but no less astonishing) reference to the possibility of an ethics of deliverance, salvation, and radical conversion (quoted at the head of this chapter). Yet to be provided with a phenomenological description of fallen relationships may even be of benefit to Christian theologians or churchmen who sometimes appear also to lack these distinguishing categories of creation, fall, and redemption, and who (in the opposite direction from Sartre's realism), being ignorant of the corruption of nature, improperly confound very different states of mankind.

On the other hand, not since Augustine, or the saints and thinkers of the past who have drunk deeply from his wells, has anyone seen so

truly and exhibited so forcefully the nature of the desire that is co-
present with every particular desire of the human heart. He does not
explicitly say that the goal is "eternal life in peace" or "peace in eternal
life." Yet Sartre is quite explicit about the fact that the Desire in the
midst of all desires, the Project of all projects, is the desire for a good
that is permanent, a good that is forever coincident with the will for
it and "cannot be lost against the will." No matter what the good that
nourishes us, no matter how high on the scale, or even if it is the
highest we know, its goodness alone does not satisfy—though pleasure
in it may for a moment kill the longing for eternity that was meant by
every desire. The undertow of all desire for the thousand and one
specific goods is the demand that our good be enjoyed on the ground of
that which is For-itself-In-itself. Finally, like Augustine, Sartre knows
that the mode of man's being in the world affects to the root the
modalities of sexual passion and sex relation. Here is an unfinished
Reformation in Christian thought; and in preparing the ground for it
there is question whether Christian teaching may not have more to
learn from Sartre than he from traditional views on this subject.

VI

That was not quite Sartre's last word on the subject of interpersonal
relations. We have now, therefore, to examine his famous lecture on
Existentialism Is a Humanism. In this we shall find that our author does
not succeed in giving a very clear utterance upon the relation of person-
to-person, but rather one which is without foundation in the whole of
his serious philosophical work and indeed flatly contradictory to it.
Then, finally, we shall probe again the meaning of the "We-Subject" in
Being and Nothingness. In this will be found certain meanings which,
taken seriously, would alter Sartre's entire scheme, or which suggest at
least the direction in which it should be corrected.

Toward the end of his lecture on *Existentialism* Sartre undertook to
answer certain objections that had been voiced against his position; and
among these the ethical issue was most prominent. In answer to the
question how, in his view, a judgment might be made on a person's
action, Sartre replies, first, by "pronouncing a judgment of truth" to the
effect that such and such a person may be willingly deceiving himself and
that "the attitude of strict consistency alone is that of good faith." [106]
Here he apparently demands "good faith" and by implication the integrity of a possible coincidence with self, which in *Being and Nothingness* were declared to be ontologically impossible, since the ideal of good
faith is the ideal of being-in-itself (which consciousness *is not*) and since
sincerity itself must be in bad faith, i.e., it is impossble for me sincerely

to coincide with my being-sincere.[107] Now, it is noteworthy that Sartre dropped a footnote near the end of this section, which reads:

> If it is indifferent whether one is in good [faith] or in bad faith [self-deception] because bad faith [self-deception] reapprehends good faith and slides to the very origin of the project of good faith, that does not mean that we cannot radically escape bad faith [self-deception]. But this supposes a self-recovery of being which was previously corrupted. This self-recovery we shall call authenticity, the description of which has no place here.[108] *

This note (which states that a description of authentic existence would be out of place in Sartre's chief work) refers to a "radical escape" from inward self-division and to a self-recovery of previously corrupted being; and this language is strikingly parallel to the reference to a "radical conversion which we cannot discuss here" and which alone would make possible "an ethics of deliverance and salvation" in concrete relations with others. When, in *Existentialism,* Sartre assumes that the achievement of good faith is comparatively simple, and a judgment of truth easily pronounced in terms of strict self-consistency, we can only conclude that he has begun to talk about freedom in Paradise before the Fall, or that he slides (with nothing "radical" interposed such as was promised) into viewing human freedom as already redeemed from the tangles and the corruption portrayed on almost every page of his large book. If this is true in the case of the individual's inward clarity and direction of his freedom, it is even more so in the case of the relations of freedom-to-freedom. He "improperly confounds two very different states of mankind": in *Being and Nothingness,* he confounds creation and fall, in *Existentialism,* he confounds creation-fall with redemption.

For Sartre's second answer to the question how, in his view, a judgment upon an action may be made is to "pronounce a moral judgment" that in good faith (which is *no faith* in external norms or pre-established values or God's assistance) only freedom can be chosen; and that

> in thus willing freedom, we discover that it depends entirely upon the freedom of others and that the freedom of others depends upon our own. . . . I cannot make liberty my aim unless I make that of others equally my aim. . . . I cannot not will the freedom of others.[109]

A few pages earlier he said much the same thing in terms of responsibility. To say that a man chooses himself means that "in choosing for himself he chooses for all men." Among the actions a man may take in

---

* The words in brackets are Walter Kaufmann's translation, *op. cit.,* pp. 319, 270 n. 10, which may be questioned for the suggestion it contains that a man might simply be undeceived. Cf. above, p. 76 n.

order to create himself, "there is not one which is not creative, at the
same time, of an image of man such as he believes he ought to be."
Indeed, "nothing can be better for us unless it is better for all"; and "in
fashioning myself I fashion man." [110] Thus "every man, without any
support or help whatever, is condemned at every instance to invent
man." [111] Sartre even connects "anguish" with "the sense of complete and
profound responsibility" on the part of each moral legislator deciding
for the whole of mankind. "Who, then, can prove that I am the proper
person to impose, by my own choice, my conception of man upon mankind?" Do I really have "the right to act in such a manner that humanity
regulates itself by what I do?" This is anguish and a sense of abandonment, which would have no reality except for the universal principle
present in the free choice of freedom itself.[112]

Now, doubtless those who believe in objective values prior to choice
will find a great deal wrong with the above views. To propose such a
reply, however, seems for the moment a waste of ammunition, as do
Sartre's own contentions largely directed against the prior reality of
ethical standards. The issue is not retrospective but prospective; and the
decision about Sartre's views has to be made at the point where the self
throws its projects forward into the world. Whether "the good," "humanity," "freedom," "universal responsibility" have an a priori or any
prior status at all is not nearly so important as the question: How on
earth can the freedom of another (if what Sartre has written about being-
for-others is true) become any part of the self's prospective aim? How
can the good of the Other be in any sense my project?

The issue is the presence of being to being, not the status of standards
for their conduct. In his lecture Sartre said, "I cannot not will the freedom of others"; in his book, I cannot will the freedom of others, since
I cannot affirm the being of others unalloyed by my project to be loved.
In his lecture he declared that by making liberty my aim I make that of
others equally my aim (which presumably may be reciprocal); in his
book, however, he wrote that "we shall never place ourselves on a plane
of equality; that is, on the plane where the recognition of the Other's
freedom would involve the Other's recognition of our freedom." [113] The
reason for this is very simple, so simple one wonders how Sartre came
to forget it: even if I wanted to take the Other's freedom as my goal,

still this freedom would become a transcendence-transcended by the mere
fact that I make it my goal.

Thus respect for the Other's freedom is an empty word; even if we could
assume the project of respecting this freedom, each attitude which we adopt
with respect to the Other would be a violation of that freedom which we
claim to respect.

Whatever I may do for the Other's freedom . . . my efforts are reduced
to treating the Other as an instrument and to positing his freedom as a
transcendence-transcended.[114]

Even if the pursuit of the ideal of "humanity" may as a vertical movement determine every one of our flat movements towards particular
men, "this concept is the same as that of the being-who-looks-at and who
can never be looked-at; that is, it is one with the Idea of God." [115] By
contrast to the missing God, the missing Humanity, or the missing
Universality or Freedom, every actual individual is *both* a being-who-looks
and a being-looked-at, even (or especially) when I undertake to launch
my action toward respect and support for his freedom. ". . . The
humanistic 'Us' " is "an ideal impossible to attain—an empty concept." [116]
   What was in Sartre's book merely an argument against solipsism, an
abstract proof of the existence of other selves, becomes in his lecture
a way of showing that the individual stands in the very presence of the
Other who is revealed to him. ". . . When we say 'I think' we are attaining to ourselves in the presence of the other, and we are just as
certain of the other as we are of ourselves." An "intimate discovery of
myself is at the same time the revelation of the other as a freedom which
confronts mine." Moreover, the discovery of others as the condition of
one's own existence no longer seems to put one in peril by the Other's
view: a man simply "recognizes that he cannot be anything . . . unless
others recognize him as such." How radical the change that has taken
place without anything radical happening, like conversion, recovery, or
salvation! For in the book, the existence of the Other was known only
in a lived wrenching away: my wrenching away from his wrenching
away. When consciousness limits consciousness, I am *not being* the one
who is simultaneously engaged in *not being* me. As James Collins puts
the matter, "The Sartrean consciousness . . . affirms not the being of
the other as other but its own otherness from being." [117] Yet, in his
lecture Sartre portrays man as if he can affirm the being of the other.
This is simply without foundation in his philosophic work; and can be
taken seriously no more than the fact that Sartre may himself be a
generous man can serve to alter his basic definition of generosity as a
form of primordial destructiveness.[118] In his lecture Sartre heaped scorn
on those secular moralists who have tried "to suppress God at the least
possible expense," by inventing pre-established values to take his place.[119]
Yet Sartre himself invents a pre-established harmony of freedom with
freedom, and does not pay the full cost he reckoned up in *Being and
Nothingness.*
   There is one way by which Sartre might perhaps be defended against
the charge of utter inconsistency at this point, and against the accusation
that he simply assumes the redemption of freedom without obtaining it

through radical conversion of the modalities and relationships he described. This is the possibility that his analysis of the "We-Subject" may already contain suggestions which, if stressed and developed, would provide a basis for an understanding of interpersonal relations beyond that which Sartre has given, indeed contrary to most of what he has said. Sartre, of course, denies himself and us the right to take this exit:

> . . . The experience of the "We" and the "Us," although real, is not of a nature to modify the results of our prior investigations. . . . The We-subject . . . is a psychological experience which supposes one way or another that the Other's existence as such has been already revealed to us [this has been proved false]. It is therefore useless for human-reality to seek to get out of this dilemma: one must either transcend the Other or allow oneself to be transcended by him. The essence of relations between consciousnesses is not the *Mitsein;* it is conflict.[120]

There is, of course, more to the "We-Subject" than two people combining against a third;[121] there is also an experience of "shoulder to shoulder" existence of a different order from a merely defensive reaction to the Third Look. Yet, for all the we-ness of shoulder to shoulder existence, Sartre denies that the two transcendences are involved as deeply as they are in "face to face" existence; and when they are face to face we already know what that means! As we now try briefly to unpack what Sartre says on this subject, we must, of course, respect the conclusions he affirms. Yet it will become clear that the "We-Subjects" who are related shoulder to shoulder are not merely items in a mass, nor are their transcendences altogether suppressed or without some sort of relation; and the question may legitimately be raised whether some of Sartre's language about their relationship may not be transferred to "face to face" relations to the end that these may be regarded to be of a different order than Sartre always supposes they are.

The lowest level (is it the only level?) of the We-Subject (apart from mere common defense against another's gaze) arises when a man discovers himself "as *anybody* [*Das Man?*] in the center of some human stream." My relation to others is that "I have a lateral and non-positional consciousness of their bodies correlative with my body, of their acts as unfolding in connection with my acts in such a way that I can not determine whether it is my acts which give birth to their acts or their acts which give birth to mine." [122] "I am engaged with others in a common rhythm," which "is the meaning of the cadenced march of soldiers; it is the meaning also of the rhythmic work of a crew." [123] The question is whether, when "the enveloping of my rhythm by the rhythm of the Other is apprehended 'laterally,' " [124] and my body and actions are apprehended laterally by the other bodies and actions, there takes place also a mutual "lateral" apprehension of transcendences. If this is the case, then, Sartre has exposed a relation of person to person not fully taken into account either by shoulder to shoulder existence or by *his* description of face to face existence.

This seems to be so: *The rhythm* of the Other "surrounds me and involves me without being an object for me. I do not transcend it toward my own possibilities," i.e., this relation of mine to the *other rhythm* is distinguishable from face to face relations based on conflict. This much is clear. The crucial question is: What can be meant by saying, of "our rhythm" as the foundation of "we-consciousness," that "I slip my transcendence into its transcendence"? [125] Clearly, transcendence (while not alive to conflict) is yet not utterly submerged in the coordination of bodily acts. And does a collectivity itself have any transcendence into which mine may be slipped? What constitutes the We-subject are not only bodies, actions, rhythms laterally apprehended; but also the lateral apprehension of one transcendence by the other in the course of their common enterprise. To say so, requires not a very large (though a significant) alteration of Sartre's system. He need only say that in cooperative existence a person *exists* and *is* his body in lateral touch with another. His own contention, of course, is obvious:

> the experience of the We-subject is a pure psychological, subjective event in a single consciousness; it corresponds to an inner modification of the structure of this consciousness but does not appear on the foundation of a concrete ontological relation with others and does not realize any *Mitsein*. It is a question only of a way of feeling myself in the midst of others. . . . The experience of the "we" remains on the ground of individual psychology and remains a simple symbol of the longed-for unity of transcendences. It is, in fact, in no way a lateral, real apprehension of subjectivities as such by a single subjectivity; the subjectivities remain out of reach and radically separated. . . . It is the material channeling of my transcendence which disposes me to apprehend it as extended and supported by the other transcendences without my getting out of myself and without the others getting out of themselves.[126] *

---

* The Christian ethicist may well stand in awe of Sartre's unwavering analysis, for here again his instinct is sure and his interpretation rigorous. He therefore poses the problem in most exact terms. "Mutual" love cannot be said to be possible or real, except on the basis of having *first* established the possibility and the reality of "love," of my being present *to* and *for* the Other. It is no easier to propose mutual love as an option for human freedom (whether by nature or through grace) than to propose *agape* (except, of course, when in the other direction thought has been confused by allowing a predicate of love to override its substantive meaning, in the expression "self-sacrificial love"). Any sort of love may be only a modification within a single subjectivity which brings the person into no real relation with the Other, i.e. this may not be love at all. See p. 131ff for a more extended discussion of the meaning of Christian love.

However, it is a fair question: What is there about a man's actual experience of being with others that compels this judgment? Is it not rather compelled by Sartre's excessive demand for getting out of self wholly into the experience of the Other, for the overcoming of separation by the merger of consciousnesses, for union and identity? Why rule out the possibility that the experience of the We-subject as a modification within a single consciousness takes place on the ground of the real meeting or encounter of transcendence with transcendence? Is not the lateral apprehension of subjectivities denied only because more was abstractly set up as the goal, or rather because the goal was drawn from a phenomenology of fallen interpersonal relationships and from the self's unwillingness to allow the Other in their meeting still to remain in his mysterious otherness out of reach? To make this correction would mean to discover in the created nature of being-with-others the possibility of realizing some *Mitsein* amid all the corruption to which Sartre is not the only witness.

At one point, indeed, Sartre speaks of "the recognition of subjectivities" by analogy with the individual's self-recognition as a spectator or perceiver of facticity in the world. This analogy is important because it sets up a comparison between my awareness of the other person and the awareness of self with which Sartre is *mainly concerned,* namely, my consciousness (of) self (in which the self is *not* objectified) and not my consciousness *of* self as an object of which I am conscious. I am "laterally" conscious (of) self in being conscious of this or that spectacle in the world. Just so, the individual in the midst of others is "a spectator, who, however, in the very upsurge which makes him a consciousness of the spectacle is constituted non-thetically as consciousness (of) being a cospectator of the spectacle." [127] It is a sufficient explanation of this technical language to say that Sartre puts the word "of" in parenthesis in such expressions as "consciousness (of) self" to indicate that there is *no separation experienced* between the subject and the object of consciousness; he calls this non-thetic consciousness. He says here, then, that the self experiences a consciousness (of) being a co-spectator of the same order as his consciousness (of) self. This might, of course, still be only a modification within his single consciousness. But why should his consciousness (of) being a co-spectator not be on the ground of the real lateral presence of one consciousness to the other? To say that there can be no real apprehension of other subjectivities as such by a single subjectivity means only that this cannot be accomplished by the thetic consciousness, i.e., consciousness *of* the Other (where the absence of parentheses indicate precisely the *separation* of the subject of consciousness and the object he is conscious of). Thus in the earlier parts of this chapter we have seen the distances that open up and which cannot be traversed by any project of the self for getting consciousness *of* the Other's consciousness *of,* etc. But perhaps that was the wrong way to the wrong goal.

We have seen how Sartre in his treatment of the We-Subject borders, at least, on another alternative, namely, the lateral apprehension of consciousnesses or the slipping of one transcendence into another, which stands between the suppression of both transcendences in a lateral apprehension of bodies, rhythms, etc., on one side, and, on the other, the face to face project of transcending *over* and assimilating another which suppresses one or the other transcendence. In this connection, we find the following striking statement in Sartre's treatment of language: "To understand a sentence spoken by my companion is, in fact, to understand what he 'means'—that is, to espouse his movement of transcendence, to throw myself with him toward possibles . . ." [128] What, then, if sexuality and concrete passions were only another language by which we understand what our companion means, espouse his movement of transcendence, and throw ourself with him toward possibles . . . ?

To carry through this alteration of Sartre's scheme would give an entirely different meaning to Sartre's statement that his analysis of the passions and the relations of love goes on under "the ideal standard of the value 'love.'" He explains this by reference to the missing Fusion: "that is, a fusion of consciousness in which each of them would preserve his otherness in order to found the other." [129] By "founding the other," of course, Sartre means the project of love, by aggression upon the other's freedom, to determine his love for oneself. But this need not be the meaning of these words. Instead the Sartrean consciousness which affirms "its own otherness from being" may be put in reverse. This would mean a consciousness which affirms "the being of the other as other" (Collins) and preserves also its own otherness, because of a recognition that distancing is indispensable to relation and that a real relation cannot abolish all distance without destroying itself and missing its goal. Sartre has shown this clearly enough! The ideal standard of love, then, launches not the project of being loved but the project of preserving otherness in relationship in order to found the Other, in a sense quite different from Sartre's. There is no reason why sexuality may not be the voice of being unto being in this understanding of human relatedness as well as in Sartre's original thought-forms.

VII

The conclusions of this chapter for the Christian interpretation of sex-in-being may now be briefly stated. Throughout the previous centuries of Christian teaching there has been lacking a full understanding of the unitive ends of marriage (as distinct from the end of procreation) and there has been a prevailing tendency to disparage sexual desire and

intercourse because of their involuntary nature in comparison with deliberate and rational acts of the person. This tradition still weighs
heavily upon us. When Jeremy Taylor wrote that "the order of nature
and the ends of God" are that men and women never seek or enjoy
venereal pleasure apart from "a desire of children, or to avoid forni-
cation, or to lighten and ease the cares and sadnesses of household
affairs, or to endear each other," [130] he made (in the last words) what
Sherwin Bailey calls "probably the first express recognition in theological literature of what may be termed the relational purpose of
coitus." [131] This statement, in its general implications, may be disputed,
but it can hardly be falsified. Moreover, the words "to endear each
other" express a fine sentiment, but they do not provide an articulated
analysis of the meaning of sexuality for the specifically human mode of
existence.

Not without a fully structured anthropological and theological encompassing of the nature of sex relation will the unfortunate and still
powerful consequences of the thought forms of the past be overcome.
There may be a reformation of the church's teaching in preparation in
the appeal to biblical perspectives in the writings of Otto Piper, Emil
Brunner, and Sherwin Bailey, and in the historical researches upon which
the latter and a number of other persons and commissions are engaged.
But a greater constructive effort will be required before (if ever) the
literature and spokesmen of the church do more than present to the
modern age a transsexual interpretation of the unitive ends of marriage
(comprised of platitudes about "the family") combined with a somewhat
more refined cult of romantic love than that dispensed by Hollywood
and its Temples* and with a biblical or traditional positivism about
monogamy. In all this, as it turns out, sexuality as a *human* capacity and
relationship never comes into view, and it may even continue to be
considered a lower aspect of our natures—when, for example, church
pronouncements subtly reintroduce dualism by replacing the biblical
"one flesh" unity by the "explanation" that this means "one person"
unity.

It is well known that for St. Augustine sexual desire was a result
of the distortion of our humanity, and the sign of this was that deliberate
action and rational consciousness were engulfed at the height of passion;
and in one degree or another theologians since his day have in the main
not succeeded in saying anything *decisively* different from this. Sartre
puts a final end to the disparagement of involuntary, nonrational acts
as somehow not centering in the person or bearing from him his
meaning. He provides us a way of seeing, and perhaps of saying, that

---

* Concerning which it has only to be said that this is not a very serious cult in
comparison with the passionate heroes and heroines of the past, and not a very
rigorous exercise of idolatry in comparison with Sartre's.

precisely because in sexual desire the transcendences of a man or a woman are "clogged with facticity," and *precisely because* the self remains no longer aloft in deliberate action playing its various roles but has become incarnate in the "flesh," he or she *for this very reason* has become accessible to another in this world for communication and creaturely participation with the other. Having made the alteration suggested in Sartre's scheme permits us to draw a different conclusion concerning coitus itself. Desire failed, in coitus, we saw, because of what was wanted. On the ground of understanding covenant-meeting to require the maintenance of distance in the relation of selves, coitus may be regarded rather as the expression of the "lateral" communication of subjectivities (a communication of persons not fraught with the difficulties of the rational consciousness transcending the transcendence of the Other); it means espousing the Other's movement of transcendence, launching oneself with the other toward his, toward *our,* possibles. . . . The real "shudder before *The Other Person*" is the tremor before his *presence* in desire and in coitus.

By way of contrast, theologians have commonly spoken as if God made a great mistake when male and female he created them for the cure of human aloneness; or else they have understood the relational, unitive ends of marriage as transsexual (i.e., subhuman) because they have meant by this only a doctrine of domestic relations, to the end of "lightening and easing the cares and sadnesses of household affairs." If it is not quite proper to speak of all transsexual interpretations of the unitive aspects of marriage as subhuman, it is remarkable how Christian thought has avoided speaking positively of sex in this connection. Sex has been regarded as a biological necessity, having a place only in monogamy, of course, where it is surrounded by those reciprocal benefits which are for us as human beings the really unitive functions marriage was meant to provide. Little was said about the sadness of having any household affairs at all (except, of course, as an encouragement to the flight of monks to islands in the Mediterranean) which sex in its human, relational function was, in large part, meant to justify. Thus, the theologians have spoken contrary to Genesis—and to Sartre.

To accuse Augustine and the tradition of Platonic idealism of dualism in regard to the "body," or of even worse errors in regard to the evilness of desire and venereal pleasure, accomplishes very little, if then appeal is made only to the Aristotelian-Thomistic reformation of the church's teaching about sex. It is true that, from the Thomistic viewpoint, soul is not separate from body, desire or passion are "natural" and not to be explained as a consequence of the Fall, and pleasure is only the natural concomitant of any activity attaining to its goal. There might even have been more intense pleasure experienced by unfallen man. Nevertheless, it is a consequence of the hierarchical structure of Thomistic anthropology and its world view that, however natural and good the sexual life may be, this is always subordinate to the soul in its spiritual or rational exercise, and sexuality cannot go to the heart of human existence. St. Thomas displays about the same preference for the deliberate, the voluntary, the controlled and quiet functioning of the soul as did St. Augustine. That woman, then, is not altogether commendable who, amid the stresses and distresses of communicating rationally and at the "more human" levels of consciousness, allows herself to be "endeared" by an Aristotelian though her husband. This would be something of a violation of her person, unless human sex communication goes to the very existence of the person as much as or more than does the mind.

Finally, we may note what *tours de force* result when the attempt is made to break radically with traditional teaching and heal the wounds it has inflicted by a simple appeal—with no more philosophy than that —to the biblical viewpoint. Thus, William Cole[132] sweeps away all "dualism" by an appeal to what is called "biblical naturalism"; and the word "naturalism" promptly resumes its current meaning, somewhat in the mind of the writer and even more in the minds of his readers. He discusses, without batting a term, the proposals of some of the ancients about "doing without sex." To which I suppose the proper answer is: I wouldn't think of attempting such a thing, not even for a moment! This answer will be forthcoming if we have been instructed by Genesis that men and women are in their creation, or instructed by Sartre that they are in their upsurge as consciousnesses in the presence of other consciousnesses, primarily and completely sexual—not simply that they have or have to do with sex. The anthropology and ontology being developed by the existentialists has this great value: it may enable us to think of sexuality as central to the unity of human personality without falling into either the language, or the consequent meanings, of a naturalistic reduction of the transcendence of the human self to the level of that-which-is.

Upon the reformation of the church's sexual teaching depends not only the saving of Christianity from very much of its past, but perhaps also the prevention of the disappearance of passion from the life of modern man in our increasingly technical civilization.

The expression of sexual emotion is becoming, according to the testimony of psychologists, increasingly a purely technical affair. Doctors bear witness to the increase of impotence among men between twenty and thirty years of age. This may be because today one can no longer expect to meet one of Tolstoy's vital barefoot peasant women on the streets of any of our large cities, or even in any of the monotonously commercialized small towns in this nation where once men and women lived still in touch with the energies of nature. I do not pretend to know the full explanation of these tendencies in our society. I only know that it is quite impossible to tell whether modern men or women are "dualist" or "naturalist" in the interpretation of their bodily life. We can only tell *when:* college students generally are naturalists on house-party week-ends, and dualists at the senior prom when they congregate each with his soul-mate, to the relation with whom, as to oneself, what has pre-viously happened in the body does not much matter, nor ever does it. On the whole, we seek I-Thou relations in coffee breaks; and of course in the transsexual aspects of marriage, in enjoying art or music together, and we do need the nurse's care somewhere referred to in the marriage ceremony. Of course, sexual satisfaction—which is a biological good we can scarcely do without—belongs in marriage, which a good society can scarcely do without (if we may state a generalization it would be harsh to think of applying in all cases). So, we Americans are the most married people in the world, and married the most. How shall pronouncements about God's great and good gift of sexuality inhering in our creation, and the human meaning of the passion of being for being, be addressed to people in such a cultural situation as ours? Surely not by silence, nor by the gibberish about the family which fills our church literature, nor by simply repeating words that bring God and the existing person into the talk about sexuality—but without explaining the cipher.

Five

Reinhold Niebuhr:
Christian Love and Natural Law

Throughout the writings of Reinhold Niebuhr there are strictures against the theory of natural law in Roman Catholic moral theology and the form it has sometimes taken in Protestant thought. There are also strong commendations of this view, with the plain implication or statement that some revision of the traditional concept of natural law is valid and necessary for the elaboration of a Christian ethic relevant to all the concrete problems of the moral life. And one essay in a recent volume deals profoundly and at length with the issue of "Love and Law in Protestantism and Catholicism." [1] Because of the importance of the relation between love and the natural moral law, both for personal and for social ethics, what Niebuhr has to say on this subject needs to be singled out for special consideration. Such an undertaking has also a practical significance for the present-day theological situation, since there are a number of persons, more or less of the neo-orthodox persuasion, who appear resolved to swelter out the present moral crisis with their own personal decisions impaled on the point of the existential moment or suspended wholly within a solution of justification by faith.

I. The Natural Law for Freedom

Fortunately or unfortunately, we today have a way of finding out whether anything akin to the traditional theory of natural law still remains central in a man's thought or to what extent this still governs what he has to say about man and morals. We can compare him with a viewpoint which in fact drops out altogether every remnant of the natural law and breaks decisively with the Western tradition in this regard: the viewpoint of atheistic existentialism. By contrast with Jean-Paul Sartre, the divergence of views among Christian theologians appears as only a family quarrel over the *meaning* of the natural law or the moral law God gives us for living in his human family.

Sartre quite rightly points out that according to traditional theism "the individual man is the realization of a certain concept in the divine intelligence." [2] This was the import of the doctrine of creation, and of the theory of natural law built upon it. By contrast Sartre may also help

us to realize what has been insufficiently acknowledged: that some view
of the essence of man is also implied in God's purpose for his creatures
in their final redemption seen in Christ. Whether the stress be placed
on creation or on redemption, man has in either case an essential nature.
The "essentialist" tradition was only cowardly attenuated, according to
Sartre, in all nonreligious views of natural law or theories of a priori
values. He breaks decisively with all this, and instead begins with bare
existence.

Man only is. He is not this or that *kind* of being. Having no essence
behind him or *before* him which defines what he ought to be, the individual man defines himself by his own engagement in choice. *Opto
ergo sum.* "Man is nothing else but what he makes himself." [3] Man
creates himself by the limitless rebounding effect of his own self-understanding. "Not only is man what he conceives himself to be, but he is
also what he wills himself to be after this thrust toward existence." [4]
For Sartre "there is no explaining things away [or, dropping out that
last pejorative word, there is no explaining things] by reference to a
fixed and given human nature." [5] "Man makes himself. He isn't ready-
made at the first. In choosing his ethics he makes himself, and force of
circumstances is such that he cannot abstain from choosing one." [6] Choice
creates value and essence. There is no pre-existent value or essence or
structure of reality or God which justifies choice; and it would be fruitless
to try to justify by a value the action which alone creates value. Man is
a free, self-manufacturing being whose freedom "in every concrete circumstance can have no other aim than to want itself." [7]

It is true that by probing to a freedom whose only aim is to want
itself, Sartre here discovers a kind of limit: "When in all honesty, I've
recognized that man is a being in whom existence precedes essence, that
he is a free being who, in various circumstances, can want only his freedom, I have at the same time recognized that I can want only the freedom of others." [8] But this shows that even a man who takes the most
extreme measures to lighten the boat by emptying it of every concept
that hampers free movement by legitimizing only some forms of conduct
must still remain in the boat. To think at all about the nature of man
Sartre must think with essences, even if that be only the thought that
man essentially consists of an entirely dynamic and limitless freedom.
However radically reshaped, here surely there is a modicum of the natural
law. It may even be affirmed that any conception of the nature of man
is so far a conception of the natural law. This becomes even more
evident in the universal principle that individual freedom (which can
have, because of its self-creative nature, no other aim than to want itself) is implicitly obliged at the same time to recognize that it can want
only the same freedom for others. So hard it is as to be well nigh im-

possible to break with the Western tradition of moral theology without standing on its shoulders!

Nevertheless, a comparison of atheistic existentialism with the theistic existentialism of Reinhold Niebuhr (if this be an apt way to characterize his view) shows how vastly more the latter is dependent upon the essentialist tradition and the theory of natural law. Or rather, it shows how his judgments are grounded in the same facts of moral experience and truths grasped by reason (or by reason illuminated by revelation) which were enshrined, with more or less adequacy or inadequacy, in this ancient teaching. Without blurring any distinctions or overlooking the additional complexity which Niebuhr rightly points out, we can see that he is actually proposing an interpretation of the nature of man and of the natural moral law which enters into continuing conversation with all the other viewpoints of this type that have been under the sun.

Readers of any of Niebuhr's books need not be reminded that he too believes that there is no explaining things by reference to a fixed and given human nature. Man is largely what he becomes; he isn't ready-made at the first. There are no fixed structures of nature or reason or history which man does not transcend by virtue of his spiritual freedom. What Niebuhr actually objects to when he rejects the idea of natural law is the view ordinarily associated with it, that human nature conforms wholly to stable structures and nicely reposes within discoverable limits. The thread running through Niebuhr's criticism of naturalism, rationalism, and romanticism in *The Nature and Destiny of Man* is his contention that man's self-transcending freedom rises above the limits or even the vitalities of physical nature and above the patterns of reason or the uniquely individual organic structures discovered by romantic idealism. Man stands before possibilities for action which are not to be calculated in terms of the potentialities of a fixed essential nature of any sort. His freedom means that his self-understanding affects what he is or is to become; and he grasps after possibilities only envisaged when, from the heights of self-transcending consciousness of himself and the present historical actuality, he seeks to reshape both himself and his social environment.

Is not such a dynamic interpretation of the indefinite possibilities of human freedom just as reasonable a conception of the nature of man as more static interpretations of his essence, and insofar does it not like them entail a (revised) conception of the natural moral law? The answer to this question, often explicit and certainly implicit in Niebuhr, is Yes.

To parley this issue at the summit, it is noteworthy that Niebuhr contends that for such a free spirit as man love is the law of life. In the search for ethical principles, as well as in other areas of his thought,

Niebuhr's apologetic procedure is the technique of demolition. This is to say, he attempts to show that all other views of the moral life fail by not taking fully into account the dimension of freedom or self-transcendence in man. In a sense this is a negative method; but, as Socrates long ago discovered, significant and rich conclusions may be drawn from a negative voice. Thus, something like the older conception of natural law might be established by reference not to man's sense of justice but to his "sense of injustice," or the basic judgment that some situations are not meant for man nor he for them. Likewise, love is the moral law for man, whose nature is what is indicated in Niebuhr's writings; and his way of pointing us to this conclusion is by showing that the natural moral law elaborated in the philosophies of naturalism, rationalism, and so on, fails and must fail to captivate and fulfill the special dimension of freedom in man's essential nature. Among the ruins of these systems love still stands as the relationship in life which was meant for man and for which man was intended. Despite the complexities that arise when we later consider the relation of love to the structures of nature and reason, and despite the fact that love at its pinnacle requires a heroic self-sacrifice which finds a nesting place in human history only at the foot of the Cross, what can be more grounded in "nature" than the assertion that man is made for life-in-community whose quality is love?

There is in nature or reason, for Niebuhr, no form or structure to which the self ought to return from its freedom; but this is true because the dimension of freedom already points the self toward a more ultimate harmony. "While egotism is 'natural' in the sense that it is universal, it is not natural in the sense that *it does not conform to man's nature,* who transcends himself indeterminately and can only have God rather than self for his end." [9] Similarly an ethics built mainly upon certain fixed structures of human nature is "not natural in the sense that it does not conform to man's nature" as indeterminate freedom. Therefore, "the law of love is the final law for man in his condition of finiteness and freedom because man in his freedom is unable to make himself in his finiteness his own end. The self is too great to be contained within itself in its smallness." [10] Although the self does not get radically beyond itself and into a relationship of love simply by taking thought, in its freedom the self is always already so far beyond itself that it cannot without damage to its essential nature return and live within "the cask of self stopped with the bung of self." [11] *Agape* is "the final law of human existence because every realization of the self which is motivated by concern for the self inevitably results in a narrower and more self-contained self than the freedom of the self requires." [12]

This is not, as for Sartre, a mere implication that one should want the freedom of others drawn from the primary and logically more ultimate fact that he always aims at his own freedom. It is rather the heart of the matter, based on the human essence in existence, or on the fact that man is made in his created freedom so that he comes to fruition only in covenant with others and in steadfast love for them. His transcendent freedom is *in order to* love; and love is ordained as the law for his life in freedom. "Materially," that is, in its content, love is the chief part of the natural moral law; and consonant with the dynamic nature of freedom this is a dynamic conception of the moral law. Love contains no code or fixed form to be imposed upon human freedom. Nor is it the law for life only in some supernatural realm. It is rather, as Principal Micklem suggests, "more like that *vis sanatrix naturae* whereby a body that is injured seeks to adapt itself to the unforeseen circumstances and to regain health, or like that law or instinct whereby if an ants' nest is disturbed its denizens set about its restoration. It is a binding obligation to loyalty under all circumstances. But, since circumstances are infinitely variable, it is neither positive Divine law nor a code. But it is in some sense law and obligatory in principle upon all men; it belongs therefore to the nature of man." [13]

Of course these analogies are drawn from biological nature, and only *mutatis mutandis* do they become illuminating for the realm of human freedom. There is also another law in our members which wars against the law in our minds. Of course, we are now speaking only of the material content of the moral law; and it need not be supposed, as the foregoing quotation might suggest, that human nature possesses self-curative powers in this respect. Because of that other law that holds sway within, the resources for living as we ought may flow only from common grace and the grace of the Gospel—and beyond grace as power, from grace as forgiveness which brings in us who remain halt, lame, and blind. Nevertheless, when by sin freedom injures itself and its life in love, there still remains a silent pressure toward love as the *vis sanatrix naturae* in the very constitution of man's transcendent spiritual freedom determining the *direction* in which alone health is to be found. Love belongs therefore to the nature of man. From thus defining the essence of man we at once define the natural norm for man. Niebuhr validates "the law of love as a vision of health which even a sick man may envisage, as the original righteousness which man does not possess but which he knows he ought to possess." [14]

The fact that Niebuhr is saying something not unlike this is shown also by the common ground between his thought and the impressive evidence from psychotherapy that man's most fundamental need, in sickness or in health, is to have the strength to love. In a review of Erich Fromm's *Man for Himself*, Niebuhr expresses succinctly the self's freedom and the consequent moral law: "The self in its freedom is too great to be contained within the self in its contingent existence. It requires an object of devotion beyond itself, and an indeterminate field of fellow-

ship." Such a statement is clearly grounded in a more adequate understanding than Sartre's (or, as we shall see, than Fromm's) that love is,
materially, the law of life. "Actually the Christian view is based," writes
Niebuhr, "precisely upon an estimate 'of the proper functioning of our
total personality' which Fromm regards as the hallmark of humanistic
ethic." [15]

Because of the significance of such statements as the above, it may be
suggested that much would be gained from saying that love with its
indeterminate possibilities is Niebuhr's radical revision of the conception
of the natural law for human personality with its indeterminate freedom.
The gain is not merely a clarification of terms, or that hereby Niebuhr's
ethics is clearly set in definite continuity with every other attempt under
the sun to rest morality upon some conception of man's essential nature
and in direct engagement with these other viewpoints. The result will
also be to remove some unnecessary complexity and paradoxicality from
his own thought. For it will be seen at once that in defining the material
content of man's whole duty there is no such thing as love beyond all
law.

The essay on "Love and Law" consists of a discussion of "love as law
and love at the limits of law and love beyond the limits." [16] As far as I
can see, "love at the limits of law" is never given further conceptual
definition. The essay is therefore a discussion of "love as law" and "love
beyond the limits of law." *Subjectively,* of course, these are the exact
terms in which the problem can be stated. This is the problem of the
relation between duty and inclination, or between love as a commandment and the spontaneity of the grace to love. Subjectively there is in
human experience such a thing as "love beyond law." This was perhaps
better expressed in an earlier book:

> Now love implies an uncoerced giving of the self to the object of its de-
> votion. It is thus a fulfillment of the law; for in perfect love all law is
> transcended and what is and what ought to be are one.
> To command love is a paradox; for love cannot be commanded or
> demanded. To love God with all our hearts and all our souls and all our
> minds means that every cleavage in human existence is overcome. But the
> fact that such an attitude is commanded proves that the cleavage is not
> overcome; the command comes from one side of reality to the other, from
> essence to existence.[17]

Subjectively there is tension between love as law and love beyond law.
But the author puts this issue largely behind him after the second section, which is five pages long. The same is not the case materially. When
from the third section onward in this essay Niebuhr turns to an attempt
to define the content and meaning of Christian ethic, he delineates four
points concerning the indeterminacy of love and of human freedom. In

each case he confuses the subjective with the objective problem, and this leads him mistakenly to call these instances of the material transcendence of love over all law. Since he believes that in fact these points of indeterminacy correspond to the character of human freedom, and knows that ultimately the natural law has to be defined in terms of man's essential nature, he cannot with consistency affirm that, materially speaking, love ever goes beyond law. Consequently he hedges: "This first element in the indeterminacy of love has already been described as being, *in one respect at least,* within the limits of law. *For it describes the sum total of all our obligations to our fellowmen without specific detail. It is thus the summary of all law.*" "Law *in the determinate sense* must stop with distributive justice." Heedless love "cannot be separated from the realm of natural love by a neat line. It transcends the line of natural love. Yet without an element of heedless love. . . ." "Yet even forgiveness comes *partially* into the category of love as law." The context here makes it plain that materially forgiveness falls within love as law, while only subjectively does it transcend law: "Our forgiveness of our brethren is primarily *a grateful response* to God's forgiveness." "This kind of love is a matter of law in the sense that the essential nature of man, with his indeterminate freedom, requires that human relations should finally achieve such intimacy." This is to say that, materially, indeterminate love is the law of life. "But it is also a matter of grace because no sense of obligation can provide the imagination and forbearance by which this is accomplished." This is to say that, subjectively, love never flows from law but from beyond it.[18]

Thus are the "dialectical relationships" multiplied, or at least the expression of them rendered unclear, by failure to carry through terminologically the actual reconstruction of the theory of natural law in terms of love. Freedom and love as corresponding nature and norm belong within the essentialist tradition of moral theology despite the difference from traditional views. This is especially true if Niebuhr allows that natural reason may know of love as the requirement of freedom. There would perhaps be something lost in "dialectic" brilliance but substantial gain in clarity of thought if the revision of the traditional theory of natural law were made more explicit. Moreover, his other writings support this, in that he does not elsewhere toy with the idea that *materially* love transcends its status as the law for man's existence in freedom.

Incidentally, Niebuhr's brief remarks about Kierkegaard in this essay are wrong for the same reason. He accuses Kierkegaard of presenting "a legalistic version of universal love in his *Works of Love.*" [19] It is true that Kierkegaard in one chapter rhapsodizes about the word "shalt" in the love commandment. But this is because he knows that love is the highest law, not materially beyond all law. His "second ethic" transcends abstract Kantian norms or the universalities of traditional natural law based on the fixed structures of human nature (these are "suspended" in *Fear and Trembling*). Where Kierkegaard is weak, and where Niebuhr proves most helpful, is in clarifying the relations between love, the natural law for freedom, and the "first ethic" based on determinate aspects of human nature and society. These tensions fall within the totality of the natural law as now re-viewed; they do not fall between the natural law (or love as law) and love beyond law. It is also inaccurate to say that Kierkegaard would have us regard "the loved self as anonymously as possible." He suggests that in Christian love we "close our eyes" to every selfish preferential relationship and then open them and "love the man we see," that is, our neighbor in all his concreteness and full identity. Kierkegaard is right in thus defining the material meaning of the law of love. He is weakest, and here again Niebuhr proves most helpful, in clarifying the relations between such love as the law of life and the intimate, preferential loves which clothe us in daily life. But this is a problem which falls within the totality of an ethics built upon the law of nature or on an estimate of the proper functioning of human personality.

No more words should be written on the subject of Christian ethics unless it is right to separate the material from the subjective problem of love and law. If we persist without this distinction Augustine's *On the Spirit and the Letter* will haunt our dreams. For it is the letter of the Gospel and not the old law only which kills. Love as law or duty condemns our actual inclinations. In this sense any actual love goes by the Spirit beyond law. Yet in the material sense love is the law of life and not more than the law; and this is the concern of Christian ethical analysis.

II. The Law for Man as a Determinate Creature?

The relation between Niebuhr's thought and traditional moral theology based on the known structures of human nature is indicated by his own summary: "What is usually known as 'natural law' in both Christian and Stoic thought is roughly synonymous with the requirements of man as creature, and . . . the virtues, defined by Catholic thought as 'theological virtues,' that is, the virtues of faith, hope and love, are the requirements of his freedom and represent the *justitia originalis*. . . . There is no uncorrupted natural law, just as there is no completely lost original justice." [20] We have considered love as the natural law for freedom, and turn now toward what is more familiarly known as "natural law" or "the requirements of man as creature." By this characterization Niebuhr can only mean the requirements of man insofar as he is a determinate creature living within social and historical structures, since the freedom by which he exceeds these limits is also finite, creaturely freedom. Both these aspects of the natural moral law, as it is modified and understood in Niebuhr's thought, belong inseparably together and constantly interplay with each other. A typical passage illustrating this interaction is found in the essay on "Love and Law in Protestantism and Catholicism":

> These points of indeterminacy in the law of love correspond to the indeterminate character of human freedom. Insofar as man has a determinate structure, it is possible to state the "essential nature" of human existence to which his actions ought to conform and which they should fulfill. But insofar as he has the freedom to transcend structure, standing beyond himself and beyond every particular social situation, every law is subject to indeterminate possibilities which finally exceed the limits of any specific definition of what he "ought" to do. Yet they do not stand completely outside of law, *if law is defined in terms of man's essential nature. For this indeterminate freedom is a part of his essential nature.*[21]

Thus sometimes Niebuhr allows that, insofar as man has a determinate structure, it may be possible to state the "essential nature" of human existence in these respects and to gain some understanding of the natural law for man as a determinate creature—subordinate, of course, to the law of love. Yet sometimes he makes the sweeping assertion that "fixed historical structures and norms . . . *do not in fact exist*" and that therefore "the moral certainties of natural law in Catholic thought are *all dubious.*" [22] The issue here raised really cannot be left vague by merely qualifying the strictures and saying that traditional natural law is "less valid" than was supposed or that "both Catholic and Reformation thought are *too certain* about the fixities of the norms of law." [23] Niebuhr writes:

> The development of natural law theories in Christianity has been criticized as an apostasy from the Christian ideal of love. But all such criticisms are informed by a moral sentimentalism which does not recognize to what degree all decent human actions, even when under the tension and inspiration of the love commandment, are in fact determined by rational principles of equity and justice, by law rather than love.[24]

Are we, then, to take most seriously Niebuhr's commendation of the theory of natural law? If so, this means that there are two inseparable but distinguishable sources and bases for the first principles of human conduct: there is, first, love as the norm for freedom in view of the fact that "the quintessence of a human personality is never in time or historic actuality" or contained in determinate structures.[25] Then secondly, there are principles based upon definition of the human essence insofar as man does have his being within determinate limits. *Together* these would comprise the entire natural law or the revised equivalent of it in Niebuhr's thought.

Or on the other hand, are we to pay more attention to the other aspect of his thought? Man's life in time itself seems subject to the all-embracing flux of historical change. In addition, human self-transcendence and freedom are capable of unsettling every determinate structure and setting it in motion and commotion. Moreover, sin obscures our vision of the essential nature of man and leads us to mistake for the moral law structures destined only to last for a day. On this interpretation there is only one fundamental principle for Niebuhr—the law of love itself, which, since it stands in relation to the very essence of man, we have called the primary natural law. "It is true that reason discloses the 'moral law,'" writes Niebuhr, and then goes on to explain: "It reveals, or at least suggests, the total field of life in which obligation moves." [26] Principles proximate to this are the equivalent, not of the older natural law as one element in his thought, but of the *jus gentium* or *jus civilis*. Proximate principles then are *applications* of the natural law (which requires that freedom have an indeterminate field of fellowship) to certain conditions of fact.

In paying tribute to the traditional theory of natural law, it may be said, Niebuhr does not mean to affirm that there actually is a secondary source of *first* principles. He means only to emphasize the necessity of keeping love relevant to actual life, and to say that when love goes in search of a social policy and into action, it gives rise to more specific principles or schemes. Thus reflection upon the concrete situation is only a secondary source of *secondary* principles. This traditionally was not the role of natural law but of the *jus gentium,* or with greater particularity, the *jus civilis*. As Maritain sums up: "The Law of Nations, or the common law of civilization, deals, like natural law, with the rights and duties which follow from the first principle in a *necessary* manner, but this time *supposing* certain conditions of fact." And *"positive law* (statute law), or the body of laws in force in a given community, deals with the rights and duties which follow from the first principle, but in a *contingent* manner, by virtue of the determinate ways of conduct."[27] It may be instructive to try this second interpretation on for size, to see whether proximate principles in Niebuhr are not more correctly to be regarded as applications of his first principle (freedom and love), "this time supposing certain conditions of fact," or as "determinate ways of conduct" related contingently to contingent factors and not to any fixed or determinate mode of man's being in the world.

However, before undertaking in the next section to substantiate this interpretation, a small degree of truth should be noted in the first. Niebuhr criticized modern relativists for not recognizing a permanent structure of human personality because of "their obsession with the changing aspects in the human situation." [28] But he ordinarily needs only a single sentence to draw up the bill of particulars. He cites the practical universality of the prohibition of theft and murder, and even then points out that these are minimal requirements. (Sometimes he suggests that these, too, have their source in love.) Announcing that, despite his freedom, man is "a creature of nature who is subject to certain natural structures," he affirms at once that "these natural structures have negative rather than positive force." [29] Then with bewildering rapidity the reader finds himself back in the midst of the other dialectic—against the fixed structures of natural law. Still, that one sentence will have made plain that the minimal, negative, and most universal aspects of morality are grounded for Niebuhr in certain immutable aspects of human existence, and that here man's knowledge of nature and norm supplements the law of love.

At only one other point do I find that Niebuhr actually defines the determinate character of human nature to any significantly greater extent. Objecting to Bertrand Russell's views on sex morality, Niebuhr writes that he "obviously disregards one important immutable aspect of the human situation, namely, the organic unity between physical impulses and the spiritual dimension of human personality. This organic unity means that sexual relations are also personal relations." [30] This aspect of the natural moral law for man as a determinate creature was applied with telling effect by Niebuhr in his analysis of the Kinsey reports,[31] and it was central in his analysis of sexuality in relation to sin and anxiety in the first volume of the Gifford Lectures. This comprises a by no means small and insignificant purchase upon traditional notions of natural law. Still, one cannot escape the conclusion that Niebuhr's frequent tributes to the meaning he still finds in natural-law theory outnumber and outweigh his actual use of such determinate moral knowledge, and are therefore largely verbal. Likewise, his criticism of relativism's stress on novelty and creative emergence somewhat disguises—but for the law of love—his own.

Niebuhr may be quite correct in finding few immutable norms for man's moral behavior, or in relating all principles to the law of love rather than allowing them to stand on their own base. This chapter is concerned only to clarify and interpret his views on love and law, and not to defend a greater use of the supposed findings of the traditional theory unrevised. One step in the direction of properly grasping Niebuhr's thought is to understand love as the natural law for freedom. Another is to understand that what he often calls natural law, or its equivalent in his thought, is not that at all, but an application of the fundamental law of love. This has to be qualified only to the extent that we have now indicated an actual spelling out of the determinate structures of human existence.

The best summary of Niebuhr's position on the issue now under consideration is his statement:

> There is not much that is absolutely immutable in the structure of human nature except its animal basis, man's freedom to transmute this nature in varying degrees, and the unity of the natural and the spiritual in all the various transmutations and transfigurations of the original "nature." [32]

Because of the unity of the spiritual and the natural, or of indeterminate freedom with the determinate in man, men are always engaged in introducing creative emergents (as well as sinful elements) into the "various historic configurations of human vitality." [33] Freedom endows all natural impulses with new dimensions, and transmutes and transfigures almost every given structure. Therefore every norm which seems to be validated by experience or to be expressive of something immutable about the human essence "must be held with some degree of tentativity and be finally subordinate to the law of love." [34]

III. Jus Gentium, Jus Civilis

Several times in *An Interpretation of Christian Ethics*, which contains the justly celebrated chapter on "The Relevance of an Impossible Ethical Ideal," Reinhold Niebuhr remarks that love and even minimal standards of justice "logically" involve each other and are "organically" related.[35] These words do not throw much light. More illuminating is the statement, also repeated in several forms, that "every moral value and standard is *grounded in* and *points toward* an ultimate perfection of unity and harmony not realized in any historic situation," or that a "minimal standard of moral conduct is *grounded in* the law of love and *points toward* it as ultimate fulfillment." [36] While establishing the transcendence of love, he also seeks to point out the relevance of the transcendent as "both *the ground* and *the fulfillment* of existence," as *"a basis* of even the most minimal social standards," "not only as *the source* of all norms of justice, but as an ultimate perspective by which their limitations are discovered." [37]

Now the statement that justice "points toward" and finds "fulfillment" in love suggests that justice itself may properly be grounded in structural reason and nature, independent of love which transcends these things. Justice, then, would stand on its own base, even though it reaches up toward heaven and is subject to Heaven's judgment. This seems to be Niebuhr's view or at least his expression, when he discusses the relation of justice to love in the chapter titled "The Kingdom of God and the Struggle for Justice" in his Gifford Lectures.[38] There, without indicating any perceptible difference, he passes from "the practical universality of the prohibition of murder," one of the minimum, negative requirements which form, as we have seen, the determinate natural moral law, to "essentially universal 'principles' of justice"; and he counts heavily on the evidence that "both 'equality' and 'liberty' are recognized in Stoic, medieval and modern theories of natural law." [39] Does this mean that here at last he elaborates more fully what comprises the determinate natural law? This conclusion might be drawn from the fact that the emphasis falls on natural or historic achievements of justice "approximating" or "pointing toward" love; and from the fact that (although he does say that "systems and principles of justice are the *servants* and *instruments* of the spirit of brotherhood insofar as they extend the sense of obligation toward others" [40]) there is not nearly so much said about love as the "ground," "basis," and "source" of justice as is the case in *An Interpretation of Christian Ethics*.

The question at this point is not whether all men possess some "sense of justice," but whether their sense of justice is mediate or immediate—whether, in short, the sense of justice is grounded in man's sense of the love requirement upon his freedom or grounded in itself by virtue of what he knows concerning the natural requirements of his determinate nature and the fixed structures of human relationships. The earlier book, *An Interpretation of Christian Ethics*, spells out the way "justice" stems from "love" as well as how justice (be it dependent or independent in origin) points toward and approximates the law of love; and this viewpoint, I believe, is most characteristic of Niebuhr's thought in general. Love as "ground," "source," or "basis" suggests the relationship in the traditional theory between natural law and the principles men may devise for applying the fundamental law (love) to actual existence. "Reason, in short, discovers that life in its essence is not what it is in its actual existence, that ideally it involves much more inclusive harmonies than actually exist in history. This is what the Stoics meant by the natural law." [41] This is also, in large part at least, what Niebuhr means by love and the vision of the ideal possible for man in the moment of transcending himself and his world.

The author also sets up a scale comprised of several terms: love, freedom, equality, equal justice (which in his usage sometimes leans toward transcendent equality, sometimes toward concrete justice), justice, and "schemes" of justice. Read in one direction—in the order given—love is the ground, source, and basis of these proximate principles. Read in the reverse direction, these proximate principles point toward love as their end and fulfillment as well as critical standard. They represent "an ascending scale of moral possibilities in which each succeeding step is a closer approximation to the law of love." [42] The latter reading, in the ascending direction, would have to be regarded as primary for certain purposes *if* Niebuhr believes that these more particular principles are actually grounded in some sort of natural law for man as a determinate creature within the structures of nature, reason, or history; and this would then be moral knowledge, supplementing that gained in freedom, of man's destiny for an indeterminate life-in-love.

It is significant that in the order of validation or justification, the opposite or descending order is the one adopted: love is the source and ground, and these other directives follow from it.

> The ideal possibility for men involved in any social situation may always be defined in terms of freedom and equality. Their highest good consists in freedom to develop the essential potentialities of their nature without hindrance. . . . Since human beings live in a society in which other human beings are competing with them for the opportunity of a fuller development of life, the next highest good is equality; for there is no final principle of arbitration between conflicting human interests except that which equates the worth of competing individuals.[43]

In other words, since love requires that human life be affirmed, positive freedom to possess the affirmed fruition is the first implication and—in a world of competing claims—equality of opportunity is the second implication drawn from the law of love itself.

Infrequently Niebuhr states that in drawing these conclusions reason is simply at work building a coherent system of relationships. Such statements occur when, reversing the direction, he is concerned to point out how rational consistency "points toward" love as its end and fulfillment:

> Reason tries to establish a system of coherence and consistency in conduct as well as in the realm of truth. It conceives of its harmonies of life with life not only in ever wider and more inclusive terms, but also works for equal justice within each area of harmony by the simple fact that the special privileges of injustice are brought under rational condemnation for their inconsistency. Under the canons of rational consistency men can claim for themselves only what is genuinely value, and they cannot claim value for any of their desires if they are not valuable to others besides themselves. Reason thus forces them to share every privilege except those which are necessary to insure the performance of a special function in the interest of the whole. A large percentage of all special privilege is thereby ruled out by the canons of reason.[44]

To the contrary, it is perfectly possible for reason (unless under the sway of love and the conviction that all persons are equal before God—and sometimes even then) to imagine a much more coherent world without the principle of equality than with it, according to some of the hierarchical arrangements or caste systems which have been the system of coherence in actual existence at most times and places.

Moreover, if only the "canons of reason" are here at work according to the intrinsic requirements of any viable social structure, and if Niebuhr is here elaborating the parallel in his thinking to the natural law for man as a determinate creature, then he proves to be more the rationalist than Maritain the Thomist. For in his latest statement Maritain defines our way of knowing the fundamental law as "knowledge through inclination" and not through reason.[45] This is to say, man's sense of justice consists of his inclination toward that which is suitable to the human essence, and his sense of injustice arises from disinclination to that which is averse to his essence. And Maritain declares flatly that "the only reason on which the natural law depends is divine Reason," [46] not human reason at all. The actual situation, I suggest, is that there is a close parallel between what Maritain means by knowledge through inclination (or disinclination; for example, our innate horror when confronted by inhuman evils in the world such as genocide) and Niebuhr's belief that because of freedom and man's self-understanding in the moment of transcendence "all human life is informed with an inchoate sense of responsibility toward the ultimate law of life—the law of love." [47] This is not known by discursive reason, but it is for Niebuhr the natural law based on a radically different conception of the quintessence of human nature. On the other hand, the principles of equal justice, which are arrived at discursively or by immediate inference from the law of love, correspond closely to Maritain's definition: "A precept which is known through rational deduction, and as a conclusion conceptually inferred from a principle of natural law, is part of jus gentium." [48]

The fact is that in his An Interpretation of Christian Ethics Niebuhr fully elaborated the position sketched as a possibility in the later essay we have had occasion before to comment on: "It may well be," he writes, "that everything defined as the 'sense of justice' is an expression of the law of love within the limits of law." [49] Numerous passages in the earlier book make this his evident view. A few of these may be cited here, since it is of considerable importance to establish once for all that the relevant principles of social ethics have their ground and source in the law of love, and not in the concession of a degree of validity in the older forms of natural law nor simply as the products of technical reason contriving temporary "schemes" of justice:

Equality is always the regulative principle of justice; and in the ideal of equality there is an echo of the law of love, "Thou shalt love thy neighbor AS THYSELF." If the question is raised to what degree the neighbor has a right to support his life through the privileges and opportunities of the common life, no satisfactory, rational answer can be given to it, short of one implying equalitarian principles: He has just as much right as you yourself.

Since the law of love demands that all life be affirmed, the principle that all conflicting claims of life be equally affirmed is a logical approximation of the law of love in a world in which conflict is inevitable.

As the ideal of love must relate itself to the problems of a world in which its perfect realization is not possible, the most logical modification and application of the ideal in a world in which life is in conflict with life is the principle of equality which strives for an equilibrium in the conflict.

Equal justice remains the only possible, though hardly a precise, criterion of value. Since no life has value if all life is not equally sacred, the highest social obligation is to guide the social struggle in such a way that the most stable and balanced equilibrium of social forces will be achieved and all life will thereby be given equal opportunities.[50]

Evidently these are not conclusions drawn by pure reason discerning, at least with "partial validity," the fixed structures of human existence. Nor are they the product merely of technical social reason contriving schemes of equilibrium while blind to the ultimate moral law. What are they then, if not principles which follow in some manner if not "in a necessary manner" * from reflecting upon the nature of man as man and the love requirement of his quintessential freedom, but "this time *supposing* certain conditions of fact, as for instance the state of civil society or the relationships between peoples"? Freedom, equality, justice—these are universal principles, "at least insofar as these conditions of fact" in which the fundamental law has to be applied "are universal data of civilized life." They are, in fact, the *jus gentium* or "the common law of civilization." [51]

It ought to be noted that Niebuhr locates equality in the realm of (relevant) transcendence, along with the law of love:

Equality, being a rational political version of the law of love, shares with it the quality of transcendence. It ought to be, but it never will be fully realized. . . . The ideal of equality is thus qualified in any possible society by the necessities of social cohesion and corrupted by the sinfulness of men. It remains, nevertheless, a principle of criticism under which every scheme of justice and a symbol of the principle of love involved in all moral judgments.[52]

* This vestigial remain of the rationalistic, deductive theory of natural law must also be removed (see Chapter Eight from Maritain's revision of his treatise on natural law in *Man and the State*. When the idea that, in finding and making law, men proceed to conclusions in a *necessary* manner is finally removed from Maritain, it is clear that his position and that of Niebuhr approach one another, even when the latter writes: ". . . Nothing in history follows in a necessary manner" ("Reply," *Reinhold Niebuhr: His Religious, Social, and Political Thought*, ed. Chas. W. Kegley and Robt. W. Bretall. New York: The Macmillan Company, 1956, p. 433). It is also clear that nothing in the findings of fact and of law on which these thinkers agree prevents social ethics from being founded in man's natural sense of justice and love, by applications of this in decision-making. Both Maritain and Niebuhr are revisionists among natural-law theorists.

Yet equal justice comes closer to existence than love; and to point this out Niebuhr even uses the opposite language and denies it transcendence: "The principles of equal justice are thus approximations of the law of love in the kind of imperfect world which we know and not principles which belong to a world of transcendent perfection." His meaning, clearly stated on the same page, is that "the ideal of love and the ideal of equality . . . stand in an ascending scale of transcendence to the facts of existence." [53] This in turn means that in Niebuhr's view the notion of equality "presupposes the resolution of the conflict of life with life, which it is the concern of law to mitigate and restrain." [54]

When Niebuhr corrects the lack of precision in equality and justice as criteria of value so as to apply them to more particular historical situations, he discovers of course that "so many contingent factors arise in any calculation of the best method of achieving equal justice that absolute standards are useless" [55]—this is to say, useless in that they provide no detailed map of the historical terrain. But this does not mean that principles have been abandoned as no longer relevant. It means only that a man is now engaged in applying them. He has, in short, entered the realm of *jus civilis* where he must deal, as Maritain says, "with rights and duties which follow from the first principle, but in a *contingent* manner, by virtue of the determinate ways of conduct set down by the reason and will of man when they institute the laws and give birth to customs of a particular community." [56]

Not noticing clearly enough that his thought actually follows the traditional ordering *jus naturale—jus gentium—jus civilis*, Niebuhr makes the mistake of interpreting his accommodation to historical contingency and relativity as a revision of the distinction between absolute and relative natural law. He points out correctly that the so-called relative natural law was an adjustment of moral requirements to human *sinfulness*. He criticizes the unqualified and absolute nature of this distinction between the two laws because it removed to too great a distance the ferment of the absolute ideal and led to complacent acceptance of arrangements based on inequality:

> The difficulty in the Christian application of the theory of natural law . . . is to be found in the undue emphasis placed upon the relative natural law which was applicable to the world of sin, as against the absolute natural law which demanded equality and freedom.
> The principle of equality was thereby robbed of its regulative function in the development of the principles of justice. It was relegated to a position of complete transcendence, with the ideal of love.[57]

Such relegation either of love or of equal justice is always a disastrous mistake. But when Niebuhr restates the truth there is to be found in this distinction between absolute and relative natural law, he explains its meaning in terms of the adjustment of the moral law more to the *contingencies* in historical situations than to the sinfulness of man:

> A rational analysis reveals both the ideal possibility and the actual situation from which one must begin. In that sense there are really two natural laws—that which reason commands ultimately and the compromise which reason makes with the *contingent* and arbitrary forces of human existence.[58]

This is not what was ever meant by two natural laws, one absolute, the other relative. It is, however, what was meant by *jus civilis*. There is then in Niebuhr only one natural or essential law, the absolute law of life (love); and there are principles of equality and justice by which love takes shape for application to historical situations; and finally there are relative schemes of civil law and economic and other institutions which fully embrace the particularities in various constellations of human relationships in history. His aim is so to relate the principle of equality to the law of love, on the one hand, and to the problems of relative justice, on the other, that complacent conservatism may be avoided, and man's allegiance to existing schemes of justice be always in danger of being set in motion toward some higher possibility. One might therefore summarize the meaning for Niebuhr of the sense of inequality or injustice, whether taken most generally or most particularly, as the reaction of love to everything which is not love. For everything defined as the "sense of justice" is an expression of love with greater specification as law.

In some of Niebuhr's later writings there may be detected a tendency to skip over the correlation of love with freedom, and following that with equal justice, and to pass at once to the way in which man's indeterminate freedom shatters every structure in history and escapes all fixed norms. This leaves him in a poor position for showing, as he is fond of saying, that "the final dike against relativism is to be found, not in these alleged fixities, but in the law of love itself." [59] At one point in his "vindication of democracy and critique of its traditional defence," for example, the author says: "One of the facts about man as man is that his vitalities may be elaborated in indeterminate variety. . . . It is man's nature to transcend nature and to elaborate his own historical existence in indeterminate degree." [60] These statements, which the author deliberately juxtaposes with Maritain's definition of natural law, are to be recognized, of course, as Niebuhr's central affirmation about the nature of man: freedom. But in this context he is concerned to point out the negative consequences of transcendence and not the positive requirement of "an indeterminate field of fellowship"—what freedom wrecks and not what freedom works through love. Freedom, of course, remains an ultimate; and the author has the positive and worthy intention of vindicating democracy. But "social freedom" proves to be as indeterminate and limitless as the ontological freedom on which it is based.

This becomes clear when the author asks "the final question to confront the proponent of a democratic and free society": "whether the freedom of a society should extend to the point of allowing these principles to be called in question." He answers that "the ultimate freedom of a democratic society" requires that "not even the moral presuppositions upon which the society rests are withdrawn from constant scrutiny and re-examination." [61] We must tread cautiously here, for what Niebuhr says is mostly valid. He does point out that "every society needs working principles of justice [are they not in the earlier book much more than mere working principles?], as criteria for its positive law and system of restraints. . . . But every historical statement of them is subject to amendment." [62] Certainly no "historical statement" or "scheme" of justice ought to go long without amendment, on account of both the vested interests and the limited imagination of any historical epoch. But this is a far cry from saying that the "moral presuppositions upon which society rests" are never to be withdrawn from constant scrutiny and re-examination—if this means not to find out better what these presuppositions require in a new day but to call them fundamentally in question and to challenge them. Such unlimited freedom means unlimited war, or a perpetual and unqualified inclination thereto, among all us Hatfields and McCoys; and there would then have been found no positive basis for community.

Of course, Niebuhr cannot adhere consistently to this answer even with regard to the single presupposition he has in mind in this context. If "the freedom of society" is really vindicated and *made necessary by the fact that human vitalities have no simple definable limits*," [63] then here is a moral presupposition so firmly grounded that objection to it by the primitives of our time ought not to be genially tolerated, even though particular proposals for adjudicating between freedom and order may be multiplied without number. It may be suggested that if what Niebuhr wrote earlier in *An Interpretation of Christian Ethics* about love as the law for freedom, and about positive freedom as love's first discernment concerning the neighbor's need, and equal justice as the next following perquisite, were all brought fully into relation to this issue, his answer would gain still greater substance and clarity. For there he wrote of "equal justice" as "the simplest of all moral principles" and said:

> That principle has been operative in all the advances made by human society, and its application to the modern social situation is obviously valid. In a struggle between those who enjoy inordinate privileges and those who lack the basic essentials of the good life it is fairly clear that a

religion which holds love to be the final law of life stultifies itself if it does not support equal justice as a political and economic approximation of the ideal of love.[64]

Yet this is Niebuhr's viewpoint in books later than the one on Christian ethics in 1935.* The chapter "Beyond Law and Relativity" in *Faith and History* (1949) says in effect that there is only one natural and essential law; the rest is application:

> The principles of "natural law" by which justice is defined are, in fact, not so much fixed standards of reason as they are rational efforts to apply the moral obligation, implied in the love commandment, to the complexities of life and the fact of sin. . . . Any definition of moral rules beyond the minimal obligation of the self to the neighbor are discovered, upon close analysis, to be rational formulations of various implications of the love commandment rather than fixed and precise principles of justice. . . . Equality stands in a medial position between love and justice . . . Thus equality is love in terms of logic. But it is no longer love in the ecstatic dimension. . . . Therefore equal justice is on the one hand the law of love in rational form and on the other hand something less than the law of love.[65]

---

* The reader should pay special attention to the fact that the interpretation of Niebuhr's thought here proposed by no means depends exclusively upon his earlier work *An Interpretation of Christian Ethics*. Not only does the paragraph above make this evident by drawing upon later works, but also the text above at footnotes 38-41 and 49, as well as the use I have made throughout of his 1953 essay on "Love and Law in Protestantism and Catholicism." It is necessary to stress this point because Mr. Niebuhr, in his "Reply" to my interpretation when it was first published, sought to "eliminate some points of difference between us" by "failing to support any idea which I propounded in my earlier work, *An Interpretation of Christian Ethics* . . ."; and then went on to state: "I was only dimly feeling my way in this book toward a realistic and valid Christian ethic. I disavowed some of my ideas and amended others in later works, which roughly represent my present position. I am therefore not able to defend, or interested in defending, any position I took in *An Interpretation of Christian Ethics*" (*Reinhold Niebuhr: His Religious, Social, and Political Thought*, ed. Chas. W. Kegley and Robert W. Bretall. New York: The Macmillan Company, 1956, pp. 434-435). Some readers seem to have taken this sweeping renunciation at face value, despite the fact that it was estopped by the passages in my original chapter cited above, and also despite the fact that Niebuhr himself proceeded to say that "the elimination of these points of difference leaves still the basic point of Professor Ramsey's criticism of my thought" (I should have said: "*interpretation* of his thought"). In the substantive reply that followed, Niebuhr plainly restated as his own present viewpoint the interpretation which I have given (see especially his final two paragraphs, *ibid.*, pp. 435-436). Any discerning reader would know that the development of a more "realistic" Christian ethics in the later Niebuhr could only affect concepts of justice based on the determinate structures of human nature and society (or their displacement by an increasing pragmatism), but that this does not touch love as the law of human freedom and justice as the application of this law, which are the chief points that, when clarified, make Niebuhr a radical revisionist among natural-law theorists.

Likewise, in the later volume of Niebuhr's essays published in 1953 there is a passage in the chapter on "Augustine's Political Realism" that is obviously his own viewpoint and which may be regarded as a précis of the foregoing. He is speaking of the "sense of justice" on the part of various interest groups in a nation, and then declares that the "spirit of justice is *identical* with the spirit of love except at the highest level of the spirit of love, where it becomes purely sacrificial and engages in no calculation of what the due of each man may be. . . .* Certain 'principles' of justice, as distinguished from formulas or prescriptions, were indeed operative, such as liberty, equality, and loyalty to covenants; but these principles will be recognized as no more than the law of love in its various facets." [66]

IV. THE MEANING OF CHRISTIAN LOVE

There may be readers who will be of the opinion that the foregoing interpretation has leveled the towering summits of the Niebuhrian mountain range, with its gathering storms and lightning flashes, to about the height of the mountains Wordsworth loved best. What has happened, they may ask, to the pinnacle of self-sacrificial love which seems in its ecstatic heroism and spontaneous heedlessness to be such an "impossible possibility" for men and nations?

Two main interpretations of the meaning of Christian love are contending for acceptance in present-day theological discussion. One is the view that the primary meaning of love is to be found in self-sacrifice. This is Niebuhr's position, and he believes the critical relevance of such love to ordinary human motives is to be found in the fact that "without an element of heedless love every form of mutual love would degenerate into a calculation of mutual advantages, and every calculation of such advantages would finally generate resentment about an absence of perfect reciprocity." [67] In demonstrating that such a redemptive relationship exists between self-sacrificial love and all forms of mutual love, Niebuhr has been accused of holding a conception of mutual love that is "neither mutual nor love." Theologians who raise this objection themselves are in general adherents of the second interpretation of the intrinsic meaning of Christian love. They believe that "community," or the highest and truest form of mutual love itself, is the basic notion in Christian ethics. In support of this viewpoint one might cite the notion of "covenant-community" so fundamental in biblical ethics, and the New Testament *koinonia,* the "fellowship" of the early Christian *ecclesia,* or the

---

* Although at its highest level the spirit of love is heedless of the self's due, it may be questioned whether love ever "engages in no calculation of what the due of each man may be."

"kingdom of God" interpreted as "the beloved community" in which God's will reigns.

A notable example of the latter interpretation of the meaning of love is Daniel Williams's Rauschenbusch Lectures *God's Grace and Man's Hope*[68]—a book which otherwise shows so much acceptance of Niebuhr's general analysis that many readers may not have noticed the most signal difference. Williams describes our present human situation with its omnipresent evil and distress admixed with good as "the embattled reign of Christ." [69] The meaning he assigns to this New Testament concept, however, may be more adequately expressed as "the embattled reign of mutual love." "Community," he writes, is the "order which is sought by love"; and "the one absolute demand is that we serve the growth of community." [70] "Here, then, is the distinctive task of Christian social philosophy: to raise in every social order the question, 'What is its consequence for the community of mutuality among men?' " [71] In passing, and if it be a virtue that the task be "distinctive," one might conclude that this has not been adequately defined by the category of mutuality, since utilitarians and self-realizationists and many other types of social philosophy propose for themselves the same task. Among these schools, and between them all and a Christian ethic of "community," there may remain significant differences; but are they fundamental enough to warrant the use here of "the embattled reign *of Christ*" as a religious label for the notion of mutuality common to them all?

When Williams asserts that "actually all love does combine the desire *of the self* with the good of another," [72] he is right in one sense of the ambiguous genitive case he uses, wrong in the other. "The desire of the self" contains two possible meanings which should be sharply distinguished: the self's desire for its own good and the self's desire for the good of another. Either may be the self's desire or the desire of the self. All love does actually express the self's desire and some love combines the self's desire with the good of another, but not all love combines the self's desire for its own good with its desire for the good of another: only mutual love sets out to do this. And if Niebuhr is correct, such love will fall short of mutuality unless it lives under the tension, correction, and constant redirection by a love that combines the self's desire, heedless of the self's own good, with the good of another. Doubtless every self is or ought to be, to borrow Tillich's phrase, "a centered self"; but not self-centered or centered only on mutuality—nor through mutual or communal love centered at the same time on one's own good and the good of another by some sort of calculating reciprocity.

Daniel Williams asks "the simple question, 'What is the good which the spirit of *agape* seeks—what does Christian love intend?' " and answers, "The Kingdom of God." Again, these biblical expressions have already been loaded with the meaning he takes from them—when he concludes that "in intention universal mutual love and sacrificial love are one, for what is intended is the mutual good of all." He sees plainly enough that mutual love is not intrinsically self-sacrificial; yet it readily becomes so, for where and whenever this kingdom of mutuality "is really intended, the self is ready to sacrifice anything for that good except the good itself." [73] Mutual love becomes sacrificial only under the present conditions of Christ's "embattled reign." It is always sacrificial because of the omnipresence of evil in human history, and this, we may readily believe, is no momentary state of affairs. Still, mutuality is the very substance of love, while sacrifice is—in the philosophic sense of the word— only an "accidental" part either of the intention or of the behavior of love. Under the present conditions of history, self-sacrifice becomes a "universal property" of mutual love, but this still is a "property," not the essence of the matter.

By contrast, Niebuhr believes that the motive and direction of Christian love is essentially sacrificial, at its highest heedless of self and containing none of the self-referential motives which are co-present with other-regarding motives in mutual love. Surely this is the more correct reading of biblical and New Testament ethics. While the national life of the people of the Old Testament was based on covenant, this covenant among men was in turn measured by the standard of the extraordinary righteousness of God. God's *hesed,* or his steadfast faithfulness to men even when there was on their part no returning love, gave the standard for the covenant. This was, so to speak, the cement of community. And we know well enough what was the basis of the New Testament *koinonia*. Here there was plenty of mutuality and strong visible bonds of community, of course; but the supporting substance of this was another sort of love which gave definitive meaning to the *agape*-community of the early church. When the Scripture enjoins: "Let love be among you," it does not mean, "Let 'among-you-ness' be among you." It is one thing to say "Let mutual love be mutual," and quite another to say in the New Testament meaning of the word, "Let *love* be mutual." For the love in question takes its measure from Christ's love for the Church when he "gave himself up for her," nourishing and cherishing her more than his own life (Ephesians 5:25-29). It is one thing to say, "Have a mutually loving mind among you," and quite another to say, "Have *this* mind *among* yourselves, which you have in Christ Jesus," for the apostle goes on to explain the meaning of such love in terms of One who "emptied himself" (Philippians 2:5-8). When Jesus said to his disciples, "A new commandment I give to you, that you love one another," so far that was no new commandment; and it only became a new word when he went on to explain the love wherewith they were to love one another: "Even as I have loved you, that you also love one another" (John 13:34).

Notice that "mutual love" or any other sort of love may be the attitude of only one party to a relationship and not of the other. Therefore it is a significant moral injunction to say, "Let mutual love be *mutual*" (or let enlightened selfishness be mutual, or let Christlike love be mutual). Niebuhr certainly grants that mutual love is a genuine sort of *love,* and he is considering the more perfect instances in which it may be truly *mutual,* before subjecting it to criticism. His position may be put in this way: There must be present some degree of the sort of love which is heedless of the question whether it is mutual or not and which nevertheless affirms the being and well-being of the other, or else a person whose attitude toward another includes that other's good (whether out of mutual love or a wise egoism) will sooner or later begin to wonder whether his own good is in turn included in the attitude of the other to the same degree, and thus human community will finally end in resentment about the *possible* absence of perfect reciprocity and in mutual recriminations over the possible or actual lack of mutuality from the other's side.

A few of Niebuhr's definitions lend support to the charge that his conception of mutual love is "neither mutual nor love." Criticizing reductive substitutes for suffering love in modern liberal Christianity, he describes these surrogates as on "the level of mutual love *or the love which calculates its relations to others from the standpoint of its own need of others.*" [74] Mutual love, he writes in his most extended discussion of this issue, is "always arrested by reason of the fact that it seeks to relate life to life from the standpoint of the self and for the sake of the self's own happiness." [75] This attitude may be mutual enough, yet it is certainly not love but a wise self-love. Here mutual love has already suffered alteration. However, Niebuhr's real definition, perhaps regrettably not used frequently enough, is qualitatively higher than this. For example, he writes that "mutual love (in which *disinterested concern for the other* elicits a reciprocal response) is the highest possibility of history; . . . such love can only be initiated by a type of disinterestedness (sacrificial love) which dispenses with historical justification." [76] In other words, both mutual and sacrificial love are types of "disinterested concern for the other," which is simply to say both are genuine love. But mutual love *also* intends the elicitation of a favorable self-referential response, and without the element of sacrificial love may soon *come* to depend on such a response; while sacrificial love intends the good of the other even in face of the necessity of sacrificing the response. What Niebuhr says of the initiating and redemptive relation between sacrificial and mutual love remains true when the latter is taken in its best possible meaning: "The consequence of mutuality must, however, be the unintended rather than the purposed consequence of the action. For it is too uncertain a consequence to encourage the venture towards the life of the other." [77]

Nevertheless, something may be lost from sight in our passion for distinction among different types of love. In speaking of "mutual" and "sacrificial" love there is danger that the adjective may overpower the substantive in our understanding of the terms. Niebuhr suspects that this is the case with mutual love in the first step in its inevitable declension from disinterested concern for the other. The good of the beloved, and not "community" as Williams apparently believes, is what love seeks. The one absolute demand is that we serve the growth of the neighbor God gives us; that we bend and redirect community to serve this end, and not that we serve "the growth of community." Love is just love, the genuine article, for which perhaps one univocal word should be reserved. The word "love" is surely not deserving of use for the self's relation to itself; and what makes the term inappropriate for use in this connection is its univocal meaning no matter what adjectives are attached to it; namely, love is a bond of life with life by which one person affirms the being and well-being of another.

There is also some evidence that the primary meaning of love has been outweighed by the adjectives Niebuhr uses. He speaks of "heedless," "suffering," "self-sacrificial" love. There can be no frontal objection to these descriptions of the *inner* attitude by which a person cleaves to the other. But without a whole cluster of other qualifications they too readily imply *rigor mortis* at the very heart of love, and soon may be taken as literal descriptions of the *external* behavior love will adopt on all occasions, or *should* adopt if only it were strong and pure enough. No doubt love is "heedless"; but there is also nothing more heedful, careful, and flexibly wise than love. No doubt love "suffers" all things; but also love rejoices with those that rejoice. Love proves willing to sacrifice the self to the needs and good of neighbors and companions in God; but love also endures in the very loving.

In his *Commentary on Galatians* (6:2) Luther writes that love is not merely "to wish well one to another, but for one to bear another's burdens; that is, to bear those things which be grievous unto you and which you would not willingly bear. Therefore Christians must have strong shoulders and mighty bones, that they may bear flesh, that is, the weakness of their brethren; for Paul says that they have burdens and troubles." But Christians need more than strong shoulders and mighty bones to bear flesh. They need also wide and sensitive hearts to rejoice in another's small joys, unenvious hearts to rejoice in his great ones, and powerful currents of vitality within themselves to embrace as their own all things human. If they are to bear flesh they must also bear those things which may surprise them with sudden and unexpected joy in another's good fortune. All this is by no means lacking from Niebuhr; and he certainly believes that love is spontaneous, even ecstatic. Yet one suspects that "sacrifice" and "suffering" tend to overcome affirmation of life in the meaning of love, and that when these are then soon rated as the clearest evidence of the presence of love in the heart, Niebuhr gains too easy a victory, and by a somewhat mistaken strategy, in his campaign to demonstrate the (relevant) *impossibility* of love. Love is mainly intent on the good of another. It is not intent on the *overt* sacrifice or the suffering this often entails, any more than it intends the mutuality that sometimes (perhaps often) follows.

For surely it must be said that Niebuhr exaggerates the "impossibility" of such a reconciling love among men, under the momentum of his polemic against a sentimentalism which supposes it to be too easily possible. No doubt such love fully and constantly incarnate in a human life ends, as he says, upon a Cross out on the edge of human history. Yet we are here dealing with the motive or intention of the act, and not only with external acts of visible self-sacrifice. Just as love which is mutual in essence or intention becomes sacrificial even in spirit only by "accident," so it ought to be said that a love whose essential spirit and intention impels one, heedless of self, steadfastly to affirm the well-being of another requires the actual act of self-sacrifice only when the occasion warrants it in terms of actually advancing the neighbor's good. The numerical infrequency of self-sacrificial acts open to external view does not necessarily indicate the absence, much less the impossibility, of the motive of self-giving love in the mundane lives of ordinary people, who may not have found in themselves the strength for martyrdom simply because they have not found reason for it or a situation actually calling for it. No doubt self-giving love sometimes expresses itself in actual sacrifice of self and of one's life, and most often weakness or selfishness holds us back from such a course. But there is also no doubt that self-sacrificial love ought often to "sacrifice the sacrifice," and then only weakness or selfishness or simply conformity to what our own bravado has led people to expect of us would plunge headlong on toward actual sacrifice. It must never be forgotten that Christian ethics casts *no more* suspicion upon the motive that may lead a man to stay at his post and "sacrifice the sacrifice" than it does upon the motive that may lead to giving one's body to be burned—and, of course, no less.

This is especially significant for the morality—or the immorality—of group actions. Niebuhr is fond of saying that the action of nations can never go beyond the area where there is actual congruence between national self-interest and concern for the needs of other peoples or of the world community (although the latter motive widely held by a people may make them and their statesmen more enlightened and in-clusive of the good of other nations when deciding what is in their own national interest). The implication is that it is always a defection from the ultimate ideal, and proof of the impossibility (though not of the irrelevance) of love in intergroup relationships, for us never to be able to point to a national policy which persists in going beyond national self-interest. This may be true; and it is the case that nations never commit suicide—except by living below, not beyond, the limits of group self-interest. By measuring the facts of history against the law of love, Niebuhr arrives at his celebrated "relevant impossibility." This is stated in a typical passage:

> Only a forgiving love, grounded in repentance, is adequate to heal the animosities between nations. But that degree of love is an impossibility for nations. It is a very rare achievement among individuals; and the mind and heart of collective man is notoriously less imaginative than that of the individual.[78]

Nevertheless, this analysis leans toward error because Niebuhr switches too easily from the delineation and castigation of the motives of men and nations to the data supplied by their external conduct and (with little or no warrant from our religious ethics) finds in the latter evidence of the nature of the former.

Two things should be pointed out in this connection: One is that there is no such thing as "the mind and heart of collective man," but only individual men and women engaged in collective action by means of a gradation of leaders who also are individuals with a mixture of motives in what they do in public and in private life. Although people always act together upon a stage set by the nature and momentum of their traditions and heritage, at the moment of action and in their public, no less than in their private capacities, people may be just as loving, forgiving, repentant and imaginative as nature and grace enable them to be. Perhaps there are no saints in private or in public. Nevertheless, what they, or we of mixed motives, should do overtly is another matter. For what sort of behavior or public policy self-giving love will lead men to undertake may be quite the opposite of what they would do were they alone involved in the issue. As one Irishman said to his friend with whom he was discussing the problem of evil in the world: "Faith, and there be many things which God does in his official capacity which he wouldn't think of doing as a private individual." This is also true of the statesman—not only regrettably but because whatever love requires for the preservation of human life in the world must be done. Perhaps where we fall short of the ideal of love in private and in public life is a subject that should only be approached confessionally, throwing the mantle of charity over the sins of others, as Luther said, and not curiously spying them out, much less laying down in advance for them or for ourselves how far sin must abound.

The second point is that it is exceedingly doubtful if ever nations *ought* to allow themselves to be nailed to a cross. Or, expressed more accurately since only individuals bear personal responsibility, it is doubtful whether the leaders or citizens of a nation *ought* ever to read from the law of love, which defines the ideal motive for their conduct in their public capacities, no less than in private, the conclusion that they should render functioning in these capacities no longer possible for themselves or others by voluntary suicidal abandonment of the system of vocations in which God has placed them in responsibility. This judgment is not just a matter of collective self-interest or the group will-to-live, which (while necessary) is then subject to either cynical or redemptive wholesale criticism by the theologian in the light of the transcendent possibilities of self-sacrifice.

Since self-giving love is a matter of motive, and not first of all of external action, defining its own hard course of action—sometimes to the death and sometimes to stick to one's post—are not nations, in the light of their total task in behalf of their own people and all the future generations and their possible contribution to the community of mankind, duty-bound to "sacrifice the sacrifice"? At least we can all be thankful that Themistocles persuaded the Athenians to use the funds from a newly discovered vein of silver in their mines, not for democratic distribution and consumption, but for building a stronger navy by which they were able to hold off the power of the despotism from the East for a few more decades in which Greek culture came to flower. Whether or not there was a Marshall Plan for strengthening the Ionian isles we need not inquire; but if there was, this was not only called for by a wise collective egoism assisted *up to that point* by genuine enough concern for the Ionians; nor was it simply demanded by concern for the Ionians *enlarging* the Athenians' conception of their own actual interests. It was called for also, as we can see from the perspective of a later age, by a concern to affirm the being and well-being of many others for generations to come and by the performance of an actual historic mission. The Athenians might conceivably have been unmindful of their own interests and thereby not mindful enough of their vocation in the world.

The point is not that the motive of love can ever be taken alone, any more than self-interest can, but that we ought not to say that only the admixture of collective self-interest prevents love in group action from leading on to overt self-sacrifice. It is true that Christianity has enlarged the field of concern to the Christian statesman's vocation, particularly with regard to including the enemy. But unless we are to say that the enemy always truly needs to succeed in aggression, we ought not to say or seem to say that it is only our own inevitable self-interest or some mysterious limit upon collective action in history, and not also our best judgment (very possibly mistaken) about what the enemy and all the rest of the world need, which demands that he be resisted. Just as sin is so inevitable that it is bound to happen, likewise the neighbor-claims which surround the Christian statesman and define for him his duty are so inevitable and numerous that it may be that he is always bound to sacrifice sacrifice, regardless of what he might be willing to do were his own life alone at stake. This may be the primary motive for what he does, and not just the desire to stay in office as the political leader of a collectively selfish people. Niebuhr is right in pointing out that individuals hear and heed the call of their appointed opportunity for actual sacrifice of life more often than groups do (perhaps the latter never). He is wrong in implying that this is always because of the greater strength of collective self-interest or necessary lack of creative imagination in public policy-makers, and not quite possibly also because statesmen and citizens see that for them *as such* there is no such responsibility and for their groups no such appointment.

At one point Niebuhr nearly cuts through the Gordian knot he himself has tied. Since, he writes, an unconditional perfection in history is impossible,

> *it is not even right* to insist that every action must conform to *agape,* rather than to the norms of relative justice and mutual love by which life is maintained and conflicting interests are arbitrated in history. *For as soon as the life and interests of others than the agent are involved in an action or policy, the sacrifice of these interests ceases to be "self-sacrifice."* It may actually become an unjust betrayal of their interests.[79]

Pondering this paragraph will suggest its own revision and improvement as a Christian analysis of the statesman's or the citizen's vocation. What can be more "right" and "conformable to *agape*" than a wise concern for the life and interests of others? Here plainly Niebuhr derives a too literal, external description of acceptable Christian action from what was never meant for such, that is, the test of conformity to *agape;* and this makes necessary his recourse to relative justice and mutual love for deciding what is actually right. Yet the passage shows also that *agape* itself, and not just these lower, less transcendent standards, requires that the interest of all involved in the policy be not "unjustly," that is to say *unlovingly,* betrayed.

No doubt cleavages and tensions remain. If perfect love means the cessation of all inner contradictions within the self, and the overcoming of all conflicts and tensions between the self and the other and between one group and another, by the complete obedience of all wills to the will of God,[80] that will have to wait on heaven or the age in which the kingdoms of this world become the kingdom of Christ—and also where there will be neither marrying nor giving in marriage. We were not appointed to be first-coming or second-coming Christs who will close the books on God's historical calling to the nations. Yet we are called to readiness to let love reign; and in face of the requirement of simple discipleship Niebuhr's rigid dualism between "within history" and "beyond history," or between what may be true "in principle" and "in fact," may prove more disastrous than all the supposed rigidities of the traditional theory of natural law, since the former places limits upon God's *agape* and providential redemptive power while the latter only indicates a recalcitrance in the human nature and history which are subject to redemption. As for what we wayfaring men do exteriorly in private or in public capacities, let not him who does this despise him who does that, "for God has welcomed him. Who are you to pass judgment on the servant of another? . . . Let every one be fully convinced in his own mind. . . . So do not let what is good to you be spoken of as evil. . . . The faith that you have"—and the love that you have—"keep between yourself and God; happy is he who has no reason to judge himself for what he approves. . . . For whatever does not proceed from faith"—and love— "is sin" (Romans 14:3, 5b, 16, 22, 23).

V. Faith and Reason in Love

The question which next arises is this: How does Niebuhr, and in his view mankind, know that love is the norm for human life in freedom? Is it entirely from a reasonable "estimate of the healthful functioning of total human personality"? Is it the positive conclusion that remains after showing that no other view proves suitable to the full measure and the indeterminate possibilities of human freedom? If so, then love is established as the moral law, as Maritain says of his own more traditional viewpoint, "*from the simple fact that man is man,* nothing else being taken into account"—although the natural law is now one single norm and no longer to be defined as an "*ensemble* of things to do and not to do" which follow from the fact that man is man in logically necessary fashion.[81] More correctly stated for Niebuhr, love is known to be the moral law for freedom by a man's reflection upon *himself*, or by an act of self-understanding. For Niebuhr locates *the consciousness of* original righteousness "in the self in the moment of transcending itself." [82] He writes: "reason itself is not the source of law, since it is not possible to prove the self's obligation to the neighbor by any rational analysis which does not assume the proposition it intends to prove. Yet reason works helpfully to define the obligation of love in the complexities of various types of human relations." [83] By this he means discursive, contriving reason or the sort of reason which applies the law of love in principles and schemes of justice. This does not exclude but calls for an act of reasonable self-understanding which apprehends the law of love itself in the moment of self-transcending freedom.

There are still would-be system-builders who may be heard to say rather petulantly that Niebuhr is an anthropologist or social analyst or psychologist and not, after all, a theologian. I would insist that at all points he is at the same time a rational analyst of human nature and a Christocentric theologian. There is in his thought a constant dialogue between man's knowledge of himself and the moral law when he views himself in the moment of self-transcendence or when studying alternative interpretations of his historical existence on the one hand, and on the other the knowledge that comes from encounter with the revelation in Christ and from viewing himself in the mirror of the Word. For this reason, having associated the Christian view closely with humanistic ethics in attempting to estimate the proper functioning of total human personality, he goes on to point out that "the Christian view recognizes that it is not easy to measure our total personality. . . . The self, as interested participant, is always involved in these processes; this is why self-knowledge is more ambiguous than the proponents of scientific objectivity in the study of human nature realize, and why self-love is more dubious than Dr. Fromm realizes." [84]

Yet there is a remaining ambiguity—perhaps a necessary one—in the uses of autonomous reason and Christonomous reason in discerning the law of love. The notion of constant "dialogue" between them just suggested may help somewhat—but only somewhat, since this tells us nothing of the contributions of each to the conversation. Niebuhr's own terms are not much better for what the revelation does to "accentuate," "clarify," and make "fuller" our natural self-knowledge and knowledge of the moral law.[85] Would the best thing be to rewrite him as more explicitly an Augustinian on this point: *Fides praecedit rationem, nisi credideritis non intelligetis, credo intelligam, fides quaerens intellectum?* This would mean that reason does not of itself alone discern that love is the natural moral law for freedom, but nevertheless that when we begin by faith we, that is, our reasons, do end in sight of this truth. Thus it would be *illuminated* reason that knows the self and freedom's requirement; yet, as Augustine believed, these would be truly known, and by reason. Such an interpretation to a degree runs counter to the credit assigned by Niebuhr to the powers of autonomous reason in anthropological and social and self-analysis. Is his procedure of joining to the extent he does, in dialogue with secular rationalistic viewpoints, to be taken as only an apologetic method, or as an indication of the balance between faith and reason in his own thought? If the latter, faith would appear as much more a dialogic supplement to reason than a corrective and redirection of reason from the beginning and throughout all the notes in the scale, as it was in Augustine. Perhaps the truest description would be to return to the notion of dialogue, and to stress the degree to which faith and reason each *confirms* what the other discerns of how love is native in the land of human freedom, while faith "firms up" and enlarges what self-consciousness alone would experience as the claims of others.

At the summit of love as a self-giving affirmation of the being and well-being of another, perhaps we can better delineate the problem of faith and reason raised by Niebuhr's ethical position. Reason, he says, or man's self-awareness in the moment of self-transcendence, has an "inchoate" knowledge that love is the law of human life, or that only an indeterminate field of fellowship really corresponds to the dimensions of freedom. This awareness is "accentuated," "clarified," "made full" by the revelation.

There are three possibilities as to how this should be understood, of which the second should be chosen (if the first two exhaust the alternatives) or (if they do not) the third should be chosen as both closer to the truth of the matter and also most accurately and consistently representing Niebuhr's point of view.

1. It may be that man has an "inchoate" knowledge of the requirement of *self-sacrificial* love, or that he dimly knows that he should heed not his own but his neighbor's good. If this be what Niebuhr means, then the revelation enters into "dialogue" with natural knowledge of the moral law; and, while we cannot separate their distinctive contributions to the ongoing conversation but must confine ourselves to saying that faith "accentuates" what reason already forecasts, both or both together come to the same conclusion: namely, that such love as was seen in the flesh in Jesus Christ is the very *imago Dei* or essence of our common humanity. On this interpretation, Niebuhr's position would be un-Augustinian in crediting so much to natural knowledge unillumined by precedent faith. At the same time it would be quite authentically Augustinian in refusing to remove from reason's sight any of the ultimate meaning of Christian faith or ethics (as St. Augustine in the *De Trinitate* still sought to understand what he began and continued in by believing, rather than separating a number of mysteries as a supplement altogether beyond reason). For this combination of motifs I can think of no better word than ceaseless dialogue; and this may appear to be what Niebuhr is saying in the main when both his autonomous anthropological analysis and his Christocentric moral theology are viewed together.

2. Perhaps a more definite meaning should be precipitated out of these words "inchoate" for natural knowledge and "accentuation" or "clarification" for the revelation, or put in their place. It may be that in his free spiritual self-awareness man has a sense of *mutual* love, and that only by faith in Christ does he know himself to be judged in terms of the *self-giving* love which seeks to save him at such cost. This then would be the distinction between love as the natural law naturally known and

love as the revealed law of life; and a reconstruction of the truth there was in the traditional distinction between infused love and the other theological virtues "living beyond reason," and natural love and the natural virtues "living within reason." If we did not know ourselves as known by such love we would not know that any such love were required of us, nor would we know that the fulfillment of our own human essence is to be found in covenant-love which adheres to the well-being of another with such costly fidelity. The continuity that may exist between this love and the community of mutuality adumbrated by nature and reason can still be emphasized. Yet the contribution of faith and reason to morality through their dialogue with each other would be more clearly indicated or confessed. Moreover, it hereby becomes evident that at every point faith precedes reason if reason ends in sight of sacrificial love.

The former of these two possibilities seems more explicit in Niebuhr when he is at work seeking to show that Christian ultimates are fulfillments of the truth there is in secular outlooks, and the latter when he is seeking to show that Christian love is the correction of the defects in secular alternatives. Yet it may be that he actually makes substantially more use of the rationally persuasive power of *mutual* love in all these polemics, while only tangentially indicating the bearing of self-sacrificial love. His review of Fromm's book, already cited, may be taken as an example of the problem.

There Niebuhr was able to correct the self-regarding imbalance in the psychologist's opinions about the source of love for others in proper love for self. The theologian's agreements and disagreements with the psychologist are quite revealing of how each may have arrived at his respective estimate of the healthful functioning of total human personality. The two are wholly in agreement in regard to the futility of moral pronouncements for securing obedience to the law of love. But there is a subtle and significant difference which springs from the fact that the psychologist, in Niebuhr's opinion, does not adequately grasp the truth that the human personality needs to abide in love and affirm the being and well-being of another. Fromm approaches the problem obliquely from the point of view of the self's own love or hatred for itself and so never quite arrives at the center of the issue, which is the bond of love itself; or else he gets there only indirectly. If man is made for covenant, then the relationships comprising his "indeterminate field of fellowship," and the defects in them, may be grasped from either end—either from the side of the self or from the side of the other. Or better, both must be held together. Fromm, however, affirms that the self's love for itself must come before he can have the strength to love another, just as some form of self-hatred precedes hatred for others. This slant only reveals that he does not really understand that the self lives always in relation-ship. Thus Niebuhr writes:

> From the Christian standpoint the self-hatred which is supposed to make love impossible is actually the consequence of a too anxious pre-occupation with self. The self-love which is supposed to make the love of others possible is actually the by-product of a genuine self-giving. Fromm is quite right in seeing that it is not possible to move from self-hatred to love by moral injunction.
> Actually both admonitions, that the self ought to love itself and that the self ought to love others, are spiritually impotent. An insecure impoverished self is not made more secure by the admonition to be concerned for itself; for an excessive concern for its security is the cause of its impoverishment. Nor is it made secure by the admonition to love others because that is precisely what it cannot do because of its anxiety about itself. That is why a profound religion has always insisted that the self cannot be cured by law but only by grace; and also why the profoundest forms of the Christian faith regard this preoccupation as not fully curable and there-fore as requiring another kind of grace: that of forgiveness.[86]

On the face of it this sounds like an unqualified reference to intentionally self-sacrificial love, or to a "genuine self-giving" of which proper self-love is only a by-product. Unquestionably Niebuhr's view is grounded in a more adequate understanding that self-giving love is, materially, the law of life. Is he therefore relying on an "inchoate" knowledge of this as the essential truth about human interrelatedness on the part of the psychologist and in the minds of his readers?

On the other hand, may not the excellence and persuasiveness of this brief analysis actually silently depend upon the concept of mutual love common to them both? For mutual love also would indicate a correction of Fromm's unbalanced concern for the isolated individual's self-love or self-hatred—unless they are correct who say that what Niebuhr *calls* mutual love is neither mutual nor love. At another place in his writings Niebuhr makes substantially the same criticism of the psychologist's views. He says that Fromm

> fails to measure the freedom of the self in its dimension of transcendence over self, which makes it impossible for it to be rich within itself. What-ever spiritual wealth the self has within itself is the by-product of its relations, affections and responsibilities, of its concern for life beyond itself.[87]

But it is significant that this contention was put forward after a para-graph in which Niebuhr cited various ways in which Christian *agape* has been attenuated into forms of mutual love and rational-prudential ethics. His disagreement with Fromm is elaborated in order to illustrate the fact that "even when the norm of love is thus reduced to the dimension of a prudential ethic, it falls under the stricture of modern psychiatry." In other words, any genuine conception of the bond of love as the norm for human life (and mutual love is one such conception) is able to correct the defects of an overly individualistic concern for the health of the private person who, apart from prior relation to life beyond himself, is trying to muster the strength to be able to love.

The true situation may, then, be this: The operational concept in Niebuhr's position when he is engaged in dialogue with secular points of view is mutual love "accentuated" by self-giving love, or self-sacrificial love in "organic" relation to other types of love; and this arises from a more fundamental inward encounter between self-sacrificial love and the love of mutuality, or from a perpetual dialogue of faith with reason. The review is an excellent illustration of the effectiveness of what Niebuhr regards as the actual relationship between self-sacrificial and mutual love. It shows that because of the element of heedless love controlling his own thinking about man and morals, he was able to point out Fromm's failure to give heed to perfect reciprocity. It shows that mutual love of itself has not the power for long to sustain true mutuality; and that unless people love one another beyond the point of being concerned about mutuality, then a love which at first was really mutual or aimed at mutuality tends to degenerate into calculations about which party is most given to the community between them or gives most to the other. This soon leads to actual withdrawal from the bonds of mutual love, which becomes evident whenever the first concern is to calculate how a person needs first to love himself properly and then go on from there to engage his own being intimately with the being of another.

In short, we have here an instance in which Niebuhr was able to outthink the secular psychologist, as St. Augustine out-thought the pagans, not necessarily because of greater rational powers or perception of what rational self-awareness adumbrates as the law of life, but because of love- or faith-illuminated reason. Thus he is able to a great degree "to heal the wounds inflicted by man on himself and on his life-in-community in modern times and, by transcending while still doing justice to the elements of truth contained in philosophic and psychological theories of man and society, to revive and give direction to the expiring spiritual ideals of the contemporary period." [88] More important that what happens verbally is what may happen in actual life. In order to maintain a person's stance or mode of existence in the world under the full sustaining, transforming, and redirecting impact of the love of Christ, it seems that much would be gained from clearly acknowledging the difference between his own ordinary sense of justice or sense of the meaning of love and the meaning of love which Christ brings to life.

The dilemma in which we now find ourselves in seeking a sound interpretation of Niebuhr's viewpoint, and of the truth of the matter, can be resolved in some measure by following a suggestion made in the preceding section of this chapter. The expressions for love which set the terms of the problem need to be *de-adjectified,* for the predicates of love are threatening to obscure the substantive. Love is simply love, the genuine article; and it intends the good of the beloved one and not the response of mutuality; it intends the good of the other and not its own actual self-sacrifice or suffering. It is the *neighbor,* and not mutuality or heedlessness or sacrifice or suffering, who stands ever before the eyes of love. This leads us to formulate a third possible interpretation of Niebuhr's viewpoint, and of the situation with regard to faith and reason in love.

3. It is simply love that is known as the norm for human existence by the self in the moment of self-transcendence and self-understanding. And in Christ we have revealed not another sort of love, nor for that matter a "pinnacle" of love, a species of love that can be clearly demarked from other classes of the same genus. The revelation shows us just the meaning of love itself. This is why Niebuhr must speak of an "inchoate" natural knowledge of the law of love and of the "accentuation" of this by revelation. Every effort to clarify the situation by stressing the predicates "mutual" and "sacrificial" only obscures the substance of the love-relation and gives rise to the first two alternatives we have considered. In these terms, indeed, there is ground for supposing *either* that self-understanding apprehends, albeit dimly, the requirement of suffering love (thus making revelation only a companion in dialogue with reason) *or* that natural knowledge goes only as far as mutual love (thus making revelation a supplement or radical redirection of human self-understanding). In these terms Niebuhr can be interpreted both ways.

He does say that "the ethical norm of history as comprehended by the 'natural' resources of man, by his sober examination of the facts and requirements of life in human society, is *mutual* love." [89] Yet among "the natural resources of man" is the capacity to transcend both himself and history; and in the moment of self-transcendence Niebuhr locates *the consciousness of* original righteousness, which means the law of love—love substantive, the genuine article. While he sometimes inadequately and less typically defines mutual love as the effort to relate life with life from the point of view of the self, on the other hand he declares that while "non-Christian conceptions of love do indeed seek to justify love from the standpoint of the happiness of the agent," still "the freedom of man is such that he is not without some idea of the virtue of love which does not justify itself in terms of his own happiness." [90] Shall we call this a higher definition of mutual love or a dim awareness of the requirement of suffering love? The answer to this question is Either, or better, Neither, for the awareness is just of the requirement of love itself. And in an ironic note directed against Brunner he attributes to children a sense of justice and of equality in which they "may lack proper reverence for the Creator of inequalities; but on the other hand they have certainly never heard of, or been spoiled by 'Stoic rationalism.' " [91] We have already seen that the sense of justice and the norm of equality are nothing less than human nature's sense of love taking shape for application.

In the revelation of suffering love in Christ visibly sacrificing himself, we stand face to face not with the revelation of another or specially self-sacrificial sort of love, nor with a fast-bounded species of love which then must be brought into some relationship with another type of love which naturally commends itself to us, nor even with a "pinnacle" of love which goes so far beyond the love we know as to amount to a difference in kind. We stand before love itself. Here existing human beings meet essential humanity undistorted, for Christ is, as Berdyaev says, the truth about freedom. The contrast between us and Him is so great, not because true love in us is admixed with other types of love structured in history, but because true love in us is mixed with no love at all, with what is not properly love at all. Such an encounter supplies our deepest need, for in all our so-called loves we underestimate how far we have come short of love; "we underestimate how far we have come short of what is necessary for a genuine understanding of the other party's case."

At our natural best we still may not understand our neighbor nor be able to feel with him, because we do not know that we have to "give something of ourselves in order to achieve real apprehension." [92] We have not broken through the sound barrier of self, and yet we think we love. This does not only fall short of suffering love, it falls short of love. In the visibly suffering love of Christ we know that God gives something of himself in order to break through the barrier and to take upon himself a genuine understanding of the other party's case. If anyone imagines that he knows something of love in his own life and has stepped existentially over to the side of another, from encountering Christ he may discover that he does not yet know as he ought to know (I Cor. 8:2).

H. Richard Niebuhr:
Christ Transforming Relativism

It has been said that, strictly speaking, the Bible contains no doctrine of man. Instead, it everywhere shows forth an understanding of man in the light of his relationship to God. In the same sense there is no biblical ethics, but only a viewing of the problems of morality in the light of God. This is pre-eminently true, also, of the thought and writings of H. Richard Niebuhr. In the ground bass and not simply in the grace notes this is the difference between Richard and Reinhold Niebuhr, or between Richard Niebuhr and many another contemporary thinker who by contrast is more an anthropologist and an ethical or social analyst. ". . . The spirit of Evangelical ethics," Richard Niebuhr writes, "is not discernible in men; it exists only in the relations of men to God and of God to men. It is as erroneous to look for it in men or churches as it is fallacious to look for manifestations of magnetism in steel filings in the absence of a magnet." Of course, sin and other actualities of human existence are subjects for theological reflection. Indeed, "the negative counterpart of the realization that God is holy is the realization that men are all profane and that they fall short of his glory in everything they do."

> But an ethics which starts with the realization of human ingloriousness, profaneness and sinfulness and in which men keep their eyes centered on the sin which stains all human acts will be profoundly different from the ethics of the glory of God. Evangelical ethics is God-centered, not sin-centered. When our fundamental orientation in life is that of persons who live *vis-à-vis* our own sinful selves rather than *vis-à-vis* God, the spirit of Evangelical ethics takes flight no less surely than when we live in the contemplation of our own righteousness.[1]

The task of this chapter will be to explore the consequences of such "radical monotheism" for our understanding of man and morals.

It will be convenient to begin with Niebuhr's formulation of a theory of value and then trace his thought concerning the "transvaluation" or "transformation" of value under the impact of monotheistic and Christocentric faith. No doubt, for the Christian theologian there must be

decisive reference to God in the formation no less than in the transformation of all thought about values. Nevertheless, these may be distinguished and a general theory of value formulated which may possibly
commend itself to the consideration of philosophers who hold and are
held by other faiths.

I. Value and the Transformation of Value

On the issue drawn between ethics and metaphysics, or between an
ethical theology and theological ethics, by the currency in modern times
of theories of abstract or "objective" values, Niebuhr ranges himself
with those who affirm the primacy of "being" both in the way we know
values and in the way value has its being. Unlike the Thomists, however,
who define values (*verum, bonum, pulchrum*) as among the "tran-
scendental" or universal attributes of being *as such* (no matter where or
when), for Niebuhr value is an attribute of being-in-relation-to-being.
". . . A relational theory of value . . . defines good by reference to a
being for which other beings are good." In the midst of plural, inter-
acting, becoming existences, "value is present wherever being confronts
being." It is "a function of being in relation to being." Value may
always be defined as "the *good-for-ness* of being for being in their
reciprocity, their animosity, and their mutual aid," or as "what is fitting,
useful, complementary to an existence." Apart from existences in interre-
lationship there are no values.

> . . . Value is present wherever one existent being with capacities and
> potentialities confronts another existence that limits or completes or com-
> plements it. Thus . . . value is present objectively for an observer in the
> fittingness or unfittingness of being to being. . . . Good is a term which
> not only can be but which . . . must be applied to that which meets the
> needs, which fits the capacity, which corresponds to the potentialities of an
> existent being.[2]

Other ethical terms are to be located in a similar fashion. "Right," for
example, means "that relation between beings, good-for-each-other, in
which their potentiality of being good for each other is realized"; and
"ought" means "what is owed to another being." [3]

Such "relational value-theory" avoids *psychological* relativism, since
"good-for-ness" and the required response vary not with desire but according to the conjunction of being with being. Niebuhr never uses the
word "relative" in the psychological sense of relative to consciousness
or desire, as if there were nothing either good or bad but thinking makes
it so. The words "relational" and "relatedness" represent Niebuhr's position better than the words "relative" and "relativism" which he uses
more frequently. Indeed, the technical philosophical designation "ob-

jective relativism" is not really adequate to describe the point of view of relational value-theory; and ought perhaps to be replaced by some such expression as "objective relatedness" or preferably "relational objectivism." Niebuhr's penchant for the word "relativism" is in part only a terminological matter of no great importance. However, it also shows the influence of the excessive contextualism of much modern social philosophy, idealistic and pragmatic, and the continued influence of Troeltsch's cultural or historical relativism upon Niebuhr's thought, which at many points is obviously breaking through the self-contradictory confines of these points of view. Relativism, and not as the term only, continues in play more than is warranted as one of the important themes in Niebuhr's writings, because of his belief that relativism of some sort is a direct implication of radical monotheism and of the "conversionist" motif in Christian ethics. The correctness of the latter opinion may and should be questioned. We shall return to these issues in the second part of this chapter.

If the "objective relativist" (or preferably the "relational objectivist") sets out to give a consistent and systematic account of what is right, his relational value-theory must have some "center of value." This center in being will be the "dogmatic starting point" for all ethical inquiry, so that every relational value-theory is a "dogmatic relativism" defining good-for-ness in terms of some presupposed center of value, such as society, man or life.

> . . . Relational value-theory . . . is evidently *dogmatically relativistic* since it is necessary to take one's standpoint with or in some being accepted as the *center of value*. . . . In view of this necessity of beginning with a value-center it seems evident that every theory of value, so far as it is relational, is religious in character. Every such theory adopts as its explicit or implicit starting point some being or beings in relation to which also the rightness or wrongness of its relation to other beings is examined.[4]

Thus, the value-center for evolutionary ethics is life itself, and all questions within ethics are about the good-for-life. The question "What is life good for?" can be raised only by shifting to some being other than life as the center of value; as a consequence all ethical questions then become relative to this new center in being. Utilitarianism seems to have two centers of value—the individual and society—and questions in this ethics are conversant about both the good-for-the-individual and the good-for-society. Questions about what the individual is good for, or what society is good for, can be raised only by momentarily shifting to one of these centers of value as that relative to which all good-for-ness is to be defined, and which itself at the moment is not regarded as good for any being beyond itself.

Thus, "the starting point of all [ethical] inquiry lies in the recognition of *that which is*";[5] and systems of ethics are distinguishable first of all according to the paramount being or beings in which they center, and by the prevailing ontic orientation discoverable within every value-system. Thus Niebuhr wrote in the volume of essays in honor of D. C. Macintosh: ". . . Every ethic rests at last upon a dogmatic basis." ". . . The dogmas of ethics are religious." [6] Here, as in the above use of the expression "dogmatically relativistic," Niebuhr does not mean a dogmatic *conclusion,* but dogma in the exact sense of the word: a framework of interpretation or center in the midst of being from which all reasoning proceeds.

Theological ethics arises from the recognition that God is *He who is* and the only proper center of value. "Critical thought based on theocentric faith," Niebuhr writes, "objects only but strongly to the religious foundations of these relativisms," and it replaces one center by another.[7] But once this acknowledgment has been made, the procedure of ethical reflection remains the same: "Such faith no more begins by asking what God is good for than humanistic or vitalistic ethics begins with the inquiry what man or life is good for." [8] It asks rather what man is good for, what is the good for man, and what are his responsibilities in the light of his being in relation to God.

When God's reign is thus acknowledged, man's understanding of his situation and his values begins to be changed. Something like this is true no matter what being has the value of God. The individualist who takes his standpoint with or in the being of society "may indeed discover that his values are included in the values of society, but the included values are not the same as those which he defined when he made his beginning with himself and sought to proceed from the values relative to personality to the values relative to society." [9] If this is true when one shifts from one finite center to another finite center of value, how much more thoroughgoing will be the impact of the shift from finite centers to the Infinite center of value. "The experience of the ground and source of all value leads to the criticism and reconstruction of the ethical system rather than to the support of one which has been accepted as absolute prior to the experience." [10] *

* This chapter in the Macintosh *Festschrift*, published in 1937, clearly demonstrates that for many years the motif "Christ Transforming Culture" has governed Niebuhr's theological reflection, only to be developed climactically in *Christ and Culture*. It is the basis for his criticism of value-theology from Ritschl to Wieman and Macintosh on the ground that in this movement "values gained from nonreligious experience are employed as the absolute criteria of theology." He calls for the complete abandonment of this procedure of defining God by picking and choosing from among attributes we would like to assign him in order that he may the more readily subserve these same unaltered values. In a radically monotheist theology, God is seen to transform values rather than being transformed or known only by means of them: "A faith which

A relational value-theory firmly grounded in related being fits into context with a number of other approaches which Niebuhr makes to an understanding of the nature of man, of the "good for" him and of his responsibility. Of all ethical notions none is more congenial to Niebuhr's main perspective upon man and morals than the concept of "responsibility." In brief, to be ethically responsible means to be a re-spond*ing* being in relation to other beings:

> To be responsible is to be a self in the presence of other selves, to whom one is bound and to whom one is able to answer freely; responsibility in-cludes stewardship or trusteeship over things that belong to the common life of the selves.[11]

Responsibility as the response of being to being is made up of two com-ponents: *to whom* and *for what or whom* one is responsible. There is a corresponding double reference in *ir*responsibility: not responding to those *to* whom one owes response, and in answering giving a wrong account of the things or beings *for* which one is responsible. Responsi-bility is always *to* being, and responsibility *for* includes not only things but also beings who are selves. In man's ultimate relationship to being, he knows himself to be responsible *to* God and responsible in some sense *for* everyone and everything that has being.

It may be noted at this point that there is a dynamic connection between these two aspects of responsibility running mainly in one direction: *to whom* we are responsible alters our understanding of the *for what* or *for whom* we are accountable. "What a man is responsible for depends in part at least on the being to whom he is accountable." [12] This fact is significant for the "transformation" of the ethics of responsi-bility in the light of God as the being to whom man is finally accountable.

Thus, the concept of "responsibility" shows most clearly the transition from Niebuhr's general theory of ethics to his concern for re-viewing values and duties in the light of monotheistic faith. "The content of responsibility varies with the nature of the society to which men under-stand themselves to belong." This general truth about how *duty to* affects the *scope* of responsibility provides the basis, in Niebuhr's view,

---

finds in God the source and center of all value, which values personal existence only because it makes the enjoyment of God possible, and hopes for immortality only be-cause it hopes for the vision of God, which founds its morality upon the sole value of God and the sacredness of his creatures because they are his creatures—such a faith must remain dissatisfied with an approach which, however disguisedly, makes him a means to an end, however noble the end in human esteem." "Value Theory and Theology" in *The Nature of Religious Experience* (New York: Harper and Bros., 1937), pp. 103, 110.

for the theocentric "conversion" or "transformation" of responsibility; and this takes place both extensively and intensively:

> If a man responds to the demands of a universal God then the neighbors for whom he is responsible are not only the members of the nation to which he belongs but the members of the total society over which God presides. If one gives account to a God who tries the "heart and reins," then one must answer for invisible as well as overt acts. . . . In the company of God and of immortal souls even family responsibility is greater and more inclusive than in the company of nations and of men who are regarded as purely temporal beings. When men know that they stand before an infinite judge and creator the content of their obligation becomes infinite.[13]

From thus describing the *theo*centric transformation of ethical responsibility, Niebuhr moves on by an almost imperceptible step (perhaps because the notion of the Triune God is the most radically monotheistic idea of God there is) to speak of how *Christo*centric faith affects the scope and nature of responsibility. He defines "the Being to whom" Christians and the Church are "answerable as *God-in-Christ* and *Christ-in-God*," or as "the redemptive principle in the absolute." This means immediately that "the content of responsibility is always mercy"; and that men must give account "for their treatment . . . of all the sick, imprisoned, hungry, thirsty men of the world—the neighbors, brothers and companions of an omnipresent being" Jesus Christ, to whom they are responsible. Here, again, the *to whom* both intensifies and also makes more extensive the *for what* or *for whom* we are ethically responsible:

> Whatever is, is good in the world of this God-in-Christ. It may be perverted, sinful, broken; but it is not bad, for God-in-Christ has made it and maintains it. Such universal responsibility is incompatible with a spiritualism that limits the Church's concern to immaterial values, with a moralism that does not understand the value of the sinner and the sinful nation, with an individualism that makes mankind as a whole and its societies of less concern to God than single persons, and with any of these particularistic and polytheistic theories of value and responsibility which substitute for God-in-Christ some other deity as the source of valuable being.[14]

The above quotation also makes plain what may have been obscured in this brief sketch of Niebuhr's viewpoint: the response is not only *to* God. Instead, the extension and intensification of the scope of responsibility *for* is largely also a matter of response *to* every one of the creatures of God. The significance of such a theocentric transformation of ethical responsiveness can be seen by comparing the resulting view with those theologies which, having only a little god made to order from preconceived specifications about what is valuable enough to be called divine, as a consequence inculcate positive response to only part of what God has evidently made.

The motif of "conversion" in ethics has been succinctly summarized by Niebuhr:

> . . . *Conversion is antithetical to substitution.* In the Christian life human *eros* is not supplanted by divine *agape* but the divine *agape* converts the human *eros* by directing it in gratitude toward God and toward the neighbor in God. The community of the family is not supplanted by a monastic society but the hearts of fathers and children and husbands and wives are turned toward each other in reconciliation because of the divine forgiveness. The gospel restores and converts and turns again; it does not destroy and rebuild by substituting one finite structure of life or thought for another.[15]

Nevertheless, human *eros,* or the best in man's spiritual aspiration, in no way remains untransformed. When wholly converted, *eros* becomes "nonpossessive *Eros*": loving God with pure adoration, gratitude, "consent to Being." Christlike love for God and man, therefore, does not mean a "like-minded interest in two great values, God and man." There is between love for God and love for neighbor "no common quality but only a common source." Love to God means "nonpossessive *Eros*"; love for neighbor, pure *agape,* compassion, "powerful pity." [16]

By analogy with the five main historical types of Christian attitudes toward culture suggested by Niebuhr in *Christ and Culture,* the following analysis might be made of the possible relationships between *agape* and *eros:* (1) *agape* "against" or in contradiction to *eros,* (2) the "identification" of *agape* and *eros;* (3) *agape* "above" and fulfilling *eros* in "hierarchical synthesis"; (4) *agape* and *eros* in paradox or continual tension and dialogue; (5) *agape* "transforming" *eros.* Adopting and elaborating the fifth, or conversionist, type of approach as the one most obviously implied by radical monotheism and the complete Lordship of Christ would put to rout the anti-Nygren Nygrenites of the present day —those theologians who first mistake Anders Nygren's *history* of the idea of Christian love for a *complete constructive* system of theological ethics and then sharpen excessively the dualism of the point of view they oppose, all to the end of raising a banner for the defense of ideal human *eros* untransformed, usually in "hierarchical synthesis" if not in "identification" with *agape.* As Niebuhr has said: "Conversion is antithetical to substitution" or to the uprooting of *eros.* But conversion is also antithetical to identification or to any synthetic points of view in which human *eros* is fulfilled but remains untransformed. The transformation of human *eros* into *nonpossessive eros* means, of course, "the perfection of *eros*" toward God and invariably also *agape* toward man: because Jesus "loves the Father with the perfection of human *eros,* therefore he loves man with the perfection of divine *agape* since God is *agape*." [17]

The same "conversionist" motif is restated in Niebuhr's discussion of the impact of "the deity of God" upon man's situation and values in *The Meaning of Revelation*. "The first change which the moral law undergoes with the revelation of God's person is in its imperativeness." [18] We know that the moral law is not what we demand or society demands but what *God* demands of us. In the second place, "the moral law is changed . . . by the revelation of God's self in that its *evermore extensive and intensive application* becomes necessary." [19] What this means has perhaps been sufficiently explained in connection with the transformation of moral responsibility. Niebuhr emphasizes that in being universalized and intensified the moral law is "reborn": "A *revolutionary transvaluation* occurs not in addition to the personal revelation (of God) but because of it." [20]

Thirdly and finally, the transformation of the moral law under the impact of "the deity of God" reveals to us our *always already* sinful use of the moral law. ". . . A restoration is begun, for . . . we recognize that the moral law as we had entertained it, was always a corrupted thing. . . ." [21] In particular, we see that we have made offensive and defensive use of the moral law "as interested men who served a creature rather than the creator." Revelation serves to "point the moral law at us, saying, 'Thou art the man.' " [22] The "conversion" of morality means therefore not only enhanced, more extensive and intensive imperativeness, but also "the conversion of the imperative into an indicative" in which we see that it is we and not only our neighbors who serve idols even by moral goodness; into an indicative in which also we see the possibility of free love of God and of the neighbor in God replacing, as the greatest change, the love demanded by the law.[23] In sum, Niebuhr envisages as the significance of religion for ethics, not the "republication" by divine authority of the law of nature nor the giving of supplementary divine decrees, but "the beginning of a revolutionary understanding and application of the moral law rather than the giving of a new law." [24]

The end toward which the transformation of man and morals is directed in the ethics of Christocentric monotheism can be clearly seen in Niebuhr's consideration of "the virtues of Jesus Christ" in the section "Toward a Definition of Christ" in *Christ and Culture*[25] and in an unpublished paper on the theological virtues, "Reflections on Faith, Hope and Love." At these points in his writings, relational value-theory evidences to the maximum the impact of the "deity-value" of God as the center which man meets in the midst of being and in his ethical reflection and action. The distinctive character of "the virtues of Jesus Christ" and of the so-called theological virtues, faith, hope, and love, arises from being-in-relation-to-God and not from any quality they may or may not have in common with other virtues which have the same name but which prove to be attributes of being in relation to some other being.

The "theological virtues" are not, Niebuhr believes, "achievements or products of training" and "not habits somehow established in the constitution of the agent," which is the traditional philosophical understanding of the word "virtue." They "are given not as states of character but as relations to other beings and particularly as relations to God," "relations which depend for their duration on the constancy with which the objective good, to which the self is related in these ways, is given." In short, faith, hope, and love are "gifts" and "responses"—gifts of the presence to the self of the "deity-value" of God and "responses" to God the center of value, gifts from and responses to the valuation of the self from beyond itself:

> The self does not think rightly or humbly of itself until God discloses himself in his majesty and graciousness and reveals the neighbor in his Christlikeness. Love is given in the gift of the lovely, the love-attracting; it is called forth by the gift of God himself as the supremely and wholly desirable good; by the gift of the neighbor, as one beloved by God, as lovely, and as loving the self. . . . Faith as trust is given with the self-disclosure to a person of God as the faithful One. . . . Faith as loyalty or faithfulness is given with the revelation of the supremely challenging cause, the cause of the Kingdom of God or the cause of Christ. Hope is given with the gift of a promise or with the gift of a future. . . . As responses (faith, hope, and love) are personal both on the side of the agent and on the side of the object, that is they are responses of a person to personal actions such as faithkeeping, love, promise.[26]

Faith, hope, and love, as attitudes or functions of being in relation to being, engage the *whole* being of man in relation to God, and this is what is meant by the interrelation of the theological virtues. These relational virtues "are as interconnected as are their bases in the creaturely constitution of the self as being devoted to value, as covenanting being and as being in time" (for "hope" engages a "being that has time in it"). As responses of man's total and concrete being to the self-disclosure of God, the responses or relational virtues are themselves aspects of one response. "Insofar as the unity of the self in Christian life needs to be defined, this can be done only" by reference to the complete presence of being with being in which man "responds faithfully, lovingly, hopefully to God-in-Christ and [the] companion-in-Christ."

Moreover, these relational virtues engaging the whole being of man in unified response cannot be adequately described as each a *donum superadditum*. Instead, they transform man's being and valuations to their roots. At the bottom and in the beginning of man's relationship to other beings and centers of value there were all along corresponding natural virtues of a relational sort. The theological virtues originate in the "conversion" and redirection of these relationships.

> They seem . . . to represent the restoration and the perfection to its true activity of a personal capacity for response which has been perverted. The love of God and of the neighbor in God are not foreign to man's nature, or, better, to man in his natural situation; but in our fallen situation they are present as love of idol and love of the neighbor in relation to idols. Man does not exist without love of an objective good which is, in a momentary way at least, the object of his greatest concern. Nor does he seem to live without relation to the Ground of Being, though in the fallen state this relation is one of hostility. The love of God is the restoration and perfection of a response which has always been present in misdirected and inverted form; this seems also to be true of love of the companion.[27]

The theological virtues are not a set of supernatural character traits supervening upon natural morality ("Christ above cultivated morality"). They are rather aspects of the ethics of redemption which engage the total being of man in a new relationship with God and with his companion in God. The redirective power of being in the presence of God reverberates throughout the whole and descends to every note in the scale ("Christ *transforming* natural or cultivated morality"). The theological virtues are directions in which man is undergoing transformation.

In defining the virtues of Jesus Christ in *Christ and Culture*, Niebuhr discusses love, hope, obedience, faith, and humility. Here he gains too easy a victory over contemporary Christian ethicists who have regarded love as the key to Jesus' ethics, by associating them with "religious liberalism" in this regard.[28]* In the first place, in some of the writings of religious liberals—e.g., E. F. Scott, *The Ethical Teachings of Jesus*—it is surprising how little attention is paid to love as the organizing principle of Jesus' teachings. In the second place, Reinhold Niebuhr, Anders Nygren, and others who today stress the perfection of love in Jesus' life and teachings have not magnified this to the exclusion of all

---

* In addition to the reasons given above for denying this association, the example of Karl Barth might be cited. He certainly cannot be accused of any lack of theological realism, or of shifting with liberalism to a stress on anthropology and man's subjective state of mind. Yet, speaking of "The Life of the Children of God," Barth sums up his views on theological ethics simply by an extended commentary on the two love commandments which, he says, mean respectively the love and praise of God; and he writes, "All things considered, the Christian life . . . consists in these two concepts of love and praise. . . . Even faith does not anticipate love. As we come to faith we begin to love. If we did not begin to love, we would not have come to faith. . . . If we believe, the fact that we do so means that every ground which is not that of our being in love to God in Christ is cut away from under us." [*Church Dogmatics* (tr. G. T. Thomson and Harold Knight; Edinburgh: T. & T. Clark, 1956), vol. 1, pt. 2, # 18, p. 371.]

other virtues. Instead, they have understood love only in vital relation
to and suffused by hope, obedience, faith, humility, and any other virtue
which it may yet appear necessary to take into account in describing
Jesus' ethical practice and teachings and which *ensemble* were a consequence of the directness and power of his relation to God. Finally,
it might be added—and this is something Niebuhr himself knows well
enough but some of his readers may not—that for the avoidance of the
"moralism" of "the love of love" it helps not at all simply to add on a
cluster of other virtues besides love. Whether the ethics of Jesus be
analyzed in terms of a number of virtues including love side by side with
all the rest, or in terms of one only, love, whose nature is clearly understood as inclusive of obedience, hope, faith, humility, and all the rest,
makes no great difference. The point is that in either case these are
relational virtues, and love is only a relation to God and the neighbor
in and under God, never a love for love itself.

In discussing each of the virtues of Christ, Niebuhr makes the same
point. These virtues, which men know in other forms in their ordinary
moral relationships, have all been transformed in the extreme in Jesus
Christ; and it is the "realization of God which makes all the virtues of
Jesus Christ radical." [29]

> Love . . . is characterized by a certain extremism in Jesus, but . . . it
> is the extremism of devotion to the one God, uncompromised by love of
> any other absolute good. This virtue in him is disproportionate only in
> the polytheistic-monotheistic sense, not in the sense that it is unac-
> companied by other virtues perhaps equally great.
>
> [Hope, radical obedience, faith, humility also were] expressed in his con-
> duct and teaching in a manner that seems extreme and disproportionate
> to secular, cultural wisdom. But he practices none of them and requires
> none of them of his followers otherwise than in relation to God. . . . His
> hope was in God and for God. . . . He hoped in the living God.
>
> The heroic character of Jesus' hopefulness does not stand alone; it is
> mated with heroic love and heroic faith; and all these have their source
> in his relation to God . . .
>
> . . . Obedience is radical when the whole man is involved, so that "he
> is not only *doing* something obediently but *is* essentially obedient." . . .
> Obedience was connected with a certain transcending of the mediate
> authority of the law, it . . . was addressed to the whole man, including
> every thought and motive as well as every overt deed, and . . . there was
> no escape from the responsibility of obedience.
>
> He is indeed characterized by an extreme faith and by a radical humility.
> But faith and humility are not things in themselves; they are relations to
> persons—habits of behavior in the presence of others.[30]

Thus, each of the virtues is intelligible in its apparently radical and
inordinate character only as a relation to God.[31] When the relation to

God as the fundamental factor in Jesus' life is left out of account, his life and teachings seem too extreme. But when relation to the one God is placed in the center, one can begin to see why in his response he could love and hope and obey and trust and humble himself before the powerful fidelity of his Father no less than he did. And insofar as God-in-Christ and Christ-in-God have "the value of God" for men, as the One who ultimately values and judges them from beyond themselves, they begin to see in him the very image of the being in response to whom they are being transformed, and to whom they are responsible for all.

CHRIST TRANSFORMING RELATIVISM OR CHRIST TRANSFORMING RELATIONALLY OBJECTIVE NORMS

The title of this section is a *question,* and will remain so to the end. It is, however, a query which H. Richard Niebuhr and we who have studied with him or been influenced by him should constantly press.

We have now to suggest that a more adequate understanding of Niebuhr's thought is to be gained by emphasizing the objective element in his relativism. Also, insofar as the word "relativism" in anything like its ordinary meaning still may be regarded as appropriate, we shall point out that relativism has only been presupposed as a (perhaps thoughtless) conclusion within the present age; and indeed that such a general position cannot even be proposed by anyone as the truth about man's situation and truthgetting without cutting out the ground upon which it itself stands. But this interpretation of Niebuhr's relationalism, and apparently severe criticism of Niebuhr's relativism, can never become our main concern. If the exposition and rejection of Niebuhr's relativism were of principal importance, then we would be responsible for developing and enforcing an alternative point of view concerning the truth of ethical judgments, or else we would be responsible for showing that his relationalism is valid. It is not necessary to undertake this here, since what must first be done is to give full and direct attention to the theme of the "conversion" of ethics which takes place whenever ethical reflection and decision come to be centered theologically in Christ. This is without any doubt Niebuhr's peerless contribution to Christian ethical analysis— the significance of which stands out all the more clearly because anyone who studies this theme as it is developed, for example, in *Christ and Culture* will see at once that it is simply *there* in Christian history and in the major documents of the Church's life. When this motif is isolated and carefully examined, it will become obvious that the problem of ethics is the problem of its conversion or redirection, not of its replacement. The transformist theme needs now to be distinguished from, or within, the context of Niebuhr's relativism, precisely because only so can the free lordship of Christ in encounter with every possible system of ethics be properly praised.

The reader's attention has been called to the fact that Niebuhr rejects subjective or psychological relativism in taking the point of view of "objective relativism." In one of his earliest and most well-rounded statements of this position, Niebuhr points out that it entails no prejudice whatever against the objectivity of value:

> Such a value-theory would recognize . . . the relativity of values without prejudice to their objectivity. The interpretation of values as relative to structure and organic needs, rather than to desire and consciousness, provides for such an objective relativism. The value of deity would appear, on the basis of such a theory, to be quite independent of human desire and the consciousness of need, but not independent of the human constitution and its actual need.[32]

What is denied is the view that "values are independent of structure and process." What is denied is not that values are objective but the "vitiating abstractionism" which separates, for example, truth and justice "from any being for whom they are valid" and teaches "that *they* ought to be rather than that *man* ought to be truthful and just. . . ."[33] In short, "objective relativism" excludes, on the one hand, subjectivism and, on the other hand, the ethical theories of Plato or Hartmann with their value-essences.

Only once in this statement of his case does Niebuhr mention "the relative standpoint of the observer," [34] which is relativism of quite another kind and which does not enter at all into the exposition and defense of the relation of value to structure, process, actual need, being. For this reason I have suggested that Niebuhr's general theory of value be called "relational objectivism" and that the misleading word "relativism" be no longer used. Not only his early essay, published in 1937, but also the recent statement of relational value-theory in "The Center of Value," published in 1952, lends support to this suggestion.

Yet at many other points in his writings Niebuhr expresses beliefs for which the word "relativism" is to great extent warranted. This is particularly true of *The Meaning of Revelation*. The thematic presupposition of this book is "the religious as well as the historical bondage of theological reason," [35] and in it Niebuhr proposes to draw out "the consequence of this understanding of theology's religious relativity as well as of its understanding of historical relativity." [36] The relativity entailed in the standpoint of the observer has special bearing upon the problem of man and morals. Yet the relativism of the historical and cultural point of view which a man occupies is nowhere established in this book, or elsewhere in Niebuhr's writings. It is simply assumed to have been established by some "prior science." The reader is asked to presuppose that a volume entitled "The Critique of Historical Reason" has already been written, and has clearly established itself in a consensus of "critical philosophers."

> Theology . . . is concerned with the principle of relativity as this has been *demonstrated* by history and sociology rather than by physics, and if it is developing into a relativistic theology this is the result of . . . an attempt to adjust itself to a new self-knowledge.[37]
>
> Critical idealists and realists knew themselves to be human selves with a specific psychological and logical equipment; their successors know themselves to be social human beings whose reason is not a common reason, alike in all human selves, but one which is qualified by inheritance from a particular society. They know that they are historical selves whose metaphysics, logic, ethics and theology, like their economics, politics and rhetoric are limited, moving and changing in time. . . . Our reason is not only in space-time but . . . space-time is in our reason.[38]
>
> . . . Our historical relativism affirms the historicity of the subject even more than that of the object; man, it points out, is not only in time but time is in man . . . the time of a definite society with distinct language, economic and political relations, religious faith and social organization.[39]
>
> . . . If reason is to operate at all it must be content to work as an historical reason.[40]

In all this there are dangers confronting human thought, Niebuhr admits, dangers such that "it is not strange that men today seek to avoid the problem by damning historical relativism itself as an aberration." [41] I propose at most to damn it as a relativism; and moreover as a relativism that has not and cannot establish for itself ground on which to stand.

We must proceed cautiously here, for Niebuhr himself believes that agnosticism need not be the conclusion drawn from historical relativism. He calls rather for "a new type of critical idealism which recognizes the social and historical character of the mind's categories and is 'belieffully' realistic. . . ." [42] Niebuhr urges that we distinguish between "universal views" and "views of the universal." A critique of historical reason must deny that man possesses "universal views"; but, Niebuhr believes, such critical idealism (or critical realism) may remain "belief-fully realistic" in the confidence that, despite "the social and historical character of the mind's categories," each of these gives a "view of the universal."

> It is not evident that the man who is forced to confess that his view of things is conditioned by the standpoint he occupies must doubt the reality of what he sees. It is not apparent that one who knows that his concepts are not universal must also doubt that they are concepts of the universal, or that one who understands how all his experience is historically mediated must believe that nothing is mediated through history.[43]

Here Niebuhr appeals to his notion of dialogue (or trialogue) in the verification and communication of knowledge of the universal. As the eye "cannot perceive the depth and distance and solidity of things save as it has a partner," [44] so in viewing the universal (or within the community of the faithful who receive historical revelation and bear witness to the meaning of Christ) there is "the test of experience on the part of companions who look from the same standpoint in the same direction." [45]

Niebuhr's "relativism of the subject" does not lean as far as might appear in the direction of skepticism—nor, in my opinion, as far in the direction of relativism as seems at first to be the case. At first it may seem that only an irrational act of faith forestalls skepticism. The empirical sciences assume with "animal faith" that the sense impressions give us relative perspectives on the real world (or that each is a view of the universal), although there is no sense beyond the senses to tell us that this is true (i.e., there is no universal view). "Without this animal faith in a dependable external world we literally would not live as bodies, for if we were true skeptics we would be errant fools to eat food made up of sense-data only, to breathe an unsubstantial air with unreal lungs, to walk with unreal feet upon a non-existent earth toward imaginary goals." [46] In a similar fashion, there is no point of view beyond historically relative points of view which can inform us that our viewpoints give us concepts of the universal or that something objective is mediated through historical experience. Only by an act of faith, it seems, do we break through the confines of our historically conditioned categories and lay hold on the real.

> The acceptance of the reality of what we see in psychologically and historically conditioned experience is always something of an act of faith; but such faith is inevitable and justifies itself or is justified by its fruits. A critical idealism is always accompanied, openly or disguisedly, by a critical realism which accepts on faith the independent reality of what is mediated. . . . So an historical relativism can and must proceed with faith in the midst of all its criticism of historical subjects and objects mediated through history.[47]

If this be the meaning of "belief-ful realism," if only an act of faith makes the difference between this position and skeptical relativism, then one might be forced to conclude that Niebuhr's objective relativism amounts to no more than skeptical relativism plus Hume's flair for playing the game of backgammon despite the inability of reason to justify the beliefs he invariably held while doing so.

But in interpreting Niebuhr one can lean just as far in the other direction, in the direction of objectivism. It is important to say whether the human mind or only an act of animal faith breaks through the charmed circle of the categories of historical reasoning and lays hold on reality. David Hume, even when at table with his friends, never believed *that the mind* could know anything; he *only believed,* with the animal faith requisite for backgammon, in the reality of friends, table, dice. The faith Niebuhr mentions is by contrast the faith that, in its views of the universal, the *mind* knows the real world. The belief of his "belief-ful realism" is actually the belief of a "critical realist." Amid relative historical perspectives, something of the universal is really grasped by reason. When Niebuhr writes that "we discern in all such formulations *elements* which are thoroughly relative to historical background," [48] does he not—perhaps inadvertently—allow for the discernment of elements in knowledge which are not so thoroughly relative? Moreover, he states positively that "we need not doubt that the categorical imperative *contains* a universal meaning but Kant's formulations of it are historically relative and when we, in our later historical period, attempt to reformulate the Kantian thought we also do so as historically conditioned thinkers who cannot describe the universal save from a relative point of view." [49] Will not our attempts today to reformulate Kant's thought also "contain a universal meaning"?

Indeed, the notion of "dialogue," which is so fundamental in Niebuhr's thinking, presupposes that each participant grasps something of the universal from his peculiar perspective and contributes this to, as well as receives correction from, the community of knowing minds. In fact, there is no impenetrable wall of separation between the point-of-viewing taken by one historical community and that of another. When describing the "religious relativism" of the Christian faith, Niebuhr is careful not to make this point of view impervious to other points of view: "To see ourselves as others see us, or to have others communicate to us what they see when they regard our lives from the outside, is to have a moral experience. Every external history of ourselves, communicated to us, becomes an event in inner history." [50] *To the extent* that such external accounts are communicated to us, has there not been actualized, through the dialogue of persons occupying different standpoints, a more inclusive community of interpretation? Here we see clearly the influence of Royce's idealism upon Niebuhr, and of the absolute community of interpretation which Royce believed to be presupposed in all human communication. Niebuhr as much as Royce accepts the *reality* of such an all-inclusive community. He simply denies that any finite perspective possesses such absolute comprehension of the truth. How much difference is there between Royce's "presupposition" or argument, that there must be such a universal community of interpretation even for error to be possible, and Niebuhr's when he writes the following?

> The church's external history of itself may be described as an effort to see itself with the eyes of God. The simultaneous, unified knowledge from

within and from without that we may ascribe to God is indeed impossible to men, but what is simultaneous in his case can in a measure be successive for us. The church cannot attain an inclusive, universal point of view but it can attempt to see the reflection of itself in the eyes of God.[51]

The crucial difference between Niebuhr's absolute monotheism and absolute idealism is not the reality of this last interpretation, which each presupposes, but the ultimate identity of the self in its wholeness with the Absolute. There is good reason, therefore, for interpreting Niebuhr in the direction away from relativism toward objectivism, and for denying that the word "relativism" adequately expresses what he means to say, as well as for replacing the term "objective relativism" with some such expression as "relational objectivism" (when the "relativity of the object" is at issue) or "perspectival objectivism" (when, as at present, the historical "relativity of the subject" has to be stressed).

"We are in history as the fish is in water," Niebuhr writes in one of his unguarded relativistic moments.[52] But no fish wrote that such was its condition. No fish ever discoursed at length on the bondage of its reason to liquidity, or on the relativity of its point of viewing from the depths. "The Critique of Piscatory Reason" has not yet produced the thesis that fish are not only in water but water also in fish, wholly determining the categories of fish understanding. Indeed, we can set it down in advance that, were such a literary event to occur, the author would thereby have refuted himself by evidencing incontrovertibly that his own reason is not, to the whole extent of its being, bounded by liquidity.

The same fate overtakes "The Critique of Historical Reason," if indeed it is being written today. "Men who assert that all moral standards are relative," Richard Niebuhr wrote on one occasion, "still believe that it is right to speak the truth about the relativity of moral standards." [53] Likewise, men who assert that all moral standards are "objectively relative" still believe that it is right to speak the truth about objective relativism. Men who believe in the entire historicity of the subject still believe that *it is true* that human reason is only a historical reason, which means that in knowing *this* truth the reason was not wholly determined by the historical seasons. To be true, historical relativism must manifestly be false, or rather the truth of the theory would manifestly contradict what it says about the human mind. If true, then this theory itself would have truth not wholly "limited, moving and changing in time," and the capacity of the mind to know this would at least be something, something transcending the confines of the categories of historical reason. It may be that absolute idealism drew extravagant consequences from this argument against the earlier "critical idealism" of Kant. Nevertheless, the argument that reason, in knowing its historical limits, has already in some sense transcended those limits still holds true, even though, as Richard Kroner has pointed out,

> It is not true that the acknowledgment of the limit allows me to penetrate into the realm beyond with limitless conquest. . . . Thus, philosophy in this definite sense transcends its own limits in knowing that it is limited. The land beyond its limits cannot be conquered, however; it can only be visited, as it were, and abandoned again with the consciousness that it always will be a foreign land, impenetrable and unfathomable as a whole.[54]

"Objective relativism" must have paid significant visits to the country where universal truth abides and brought back increased human discernment; or else at least some forms of absolutism would have equal truth when in season. As Niebuhr partly confesses in the preface to *The Meaning of Revelation,* he has indeed seized both horns of the dilemma[55] which knowledge confronts in facing up to the relativity of the historical standpoint of the observer; but it should be clear which horn he will have to let go as the discussion of the situation and problem of human knowledge proceeds. As precondition of his speaking the truth to us, even as precondition of the possibility of our significant disagreement with him, he can only mean "perspectival objectivism." This expression retains the full force of what he says about our "views of the universal" as distinct from "universal views" better than the oft-repeated use of the word "relativism."

However, the chief reason for Niebuhr's penchant for relativism is that he regards it as a direct consequence of radical monotheism and of the conversionist motif in Christian ethics. The faith of radical monotheism, he says, "makes relative all those values which polytheism makes absolute, and so puts an end to the strife of the gods." It is true that, as Niebuhr points out, faith in God does not relativize values in the way that self-love does. Since for monotheism "whatever is, is known to be good," this faith also upholds man's positive response to all being, so that "a new sacredness attaches to the relative goods." [56] Still, radical monotheism also subjects every value to radical scrutiny, making relative what polytheism absolutizes. Perhaps the best statement of the bearing of love for the one God upon relativism is to be found in the following paragraph in Niebuhr's essay on "The Center of Value":

> . . . The value-theory of monotheistic theology is enabled to proceed to the construction of many relative value systems, each of them tentative, experimental, objective, as it considers the interaction of beings on beings, now from the point of view of man, now from the point of view of society, now from the point of view of life. But it is restrained from erecting any one of these into an absolute, or even from ordering it above the others, as when the human-centered value system is regarded as superior to a life-

centered value system. A monotheistically centered value-theory is not only compatible with such objective relativism in value analysis but requires it in view of its fundamental dogma that none is absolute save God and that the absolutizing of anything finite is ruinous to the finite itself.[57]

Now, we should not only note but proclaim the significant fact that Niebuhr says that all these "many relative value systems" are, among other things, "objective." Nevertheless, not all of what is said above follows necessarily from a serious effort to view morality in the light of God. To have "an absolute" in value-theory is not necessarily to substitute it idolatrously for *the* Absolute. And it is difficult to see why "ordering" one value system above another of necessity infringes the sovereignty of the one God, or why regarding one value as "superior" to another puts in question the "fundamental dogma that none is absolute save God." This may happen, but not inevitably. Monotheistic faith is incompatible only with idolatry, not with all ordering and rank among the (now subordinate) centers of value in various value-systems.

Consider the suggestion that a human-centered value-system may be regarded as superior to a life-centered value-system in theological ethics. Of course, if by "centered" is meant that we attribute the value of God to "man" or "life," this and every other idolatry monotheism purges away. But from this purging it by no means necessarily follows that all value-systems are absolutely leveled, or that the Christian living in the midst of these beings and values is reduced to viewing everything "now from the point of view of man, now from the point of view of society, now from the point of view of life" with considerable indifference to whether one of these relative centers may not be superior to another. It is true that in his total response to all the beings who are his companions in God, he will be sustained by a new sense of sacredness attaching to all relative goods. But neither does the limitation which monotheism places on all relative goods reduce the human-centered value-system, nor does the extension and intensification of the sense of the sacredness all beings have in God necessarily raise the life- or society-centered value-system, each to a qualitative parity with the other under God.

In his essay on "Value-Theory and Theology," Niebuhr found an ally in D. C. Macintosh in linking value with structure, being, or process, as against theories of abstract values or objective essences. The criticism of Macintosh's theology which Niebuhr succeeded in pressing home was his objection to making human values the starting point of the theological system or the antecedently known criteria of the divine. Such procedure Niebuhr rightly rejected. But he did not seriously take issue with Macintosh's view that there is a certain "absoluteness of values relative to persons" or values "universally and permanently valid for persons." [58]

This affirmation may still be true even when God is taken as the uncon-
ditioned starting point of a wholly disinterested theological science.

At the heart of Niebuhr's own theology, indeed, he acknowledges that
a human-centered value-system may possibly be ordered in God's view
above life- or society-centered systems. We stood once before at the heart
of his theology when indicating how a redirecting influence and transforming power flows from man's responsible engagement with God as
the center of value. This is only part of the meaning of God in human
experience. Another at least equally significant element consists in the
"valuation" involved in what Niebuhr calls "deity-value" or deity-
potency. "It is possible and necessary," he writes, "to interpret religion
as an affair of *valuation* without assuming that such valuation must or
can be made on the basis of a previous established standard of values." [59]
It is not now a question of man's disinterested (but not uninterested)
response to the Other whom he meets in the midst of being, but of this
Other's action toward him through his sovereign call and divine judgment:

> The religious need is satisfied only in so far as man is able to recognize
> himself as valued by something beyond himself. That has the value of deity
> for man which values him. The valuation of which man becomes aware in
> religious experience is not first of all his evaluation of a being, but that
> being's evaluation of him. The latter evaluation does not need to be positive;
> on the contrary, in his experience of deity man frequently becomes aware of
> his disvalue, but he does not become aware of his unvalue. . . . The content
> of revelation is not the self-disclosure of an unknown being, but the un-
> veiling of the value of a known being. What is revealed in revelation is not
> being as such, but rather its deity-value, not that it is, but that it "loves
> us," "judges us," that it makes life worth while.[60]

This same view of deity-value is restated in *The Meaning of Revelation:*

> Revelation means the moment in our history through which we know
> ourselves to be known from beginning to end, in which we are apprehended
> by the knower. . . . Revelation is the moment in which we find our judging
> selves to be judged not by ourselves or our neighbors but by one who
> knows the final secrets of the heart; revelation means the self-disclosure of
> the judge. Revelation means that we find ourselves to be valued rather
> than valuing and that all our values are transvaluated by the activity of
> a universal valuer. When a price is put upon our heads, which is not our
> price, when the unfairness of all the fair prices we have placed on things
> is shown up; when the great riches of God reduce our wealth to poverty,
> that is revelation. When we find out that we are no longer thinking of
> him, but that he first thought of us, that is revelation.[61]

Looking back upon the alternative idolatrous centers of relational value-theory it is possible now to say that what was sought in and through them all was not only value, or even some center in being in relation to which good-for-ness might be judged. What was sought was *reciprocal* being in relation to being. What was sought was being, power, purpose, judgment, deity-potency, and "deity-value" in the sense of an evaluation from beyond oneself (such as "the people" are endowed with capacity to make, when democracy is regarded as the source of ultimate judgment and redemption). What was sought was not only a center for our own relational value-judgments, but Being's relation to us in terms of which ultimate worthwhileness is given to us and purposed for us; not only a focus for our participation in being, but primarily the participation of Being in even our own existence.

In what Niebuhr calls "deity-value," value and being completely coalesce. In the need for God the question is not "whether a god exists, but rather what being or beings have the value of deity" and the potency of deity. ". . . It is a being which is sought, not value as such." [62] "We would not use the word God at all if all we meant were designated by the word good, but neither would we use it if we meant only power. To say that God and faith belong together is to maintain that no power could be apprehended as God save as its value were made manifest." [63] And elsewhere he writes that "Faith . . . always refers primarily to *character* and *power* rather than to existence. . . . Faith is an *active* thing, a committing of self to something, an anticipation. It is directed toward something that is also *active,* that has *power* or *is* power." [64] Thus, in the foregoing illustration, if "the people" has deity-*value* and deity-*potency* as in some forms of democratic faith, this refers both to the character *and* to the power of the people; "the people" is active, it has power or is power to give value and to sustain the meaning it gives to life.

Now, some sort of endorsement of the judgment of "a human-centered value-system" seems involved at the very core of what Niebuhr says about "value as valency" placed upon man from beyond himself by that being which has the valuation-potency of Deity. The infinite or sacred value of human selves cannot, it is true, provide the starting point of a system of theology, since "it cannot be true that the proposition about the infinite worth of persons is self-evident unless there be some infinite being to whom they are valuable." Nevertheless, Niebuhr writes, "*It is very true* that recognition of the infinite value of souls is a concomitant of revelation, but it could not be given were not something else given in that event—the infinite self for whom all souls are valuable." [65]

Without claiming that in this perspective upon the universal *we* have completely vanquished the land where dwells the universal view of all things, is there not something *given* here which is entirely compatible with the view that the human-centered value-system is superior to the life-centered system even when human life has been displaced from *the* center? As a gift within man's God-relationship, all idolatry is of course excluded—as well as any proposal to use the value of the self to establish the value of God, and any *self-interested* insistence on the value of one's own person as the elected center from which the rest of life may be exploited. But was Jesus any the less mindful of the sacredness of persons only in the eyes of God, or any the less regardful for the sacredness also bestowed on all their natural companions under God, when he said of people in comparison to sparrows, "Are you not of much greater value than they?"

Finally, a careful inspection of Niebuhr's fundamentally conversionist outlook proves it to be harmonious with the objectivity of certain value-relationships and their possible ordering in some scale. It may be that in describing the transformation of man and his morals Niebuhr again "seizes both horns of every dilemma." His outlook, when properly grasped, however, may be interpreted more in the direction away from "Christ Transforming Relativism" toward "Christ Transforming Relationally Objective Norms." Perhaps this says more than he intends, and would alter the force of what he says at many points; but I would argue that it is quite in line with what he says in at least an equal number of other points. This is what he ought to say more definitely and clearly in all his writings.

"Transformation" does not mean the "republication" of the law of nature, and thus merely the provision of divine sanction for a moral law quite intact as it was already known to us. Nor does it mean *identification* with or mere *supplement* of such intact, untransformable moral principles. But neither does transformation mean *substitution,* the *replacement* of the moral law—whatever it is—by the demands existentially encountered in Christ. Morality (whatever its principles are found to be) should rather be subject to transformation in the light of these demands in Christ. If moral values are only relative, then the impact of Christocentric faith upon the moral life would mean "Christ transforming relativism." If, however, there are discoverable moral values and relationships, then this would mean "Christ transforming relationally objective norms." Nothing in the nature of radical monotheism or the conversionist-motif itself, but only a certain philosophical conception of human historical reason, seems to require that large concessions be made to relativism. What Niebuhr wrote concerning reason in general may also be said concerning man's capacity for moral judgments: "The pure reason does not need to be limited in order that room be made for faith, but [as one of the chief changes wrought by conversion] faith emancipates the pure reason from the necessity of defending and guarding the interests of selves, which are now found to be established and guarded, not by nature, but by the God of revelation whose garment nature is." [66] Man needs to be redeemed from sin and idolatry and all his values made responsive to God-in-Christ; he need not be delivered from his competence to make objective-enough value-judgments.

In *Christ and Culture*, Niebuhr again proclaims his "acceptance of the relativity not only of historical objects but, more, of the historical subject, the observer and interpreter." This is the lesson he learned (too well?) from Troeltsch, but Niebuhr distinguishes his own view from that of Troeltsch by reference to his effort "to understand this historical relativism in the light of theological and theo-centric relativism." [67] (This, it has been suggested above, were better called theological "relatedness," which is to go a long way toward the correction of relativism.) He speaks of "the reason which prevails in culture" and of "the understanding of right and wrong developed in the culture" [68] as one contender in the double-wrestle of Christian conscience with Christ and culture.

Stated in this fashion, the ethics of natural or moral law seems to be a cultural work of man, indistinguishable from partial institutions like middle-class or workingmen's churches or like specific social policies once effective, such as the legislation of national prohibition. It cannot be too strongly emphasized that there would never have been any reason prevailing in culture if men of the past who placed a degree of confidence in reason had been persuaded theirs was only cultural or historical reason. Unless reason reaches beyond culture, culture prevails in reason and not reason in culture. Likewise, it cannot be too strongly emphasized that there would never have been any understanding of right and wrong developed in culture had men been of the opinion that all conceptions of right and wrong are moving and changing in time. Niebuhr defines culture as "the work of men's minds and hands"; [69] but men of the past who have championed right against wrong have ordinarily conceived their task as having in view what was most decidedly not the work of their own minds alone, and for all the flux of history they have believed it possible for two men to step twice in the same river.

Moreover, concerning the other contender in the wrestle of Christ with culture it is impossible to say anything "which is not also relative to the particular standpoint in church, history, and culture of the one who undertakes to describe him." Thus, Christ also is subject to a religious and a historical relativism—so much so that the reader may occasionally wonder whether in the long run Christ transforms relativism or relativism transforms Christ.

With one horn of the dilemma firmly in his grasp Niebuhr then seizes the other; or to change the metaphor he gives back with one hand what he appears to have taken away with the other. Concerning views of right and wrong, he says, as we have seen, that though each is a relative view, each

may still be a view of the universal. Here reason breaks out from among
the categories of historical reason and lays hold on the real. And concerning Christ, he writes that "though every description is an interpretation, it can be an interpretation of the objective reality." [70] Here faith
breaks through religious relativism and knows in whom it has believed.
The Christ of Christianity is indeed one Lord seen from different perspectives, yet he is discernibly one. Humility before the one Lord requires
us not to absolutize any one of five possible positions on the problem of
the Christian's loyalty to the work of reason and culture. "Christ's answer
to the problem of human culture is one thing," Niebuhr affirms at the
outset, "Christian answers are another; yet his followers are assured that
he uses their various works in accomplishing his own. . . . Christ as living Lord is answering the question in the totality of history and life in
a fashion which transcends the wisdom of all his interpreters yet employs their partial insights and their necessary conflicts." [71]

To the end Niebuhr endeavors to stick by his resolution not to name
the Christian answer: ". . . The giving of such an answer by any finite
mind . . . would be an act of usurpation of the Lordship of Christ which
at the same time would involve doing violence to the liberty of Christian
men and to the unconcluded history of the church in culture. . . . We
should need to assume, if we tried to give *the* Christian answer, that we
are representatives of the head of the church, not members of its body
. . ." [72] Yet Niebuhr necessarily has a *view of the universal* even when
disclaiming the universal view, or when breaking the Christian answer
into five different strategies in *Christ and Culture.* Just as of necessity
Niebuhr must assert the more than historically relative truth of historical
relativism itself, so he cannot avoid affirming that these five types *together* comprise the truth about Christian social ethics. In designating
these five types and not five other or an indefinite number of other types,
he approximates, through the dialogue of these perspectives with one
another concerning the meaning of Christ, the more Christian answer. He
knows in whom Christians believe all the more from their historical discourse. Is this not better called a relational or perspectival objectivism
than any sort of relativism? In appraising each position with fine sensitivity, Niebuhr plainly has in mind not just another relative perspective,
but God-in-Christ beyond them all and discernible in part through them
all. The way he is able to penetrate to the heart of each Christian perspective and comprehend them all together and evaluate them provides
us with an example, not of the edification there is in the relativism believed to be required by radical monotheism, but an example of the
illumination there is, *credo ut intelligam,* in knowing oneself as known
by the Triune God.

The Trinity is not only the *arche* at work within Niebuhr's appraisals
of all five types in their relatedness; it is also the *arche* at work in the

transformation-motif itself. Therefore, it is not surprising to find evidence that Niebuhr's thought (despite his explicit disavowal) always tends toward conversionism as *the* most adequate Christian answer in the sense that it proves most responsive to the Triune God. The other Christian social outlooks which flank this one and help to sustain it seem discernibly less than responsive to all the meanings of this *arche*. They "belong" as possible types of Christian social witness which God-in-Christ also uses in working his will through the whole of the human story. Try as Niebuhr will, however, he cannot refrain from discriminating the flanks from the center of the line in recounting Christ's engagement with culture. In the light of this *arche*, the Triune God who is, Niebuhr cannot discover criticisms of the conversionist point of view as significant, theologically or culturally, as those he makes in the course of extremely sympathetic appraisals of other points of view.

Moreover, one cannot belong to all these positions, even though one may dimly see how they all belong. Though the fact is somewhat hidden from view in this volume by the inclusion of the fifth type along with the rest in the synoptic final chapter, which shows the author to be to a great extent a relativist, it is plain here and everywhere else in his writings that Niebuhr belongs to the type "Christ the Transformer of Culture." In articles and books, conversionism has been his constant theme. Unavoidably he affirms this to be not only one view among many, but the view which most adequately expresses the meaning of God-in-Christ in relation to culture and morals and the community of mankind. Transformism gives us no instance of the edification to be found in religious relativism, but rather of the illumination, *credo ut intelligam,* which there is for moral reflection and the perpetual revolution that may be set going in the moral life from assuming (with firm conviction that herein faith has been grasped by the truth) such a perspective on the objective meaning of Christ for the whole of life.

The final issue is whether such an objective relatedness to the being of Christ, or such a view of his universal meaning, need deny the universal and permanent validity of certain ethical principles or hierarchy of values relative to the structure of man or to his mode of being in the world. Can there be no absolute or unchanging truths if man and his morals are subject to transformation in the light of the absoluteness of God-in-Christ?

To take a loaded illustration first: Surely, at all times and places and under whatever historical circumstances or conditions of personal relationships, rape is wrong, and the use of slaves as studs and the herding of women into barracks for the purpose of producing children by selected Nazi soldiers were horrible crimes. This can be said without that "vitiating abstractionism" which separates absolutes "from any being for whom they are valid." Men and women have the right to the free exercise of their sexual powers[73]—not that such freedom *ought to be* in the abstract in some world of essences, but that people ought to be free in this capacity. This we know, as Maritain might say, simply from reflecting upon the nature of man as man, no relative considerations of fact being taken into account. When legislatures determine the statutory "age of consent," and when juries and judges help to make law by their decisions of guilt or innocence before such statutes, of course they are in part exercising "cultural reason." The degree of responsible freedom and maturity assumed by (or too early forced upon) adolescent girls in our society today, as compared to twenty-five or fifty years ago, is a significant cultural change which should obviously be taken into account. This maturity means, in all probability, that eighteen is now too old for the age of consent in the state of California; and incidentally that the jury acted wisely and justly a few years ago in acquitting a celebrated movie actor of the charge of statutory rape, even though as the law now stands he may well have been technically guilty of the charge.

But all this does not obviate the fact that a child still has a right to be treated as a child, and her "voluntary" consent at too early an age should still be regarded as forced upon her by the male. In seeking to determine some new age-figure or in tempering the application of old law, legislative or judicial reason simply asks, "When is a child still a child?" This may be partly a cultural question. However, the question would itself not be of importance to us were we incompetent to know something of the nature, meaning, and rights of human childhood and of mature human freedom in its sexual expression. The need for some new answer to the question posed by our contemporary cultural situation, or for answering it in particular cases that come before the courts, rests in part upon the moral certainty that a child has a right to be regarded as unfree and an adult person the right to be free in the exercise of sexual powers. (The foregoing does not raise the question of whether there are any norms for freedom in sexuality, such as monogamous marriage.)

Niebuhr himself gives a more significant illustration of an experienced truth or value not independent of structure and process which nevertheless seems to have permanent validity, and it is notable that he does so in immediate connection with submitting man's situation and values to radical transformation:

> The Hellenic distinction between the temporal and the eternal was accepted by the Christian movement, for it was evident that it corresponded to aspects of man's experience which the Hebrew scheme of two aeons left out of account. But the chief concern of Christian faith was to convert this Greek two-worldliness, so that the Greek might see through the revelation of God in Christ how personal were the other-worldly objects of the soul's contemplation, the form of the Good and the *logos,* and how graciously creative and redemptive they were.[74]

Here, simply by reflecting upon man as man in his being in the world, Niebuhr arrives at strikingly Augustinian conclusions which entail in part at least a "scale of being" and of value. "The temporal goods which satisfy a temporal being do not satisfy man or correspond to his nature," he writes. "That earth is not enough for him, his adventures, his crimes and glories on earth demonstrate. That an exclusively secular environment does not correspond to his nature is indicated not only by the presence in him of personal freedom and conscience but by his hunger which earth cannot satisfy with all its goods." [75] In short, St. Augustine first, and then Niebuhr himself, are accepting the permanent validity and superiority of elements in the Greek approach to and interpretation of human experience, in contrast to one-dimensional world views; yet both writers see, through the revelation of God in Christ, how personal are the other-worldly objects of the soul's contemplation, the form of the good and the *logos,* and how graciously creative and redemptive is the eternal. Kierkegaard provides another great instance of the acceptance of the juncture of the eternal and the temporal in the structure of human nature (most vividly portrayed in *Purity of Heart*[76] and whenever he considers "the lilies and the birds"), and yet at the same time the transformation of this understanding by the gospel in his *Christian Discourses,*[77] "The Anxieties of the Heathen," and "Joyful Notes in the Strife of Suffering," and in "The Lilies of the Field and the Birds of the Air: Three Godly Discourses."

The trouble with Greek-minded speculative philosophy and with the theory of natural law in ethics is not that truth has been discerned by them but that it is claimed they are autonomous, and are apt to be left so in "identification," "dualism," or "hierarchical synthesis" when brought under the aegis of Christ. Brunner's error is not that he speaks of "orders of creation" but that in *The Divine Imperative*[78] these orders may have been understood *primarily* as orders of "creation" and of "sin" refracting love, without being set sufficiently in motion and commotion by the primacy of redemption. One cannot object to Brunner's reliance on man's sense of justice in *Justice and the Social Order,*[79] but only to the fact that he keeps the realm of justice unaltered and unalterably apart from the (consequently purely personal) dimension of love and grace. This same "dualism"—of Christ and Culture or Christ and Reason in Paradox—is repeated in the ethical sections of Brunner's *The Christian Doctrine of Creation and Redemption.*[80] The primacy of redemption in converting, transforming, invigorating, and redirecting natural reason would not deliver us from accepting the substantial validity of Brunner's tabulation of basic human rights;[81] but would ensure instead that the stress would fall no longer on *minimum* rights, but on maximizing the conditions for fullest human fulfillment on the part of all for whom Christ died. This would be to see how personal, how graciously creative and redemptive are those forms and principles we contemplate when considering only "nature and nature's God." * Niebuhr's lectures on ethics, in which the Christian life is viewed as simultaneously responding to "creation," "judgment" or "governance," and "redemption," have always suggested to his students the indivisibility of these approaches, since God is he with whom we are always already engaged, and he is all these eventful acts toward us, wherever we are culturally and historically in our being in the world. In this there is promise of a dynamic ethics of redemption which does not simply build upon yet does not jettison the ethics of creation.

The relationship of Christianity and democracy provides another example of the Truth transforming truth. Without identifying Christ with liberal democracy, it may be affirmed that the growth of democracy in England in the seventeenth century was due in part to the "Christ transforming culture" motif in Puritan Protestantism. But were there not at work also principles concerning the good for man in society which have more than relative historical importance and which belong always to the good for man, even though, when account is taken of relative cultural factors, it may not be wise to attempt to realize them everywhere now? Certainly there were in the seventeenth century people who joined in transforming political life in the direction of democratic "covenant community," yet who were secular-minded enough to conclude that in the congregation, as well as elsewhere, "the odd man is the Holy Spirit." If there be any warrant for democracy as a social goal, then the present dynamic relation of Christ to the ideal of liberal democracy is that of "Christ transforming relationally objective norms," although his relation to actual democratic cultures includes with this also a large measure of "Christ transforming the relativism" of many a historical peculiarity or variant moving and changing in time.

It is easy to see, and one should be wholly sympathetic with, the reasons why Niebuhr tends to think that both radical monotheism and an unrestricted conversionism make all other things relative. The transformation-motif so easily loses its dynamic and changes into one of the other types of Christian social outlook which defend some cultural achievement or some rational principle intact as it is.

The criticism Niebuhr directs against certain of the other types might well apply to the interpretation of conversionism and moral law suggested here. Efforts to erect a hierarchical synthesis of Christ and culture or of Christ and the rational moral law into one system, he writes, tend "perhaps inevitably, to the absolutizing of what is relative, the reduction of the infinite to a finite form, and the materialization of the dynamic." In particular, the synthesist almost invariably formulates the moral law

---

* A fuller treatment of these themes in the Christian ethics of Emil Brunner is given in Chapter Seven.

"in language and concepts of a reason that is always culturally conditioned," and indeed "no synthesist answer so far given in Christian history has avoided the equation of a cultural view of God's law in creation with that law itself." [82] Once having synthesized Christ with something evanescent, soon such a Christian "will be required to turn to the defense of that temporal foundation for the sake of the superstructure it carries when changes in culture threaten it." [83] Thus, a Christian, who began with a clear distinction between culture and Christ while loyal to both, soon becomes a "culture Christian."

The peril of transforming Christ into a cockpit from which to defend a culture that is withering away cannot, of course, be exaggerated. When the synthesist recognizes this danger "he is on the way to accepting another than the synthetic answer; he is saying then in effect that all culture is subject to continuous and infinite conversion." Yet Niebuhr errs slightly when he goes on to say that the conversionist, or the converted synthesist, will necessarily acknowledge "that his own formulation of the elements of the synthesis, like its social achievement in the structure of church and society, is only provisional and uncertain." [84] Provisionally formulated, one might retort, but there is truth in the formula. Must *everything*, including reason's grasp of human being, structure, and value, be "only provisional and uncertain" in order for conversion to be "continuous and infinite?" Must "Christ transforming relationally objective norms" be programmatically ruled out in order to preserve a fully dynamic conversionism and to avoid man's self-defensive holding on to some rigid cultural form?

Niebuhr's own profound insight into man's self-defensiveness leads him to see that there is no help toward curing self-interestedness to be gained from limiting reason. This insight has only to be applied here for it to be sun-clear that men may quite as easily identify or synthesize Christ with such national legislation as prohibition or with the maintenance of early American social organization[85] (which no serious thinker would regard as directly grounded in the fundamental law) as for them to identify him for defensive purposes with any of the first principles of moral reasoning (if such there be).

Cultural or historical relativisms give no real assistance toward the avoidance of rigidities which might impede dynamic, continuous, and indefinite conversion of the moral life. The categories of historical reason are not less effective means for the self-defense of faithless men than are the truths or values in being which they may apprehend in their views of the universal. To see this clearly, let us suppose the case of a Christian ethicist who, under the impact of a radically monotheistic faith and the regenerative Lordship of Christ, allows his whole being to be transformed by the thought that God-in-Christ makes all else relative and nevertheless renews all. Imagine him a deep student of Dilthey and Troeltsch and the "sociology of knowledge." Will he not soon begin to find in these views support for the dynamic conversionist meaning he finds in Christ? From being intrinsically a conversionist he then soon becomes a synthesist, even though Christ be now synthesized with historical and other forms of relativism.

These philosophies—for such they are, on all fours with every other philosophy with which Christian faith has ever been joined—seem to him quite plausibly to contain truth which it will be helpful for men to accept, or at least a point of view for them to adopt toward truth, before or while going on to the supervening perfections given in what happens to them, to their self-understanding and their understanding of the world in the light of Jesus Christ. Subtly there already has taken place here a confusion or even an "identification" between the subordination of the human heart and life to Christ and the subordination of the mind to this way of thinking (which, only by an illusion, seems to make the former easier).

Then suppose that out of the depths there begins to take place a profound historical and cultural change. A Troeltsch, deeply troubled by certain tendencies in the German historical view of law, delivers in 1922 his address on "The Ideas of Natural Law and Humanity in World Politics." [86] And everywhere men are questing for certainties and remembering the asserted universal principles of their ancient ethical and political heritage. What happens to our Christian relativist? Why, having once synthesized Christ with something evanescent (historical relativism), soon such a Christian "will be required to turn to the defense of that temporal foundation for the sake of the superstructure it carries when changes in culture threaten it." [87] In this respect he becomes a "culture Christian." This is sufficient to show that, for preserving the dynamics of an ethics of redemption, there is no help from particular philosophies; and that no philosophical or ethical outlook can be programmatically excluded by a theology of conversion.

The theological presuppositions of the conversionist-motif are in line with the suggestion that this point of view may be held without prejudice against the possible objectivity of norms. By virtue of the conversionist's positive view of creation "he finds room for affirmative and ordered response on the part of created man to the creative, ordering work of God." [88] It is therefore not impossible that the knowledge of certain universally valid principles or hierarchy of being and value may be a part of man's "ordered response" to the ordering work of God. The conversionist puts special stress on the Incarnation of the Word who has entered into "a human culture that has never been without his ordering action." [89] It is therefore not impossible that in Christ the Redeemer of culture "the true light that enlightens every man was coming into the world" (John 1:9 RSV) for the conversion and redirection of the light already among men and in culture. While the conversionist asserts with the dualist a doctrine of the radical fall of man, he knows that "culture is all corrupted order" rather than ordered corruption: "The problem of culture is therefore the problem of its conversion, not of its *replacement by a new creation.*" [90] In all these ways it should be clear that Niebuhr's fondness for relativism is not a necessary part of his theology of conversion, but rather a consequence of the influence of Troeltsch and others upon him and an aspect of his philosophical point of view, which itself, this chapter has suggested, needs to be interpreted—*perhaps* in part corrected—in the direction of relational objectivism.

St. Augustine was certainly a dynamic and thoroughgoing conversionist who—on Niebuhr's own accounting—did not believe that this position entailed relativism.

> [Augustine] the Neo-Platonist not only adds to his wisdom about spiritual reality the knowledge of the incarnation which no philosopher had taught him, but *this wisdom is humanized, given new depth and direction, made productive of new insights,* by the realization that the Word has become flesh and has borne the sins of the spirit. The Ciceronian moralist does not add to the classical virtues the new virtues of the gospel, nor substitute new law for natural and Roman legislation, but *transvalues and redirects in consequence of the experience of grace* the morality in which he had been trained and which he taught.[91]

In brief, "Christ is the transformer of culture for Augustine in the sense that he redirects, reinvigorates, and regenerates" [92] the whole life of man, including the life of moral reason and of the spirit, which is fundamentally good but misdirected. This approach enabled St. Augustine and the early medieval period—as two leading modern historians agree—"to overcome the radical deficiencies of the classical approach to experience" and "to heal the wounds inflicted by man on himself in classical times and, by transcending while still doing justice to the elements of truth contained in philosophic paganism, to revive and give direction to the expiring spiritual ideals of classical antiquity." [93]

Christians of the present day need to take this same way of looking upon the best products of the human spirit in our own time, if there is any hope—not necessarily the hope, as Christians of the identifying and synthesist types desire, of averting the demise of Western democratic life any more than the transforming power of Augustinian Christianity saved Roman civilization—but if there is any hope of overcoming the deficiencies and wounds of the contemporary world so that beyond probable tragedy the expiring spiritual ideals of modern democratic society may be revived and given new direction.

Paul Tillich and Emil Brunner: Christ Transforming Natural Justice

I

The chief problem for Christian social ethics is how we are to understand the relation between the law of nature and the righteousness of the covenant. There are two ways, and only two ways, of avoiding this problem. Ethics may, on the one hand, remain wholly within the "Egypt" of the natural law, deriving the standard for man solely from man and from the structures immanent in human society. This is the path taken by every humanistic ethic. Christian ethical theory may, on the other hand, pass wholly into "Exodus," taking note only of the demands upon men who live in the immediate presence of God and ignoring the fact that they live still within the ordered forms of *some* natural community which is based, in part at least, upon agreement as to inherent principles of justice based on creation. This is the path sometimes taken by the ethics of Protestantism with its radical doctrines of sin and grace; and St. Augustine came close to this point of view when he defined political society as only "an assemblage of reasonable beings bound together by a common agreement as to the objects of their love [will or interests]," omitting from Cicero's definition any reference to man's knowledge of justice.[1]

To take either of these ways exclusive of the other is to refuse some part of the political and ethical wisdom in our human or religious heritage. The undesirability of making either sort of thoroughgoing refusal (and the actual difficulty of succeeding in the attempt) is made evident by the surreptitious inclusion of the truth refused. Thus, humanistic views of social ethics consciously based only on reason and "nature" actually display an unacknowledged indebtedness to the moral insights of biblical theology. Their "reason" is always already a cultural and religious inheritance; their "nature," a transformed nature. They deceive themselves into believing that something like love or redemptive justice can be shown to be solely a product of reason. J. S. Mill cannot be understood, with utmost seriousness and consistency, to mean what he says about there being only one standard, "the greatest amount of happiness altogether."[2] That, standing alone, may mean "regardless of numbers," and Mill was prevented by a mind shaped by the Christian tradition from drawing any such consistent conclusion.* No more can any other rationalistic ethics succeed in producing what Western peoples *theodidacti* have learned to require of a system of morals.

And radical theological rejections of the law of nature generally presuppose some degree of continued reliance upon the sense of justice or injustice. They deceive themselves into believing that this flows only from God's meeting with man in covenant and belongs wholly to the sphere of redemption. Thus, Dietrich Bonhoeffer cannot be understood, with utmost seriousness and consistency, to mean what he says about the moral requirements of biblically derived "mandates," when we also observe that, throughout his sensitive reflections upon the tragedy that has happened to numberless men in our era, he actually operates with a suppressed concept of the "unnatural." [3] In short, there is always more mercy and compassion in the one refusal, and more natural justice in the other refusal, than either confesses.

This means that the outstanding problem for Christian social ethics is how we are to understand the relation between the law of nature and covenant-righteousness, or between justice and love. Not only has some connection to be asserted to exist between them; but also just how this is so, and what are the effects of it, need to be elucidated. A succinct formulation of the bearing of redemptive righteousness upon natural justice may be expressed as "love transforming the natural law." Not only increased clarity in Christian ethical analysis is to be hoped for from fully articulating the meaning of love converting, transforming, redirecting, extending, and reinvigorating natural justice; but also a release of the impulses for conduct and action on the part of men in their several vocations in our society and a resumption of connection with the gift and the task we have received through our religious history.

I propose that we step into the center of this issue by examining two points of view which attempt in opposite ways to avoid separating love and justice while relating them in an entirely transforming way. One of these is to be found in the moral and political writings of Paul Tillich, who gives what may be called for want of a better term a "monistic" view of the relations of love and justice, resulting from the grounding of the meaning of both these terms in ontology. The other is Emil Brunner's "dualistic" understanding of love and justice. When these accounts of

---

* Of course, there is no reason why happiness should not be distributed to the greatest possible number, since (as Mill says in a footnote near the end of his *Utilitarianism*) "equal amounts of happiness are equally desirable, whether felt by the same or by different persons." But, there is no reason to be found in this standard for not limiting the distribution to fewer people, provided only that their happiness can be enhanced to an amount or intensity or quality equal or greater than that experienceable by the many. Plainly, the second part of Mill's standard, "the greatest happiness of the greatest number" is a relic of a Christian love that responds to the needs of everyone.

Christian social ethics are carefully "unpacked," it can be shown that each of these writers obviously makes use of the concept of "love transforming justice" and that this is the reason each succeeds in great measure in formulating the principles of a Christian social outlook. In the course of unpacking these points of view the meaning of "transformism" will become clearer; and it will be suggested that Christian social ethics should explicitly begin with an examination of this principle, and that Christian social action means extending it in practice.

II

In his book *Love, Power, and Justice*,[4] Paul Tillich argues that we need "ontological analysis" before attempting "ethical application." He quite rightly insists that so long as we remain content with ordinary usage there is only confusion as to the meaning of these terms, "love," "power," and "justice," and apparently insoluble conflict among them. Hence arises the supposition that love is opposed to power, justice to love, and power to justice. Only by plunging deep into the reality behind the terms, by tracing the meaning of these ethical concepts from the power of "being itself," can their essential meaning be brought to light, as well as their ultimate harmony. So long as love has only an emotional or sentimental meaning, and power is understood in terms of compulsion, and justice in terms of static proportion, they are bound to contradict one another both in theory and in practice.

An ontological analysis, however, discloses the root meaning of each of these terms, and their unity. Love is not a mere emotion but the ontological drive of separated beings toward union. Power means not mere compulsion but the intrinsic power of being itself; and so "the more conquered separation there is the more power there is. . . . The more reuniting love there is, the more conquered non-being there is, the more power of being there is. Love is the foundation, not the negation, of power."[5] Justice recognizes the claim of every being to endure in its power and to unite in love. Thus "if power is reduced to [compulsion] and loses the form of justice and the substance of love, it destroys itself and the politics based on it."[6] By understanding love, power, and justice as thus grounded in being itself, the apparent conflict between them can be resolved—between, for example, loveless power and powerless love, or between justice claiming natural equality and love as chaotic self-surrender.

Now, I shall contend that Tillich's ontological analysis is actually speculation within a parenthesis first drawn by Christology. Instead of reducing love, power, and justice to the power of being itself, the fact is that love has already transformed Tillich's concept of justice, and this justice in turn has transformed his concept of power, before ever the meanings of these ethical terms consent, like the lion and lamb, to lie down together. Indeed, what is the power of being itself or "the infinite resistance against non-being and the eternal victory over it" [7] but simply a compact formulation of the idea of resurrection by the power of God? So love, power, and justice—as well as the power of being in which they find repose—all have already undergone transformation, for all are ways of viewing the universal *logos* from the point of view of the concrete *logos* in Jesus Christ.

Before undertaking to demonstrate this by unpacking Tillich's ethical analysis of these terms and their interrelationships, we should in passing note a point at which the Christian concepts he employs have in fact themselves already suffered transformation by the general philosophical insights of a particular school. An ethic grounded in ontology inclines inevitably in the direction of monism, and from the point of view of traditional theological ethics displays two related inadequacies: a defective doctrine of creation and a failure to define love unrestrictedly in terms of covenant. These criticisms clearly apply to Tillich's understanding of love. He is not content to define love as the drive of one being toward covenant-relation with another from whom it is separated. Instead he constantly calls this "*re*union." He cogently argues that "the absolutely strange cannot enter into communion." But this may mean that beings *created* for covenant-community, and not therefore strangers to each other, seek one another through love; and not that all "separation presupposes an original unity" or that in love "the *estranged* are striving for *re*-union." [8] Is it wrong to see here in the shadows the idealistic Absolute going through the undulations of separation or estrangement from itself and then rejoining itself? This point is closely related to the oft-repeated criticism of Tillich's theology for linking finite individuality too closely with the Fall; and it certainly involves a refusal to take covenant-faithfulness seriously as the one meaning of love amid all the concrete qualifications of love.

The idealistic source of this understanding of love is obvious. Without any change from the terms he himself approves and adopts, Tillich says of Hegel that "he started in his early fragments as a philosopher of love, and it can be said without exaggeration that Hegel's dialectical scheme is an abstraction from his concrete intuition into the nature of love as separation and reunion." [9] Elsewhere Tillich writes that in speaking of God as loving we necessarily make symbolic use of "our experience of love." [10] It is not surprising, then, that Tillich adopts this same Hegelian "dialectical scheme" in speaking of God as loving: "In the Son, God separates Himself from Himself, and in the Spirit He reunites Himself with Himself." [11] The model for this understanding of the inner trinitarian life of God was first drawn from human love as reunion. This is to describe love—even the love we thrust into the very heart of God—

according to the basic anatomy of idolatry; and there is every reason to believe that such an understanding of love is simply read off of the human condition in its distorted existence. As Tillich says of Freud's account of Libido, it is a "description in estrangement." [12] Since this is the case, Tillich's "ontology" somewhat blunts the transformation of human justice and love that might flow from an account of steadfast love drawn from the divine model given in the covenant God establishes and renews with his people.

Indeed in some measure such an understanding of love vitiates Tillich's fine argument[13] for abandoning the use of the term "self-love" because of the misleading metaphorical meaning the word love has when applied to the self's relation to itself. For while there is not a "separation" or a created separateness "in the structure of self-consciousness," there is in fact an inner "estrangement" and a striving within the self for "reunion." There is indeed within us all a "self which fights against another self, with which, on the other hand, it is identical." [14] There would therefore be a proper love of the self for itself, *if* love is the striving of the estranged for *re*union. Tillich's insistence that there is nothing more separate than a "self-centered" or centered-being from all other beings (which is why he *reserves* the word love for relations *between* beings) should have entered more fully into the very *definition* of love to jettison from its primary meaning the idea of a *re*union of the estranged. Tillich insists most strongly that "the centre of a completely individualized being cannot be entered by any other individualized being, and it cannot be made into a mere part of a higher unity." This makes necessary the following statements: "Love *unites* that which is self-centered and individual" and "It is the fulfillment and the triumph of love that it is able to *unite* the most radically separated beings, namely individual persons. The individual person is both most separated and the bearer of the most powerful love." These are Tillich's words, except that *he* continues to use the word "*re*unite(s)." [15]

The foregoing criticism is remotely but definitely related to an error Tillich makes at another point in his discussion of the meaning of love. He enriches much recent theological interpretations of this subject by indicating several intertwined "qualities" or "qualifications" (not "types") of love: *libido, philia, eros,* and *agape;* but he is surely wrong in saying that the typological "attempts to establish an absolute contrast between *agape* and *eros* usually presuppose an identification of *eros* and *epithymia.*" [16] Plato is sufficient to refute that. Tillich correctly argues that the mistake in analyzing distinct "types" of love lies in its obscuring the fact that "love is one." [17] Contrasting predicates may in fact obscure the single covenant-meaning of love. Granting this, it must be pointed out that by designating *more* distinctions or qualifications of love than can be comprehended under the name *eros* in its contrast with *agape,* Tillich somewhat obscures the fact that the *one* meaning he assigns to love is *re*union, which is a philosophical concept quite different from covenant-fidelity. Only when he indicates how the *agape*-quality of love "cuts into" the other qualities of love to purify and elevate them does he speak of the one covenant-meaning of love; and, significantly, this is the point at which transformation as a theme in his writings becomes most explicit. And it is not ontological analysis but biblical theology which leads to the basic assertion that love is one in this sense. If this is the *one* meaning of love, and if such aspirations as the *eros* of civilization still deserve the name of "love," then we are driven to adopt a theory which allows for several different "types" of love, and cannot accept Tillich's suggestion that these are only qualifications or expressions of a single nisus of the soul toward reunion.

As we now undertake to analyze the relations Tillich discerns among love, power and justice, it ought to be noticed that the harmony he asserts to prevail among these ethical terms (when properly grasped) does not consist of an entire identity. To this extent it is false to speak of his ontological analysis as "monistic." In his three final chapters he speaks, for example, "first of *justice*, love, and power in human relations, then of *power*, justice, and love in social institutions, then of *love*, power, and justice in relation to the holy." The order of the words is of importance for where the stress falls in each instance, and I have indicated this by the use of italics. "In the first sphere, justice is leading, in the second sphere, power, and in the third, love." [18] This would not be the case if these three words referred to exactly the same attitude or relation. Still the main tendency of Tillich's ontological analysis is to reduce the different meanings, usually assigned to these terms, each to harmony with the other two; so that the upshot is a position which affirms that love can never do more than justice requires, or justice be other than inclusive of love, and that power cannot prove unjust or unloving unless this happens because of an erroneous apprehension in the encounter of being with being.

On first hearing this summary one may wonder whether what we have here is not actually a phenomenology of the kingdom of God and of his Christ; and indeed on closer inspection this will prove to be speculation which already presupposes the transformation of all relationships in the present age by the power of redemptive justice or love. My thesis, already announced, is that love has already transformed Tillich's concept of justice, and this justice in turn has transformed his concept of power, before ever their cases come up for adjudication before Tillich's court of last resort (ontology). It will be convenient to attempt to prove this contention in the reverse order, i.e., by showing that what Tillich says about power, if acceptable, drives on to his analysis of justice, and indeed to the illuminating, transforming power of an extraordinary kind of justice; and that this conception of the meaning and nature of justice in its turn drives on to and must rely upon the transforming power of love which is pure *agape*.

Tillich presents a phenomenology of power—of unintermittent encounters of power in ever changing balance. "Every encounter of somebody who represents a power of being with somebody else who represents another power of being leads to a decision about the amount of power embodied in each of them." [19] In striking some sort of dynamic balance of power, use is made of compulsion; but compulsion is bad only if it does not express the actual relative power of being in each of the beings who meet in the encounter.[20] Now, this distinction between power and compulsion is an entirely abstract, theoretical distinction, since Tillich also affirms that it is impossible to determine before the encounter the real power of being represented by each of the contending beings. "The problem of 'justice in encounter' is given with the fact that it is impossible to say before the encounter happens how the power relation will be within the encounter." [21]

Here then appears a first problem for analysis: unless Tillich can supply a satisfactory concept of justice, his own thought will be open to an objection he seeks to avoid, namely, that he interprets justice exclusively as a function of power expressed in encounters and as in no way its judge or moral criterion.[22] It will not help simply to refer to reuniting love which conquers separation and enhances the power of being; for without some norm of justice this means only that certain combinations of power continually encounter other combinations of power, and there will still be no actual distinction between these structures of power and the compulsion they exert. Without some concept of justice, we must wait to see which compulsion succeeds before we can know "how the power relation will be within the encounter." It may not be legitimate to demand some *general principle* of justice, known beforehand and then imposed on the powers when they meet in encounter. But at the least there needs to be indicated some capacity for knowing justice *in* the encounter, some sense of injustice manifested in the prism of the actual case. Without this, Tillich's sweeping endorsement of "the power struggle" which Sartre says takes place "in the accidental look of a man at another man" as "simply a description of life processes which occur in 'heaven' as well as in 'hell' " [23] must simply be put down as an amoral view of human relationships. Either heaven is not like this, or there is no heaven; and we may say that (reversing Schopenhauer's famous remark) all the boredom has been emptied out of this view of heaven because it has been filled with all the evil will and relentless struggle in the world.

Such, of course, is not Tillich's position; but so much is at stake when his analysis of power is driven back upon his concept of justice. In fact Tillich calls for some "new foundation of natural law and justice." [24] Tillich's first definition of justice is that it is the "form" which is adequate to the movement of separated beings toward reunion.[25] While at first glance this understanding of the meaning of justice seems to be simply that which pertains to a robber band or to any larger assemblage of rational beings who are agreed as to the objects of their mutual self-interest, the fact is that included in this purely formal adequacy is a dynamic adequacy to the ever changing real powers of being in encounter. As such, this justice has to wait on the event to make evident what is adequate or inadequate to the beings in question.

The second principle of justice is equality. While this provides no normative content that would discriminate the just from the unjust before an encounter, it does suggest a sense of justice acknowledging and respecting the claims voiced by beings *in* the encounter of powers. "The basis of justice is the intrinsic claim for justice of everything that has being." [26] This means that the "unique and incomparable individual . . . expects a special justice which is adapted to his particular power of being" and that "the principle of personality" is "a principle of justice." [27]

When this is said, however, we are driven also to acknowledge that there is a hierarchical principle included in this justice, because different persons have actually different powers of being to express and these claim respect as such. Therefore, justice is mainly "tributive or proportional." [28] Tillich says "tributive"—meaning "a thing or person ought to receive according to his special powers of being"—because included under this heading are the classical types of "distributive" and "retributive" justice. Both are proportional, the former in a positive, the latter in a negative sense.[29] So far it must be granted that Tillich succeeds in including in justice a dynamic adjustment to the differences of proportional power present in encounters of beings. Justice still means formal adequacy to the (unequal) powers of being as they effect reunion—or at least some kind of conjunction, if not collision—with one another in actual encounters.

But then it must be pointed out that as yet we have arrived at no concept of justice that can be the criterion or judge of power. This justice is still a function of power. Indeed, this justice is not yet dynamic enough to sustain a formal adequacy to the changing situations met with in the actual world of concrete beings in relation. As Tillich notes, "tributive justice is never adequate to this because it calculates in fixed proportions" and never quite keeps pace with the new claims arising from the powers in being. And he repeats: "One never knows a priori what the outcome of an encounter of power with power will be." [30] Tributive justice cannot by itself anticipate all that natural justice may require. Must we, then, wait for successful compulsion to show what new degrees of relative power have actually emerged in the perpetually changing balance of historical forces?

We come, then, to a crux by which we are driven beyond the analysis of justice to the concept of love; and, moreover, to a love which converts, redirects and transforms human understanding of the problem of justice. This same turning point is indicated by what Tillich says about the natural law. No matter what principles are proposed—the "golden rule," the Ten Commandments, equality and freedom as principles of the natural law—Tillich concludes that "in the moment in which these principles are used for concrete decisions they become indefinite, changing, relative. . . . The natural law theory cannot answer the questions of the contents of justice. And it is possible to show that this question cannot be answered at all in terms of justice alone." [31]

In the course of the foregoing analysis Tillich has spoken of "the absolutely valid formal principle of justice in every personal encounter, namely the acknowledgment of the other person as person." But he acknowledges definitely and without qualification that one tries "in vain to derive contents for this formal principle" [32] from any supposed principles of natural law or natural justice. Therefore, according to Tillich, respect for the other person in encounter (or the sense of justice, effective in the prism of the concrete meeting) is wholly without content. If, then, justice is to be more than a function of power, if it is also to be in some sense the judge of power relations, this must arise from the direction or meaning justice obtains when our analysis of it drives on to the concept of love.

There are two ways in which the effect of love upon justice may be expressed from the thought of Tillich. Love keeps justice dynamic, and love makes justice creative. This twofold formulation was forecast early in Tillich's book when, observing the limitation of the Aristotelian types of justice, he raises the question, "Can perhaps the proportional element be taken into a *dynamic-creative* type of justice?" [33] The brevity of the hyphen in this expression should not lead us to suppose that dynamic justice and creative justice have the same meaning, or that the transition —from dynamic adequacy to the changing proportions to a creative changing of the proportions—is unnoticeable or unimportant. In keeping justice dynamic, love directs and reinvigorates natural justice, or love fulfills justice by extending it flexibly in every moment of encounter up to its own maximum requirements. In making justice creative, love converts and transforms natural justice by releasing upon it impulses for conduct which are not as such contained within the formal requirements of justice itself. In keeping justice dynamic, love directs the agent toward the acknowledgment of the other person as a person with precisely the claims which his *present* potential power coming into being represents. Love illuminates justice so that it *now* knows what will prove adequate as the form of the present and actually forthcoming balance of powers in encounter and of their present striving for reunion across separation.

In making justice creative, however, love breaks into the world of claims and counterclaims and freely posits some new proportion which was not there before among the requirements even of the most dynamic justice or of a justice most sensitive to the actual changes taking place in the situation. The fact that Tillich speaks of a "creative justice" as the third and last of his "levels of justice" should not mislead anyone into supposing that it belongs there for any other reason than the transforming power of love. No more should the short hyphen in the expression "dynamic-creative justice" mislead anyone into supposing that intrinsic justice (which proves less than just unless it is kept dynamic) may become a creative justice while still doing no more than a dynamic intrinsic justice requires. A proper reading of Tillich will show that dynamic justice is intrinsic but kept that way by the extrinsic pressure of love, and that his so-called "creative justice" is itself an extrinsic result within the realm of justice of the transforming power of love.

The preceding paragraphs are, I believe, an accurate statement of the elements present in Tillich's analysis. Needless to say, these elements are not so clearly distinguished in Tillich's own writing. In fact, he expressly contends that "one should never say that love's work starts where the work of justice ends" or that "love gives what justice cannot give." [34] He says that "love does not do more than justice demands," [35] and he rejects "the 'theory of addition' of love and justice." [36] Now, of course, "transformism" must also reject the theory that love is only added to justice, if this means added only as a superior righteousness hierarchically imposed upon an unaltered natural justice (as in Thomism) or added only as an inner motive to the external realm of justice (as in the dualistic view of Luther or of Brunner). But Tillich obscures and blunts the transformism that is an actual main theme of his writing by attempting to enforce a too complete unity between justice and love. This attempt succeeds in a measure only because the justice which is so closely allied with love has already been redirected and transformed by love.

Perhaps the most important single passage in Tillich's discussion of love and justice is his statement that

> Love . . . has the same relation to justice which revelation has to reason. . . . Both of them transcend the rational norm without destroying it. Both of them have an "ecstatic element." Love . . . can be called justice in ecstasy, as revelation can be called reason in ecstasy. . . . And as revelation does not give additional information in the realm where cognitive reason decides, so love does not drive to additional acts in the realm where practical reason decides. Both give another dimension to reason, revelation to cognitive reason, love to practical reason.[37]

Here again Tillich rejects the theory that love adds some specific contents to natural justice. Love does not transcend justice by its additional information about the contents of the moral life, or by the specific concrete acts it performs in addition to those justice requires. But this means only that love does not deduce its action from general principles known beforehand, any more than dynamic justice knows in advance what will prove adequate to the actual claims of persons and powers. Neither an act of proportional justice, nor an act of creative justice changing the proportions nor an act of love transforming justice is constituted by theoretical principles. What *specifically* is to be done either by love or by justice arises only from the concrete situation which supplies the content. Since this is the case, the relation of love, transforming justice, and flexible proportionate justice can in no way be a matter of adding content to content.

Nevertheless, love "gives another dimension" to practical reason or to natural justice, and it is from the determinate meaning and quality of this other "dimension" that there flows the transforming power of love upon justice which produces creative justice, and the radical conversion even of the most dynamic proportional justice and its redirection as an act of self-surrender changing the proportions.

The fact is that the statement "love does not do more than justice demands" applies only to the operation of love in *keeping* justice *dynamic*. It does not hold true to the extent that love *makes* justice *creative*. Creative justice would fall back into the merely formal adequacy of tributive justice to the dynamically changing proportions at any moment the pressures of love ceased to be toward more than a reasonable, flexible, natural justice requires.

It is true then that, in keeping justice dynamic, love simply fulfills the requirements intrinsic in the situation. In this sense both justice and love must be decisively related to the concrete situation; and "it is love," Tillich writes, "which creates participation in the concrete situation." While it is not true that love must be added to justice, it is true that love must be immanent within this sort of justice, "if the uniqueness of the situation is to be reached." Thus, "justice is just because of the love which is implicit in it." [38] Love immanent within justice keeps justice aware of the concrete contents to be taken into account if justice is to acknowledge the specific claims represented by every degree of coming change in the power of being in everything that has being. It ensures that the principle of personality shall be the principle of justice, and it illuminates the actual claims of persons as they put themselves forth into encounter. Love thus directs justice beyond formal principles to concrete situations and specific persons in their wholeness. The just, natural claims of any being have "a large margin of indefiniteness";[39] love sensitizes justice to these claims. So far love performs no greater work than justice should. Love simply "shows what is just in the concrete situation." [40]

Toward the end of his book Tillich remarks that "the analysis of transforming justice as an expression of creative love makes it necessary for

me to reject the ordinary contrast between proportional justice and super-
added love." [41] We have seen that this contrast must be rejected, not
because Tillich has shown that there is actually a type of justice which
posits the same directives as creative love but because *transforming* love
is already a *transformed* justice. This is evident in everything Tillich says
about this justice. He speaks of the justice not limited to proportional
distribution as an "act of resignation," an "act of non-proportional justice." [42] He can say that "ultimately love must satisfy justice in order to
be real love" only in the context of saying also that "justice *must be
elevated* into unity with love in order to avoid the injustice of eternal
destruction." [43] When he first introduces an explicit definition of "transforming or creative justice" he mistakenly affirms that this is "based on"
the fact that "intrinsic justice is dynamic" in its adjustment to the unpre-
dictable outcome of an encounter of powers."[44] As we have seen, this only
indicates the justice which love keeps dynamic in its reading of the
proportions. On the next page, the true basis of transforming, creative
justice is correctly expressed: "More exactly one should speak of the
resignation of proportional justice for the sake of creative justice." Here
he speaks also of "fulfillment within the unity of universal fulfillment,"
symbolized by "the kingdom of God." [45] Plainly Tillich does not know
the meaning of transforming justice from an untransformed analysis of
justice or a dynamic ontology of power. He knows this rather from the
divine model given in biblical theology: "God is not bound to the given
proportion between merit and blame. He can creatively change the
proportion, and does it in order to fulfill those who according to proportional justice would be excluded from fulfillment." [46] This statement
should have been introduced by the words (reversing Tillich's): as in its
application to God, so in its application to man, justice means more than
proportional justice.

Moreover, Tillich describes three functions of creative justice as
"listening, giving, forgiving." [47] Surely, "listening" belongs among the
functions of dynamic justice and the love that, immanent within it, does
only what justice requires; while "giving" and "forgiving" are qualities or
dimensions (not contents) in which love transforms intrinsic justice into a
creative or transforming justice which goes beyond any sort of intrinsic
justice. In either case it is love which listens, gives, and forgives.
Finally, Tillich writes that there are other kinds of self-surrender than the
chaotic self-surrender which is unjust to the self, and than even the self-
surrender sometimes demanded by proportional justice for a common
cause. There are also the acts of self-surrender demanded by love. Only
by virtue of the transformation and elevation of the concept of justice
that has already found its way into Tillich's system can he still insist that
if such acts of self-surrender are "demanded by love they are demanded by
creative justice. For the creative element in justice is love." [48]

It remains only to point out that as Tillich's analysis of the concept of justice is driven back upon the transforming influence of love, this love is no longer understood in general terms as the reunion of the separated but as covenant love or pure *agape*. The final expression of Tillich's transformism is what we may call love converting love, transforming and redirecting it. He writes:

In the holy community the *agape* quality of love cuts into the *libido, eros,* and *philia* qualities of love and elevates them beyond the ambiguities of their self-centeredness. . . . *Agape* seeks the other one in his center. *Agape* sees him as God sees him. . . . *Agape* cuts into the detached safety of a merely aesthetic *eros.* . . . *Agape* makes the cultural *eros* responsible and the mystical *eros* personal. . . . Again, *agape* does not deny the preferential love of the *philia* quality, but it purifies it from subpersonal bondage, and it elevates the preferential love into universal love. . . . *Agape* cuts through the separation of equals and unequals, of sympathy and antipathy, of friendship and indifference, of desire and disgust. It needs no sympathy in order to love; it loves what it has to reject in terms of *philia*.[49]

Tillich uses very strong language indeed for the transcendence of *agape* and its impact upon the other qualities of love: "cuts into," "cuts through," "purifies," "elevates," "loves what it is necessary to *reject*" in terms of the other loves! It almost seems that this is another *type* of love (if the other so-called qualities are also deserving of this name). This in fact is the case. Moreover, there is no way of avoiding this conclusion by attempting to assimilate *agape* again to the general notion of love as an inherent nisus of the soul toward reunion of the separated—by saying, for example, that "forgiving love is the only way of fulfilling the intrinsic claim of every being, namely, its claim to be reaccepted into the unity to which it belongs." For such union only "belongs" to a being as it is given him by forgiving love; it comes only after the proportionate claims have been discounted; or (to say the same thing after justice has been transformed by *agape*) "creative justice demands that this claim be accepted and that he be accepted who is unacceptable in terms of proportional justice."[50]

In any case, the above quotations show clearly what is meant by "love" transforming, purifying, converting, redirecting or reinvigorating "love"; and from this flows transforming or creative justice, and then finally the transformation of the very concept of power. "If this happens man's natural or social power of being becomes irrelevant. He may keep them, he may resign some of them or even all of them."[51] This leads Tillich to express in the end an eschatological vision quite different from his earlier overly enthusiastic endorsement of Sartre's view of interpersonal relations based always on struggle for power as simply a description of life-processes which will continue even in heaven. He now writes: "Love, power, and justice are one in the divine ground, they *shall become* one in human existence," [52] and this is true in a different sense than can be disclosed by ontological analysis. All this follows from the fact that symbols for God's love drawn from human experience are actually, in the main direction of Tillich's theology, radically transformed by God's revelation of himself.

While our own experience of love seems at first to be the principal point of departure for understanding the inner life of God the reverse is most of all the case: it is the divine love which "cuts into" and gives the meaning of proper human love. If we apply some general, experimental notion of love to God, "we throw it into the mystery of the divine depth, where it is *transformed* without being lost. It is still love, but it is now divine love." [53] So also with the concept of justice: "It also must be thrown into the mystery of the divine life and in it both preserved *and transformed*." [54] So also with the concept of power, which as we have seen becomes the power to resign power. Then all *shall* become one, when all these aspects of human existence shall have been transformed by conversion to God and toward every creature as God himself bends toward them.

Thus, it seems demonstrably the case that Tillich's ethical and social philosophy is throughout anchored in *agape*. It is reflection within a parenthesis already drawn by Christology. His ontological analysis is Christology cutting into ontology. *Agape* is love cutting into love. Creative justice is love cutting into justice. And finally if Tillich succeeds in arriving at a concept of justice that is more than a function of power, if instead justice is the judge and criterion of power, and if there is an actual and not merely a theoretical distinction between power and compulsion, this is only because Tillich has in the final analysis a love-transformed understanding of justice.

Still within the context of the transformism implicit and explicit in his book, Tillich might have found more substantial meaning in natural justice, and not simply have stated its meaning as empty principles or as only formal dynamic adequacy to actual power relations. Just as *agape* may be said to have content if not contents, so with justice; and the one dimension, or meaning or content, impinges upon the other in a transforming way. In order for love to triumph, it is surely not necessary first to formulate an idea of justice that knows so little of what it should do before the living encounters of powers in being.

Perhaps this point ought not to be pressed, because we have seen that, while Tillich rejects every suggestion of principles of natural justice that are more than empty forms, he does allow fully for a natural capacity on the part of man for deciding justly and rightly *within* the actual encounter when he has before him, concretely or in the prism of the case, the claims of persons. And this is the moment—the moment of decision—when the pressures of love enter into the decisions of justice to sensitize, enlighten, direct and extend them in the way that love requires. Perhaps it is inevitable that, when a philosopher delineates the place where justice is discovered and declared, what he writes will seem more formal and lacking in substance than when a professor of jurisprudence says essentially the same thing about the "sense of injustice" and about decision made in "the prism of the case." [55] For in the latter case we know that, while the judgment rendered may not be a deduction from principles, the decision joins with innumerable others to become, as it were, principles expressed in precedents and rules of law; and moreover that a present decision in the face of the concrete and novel factors in a particular case is always handed down by an individual decision-maker only after he has entered into the widest possible "discussion" with similar and contrasting decisions of the past deposited in our law. This was what Holmes meant by his remark that "continuity with the past is not an obligation, it is a necessity."

Thus it was that the English *positive* common law, a product of innumerable decisions of *judicial* reason in particular, local cases, became "higher law" binding upon kings and parliaments and embodied in charters and bills of rights; and thereafter such a justice was to be discovered and declared (not made) by judicial review. Thus there is a continuing dialogue between the principles of justice enshrined in the law (but originating from decisions in prior cases) and the particular case now before the court. In articulating a theory of justice, and a theory of love transforming the natural law, this is the correct understanding of natural justice (going from the particular to the general) to be employed in Christian social ethics; and not in the main the continental natural law which was supposed to pass from the general conclusions of "common reason and right" somehow into the particularities of positive law.

With all this in mind we can understand that radical doctrines of sin as such do not require the rejection of natural justice. Perhaps Tillich should have mentioned the need for the transforming power of grace and love to convert and purify the self-centered will not only in connection with creative and transforming justice. Surely this is also a defect in that love which is immanent in inherent justice keeping it dynamic, sensitive and enlightened as to the real claims of persons, and enabling it to do what justice itself requires. Men's need to have their culpable blindness corrected can be seen by remembering that most of the authors of the Declaration of Independence with its appeal to the inalienable rights of man saw no frontal and immediate contradiction between these and the institution of slavery. Transforming love, and an acknowledgment of the radical sinfulness which prevents justice from "listening" to the claims of personal beings, would not have called for a rejection of natural justice in this instance but would rather have made possible its fulfillment and perfection.

III

In his ethical writings, Emil Brunner has rather consistently set forth a "dualistic" understanding of the relation between biblical "righteousness" and the natural law or between love and justice. Yet a careful analysis of what he says on this subject will show that at crucial points he actually makes use of the idea of love transforming natural justice. An exhibition of this somewhat suppressed theme in the writings of Brunner, who is primarily and consciously a dualist, will again illuminate the meaning of "love transforming the natural law." At the same time, it will lend support to the constructive contention of this chapter, namely, that Christian social ethics needs explicitly to elaborate the meaning of transformism in connection with the problems of justice and law.

Brunner maintains that we should make a strict "distinction between what holds good in the world of institutions and what holds good in the relationship of persons"; and this corresponds to "a strict distinction between the justice and the *suum cuique* and the love which knows nought of rights and claims." [56] Throughout there is an essential and complete difference between the meaning and requirements of justice and the meaning and requirements of love. Love is "all-the-same" and in-spite-of-everything, it is "never love because"; while justice is always rendered *because*. Love always bestows worth, while justice only judges worth. Love is "born simply of the will to love, not of the nature of the beloved," while justice rests upon an apprehension of the nature of the one to whom it is due and upon respect for his claims. "Justice makes no free gift; it gives precisely what is *due* to the other, no more and no less." [57]

When we consider the different spheres to which love and justice belong, and in which each is supreme, it seems correct to associate Brunner's position quite closely with Luther's doctrine of the "two realms." Brunner speaks of "the heavenly law of forgiving love" and of "the earthly law of even-handed justice";[58] and this language is reminiscent of Luther's when he speaks of the "kingdom of God inwardly" and the "kingdom of this world outwardly." Indeed, their views are identical so far as concerns the dualism between faith and love on the one hand and on the other the external ordering of social and legal institutions; and Brunner is not wrong in his contention that Luther and Calvin believed there is a natural justice by which even a pagan prince should rule his realm. For Brunner as for Luther, love is the motive which impels a Christian citizen or soldier or magistrate to stay in his position in the secular order. Justifying faith and love tell him *that* his vocation is there, but *what* he should do in the vocational setting of existing social institutions is determined entirely by natural justice and by the necessities of the situation, and not at all by love. If there is any significant difference, this may arise from the fact that Brunner's *I-Thou* philosophy of personal encounter leads him to identify this as love's realm, while Luther, in speaking of the kingdom of God *inwardly,* was perhaps more conscious of the difficulty of submitting actual personal relations (as well as the legal and political order) to the rule of love. Both agree that in most concrete situations when love goes into action it takes the form of justice.

In any case, it is important to stress the correlation of love with personal relations and of justice with impersonal institutions in the thought of Brunner, because later on we shall see that, by introducing a type of justice which has a great deal to do with the *person* as such, Brunner himself opens up the bridge over which "love transforming justice" enters decisively into his thought, supplanting its explicit dualism. In the present context, however, a strict distinction between love and justice is made precisely in terms of the distinction between the personal and the impersonal. "Justice is never concerned with the human being as such," Brunner writes, "but only with the human being in relationships. Justice belongs to the world of systems, not to the world of persons." Of course, for the Christian, love is the supreme standard, but this applies to interpersonal relationships; and "in its own place" in the social system "justice is supreme." [59] The connection between love and justice (or rather, the point of transition from one to the other) can best be expressed as the *complete change* of love into the form of justice as it seeks to become effective in the social and legal order.

> . . . In the world of systems [a Christian] cannot give effect to his love except by being just. He remains loving none the less, but as long as he is active in the world of systems, his love compels him to be just. Within the world of systems, he must, so to speak, *change his love into the current coin of justice,* since that alone is legal tender in the world of systems. . . . The man of love can only serve the state with justice. He must transform his love *entirely* into justice for as long and insofar as he acts in the state.[60]

This change from the essential requirements of love "entirely" into the form of justice does not mean, of course, a complete lapsing of connection between love and justice. This must be noticed in any fair assessment of dualistic social ethics. First of all, Brunner points out that "because no man, as a member of an institution, is *only* a member of an institution, but always and only [?] a person, there is room for love even in the most impersonal of institutions, not in the actual activity of the institution itself, but 'between the lines.' " [61] This love expresses itself *as love* through the "interstitial spaces" within the social order, and beyond them; and this is not unimportant in our age when the cup of cold water given in Christ's name has to be assigned greater significance than social reformers once supposed.

Moreover, and secondly, love which expresses itself *as justice* through the impersonal framework of institutions needs always to be immanent within justice for justice to be fulfilled, i.e., "filled full," completely or perfectly what it should be. So Brunner writes that "only love can be perfectly just" because "love is the only guarantee that all the motives which stand in the way of justice shall vanish or become ineffective." [62] Love immanent within justice purges and purifies the motives of men so that they may prove just. While love may not transform justice, it *keeps* justice *just*, by its continual transforming and directing power in the hearts of men. Perhaps we may also say that love "perfects" and "elevates" justice, having in mind the figure Brunner uses for the relation of love to justice: "we can only fill a glass quite full if we are ready [as love is] to let it run over." [63] His viewpoint in many respects, therefore, approximates that of Paul Tillich.

There are two important differences, however: One is that Brunner gives us no explicit ground for saying, as does Tillich, that it is love that *keeps* justice *dynamic*. This would be an additional statement of the relation between love and justice. Instead, in his chapter on "Static and Dynamic Justice," Brunner regards the need for dynamic justice as something that has sufficient recommendation from a reasonable analysis of the "historical relativity" and "transitoriness of all earthly things"; and in this connection he employs the traditional distinction between "absolute" and "relative" natural law which takes realistically into account the consequences of the Fall. He does not indicate any positive influence of love immanent within dynamic justice.[64] The most that can be said is that his thought as a whole borders on relating love to the dynamic element within justice, and that it would not be too much altered by the inclusion of this point.

The second difference between Tillich and Brunner is that the latter, in setting forth his view that love immanent within justice perfects and completes it, adheres to a viewpoint which, as we have seen, Tillich attempts unsuccessfully to deny. "Love can only do more," Brunner writes, "it can never do less, than justice requires. . . . There is therefore no such thing as love at the cost of justice or over the head of justice, but only beyond justice and through justice." [65] They both agree that justice is a form of love; but Brunner believes that it is the nature of love to extend beyond the justice which is the first of its works.

A third and final characterization of the continuing relation of love to justice current in "the world of systems" is that, for all the strict distinction between the two "realms," they both have the same "final cause" or end. ". . . The ultimate purpose of the orders of creation is the purpose of community. Their meaning, their reason and their goal is love, even though their specific nature, being of the order of justice, cannot be of the order of love." [66] The meaning, reason and goal of social institutions and systems, and of the justice which is supreme in the sphere of the orders, is love. Justice is therefore not only the "strange work" of love from the point of view of the moral agent who can actually live according to love only in his personal relationships; it is also the strange work of the God of love who ordains justice in order that just, endurable (and just endurable) community may not perish from the earth.

Still, when all is said that can be said concerning the continuing relations between love and justice, dualism remains the position Brunner wishes to maintain; and his distinction between these two terms in Christian ethics is correlated with the distinction between interpersonal life and impersonal institutions. A summary of Brunner's exposition of this matter in *Justice and the Social Order* may well conclude with the following statement: he writes that the manifold institutions of social life "are ruled more by justice or more by love" "according as persons or things predominate in their purpose." [67] This formulation is important because we shall see that—inconsistent with the dualism fixed between love and justice—Brunner in fact defines a kind of *justice* in which persons predominate more than things, and this becomes the bridge over which "love transforming justice" makes entrance.

This happens at the point where Brunner suggests an important revision of Aristotle's two main types of justice. "Corrective" justice was understood by Aristotle to be applicable to the sphere of private law; i.e., in the case of one man injuring another through theft, the judge should simply "correct" the imbalance introduced by this crime while regarding both as abstractly equal before the law. "Distributive" or "proportional" justice, however, Aristotle regarded as belonging to the sphere of public law, i.e., when it is a question of the citizens' relation to the "common wealth," or of the distribution of honors, rewards and participation in the common good, a just ruler will recognize that one man may have more stake in the community than another and he will take their unequal contributions into account. Now, in accepting the distinction between these two types of justice, Brunner affirms that Aristotle mistook their different spheres of application. Private law, e.g., in liability cases, sometimes takes account of inequalities of persons and circumstances; while public law, e.g., in justly granting universal suffrage, sometimes regards persons as arithmetically equal before the law. Brunner therefore proposes a revision of Aristotle in determining when one or the other of the two types of justice should be in force:

> The more the person is overshadowed by the thing, the more directly measurable becomes the value of the two things which are to be reciprocally

valued, and the more justice coincides with mere equality in the value of things. . . . The more justice is concerned with the relations between persons, the less the differences between the persons can be disregarded, hence the more account justice must take of those differences, so that it is proportional and not contractual justice that must prevail.[68]

Now, it is obvious that this formula for locating proportionate and arithmetical justice corresponds exactly to some of Brunner's language in "strictly" distinguishing between *love* and justice. If human relations are ruled more by love than by justice according as persons predominate over things in the purposes expressed through these relations,[69] and if precisely the same condition determines when proportionate justice should prevail, then we may certainly conclude that love and justice are not nearly so distinguishable in their essential definitions or in their actual application as Brunner supposes. I know that, in many ecstatic expressions of the "more" which love by nature freely gives, Brunner and other writers on the subject frequently speak as if "heedless" love were really "headless" in its unconcern for persons' relation to things or for their rightful claims and counterclaims. But this is the fault of Brunner's I-Thou philosophy of existential encounter, resulting in an unsupportable abstraction of persons from their relationships in actual life. If faith discovers no such person to love, and if a reasonable justice discovers no such person upon whom to bestow his due, then *in medias res* love impinges upon justice in a dynamic, and possibly a transforming, way—whenever the person overshadows the things that belong to him and overshadows also the impersonal institutional relationships to which he belongs.

This, in fact, has already happened in Brunner's own analysis of justice. His also is a love-transformed understanding of justice. There is no other way to explain the difference between what he says "natural justice" requires and what Aristotle would probably have said. Perhaps the inequalities provided by wartime food rationing for expectant mothers and for those who do strenuous labor in comparison with the rest of the population can be brought under Aristotle's proportional justice with its wise adjustment to differences in contribution.[70] But in his most extended illustration—the weak, crippled old lady who "deserves" to be given her coat in violation of the chance order, and abstractly equal order, of the line of people waiting in front of the check room—Brunner understands proportionate justice as providing for inequalities of *need* and not of contribution.[71] What is this but love, immanent within justice, transcendently directing, transforming and extending what justice requires?

Moreover, it is in the midst of discussing the Christian understanding of *justice* and equality (*not love*) that Brunner declares, "The Christian principle of the dignity of the person is unconditionally personal," and in the same paragraph he grounds this in God's address to every man as a concrete, unique Thou.[72] It is therefore impossible to understand him to mean with utmost seriousness what he says when he writes that "justice is not concerned with the person, but with that share of something which is derived from the quality of being a person." [73] Or rather, granting that this reference of justice to a person's share in things is a valid index to its meaning, this is by no means sufficient even in Brunner's thought to hold love dualistically apart or to prevent it from manifesting a transforming effect upon justice. Love has something to do with increasing the value of the currency of justice which circulates in the world of systems; and Brunner's own reflection upon the problems of justice is already reflection within a parenthesis drawn by Christ. The only thing that remains to be said is that if this had been quite consciously a main theme of his book, then transformism might have driven beyond *minimal,* primal rights to maximizing the needs of the person which should be given the name of rights; and it might have radically altered the conclusions the author draws regarding the "inequalities" of men, which as it stands are based too much on a static view of what nature makes evident providence has ordained.

It has frequently been asserted that *Justice and the Social Order* is atypical among the ethical writings of Emil Brunner; and this has been explained by the author's concern, under the pressure of the crisis that bears the name of the modern totalitarian state, to elaborate a clear concept of justice to which all reasonable and morally sensitive men, and not Christians alone, may repair. Brunner's book on justice does seem to resemble more closely the Roman Catholic theory of natural law than was the case in his earlier definitive analysis of Christian social ethics in terms of the "orders of creation" in *The Divine Imperative.* In that work, only the natural justice of marriage seemed clearly knowable; while with respect to the other orders, such as economic or political life, *what* we should do in them seemed to be so refracted by sinfulness that we cannot know very much beforehand about what ought to be done, but must await God's particular command. In the book on justice, political justice seems as clear as before the good of marriage was said to be.

More than this development in Brunner's analysis of the social order (and its norm of justice) may be observed to have taken place between the writing of these two books. It is much more important for us to notice that Brunner is far more of a dualist in his later work, and that in *The Divine Imperative* there was much more indication of the role of love (or our response to God's Command) in transforming the orders. This is a question of the relation *between* love and justice (or the orders), and not alone a question of the meaning of justice. It goes without saying that these two may be related questions; but they are not the same, even if (as seems likely) it could be established that the more discernment of static struc-

tures of justice the less amenable a Christian social theory will be to penetration and reformation by redemptive love. It is a striking fact that when
Brunner was less articulate about justice he was more of a transformist in
his social ethics. In any case, in our pursuit of the meaning of the conversionist motif, a study of *The Divine Imperative* will prove most
rewarding, for this great work was timely when it appeared and it remains
definitive.

Throughout this work, Brunner speaks of *Das Gebot* (God's Command:
love) and *die Schöpfungsordnungen* (the orders of creation, natural orders,
created orders). The latter differ from traditional natural law concepts in
that "we only know the Divine Creation as it has been marred by sin. . . .
We know them as means by which the divine wisdom *compels* men to live
in community." [74] They are presuppositions of mankind's present historical existence, but they "still cannot be described as belonging to the
created or natural order, because they only have any meaning owing to
the fact of sin." [75] They refer not to "the order created by God" but to
"the order created by God in its broken condition due to sin." [76] The
suggestion immediately springs to mind that the ambiguity of using the
terms "created" or "natural" with such a meaning perhaps had better be
removed by calling these "sinful orders"; and this suggestion would not be
incorrect. However, this expression would indicate that the orders are
determined in their nature by our human condition and not by the
divine action. Therefore, a preferable way to summarize Brunner's meaning in a concept would be to call the orders "orders of preservation" or
"orders of providence" or of God's merciful governance of a fallen world.
The orders are "garments of skin" (Gen. 3:21). These terms are not only
useful intellectual tools for grasping the actual content or structure of the
orders. They also, far more than "creation" or "sin," set our views in
motion toward the goal of God's purpose in preserving and governing
the world, toward redemption; and this is the opening for a greater
emphasis upon transforming and redeeming the various orders in the
world than we have found to be the case in Brunner's later writings.

Although it would be wrong to speak of "dualism" in connection with
The Divine Imperative, there is of course a real "duality" or "polarity"
here between the Command and the orders.* There is, one might say,
a fruitful tension, within limits yet to be specified. Brunner is not likely to
fall into Tillich's error of supposing that throughout centuries of time
human language has in practice used two such terms as "justice" and
"love" for such closely related meanings yet without men being aware
that in actual fact the words are so nearly synonymous. The orders are
also always, because of sin, spheres in which the love that is possible in

---

* The term "dualism" should be removed, despite Brunner's explicit statement that
"there certainly *is* an insoluble dualism between the law of the orders and the
commandment of love" (*op. cit.,* p. 222).

personal relations has been "refracted"; and consequently they are places where men find themselves, for love's sake, obliged in ways different from what love alone would require.

We may expect, then, that Brunner will dwell upon the theme of love "between the lines" provided by God's preservative orders and beyond a man's "official" function in them. ". . . These orders do not obey the logic of faith or of love, but the logic of the human and rational (and that always means also sinful) positing of an end." [77] ". . . The 'orders,' as the *Lex* in an imperfect and sinful world, can only perform their service if they are understood and used in their own legal spirit; it is also true that it is nonsense to apply the Sermon on the Mount as an ideal law." [78] "Life in the 'official' orders, to perform its service of the maintenance of order, must be of coarser stuff than the life which consists in the relations between one person and another." [79] Brunner even goes so far as to say that

> . . . The Christian believer must, as it were, first of all *forget all he ever knew* about the meaning of love, in order that he may help to protect and to further the life of these "orders" themselves *in accordance with their own logic.* For although these orders are necessary *for the sake of love,* most decidedly the behaviour they require is not the kind which we would expect to mete out to our fellow-man in love, if we were dealing simply with two individuals.[80]

However, the qualification contained in the words "as it were" in this quotation is by no means negligible; and even more important are the words "first of all," for along with this first task, as we shall see, there is a second task which his faith and love sets before the Christian in the orders. Still Brunner emphasizes that true, unrefracted love expresses itself only in "personal dealings." The judge, for example, who ought in his official capacity to condemn the criminal, should "allow the accused, in some way or another, to feel that he has not personally broken off all relations with him, but that in the spirit of solidarity he bears his guilt with him, and 'believes' in him, that is, that he remembers his divine destiny." [81] The "dualism" still contained in the "duality" between love and justice again is stressed in the following summary statement: "At all times I must myself decide what are the respective claims upon me of love and of the order, at this particular moment; or rather, it would be better to say, not what 'love' and the 'order' say I ought to do, but what kind of service the command to love my neighbor requires from me both in my 'official capacity' and in my personal and direct relation with my brother." [82]

As the next step in analysis of Brunner's ethics of the orders, it is necessary to probe more deeply into their nature and purpose, and at the same time to formulate the "first duty" [83] to which men are called in them. "As *real* orders, the Creator uses them to preserve the world; He uses them in particular as a firm bond which checks the otherwise inevitable tendency of humanity to disintegrate into atoms." As the Preserver of the sinful world, God preserves it through obedience to these orders, and not through *direct* obedience to the commandment of love.[84] By recognizing and adjusting ourselves to the orders we receive from God's hands the *only* "means by which sinful humanity keeps the final consequences of sin at bay: that is, disorganization and chaos." [85] By a positive acceptance precisely on the spot of the space and time of historical institutions into which we have been called into existence by our Creator and Preserver, our "*first* (although not the highest) duty" is to engage responsibly with Him in the work of maintaining the dyke which the present existing order places in the way of the irruption of chaos. [86]

These statements make abundantly clear why it is proper to call the spheres of secular life "orders of preservation." At the same time, the accent placed upon preservation (in its correlation with sinfulness) unnecessarily obscures the more positive purpose Brunner believes also to be expressed through the orders. This positive purpose need not yet refer to redemption as the final goal toward which God preserves the world. There is also the more positive purpose indicated by the word "creation" in its unambiguous meaning which comprises, along with guarding against the unlimited ravishments of sin, a dual good furnished mankind by the orders. Although there may be some inadequacy in Brunner's general description of the nature and purpose of the orders at the outset too much in terms of restraint, this is not the case in his specific treatment of any of them. For example, in the economic order God intends to maintain human life and (in a different sense from the above meaning) to "preserve" the world, and He therefore commands man to work and engage in economic activity: this is emphasized as well as the "dark side" of the economic order.[87] Perhaps there is a certain tendency here to correlate the good of the orders mainly with sinfulness; and this is corrected—even overcorrected—in Brunner's later writings upon the subject of man's political and other cultural activities which have clear natural justice as their norm. For this reason, it is not only sinfulness but the intact and impenetrable structure of justice which refracts love in his later writings. Because of the justification which justice contains in itself, the later book is less open to "love transforming justice" than the orders are. This is not surprising, since to speak of God's governance of a sinful world as the setting in which the Christian's total response is to be made obviously requires an articulation of the ethical meaning of conversion and of redemption. To this theme we now turn, as every man must within the orders.

The "second duty" that is placed upon the Christian in every order of life is to "ignore the existing orders, and inaugurate a new line of action in view of the coming Kingdom of God." [88] Brunner dwells upon this theme—which is so evidently the ethics of social redemption and the transformation of the social order—at such length and with such passionate conviction that it may almost be said that whoever finds in *The Divine Imperative* only a static ethic of creation or a pessimistic view of sinfulness is himself probably one of those fanatics and sentimental enthusiasts whom Brunner rightly opposes. All that Brunner asks of him is that an action which has in view the actual transformation of society be located in this world and not some other; and for this a man must take care that his zeal or idealism is not a matter of high-minded rebellion against the governor and preserver of the existing world.

The religious grounds for adjusting ourselves to the orders as well as for introducing some new line of action into them is, of course, the indivisibility of response to God's action in creation, preservation and redemption. If God's preservation through the orders is inseparable from his redemptive purpose in them, then man's own action is set in motion from simply upholding things as they are to aligning them more to accord with God's Command (love). "God does not preserve the world simply in order to preserve it, but in order that He may perfect it." [89] Men who believe that they should will the good that God wills know also that, beyond acceptance, "He also demands from us something new." [90] They must not only adapt themselves; they must also resist and protest.[91] This means not only inwardly, but outwardly as well. No man has a "right to close his eyes or shut his heart to anything by means of which love is injured by the 'orders.'" [92] Here plainly love must do more than change itself "entirely" into the small coin of justice; or submit piously to the way in which someone may tell us God does his strange work of preserving the world. Since there is a teleologically dynamic connection—running backward, so to speak—between redemption, preservation and creation, Christian faith and love as qualities of the wills of men should also manifest a dynamic, redirecting and transforming influence upon the apparently given necessities of the orders of society and upon any of the standards of natural justice which may commend themselves to the minds of men. Love is immanent within justice and within the orders: "the first thing necessary is not to alter the vessel but to fill it with the new content." But love immanent within the orders also will sometimes require that they be shattered and reconstructed: ". . . there are vessels which are contrary to this content of love, and it is quite possible that such vessels ought to be smashed." [93]

Moreover, the orders, even when in the main they are to be accepted, are variable and open to improvement. The only limit upon this which the Christian should have in mind is that, for the preservation of the world, an order is worth something only if it is real, and not merely ideal. Any order is better than none at all. But this need not be interpreted conservatively. It may mean only that a man should be concerned about the "practical possibility" [94] of any "new line of action" he plans to introduce. Finally, his estimation of the practical possibility of effecting reformation need not be weighted heavily on the conservative side. The orders are variable not only so far as we are concerned, but also in themselves they are undergoing change. Therefore

> . . . This question of "possibility" is not a pre-determined actuality. It is so at a particular moment; but it is not so when we take into account a longer period of time, during which many changes, both inward and outward, may take place. Even then, however, we ought conscientiously to try to discover whether we can reasonably expect a definite change within this period or not, or even whether we ourselves may be in a position to effect this change, *by means of which that which was previously impossible becomes possible.*[95]

The judge, therefore, who in his official capacity must condemn the criminal, has at the same time much more to do than "to allow the accused, some way or another, to feel that he has not personally broken off all relations with him." [96] He may also be required, without abandoning his position in the present legal scheme, to work for the abolition of capital punishment; or in his daily life as judge and citizen to contribute to the improvement of the administration of justice so that what "was previously impossible becomes possible."

At the very least, Brunner is saying that love not only interpenetrates justice as, as it were, a static vessel, to keep it just; but also that love *keeps* justice, and the orders, *dynamic.* This itself is a good deal more than he later was concerned to point out in his book on justice. He clearly means also that love, which is the Christian's response to God's redemptive purpose, *transforms* the orders and all their schemes of justice. "Just as faith must prove its reality by searching for opportunities in which love can have free play, within the limits imposed by the official order, so also faith must prove its reality by searching for ways of making this official order itself more just, more humane, *more full of the spirit of love,* without unfitting it for the purpose for which it exists as an order." [97] This is the meaning to be read from Brunner when he says that the Sermon on the Mount "is and remains the *guiding standard* even for life within the orders," [98] and when he writes that the part faith and love play in the orders is "not constitutive but regulative." [99] The guidance, the regulation, is not set dualistically apart from the strange work of the orders, but is transformingly related to them. Indeed, it might be better to say simply that love is not the *only* response that is *constitutive* of the Christian's life in the orders, since this remains indivisibly a part of his total relation to God, including with his response to redemption a response also to creation and preservation.

Now, throughout the chapters of *The Divine Imperative* we have been examining, Brunner everywhere asserts that as reasonable, moral beings (and not alone as Christians) we can "know what is due to man as man," that "it is not necessary to be a Christian to see that a certain order is unjust," and that "the orders themselves are the subject of a *purely rational knowledge*," although only the Christian recognizes in them the creative, preserving and redemptive word of God.[100] It is a mistake, therefore, to regard the concept of justice in *Justice and the Social Order* as a novel development in his thought. The wrong turn taken by Brunner— if it be such—was not that he attempted to answer the need for a fuller articulation of the concept of natural justice already contained in his ethics of the orders; but that in doing so he abstracted this from the context of life in the orders. This meant abstraction from the totality of God's action as it is viewed by the Christian. As a consequence justice and love, or nature (creation) and redemption (love), fell into realms more apart than in the ethics of the orders; and the transformist motif which was so powerful in *The Divine Imperative* was replaced by dualism. The result was that the impulse to improve the social order now had as its sole standard the concept of justice; no longer was there a strong movement in the direction of redemptive love, since at the immigration station on the border of the social order this was "entirely" changed into another currency. Thus, the promise and the accomplishment of Brunner's great book on ethics was withdrawn: namely, that in Christian ethics— no matter what issue is being discussed—"*every* ethical consideration is . . . connected with the *whole* idea of God." [101]

Of course, Brunner rightly opposes an ethic of redemption or the transformist motif or an ethic of "the kingship of Christ," if this is supposed to mean that one "new line of action" effectively introduced and significantly transforming the social order can simply be added to another in a continuous line toward final perfection of this world. "Love transforming the orders and redirecting natural justice" does not mean an optimistic hope for the gradual penetration of the world by the Kingdom of God. But the proper answer to this extreme is not simply to reaffirm, as Brunner recently has done, the more unqualified dualism of his book on justice. There is more to be said from his own earlier point of view than that "in the world and in the State Christ must reign in a different way from that in which He rules in the Church." [102] A *maximum discrimen* between "the direct Kingship of Christ through the Gospel, in the Church" and "the indirect Kingship of Christ through the Law in the world" [103] is not the only way to avoid illusions. Another way Brunner himself supplied in his understanding of life in the orders in which the "indirect Kingship of Christ" or the "regulative" function of love as a "guiding standard" had bearing upon every possible reconstruction of the social order that would not unfit it for serving as a real order.

In the latest stage of his thought as a dualist, Brunner demands that theologians who offer what he regards as a mistaken "Christological" ethics say plainly "what a legal system derived from norms based on the message of the Cross, would be like"; and he asks rhetorically, "What for instance does it mean for a lawyer, who is working on a new penal code, to acknowledge the Kingship of Christ?" [104] In *The Divine Imperative* he himself gave an answer to these questions in everything he wrote about the Christian's "second duty" in the orders, not in terms of a "Christian state" or a "Christian code of law" but to the effect that the lawyer himself must determine precisely in what measure or way the existing order may be altered in the direction love requires and in response to the divine Command. The answer to any mistaken Christological gradualism is to connect *every* ethical consideration with the *whole* idea of God, that is to say, with man's "first duty" of ensuring that a just, endurable and just endurable order may be upheld for the preservation of human life. The answer to Brunner's dualism is again to connect *every* ethical consideration with the *whole* idea of God, this time with man's "second duty" of searching for ways of making the secular orders not only more just but more humane and more full of the spirit of love without unfitting them for the purpose for which they exist as orders. Best of all it would be to refrain from calling either one or the other of these tasks (justice or love) man's "first" or "second" duty under his covenant with God and with man, in the time afforded him by God's patience and in the place where he lives in the social order.

Eight

Jacques Maritain and Edmond Cahn:
The Egypt of the Natural Law

When General Patton's troops first burst in upon the concentration camps and cremation furnaces, his first action was—before cleaning anything up—to march through them the burghers and burgomasters of the nearby German towns. Patton's assumption was that, no matter what the political environment and a decade of "education" had done to the people of Germany, the human essence might still be stirred within them when faced with the actual evil that had been done. There is some evidence of the tendencies of human nature in the fact that tyranny always assigns at least *two* soldiers to carry out acts of special brutality. By knowledge through their own immediate *dis*inclination or aversion when they are faced concretely by acts of cruelty or genocide, the prohibition of the natural law reveals itself to the minds of men. Decision-making is then a matter of reflection and conceptualization *bound* to this knowledge through inclination or disinclination, and always has before it certain specific states of affairs which would be incompatible with human nature and human ends.

"Suppose a completely new case or situation, unheard of in human history: suppose, for instance, that what we now call *genocide* were as new as that very name. . . . That possible behaviour will face the human essence as incompatible with its general ends and innermost dynamic structure: that is to say, as prohibited by natural law. . . . Which does not mean that the prohibition was part of the essence of man as I know not what metaphysical feature eternally inscribed in it—nor that it was a notion recognized from the start by the conscience of humanity." [1]

It is commonly agreed that men and women have the right to the free exercise of their sexual powers.[2] Without raising the question how mature sex life should be freely regulated—with all the questions of cultural relativity which this involves—we say that rape is wrong, and that the use of slaves as studs and the herding of women into barracks for the purpose of producing children by selected Nazi soldiers were horrible crimes. What sexuality means for the mature human being is somehow violated if freedom cannot be expressed in this connection.

A child has the right to be treated as still a child, i.e., as unfree, even when seemingly consenting to sexual relations. When legislatures determine the statutory "age of consent," and when juries and judges help to make law by their decisions of guilt or innocence before such statutes, of course they are in part exercising a culturally determined reason. The degree of responsible freedom and maturity assumed (or too early forced upon) adolescent girls in our society today as compared to twenty-five or fifty years ago is a significant cultural change which should obviously be taken into account. This maturity means, in all probability, that eighteen is now too old for the age of consent in the state of California; and incidentally that the jury acted wisely and justly a few years ago in acquitting a celebrated movie actor of the charge of statutory rape, even though he may well have been technically guilty of the charge. But important as the decision may have been as to who was the aggressor and who the victim when a seventeen-year-old girl paid him a visit in his shower room (thereby disclosing to both inclination and reason the primacy of another sort of natural law), all this does not obviate the fact that a child still has a right to be treated as a child, and her "voluntary" consent at too early an age should be regarded as forced upon her by the male. In seeking to determine some new age-figure or in tempering the application of existing law, legislative and judicial reason simply ask, "When is a child still a child?" Even if this is partly a cultural question, the question itself would be of no import at all were we incompetent to know something of the nature, meaning and rights of human childhood and of mature human freedom in its sexual expression. If there is a need for some new answer to the question posed by our cultural situation in this "century of the adolescent," or for answering it in particular cases that come before the courts, this rests in part upon the moral certainty that a child has a right to be regarded as unfree and an adult person the right to be free in the exercise of sexual powers. "That possible behaviour"—of a fifty-year-old man obtaining the apparent voluntary consent of a nine-year-old girl—"faces the human essence" and discloses through fundamental disinclination in us its incompatibility with the well-being of the person; and we feel that full justice may not have been done when the man goes free on appeal because the indictment was not properly drawn. The possible "justice" of even such an outcome is sustained only by the countervailing knowledge through disinclination—dimly possessed by most people, with larger awareness by those who know something of legal history—when they remember concretely and imaginatively those possible forms of behavior and predicaments of the individual from which have arisen the protections of "due process." [3]

I know the man who was the first Christian missionary to live among the Dyak people in the interior of the island of Borneo. He and a British civil servant were the only white men there among tribes who only recently had advanced beyond the stage of head hunters. Another quaint custom, still practiced, was sexual hospitality; and so these two men—the missionary and the civil servant—as they made their rounds from village to village were made welcome by the chief of each village by the offer of one of his wives for the night. The civil servant accepted the gesture, and more than the gesture; my friend did not. I mention this fact to call attention not to a noble example of the virtues of Western man with centuries of the positive law and religious instruction behind him; but rather to what then began to happen behind the brow of the native chieftain. For, lo, a greater than Solomon was there! He corrected the *inequality* in that state of affairs by ceasing to offer his women to the British civil servant; whereupon, as is usual, the missionary was called in and given a lecture on the harm he was doing by contributing to the rapid disintegration of native *mores,* and told to mend his ways. What stirred in the mind of the chief, however darkly, was the sense that the unequal better be set straight. Indeed, in this noble savage there was the mind of a Rousseau with its insight that the law, to be true law, must be general in essence and in application as well as (and even if not) general in its source; and that the wise ruler or legislator will see to it that "the conditions are the same for all." 4

What will have to happen, we may ask, to incline a mind so endowed to the conclusion that the woman also should not be excepted from generality and equality of application? What would cause this chieftain to believe that males should not extend hospitality to other males *by means of* their wives, or convince him that generality of application is needed with regard to males and females alike so that no one will be tempted to make social conditions or practices more burdensome for others than he is willing to have rebound upon himself? Perhaps the traumatic experience of having one of his wives seize the initiative and offer him for the night on the occasion of the visit of the three-hundred-pound queen of a neighboring matriarchal tribe! Perhaps some imported religious doctrine that God's justice includes all alike; or perhaps simply through the long course of glacial social change. In any case, these factors will only have freed man's knowledge through inclination or congeniality for more adequate expression.

Social workers in the past have been faced with the fact that precisely the people who would most benefit by it refuse to come to birth control clinics for instruction. Perhaps in a short time now this problem will at last be solved; and it will be possible, by a tidy piece of social engineering, to sterilize a whole population by means of an additive in the water supply and to provide that people who want to do so, and are eligible, may go to parenthood stations and receive a fertility potion. "That possible behaviour will face the human essence as incompatible with its general ends and innermost dynamic structure."

Consider that possible behavior—in fact, that actual state of affairs, those concrete conditions of fact and of law which may allow a person racially an Oriental to be defrauded of his already existing marriage by the laws of Virginia prohibiting miscegenation;[5] and similar statutes of the state of Mississippi which some years ago permitted a litigant in a case involving some property matter to win his point in contention by digging back into the past and showing that the opposing party was partly descended from that enterprising Negro who during the Civil War organized the Free State of Jones (County, Mississippi) and tried to join the Union. Do we not know that in these situations and decisions, because of natural tendencies of the human being as such, natural justice was frustrated; that the time may not yet be ripe for realizing a greater justice; but that no matter how compact the decisions favoring the constitutionality of such state regulation of marriage[6] men cannot forever on a pretext put asunder those whom nature and nature's God have joined together?

I

The foregoing cases are examples of contextual decision in the matter of equality, the right to life, the freedom of mature people in the use of their sexual capacities and the unfreedom of children acknowledged by legal definitions of the age of consent, and the freedom of marriage. They also illustrate natural justice fundamentally at work in moral and legal decision. The proposition that ethical judgment in these cases confirms the theory of natural law in jurisprudence has to meet the objection that, to the contrary, this theory affirms that ethical conclusions may only be deduced logically from prior abstract principles. This stereotype about the meaning of the natural law must itself be examined and rejected. Jacques Maritain's philosophy of law, for example, itself mounts an attack upon the rationalistic, deductive theory of natural law, or against such misinterpretations of it. Especially is this the case in his latest writings, in which natural justice is said to be known only through inclination, and not primarily through reason. His view of fundamental moral and legal decision, then, makes this a matter of judgment rendered in the context of particular cases or in the midst of concrete affairs. The natural law is, therefore, essentially what Edmond Cahn refers to as the "sense of injustice" or as our competence to decide rightly in "the prism of the case." Such a view of the natural law has been insufficiently taken into account in all discussions of it.

This will be the main contention of this chapter. As a subordinate point, it will also be shown that the rigidity and absolutism usually associated with natural law theory must be attributed rather to the conviction on the part of Roman Catholics that revelation has "republished" the entire natural law and thereby made our knowledge of it certain and exact. It follows that a possible Protestant view of the fundamental nature of moral and legal decisions based on natural justice (or law) has a great deal in common with the jurisprudential understanding of judicial reasoning and moral decision in legal cases. Both accent personal responsibility for making decisions without submitting the matter to any ecclesiastical or sociological positivism. Both are confident that the good may be discovered in and by a free verdict through unlimited discussion with decision-makers of the past and present who have been confronted by similar or related cases.

II

It is true, of course, that the rationalistic, deductive interpretation of natural law has an ancient lineage. Belief in the natural law has been, for most of its history, coextensive with the belief that not very many particulars (even if more than one) are necessary for the mind to be able to abstract from them their common essence or their substantial form. The rise and the ascendancy of the theory of natural law in the West was always associated with the conviction that man has other ways of knowing than staring at the bare facts, or looking at once on both sides of the Pyrenees. Thus, rationalism and not empiricism in the modern sense has been the philosophical framework in which natural law interpretations of ethics, politics and law have seemed persuasive. This viewpoint expresses the confidence that, although there is no content in the mind that was not first in the senses, what the intellect takes from the senses is in fact the true and unchanging nature of the sensed reality.* It expresses

* It is often remarked that in the theory of natural law norms are derived by "an inductive generalization from facts" (John A. Hutchison, *The Two Cities.* Garden City, New York: Doubleday and Co., 1957, p. 175), and this viewpoint is supposed to be refuted when the specific facts, either of human behavior or of human judgment and decision, do not seem to yield conclusions which are true everywhere and always. Nothing could be further from the truth. Instead of interpreting natural law as an empirical generalization, we should remember its confidence that reason has the power to know, from one or a few particulars, the essence of a thing; and that, in the rational-deductive system of natural law, "first principles" were thought to be native to the mind, never *derived* from if also never apart from experienced particulars.

Far from factual differences in the behavior of peoples, or their decisional disagreements, at once ruling out the validity of the natural law, it might be said that men cannot even *disagree* in their judgments, they can only ejaculate, unless the human mind is competent to do more than simply retain and generalize from what the moving finger of experience writes upon it, or if it simply transmutes personal tastes or the existing preferences of society into statements about the true and the good and the just. Concerning tastes there can certainly be endless disputing; but there cannot reasonably be real disagreement or error. The spies must actually have penetrated the land beyond before they can bring back different reports about the quality of the grapes that grow there.

the confidence that we know enough about the nature of man to say that
he has a natural right to personal liberty, a right to pursue the perfection of his moral and rational being, a right to freedom of investigation
and discussion, a right to family life not subject in its entirety to political considerations, a right to friendship and free assemblage, a right to
an unmolested pursuit of his eternal End. Affirm any of these propositions
and you are in some sense asserting the natural law, whatever happens to
be your theory of knowledge. What is impossible is to assert them, and
at the same time take it all back by declaring that they are only "value
judgments." A moratorium should be declared on the use of that expression: they are simply *judgments,* and the law of noncontradiction at
least requires us not to contradict ourselves. A judgment about the good
for man cannot be both rendered and not rendered at the same time. If it
is rendered, and supposed to be within the competence of reason,
reference is somehow made to the nature of man, whatever account may
be given of how this is known. Entailed in any serious utterance about
the rights of man (unless of course one wishes to base the rights and the
dignity of man on revelation) is some conception of human nature, and
so of the natural law. Nothing hinders such judgment being uttered
in medias res in a personal moral dilemma or in judicial decision. Nature
and nature's God preside over the deliberations of ordinary people, our
courts and our legislatures, as much as over meetings of the American
Catholic Philosophical Association.

The rational-deductive scheme of natural law ought perhaps to be held
in mind as we follow Maritain in departing from it. Here one thinks especially of the notion, both in Aristotle and in St. Thomas, that be-
havioral science is based on a practical, deductive syllogism comparable to
the theoretical syllogism in the pure sciences. Reason has by the power of
synderesis the capacity for (axiomatic) "first principles" of practical conduct. From this capacity comes our knowledge of the universal truth
stated in the major premise of every practical syllogism. Specifically
identified as the image of God in man, this pure capacity for practical
first principles supplies (it appears necessary to claim) those principles of
the natural law, such as "Do no murder," *from which* all moral reasoning proceeds and *to which* reason could not hope to attain by any sort of
faculty for generalization from facts. These principles may be expressed as
universal propositions, an entire list of them; and as laws of reason they
function as the major premises in a deductive moral science. Moreover,
the major premise itself was believed to be a *proprium principia* (a proper
or specific kind of universal moral truth, such as "Do no murder") derived within pure reason from the more fundamental *principia communia*
of the natural law ("Do nobody evil").* Then in addition to all this

* Maritain calls this "the preamble and principles of the natural law." See below.
Also cf. p. 218 n. for Aquinas' view that the love commandments of the New Testament
belong among the *prima et communia praecepta* of the natural law.

theoretical knowledge, there is in "practical reason" a capacity "apt to do." The virtue or right habitual disposition of this faculty means that we know how to classify cases properly, making the judgment that "*This* is a case of murder." Thus prudence or practical wisdom supplies the minor premise of the syllogism needed before any conclusion can be drawn. After all, what is disputed in law courts is never whether murder is wrong, but whether this is or is not a case of murder, and to what degree. Thus, from some general or universal truth combined with practical wisdom in interpreting the facts, there follows as a logical conclusion: "*This* is wrong." Some such view of the contents of reason was voiced by John Cook, chief prosecutor of King Charles I, in answer to the question, By what law was the king condemned? "By the unanimous consent," he replied, "of all rational men in the world, written in every man's heart with the pen of a diamond in capital letters." [7]

III

Now, Maritain mounts an attack upon the extreme rationalistic versions of the natural law, or against erroneous rationalistic interpretations of it. Putting aside the question whether he is actually revising the theory of natural law or only correcting false views of it propounded more by its detractors than its proponents or more in the seventeenth and eighteenth centuries than in the medieval period, we need to examine carefully the philosophy of law expressed by M. Maritain.

St. Paul's statement that the "Gentiles who have not the law do by nature what the law requires" and "what the law requires is written on their hearts" (Rom. 2:14, 15) was the bridge by which Stoic and Roman conceptions of law crossed over into Christian thought.[8] "This metaphor itself"—of a law written in the heart—"has been responsible," Maritain writes in his book on *The Rights of Man and Natural Law*,[9] "for a great deal of damage, causing natural law to be represented as a ready-made code rolled up within the conscience of each one of us, which each one of us has only to unroll, and of which all men should naturally have an equal knowledge." * If this manner of speaking is retained at all, it must be severely modified by remembering that the law "written" on the heart can only mean "in the hidden depths, as hidden from us as our own heart," as hidden from us as our own essence. Plainly, then, the natural law is not from the first a content of rational consciousness; nor as such is it known to every man.

When we ask what positive position Maritain advances in this early work of his; when we ask, What then does belong among the articles with

---

* Maritain speaks also of "the bulk of contemporary jurists (particularly those of the positivist school) who, by the way, are really attacking a false idea of natural law, and in exterminating it, exterminate only a man of straw, drawn from the pages of cheap-jack textbooks" (*op. cit.*, p. 59; and cf. pp. 80-81).

which the mind is naturally furnished? we have to attend to his express statement that "the only practical knowledge all men have naturally and infallibly in common is that we must do good and avoid evil." [10]* Note well that he does not say that man naturally has *any* native *knowledge* of good and evil, but only that he should do the good and avoid evil whenever and however he comes to distinguish them. And although Maritain uses the term "practical *knowledge*" for the inward call of conscience to do the good and avoid evil should these become known, and insofar as we know them, this itself is surely not a content of consciousness but a bent of the mind toward the true and the good assumed by both classical and medieval authors to be a permanent *nisus* or tendency of the soul of man. This is not even a little bit of a scroll. However, there may be a vestige of the rationalistic framework which appears when Maritain speaks of the awareness that we should do the good as "the *preamble* and the principle of natural law." [11] This metaphor does suggest that there is a little bit of a constitution—the preamble—written within; but surely such representations are not to be taken literally.

As for the content of the natural law itself, this no man natively possesses. Knowledge of the law arises later; it is acquired. How? I think the answer is: in the course of active reflection upon man in the context of moral, social and legal decisions. Of course, Maritain (since he does not want to discuss nonsense) takes for granted that "there is a human nature" the same in all of us and that reason can discover the order according to which the human will must act if the natural ends of the human being are not to be violated.[12] But "knowing that there is a law does not necessarily mean knowing what that law is." [13] Knowing what that law is, is not already inscribed on the mind; it arises from acts of the reason gathering from experienced particulars their essential natures. "Natural law," Maritain writes, "deals with the rights and duties which follow from the first principle: 'do good and avoid evil,' in a *necessary* manner, and *from the simple fact that man is man,* nothing else being taken into account." [14] Or it is "the ensemble of things to do and not to do which follow therefrom [i.e., from the preamble or principle: do good, avoid evil] in a *necessary* fashion," etc.[15]

There is, of course, a remainder of the rationalistic viewpoint in Maritain's claim that knowledge of the natural law first arises in a *rational* apprehension of the essential nature of man; and there is a remainder of the deductive practical syllogism in the reference to something "following in a *necessary* manner." These two points should be especially

---

* "It ought to be remembered that the classical conception of 'nature' was of an active, creative force, so that the 'nature' of a thing became an innate tendency toward the realization of a certain ideal of the thing." Edward S. Corwin, *The "Higher Law" Background of American Constitutional Law* (Ithaca, N.Y.: Cornell University Press, 1955. Great Seal Books), p. 10, n. 23.

noticed, for both are abandoned in Maritain's later writing. It may be questioned whether in ethical and legal reasoning any conclusion ever follows in a *necessary* manner from presupposed principles. In the treatise we are now examining, Maritain still maintained that conclusions do so follow, in judgments as to the natural law, and as well in the *jus gentium*—the Law of Nations, or the common law of civilization—which Maritain defines as having to do with "the rights and duties which follow from the first principle in a *necessary* manner, but this time supposing certain conditions of fact," [16] such as the universal facts of social relationships and civilized life. *Jus gentium* means the "natural or unwritten law itself as exceeding the very sphere of nature and as particularized by the conditions of social life." [17] It may, in short, be questioned whether throughout the process of decision, logical necessity should not be replaced by contingency, as in Maritain's definition of the nature of the civil law and the way it arises from the judgments of legislators and people: "*Positive law* (statute law), or the body of laws in force in a given community, deals with the rights and the duties which follow from the first principle, but in a *contingent* manner," [18] in view of the very specific conditions of fact, the particular customs and institutions that have to be taken into account. Maritain admits that "there are *imperceptible transitions* (at least from the point of view of *historical experience*) between natural law, the Law of Nations and positive law." [19] What is gained by claiming that, from the point of view of logic or concepts, the transitions are wider, more perceptible or more logically necessary than in fact they are?

Indeed, it is difficult to see how anything can follow in a necessary fashion from a principle so vague as "do good and avoid evil." The case is rather that, given a mind that is "in order to" the good, knowledge of the natural law arises *from* the simple fact that man is man, or *from* what reason can comprehend of man's nature and ends, no specific conditions of fact as yet being taken into account. Nothing is deduced from prior principle, necessarily or otherwise.

In a later book, *Man and the State*, [20] Jacques Maritain carries forward his revision of traditional natural law notions, or he expounds still more radically his rejection of excessively rationalistic interpretations. He declares boldly: ". . . The *only* reason on which natural law depends is divine Reason." [21] This means not only that in the order of being the law of nature depends upon the being and will of God, the natural law upon the Eternal Law of Him who rules the entire community of creation. It also means that, in the order of knowledge, the only reason which has an immediate apprehension of the natural law is the divine Reason. To the statement that the natural law is *within* the heart of man as his inmost essence is, Maritain now adds that this "precedes all formulation, and is even known to human reason *not* in terms of conceptual and rational knowledge." [22] To say that some crime is prohibited by the natural law does not mean that the prohibition is "part of the essence of man as I know not what metaphysical feature eternally inscribed in it," [23] nor that the prohibition first becomes known through the mind's capacity for rational abstraction. ". . . Human reason does not discover the regulations of natural law in an abstract and theoretical manner, as a series of geometrical theorems. Nay more, it does not discover them through the conceptual exercise of the intellect, or by way of rational knowledge." The mind is first notified of the fundamental demands of natural law through the guidance and pressure of the *inclinations* of human nature. The human being knows natural law by "knowledge *through inclination.*" [24]* Now, this puzzling expression at least wants to say that there is a kind of knowing which is not at bottom any sort of rational knowledge. This means that man's primal apprehension of the natural law, the first disclosure of essential human nature to him, is

> not clear knowledge through concepts and conceptual judgments; it is obscure, unsystematic, vital knowledge by connaturality or congeniality, in which the intellect, in order to bear judgment, consults and listens to the inner melody that the vibrating strings of abiding tendencies make present in the subject. [25]

* This interpretation of the law of nature is not, of course, the exclusive property of M. Maritain. Indeed St. Thomas has often been interpreted in this fashion. "Aquinas' approach to Natural Law is, then, by way of man's *basic drives or inclinations*. . . . [Man] con-naturally—that is, without any reasoning—judges that all those things to which he has a natural inclination are good and ought to be sought after and that their contraries are bad and should be avoided. . . . Natural Law could be defined as the *elementary demands expressed by a man's basic inclinations which are known connaturally*" (Thomas E. Davitt, S.J., "St. Thomas Aquinas and the Natural Law," in *Origins of the Natural Law Tradition*, ed. Arthur L. Harding, Dallas, Tex.: Southern Methodist University Press, 1954, pp. 30, 34, 36). Certainly the notion of connaturality belongs to Aquinas; and his was the classical view of the "nature" of a thing, from which he concluded that "Man has a natural urge to goodness" (*De Veritate*, 22, 7). But rational, not connatural, knowledge was the basis of his treatise on law; and he even used the syllogistic model when he wanted to say that not all of the fundamental principles of the law of nature are contained in the Decalogue: the love-commandments of Matt. 22:37 f. are the "prima et communia praecepta legis naturae, quae sunt per se nota rationi humanae," and the precepts of the Decalogue "are referred to these, as conclusions to general principles" (*Summa* I-II, Q. 100, a. 3, ad primum). Nevertheless, apart from how Aquinas ought to be read, it is clear that the present interpretation of natural law has not been sufficiently taken into account in discussions of the philosophy of law. Professor Jean Dabin of the University of Louvain also holds a position comparable to that of Maritain: ". . . The rule of human conduct that is called natural law is deduced from the nature of man *as it reveals itself in the basic inclinations of that nature* under the control of reason, independently of any formal intervention of any legislator whatsoever, divine or human" (*General Theory of Law* (1944) in *The Legal Philosophies of Lask, Radbruch and Dabin*, trans. K. Wilk, Cambridge, Mass.: Harvard University Press, 1950, 203, n. 7, italics mine).

Of course, to deserve the name of *law,* the natural law must be an order of reason; but this means an order of *Divine Reason. To us,* "the normality of functioning of human discloses itself by 'knowledge through inclination.' " [26]

This way of "knowing" the natural law in the course of actual decision in concrete contexts was illustrated by the cases at the opening of this chapter. It will assist our comprehension if we now sketch in the other chief bones in the anatomy of Maritain's revised treatise on law. For it needs to be pointed out that reason only comes into primacy when we pass to a discussion of *jus gentium.* In the first book the distinction between the natural law on the one hand and, on the other, *jus gentium* and positive law, consisted simply and solely in the fact that in the first instance nothing else was taken into account besides essential human nature while in the other types of law certain conditions of fact were said to be involved. But in the second book, the statements to this effect at the end of each of the three definitions are stricken off; and the difference between them becomes simply and solely the intervention of conceptual reason in the process of law-making. ". . . The law of nations, or better to say, the common law of civilization, differs from natural law because it is *known,* not through inclination, but through the *conceptual exercise of reason,* or through rational knowledge." [27] Or again he writes, interpreting St. Thomas, that "a precept which is *known through rational deduction, and as a conclusion conceptually inferred* from a principle of natural law, is part of *jus gentium.* The latter pertains to positive law more than to natural law precisely by virtue of the manner in which it is known and because of the intervention of human reason in the establishment of the precepts conceptually concluded." [28] These definitions do not include reflecting upon "conditions of fact" precisely because natural law, known through inclination, is also known only *in medias res,* in social contexts, or in the prism of actual cases.

Moreover, in accordance with the nonconceptual way in which natural law is said to be known to us, Maritain at the decisive point now no longer talks about conclusions following from prior principles. The law of nature precisely is *not* any sort of conceptual inference or conclusion. The most that can be said is that, while the *"propria principia* or specific precepts of Natural Law are *in no way conclusions rationally* deduced, they play in the practical realm a part *similar* to that of conclusions in the speculative realm." [29] Or again, "the *propria principia* of Natural Law are *like*[30] conclusions derived from *principia communia.*" Thus, "a precept which is *like* a conclusion derived from a principle of natural law but which in actual fact is *known through inclination, not through rational deduction,* is part of *natural law.*" [31] Why Maritain should have chosen still to say that the natural law is *like* a conclusion is difficult to understand, since these statements are made precisely in the context of telling us how *unlike* are *jus naturale* and *jus gentium* because of the intervention of conceptual reason in the case of the latter only.

Maritain's new formulation is never allowed to exert its full impact upon the grammar of deductive logic taken over from his previous book. At points more is so obviously required that one is tempted to attribute the failure simply to imperfect revision of the older text that was obviously still being used. For example, I have already pointed out the insignificance of speaking as if natural law were comprised of rights and duties (conclusions?) which "follow from the first principle: 'do good and avoid evil,' in a *necessary* manner, and *from the simple fact that man is man*." The last phrase is regularly stricken out in the second book, because formerly it was the bearer of the meaning, "and from rational knowledge of the nature of man as such." Yet the rest of the formula (about "necessarily following") still is repeated; and this, I suggest, is now meaningless. So Maritain writes: "Natural Law is the ensemble of things to do and not to do which follow therefrom [from: do good, avoid evil] in *necesssary* fashion" and "*natural law* deals with the rights and the duties which are connected in a *necessary* manner with the first principle: 'Do good and avoid evil.' " [32]* But strictly speaking, nothing *follows* from this principle, and of course nothing follows in a *necessary* manner." †

Finally, it is worth remarking that the "imperceptible transitions" from one sort of law to another, "at least from the point of view of historical experience," have become even more a matter of imperceptible transitions from one definition to another. So the actual nature of decision-making threatens to wreck the traditional scheme. In the first place, knowledge of the natural law no longer is a matter of reflecting upon essential human nature in abstraction from variable factual conditions and social relationships. Knowledge by connaturality, congeniality, inclination arises only vis-à-vis quite concrete conditions of fact. Judgments as to the fundamental law, quite as much as any other sort of law, are made only *in*

---

* The now ancient frame-story continues in Maritain's definitions of other types of law: ". . . *Jus gentium* or the common law of civilization deals, like natural law, with rights and duties which are connected with the first principle in a *necessary* manner," and "*Positive Law* . . . deals with the rights and the duties which are connected with the first principle, but in a *contingent* manner (p. 99). Why not in both these definitions add—as before—"this time supposing certain conditions of fact"? Because this no longer distinguishes these phases in the specification of law. Knowledge of the natural law also arises *through inclination* only in the face of quite concrete conditions of fact. It also is a judgment made *in medias res*. Then why the distinction between a necessary or a contingent manner of drawing specific moral conclusions in making law?

† "I can think of no legal or legislative problem of American law in my lifetime that would be appreciably *advanced* toward a satisfactory determination by invoking this formula." Edwin W. Patterson, "A Pragmatist Looks at Natural Law and Natural Rights," in *Natural Law and Natural Rights* (ed. Arthur L. Harding), Dallas, Tex.: Southern Methodist University Press, 1955, p. 55.

medias res. Secondly, while insisting that the law of nature exerts a primal pressure upon social structures as it expands into the more specific forms of law, Maritain at the same time says that "knowledge of the primordial aspects of natural law was first expressed in social patterns rather than in personal judgments." This suggests, does it not, that *jus naturale* first manifests its presence in *jus gentium* and not in essential inclination? At least, this "knowledge has developed within the double protecting tissue of human inclinations and human society." [33] It was, for example, the modern political experience which *freed* the root inclinations of human nature so that there could develop knowledge through inclination that the *rights* of the person are as essential as his *obligations.*[34] Thirdly, having reserved conceptualization for the *jus gentium*, Maritain still can use the word for our knowledge of *jus naturale*, distinguishing now between *free* conceptualization and another sort: "our knowledge . . . is no work of free conceptualization, but results from a conceptualization *bound* to the essential inclinations of being, of living nature, and of reason." [35] But was not *jus gentium* defined as conceptualization precisely so bound?

Here as always the straddle position of what is called *jus gentium* becomes evident. *Jus gentium* contains *both* characteristics which belong also to natural law (i.e., known not only as rationally inferred but also through inclination) and characteristics that go beyond the content of natural law (i.e., *only* rationally inferred, and not known through inclination).[36] This suggests not so much that there is here no substance of truth as that it had better be freed from the System! Is the legislative decision against murder really strengthened or better understood when it is broken down as follows: "The prohibition of murder, insofar as this precept is *known by inclination*, belongs to natural law. The same prohibition of murder, if this precept is known as a conclusion inferred from a principle of natural law, pertains to *jus gentium*." [37] The judgment here being made is indivisibly tendential, decisional, and conceptual; it is at once natural and positive law.

In the same year that Maritain published, in *Man and the State,* his radically but insufficiently revised treatise on law, he also wrote a brief paper entitled "On Knowledge through Connaturality." [38] This was apparently a subject with which he was seriously engaged at that time, with the significant results we have noted in his theory of law. In this essay, he suggests that in mystical, poetic and ethical experience man is prerationally "co-natured" with truth in the very depths of his being. However, "moral experience offers to us the most wide-spread instance of knowledge through connaturality." [39] In comparison with such primary knowledge, moral philosophy is knowledge at a distance even as theology "makes us know divine things at a distance." [40] Moral philosophy—and as we have seen, all forms of actual law—contain "*reflective* knowledge, a sort of after-knowledge." Neither it, nor reason, discovers the moral law, which has to be "previously discovered in an undemonstrable manner, and in a non-conceptual, non-rational way." [41]

Still this is a species of knowledge; it comes within the range of reason. It is "produced in the intellect but not by virtue of conceptual connections." [42] If no conceptual connections, then we might point out again, it is no longer at all appropriate to continue to speak of "conclusions" as to the moral law following in a "necessary" manner, as from something prior; or even to speak of principles of the natural law which are "like" conclusions. While *produced* in the intellect, the intellect "has no part, either in causing it to *exist*, or even in causing it *to be known*." Thus only the reason of God, Uncreated Reason, is "at play not only in *establishing* Natural Law (by the very fact that it creates human nature), but in *making Natural Law known*, through the inclinations of this very nature, to which human reason listens when it knows natural law." [43]

All this makes for the greater "essential *naturality*" of natural law, its "greater" not less "validity," and its "more than human rationality." [44] If there are any structural principles to be derived by conceptual reason from reflecting upon the nature of man as man or by perceiving the "requirements of the normality of functioning of human nature"—however correct these may be—they are no part of the natural law. Natural law deals only with moral insight known through inclination; it "deals only with principles *immediately known* (that is known through inclination, without any conceptual and rational medium) of human morality." [45] Conditions of fact, and all the knowledge a man has acquired, are, of course, not removed. But "when a man makes a free decision, he takes into account, not only all that he possesses of moral science and factual information, and which is manifested to him in concepts and notions, but also all the secret elements of evaluation which depend on what he is, and which are known to him through inclination, through his own actual propensities and his own virtues. . . ." [46] Moral judgment, therefore, proceeds primarily from "*connaturality* or *congeniality* through which what is consonant with the essential inclinations of human nature is grasped by the intellect as good; what is dissonant, as bad." [47] It should be noted that "the inclinations in question . . . are *essentially human,* and therefore, *reason-permeated inclinations;* they are inclinations refracted through the crystal of *reason in its unconscious or preconscious life.*" [48] Thence they are produced in the intellect. Finally, in this view of knowledge of the natural law, not only is the range of reason expanded to include the nonrational tendencies whose source is in that nature of man inscrutable to the conscious intellect alone; but also that human nature on which pivots the natural law is rendered essentially historical: "these essential inclinations of human nature," Maritain writes, "either developed or were released in the course of time: as a result, man's knowledge of Natural Law progressively developed, and continues to develop." [49]

Such a view as the foregoing, Maritain admits, is to be found in Aristotle or in Thomas Aquinas in the main where the doctrine of *moral virtues* is in question. Thus, for Aristotle the virtuous *man* is the rule and measure of moral actions, not his notions; and his notions are right if they are such that a man of sound virtue would be disposed to entertain them. For Aquinas, also, knowledge of moral virtues is "the first and main example of knowledge through inclination and through connaturality." [50] Moral goodness the simple man knows simply by something in him that is the measure of it in practical cases. What the simple man knows, the wise man only knows he knows, when moral truth "co-natured" to man is produced in his intellect and reflected upon. But all this means that Maritain's present point of view stands in contrast not only with "eighteenth century rationalism" or with those eight or more new systems of natural law which made their appearance at every Leipzig booksellers' fair. It stands in contrast also with Thomas Aquinas so far as his treatise on law alone is at issue. Plainly, Jacques Maritain is a revisionist among theorists of the natural law; and a rather radical one.

Quite clearly, the expression "knowledge through inclination" represents a remarkable departure from the traditional scheme of the rational-deductive natural law. On the other hand, this expression does not enact the pleasure principle into fundamental law. Rather is inclination a distinctively *human* response; and in such spontaneous reaction to whatever is inhumane the human essence first discloses itself to our minds. Essential human nature manifests itself through innate tendencies towards its ends, and this is known to us in the context of whatever proves basically congenial to that nature. Thus, the natural law first discloses itself to our minds through the silent, preconceptual pressures of inclination or disinclination. ". . . Knowledge through connaturality plays an immense part in human existence," Maritain wrote in the essay discussed above, *"especially in that knowing of the singular which comes about in everyday life* and in our relationship of person to person." [51] This would seem to be not greatly different from man's competence to make moral judgment "in the prism of the case" as this is exhibited in the jurisprudential writings of Edmond Cahn, to which we now turn.

IV

The thesis of this section is that, unless one wants to make mighty fine distinctions, there is no significant difference between Maritain's understanding of natural law and the philosophy of law advanced by Professor Edmond Cahn in *The Moral Decision*[52] and in his earlier book *The Sense of Injustice*.[53] This is evident both in their common rejection of universal, merely theoretical principles deductively applied to cases, and more importantly by what Cahn means by the "sense of injustice" and the competence of moral judgment in "the prism of the case."

Late in *The Moral Decision* Professor Cahn remarks, "No system having been taken along with us, none has been brought back";[54] and throughout he is skeptical "whether a man has the capacity to distinguish between right and wrong *in general*."[55] But this, and comparable strictures in *The Sense of Injustice,* are only to be compared with Maritain's polemic against rationalistic versions of the law of nature. In regard to their constructive positions, it is clear that what Cahn says about a case at law operating as a *prism*[56] through which moral judgments can become clear, about the importance of *enacting* the transactions we meet with and thus coming to *care with* the persons involved,[57] and the confidence he expresses in ordinary conscience when put on its mettle and disciplined to the concrete case, bear remarkable similarity to what Maritain means by "knowledge through inclination." For both of these legal philosophers, decision-making (as I have said of Maritain) is at once natural and contextual or positive; and for both "it is realistic to look at the law . . . as a rich repository of moral knowledge which is continually reworked, revised, and refined."[58] The similarity even extends to the fact that, on the one hand, the illustrations that can be given of Maritain's point of view mainly go to show "knowledge through *dis*inclination," and, on the other hand, Professor Cahn insists that our analysis should focus not only on an *act* but an act of *wrong*,[59] and the theme of his earlier book was "the sense of *in*justice." *

A moment's glance at that earlier work confirms the comparison of Cahn and Maritain on the law; and, at the same time, it will enable us to make a fine distinction between them. Cahn writes: "*That* justice is we know before the occasion, but only the occasion discloses precisely *what* it calls on us to do."[60] This corresponds to Maritain's insistence that the being of the natural law is one thing, our knowledge of it another. The sense of injustice, of course, corresponds to "knowledge through disinclination." The same is the case with regard to judgment made through the "prismatic" case. Moreover, too much ought not be made of Cahn's negative formulation or of Maritain's illustration of the *in*compatibility of genocide with human well-being. It is plain that both have something positive, though not static, in mind; and there is agreement even in choice of words when Cahn writes that "equality . . . is a perception so *congenial* to humanity that we have to be educated to the missing of it."[61] This positive affirmation does not differ essentially from the negative statement: "The sense of injustice revolts against whatever is unequal by caprice."[62] And even he who runs while he reads should

* " 'Justice,' as we shall understand the term, means the *active* process of remedying or preventing what would arouse the sense of injustice."

realize that to say that "Ockham's razor excises natural law from our present interest; it does not excise the sense of injustice unless all the phenomena of positive law could be explained without it" [63] entails no disagreement with Maritain. Both our authors are looking for a justice that is "not in the ether, but in the courts and legislatures and in the transactions of men." [64]

What then is the difference, if there is any, between these two accounts of what is fundamental in the law? It lies, I think, in the fact that Maritain presupposes an essentialist philosophy in his treatment of human nature. However deeply hidden from view, it is still the human *essence* which *vibrantly* reacts to that which would specifically contradict it; and so the *humanum,* and natural justice, come to be known through the basic inclinations of the single individual. In contrast to this, Cahn portrays the human being somewhat more "naturalistically." He speaks of the movement and warmth of the human organism, of outrage, shock, resentment and anger preparing the human animal to resist attack.[65] So far it is not essential *manhood* but the *self* or the *agent* or an embattled animal who resists aggression; and there is as yet no sense of injustice called forth. The sense of injustice does not arise from deep within the essence of the single individual viewed as such; it arises, so to speak, "between man and man." It arises not from essential nature (which, isolated and alone in the world, would still be what it is and continue to give voice to natural law through the inclinations of its own being and reason), but rather from the emphatic being of man in relationships. Nature has equipped us not only for self-defense but also for an "imaginative interchange" by which another who is victimized really appears as one's own self in jeopardy. Thus, the sense of injustice is an indissociable blend of organic resistance, reason and empathy.[66]

This "naturalistic-relational" interpretation of the sense of injustice may be in error. At least by the time he wrote *The Moral Decision,* Cahn seems to belong more to the essentialist tradition: He speaks of "conscience's *generic* commands," "the accused's *generic* rights"; and says that "imaginative projection *uses genus* as a bridge over which we pass to see and defend the irreducible uniqueness of another." [67] In his newest book, *The Predicament of Democratic Man,* Cahn gives striking expression in successive paragraphs to *both* of these basic theories of morality (the more naturalistic theory basic to *The Sense of Injustice* and the more essentialist viewpoint of *The Moral Decision*):

> It has always been possible for the members of a society to project themselves imaginatively . . . into the place of a victim of legal oppression and share the impact of his experience. The capacity to identify ourselves with him has great survival value for us as well as for him. Our personal impulse for safety and self-preservation becomes active the moment we realize that

what has happened to him may in turn happen to us if we should be caught in the toils of a similar mischance.

In some instances, there is also a higher, more unselfish level which our identification may reach. On this level, we become eager to save Joe, not because of any collateral or contingent threat to our own safety but because any harm to Joe as a specimen of the genus homo inflicts immediate harm on all mankind, and as our larger self encompasses Joe, his injury automatically becomes ours. On this level, we are not so much preoccupied with the possibility that we may some day stand in the prisoner's dock. We are more preoccupied with the fact that we already stand there—in Joe's person.[68]

The latter position seems entirely comparable to knowledge of the natural law in Maritain by virtue of the reaction of human nature in us to anything in prismatic cases or situations not congenial to it. The first, naturalistic interpretation is not yet an adequate account of morality; while concerning the ethic of identification with the *genus,* the question to be raised is whether there is not needed some more *explicit theological* premise *active* in the moral life itself in order to sustain any such ethic or to comprehend it. This question applies equally to Cahn or to Maritain on man's supposed "natural" sense of natural justice.

It ought to be pointed out that in this interpretation of Cahn as a natural-law thinker, or of Maritain as a "Cahnian," nothing has been said, I am sure, of which Professor Cahn is unaware. "The stubborn survival of some sort of faith in *natural* justice," he wrote, "should point to a nucleus of truth." [69] The sense of injustice, knowledge through inclination, is that nucleus. "Judges may speak of 'due process,' 'equal protection,' 'general welfare,' 'reasonableness'—all somehow cleansed of natural rights or higher law. But would the decision be the same if twenty-four centuries had not preached an indwelling justice?" [70]

There is, of course, a tentativeness about Professor Cahn's writings not usually associated with natural law theory even at its best.

Is the sense of injustice right? Certainly not, if rightness means conformity to some elaborate and inflexible standard. . . . [H]ow can we know that the intellect has understood and that projection has comprehended every last relevant factor?

The sense of injustice is only one of several causes that are *constitutive* of particular answers; to find it permanently *constituted* in any single answer or series of answers . . . is to betray it.[71]

But, I would insist, there is nothing substantive about Maritain's interpretation of the fundamental law which prevents his speaking also in this cautious fashion even more than he does. Nor, at this level of analysis, do significant differences flow from the fact that Cahn calls his an "anthropocentric" analysis, while for Maritain the human order obviously depends on the divine, and natural law upon Eternal Law.

V

If there are inflexibilities and claims of absolute certainty and finality in a theory of natural law, these, you can be sure, do not ordinarily flow from the account actually given of the meaning of the law of nature, but from quite another point in Roman Catholic moral theology, namely, the claim that the natural law has been "republished" in revelation, or given determinate and specific shape in Scripture as guarded and interpreted by the positive teachings of the Church.

A recent book on Christian views of sex offers the unsolicited advice that the teaching of the Roman Church concerning the primacy of procreation over the unitive ends of marriage, and its prohibition of conception control, would be strengthened if this were declared to be revealed truth and not part of the content of natural law.[72] I venture to believe that the difficulty lies not in the fact that the claim is made that this teaching is based on natural law but rather in the fact that the "republication" of natural law in the teachings of the Roman Church guarantees the conclusion in advance and removes the matter from the province of rational inquiry and discussion which were said to be quite sufficient to establish it.* Thanks to the infallible authority of the Church, or rather thanks to the fact that the teaching commission of the Church has been extended to include reissuing the natural law (which anyone who has human sensitivity and reason in exercise was supposed able to grasp), unnecessary inflexibilities have been introduced into the theory of natural law and Catholic moral theologians are reduced simply to giving more and more subtle reasons for a position already firmly held on essentially different grounds.†

* A recent book by a Roman Catholic author appeals in a curious way to the supplementary *supernatural* source of knowledge of the natural law (needed to make the human mind *certain* as to this) as the reason Catholics ought *not* to press for the enactment of their views of the natural law in civil statutes. Norman St. John-Stevas argues not only that not all contraventions of natural law are fit subjects for legislation, he not only urges Catholics to seek to distinguish, at the level of natural morality, between what is a fit or not a fit subject for legislation. He also suggests that they, *"for purposes of jurisprudence,"* treat "the morality of birth control as within the sphere of moral theology, a science *based on revelation and the teaching authority of the Church, rather than of natural ethics."* (*Life, Death and the Law.* Bloomington: Indiana University Press, 1961, p. 30, italics added). This is not the same as the advice (above) that this teaching be regarded as a part of revealed truth *and not* a part of natural law, for it affirms rather that this teaching is both a part of revealed truth (by republication) *and also* a part of natural law.

† ". . . It is necessary that a filial and humble obedience towards the Church should be combined with devotion to God and the desire of submitting to Him. For

This, I suggest, is the only significant difference there is between Catholic and Protestant theories of natural law. It is not the scarcity of the latter, which has so frequently been pointed out. When Luther violently rejected the canon law, and even in 1520 engaged in his historic act of book-burning, consigning to the flames the whole library of canon law, this act was directed against the proliferation of oppressive exactitudes by which the Church sought to govern not only itself but society in general. He did not thereby deny the natural law elements in this structure, or deliver the state over only to the guidance of *Realpolitik*. The Christian prince—or even a pagan prince—was still competent to rule according to the principles of natural justice; and this extended even to the apprehension of the truth of many of the things contained in Scripture and often regarded as going beyond nature, i.e., not only the Decalogue, but the Golden Rule as well.* When even a modern Protestant

---

Christ Himself made the Church the teacher of truth in those things also which concern the right regulation of moral conduct, *even though some knowledge of the same is not beyond human reason*. For just as God, in the case of the natural truths of religion and morals, added revelation to the light of reason . . . , so for the same purpose He has constituted the Church the guardian and the teacher of the *whole* of the truth concerning religion and moral conduct . . ." Pius XI, *Casti Connubii*, 103 (italics mine). "For the deposit of truth entrusted to Us by God, and Our weighty office of propagating, interpreting, and urging in season and out of season the *entire* moral law, demand that both social and economic questions be *brought within Our supreme jurisdiction, insofar as they refer to moral issues*." Pius XI, *Quadragesimo Anno*, 41 (italics mine). This, of course, is the area of not necessarily infallible but none the less authoritative teachings, and of a large part of ecclesiastical positive law. In other words, between the wholly spiritual area of the Church and Sacraments and the mainly public area where Christians may make many different decisions and where they act only by the inspiration of their religion, there is an area of incidence, an intermediate plane, of partly spiritual and partly public questions (education, marriage, etc.). Here no less than in the first, the watchword for "Catholic action" is unity and authority. What is and what is not proper Catholic action is determined by the Holy See and not by "the particular judgment of no matter what person and no matter what party." (Jacques Maritain, *True Humanism*, New York: Charles Scribner's Sons, 1938, p. 297; and cf. *Freedom in the Modern World*.) Thus, the "republication" of the natural law by the Guardian of revelation aims to provide quite specific guidance on moral questions; and this republication, or making determinate, also *publishes* for the first time what does or does not form a part of the natural law and what does or does not fall within this area so closely adjacent to faith and morals that the Church rightfully prescribes what it first circumscribes. Thus, far from its being the case that Roman Catholic moral theology possesses the archetypal theory of natural law, it might be asserted that in this theology the law of nature and of reason has already had its back broken by ecclesiastical positivism.

* "But if neither is a Christian, or if either is unwilling to be judged by the law of love, you may ask them to call in another judge, and announce to them that they are acting against God and the law of nature. For, nature, like love, teaches that I should do as I would be done by. . . . Both Nature and love alike teach that I should act towards others as I wish to be treated by them." Luther, *Secular Authority, Works* (Philadelphia: Muhlenberg Press), III, p. 272. "The natural law which the Lord states in Luke 6:31 and Matthew 7:12 [is] 'What ye would that men should do

theologian, Emil Brunner, writes that "while the Catholic church, drawing on centuries of tradition, possesses an impressive theory of justice, Protestant Christianity has had none for some three hundred years past," [73] this reveals on his part not only an inadequate reading of British and American theologians for the past three centuries, but also a failure to follow his own continental Calvinistic tradition as far down as the Huguenot political theory of the *Vindiciae contra tyrannos* (1577, usually attributed to Philippe de Mornay, called du Plessis-Mornay), concerning which Harold J. Laski said that in it "practically every theory of importance in political science until the outbreak of the French Revolution found, in some sort, its expression, with the important and constant exception of egalitarianism.*

The first distinctive feature of Protestant doctrines of the law of nature —though not only of Protestantism—is the separation of the natural law from the context of the authority of ecclesiastical positive law so that the inherent meaning of natural law might come to fulfillment in the progressive discovery of new and relevant truth through unlimited discussion. One may sympathize with the plight of a judge confronted by myriad complex cases to decide and who, as a religious man, desperately desires from his church and its teachings quite specific guidance. One may sympathize without yielding to this demand, or imagining that, if the conclusion were supplied him in advance of his own decision-making, this would not be simply an abdication of his own responsible share in the discovery and the making of law that is, at least in many cases, at once natural and positive. The judge who must decide whether a crime is one "involving moral turpitude" or who is required in naturalization cases to decide as to the "good moral character" of the applicant for citizenship ought not to shift this to the "moral feelings now prevalent generally in this country" or "the common conscience prevalent at the time," [74] else he ceases to be a creative part in the making of decisions. He waits until the polls are taken before himself deciding how to vote, and so one vote at least will never be counted. The same is true of any judge who refers his decision to what the Church teaches. Just as the positive "law" current in informal popular opinion is no substitute for a renewed effort to determine the nature of the case, so also with any ecclesiastical positive

---

to you, that do also to them.' " Luther, *Three Laws for Lending, Works* IV, p. 53. By the above, I do not mean to deny that much was lost through Luther's violent break; but only to raise the question how else in that day Christendom might have been freed for new legal development, and the modern political experience (with its great achievements as well as its acknowledged evils) have been made possible. It is important to see that the conceptions of sin and grace in the Reformation, or all the fury of its opposition to Rome, did not rule out general natural law notions.

* Introduction to *A Defense of Liberty against Tyrants*. London: G. Bell and Sons, 1924. This tribute includes, of course, the whole of John Locke and the ideas fundamental to liberal democracy as it developed in England and America.

law or republication of the law of nature. It can have at most the role of a "friend of the court." The court itself must decide.

The whole procedure of marshaling and citing precedents in rendering decision does not testify to the belief that the law is something static to be found by submission to the past. Is it not rather an expression of confidence that the court is competent to determine the law natural and positive only within the widest possible, continuing dialogue with the decisions of men faced in times past with similar cases? Is this not what will in fact take place when some judge in the future has occasion to write, "Cardozo said in the opinion cited, 'Joint adventurers, like co-partners, owe to one another . . . the duty of the finest loyalty . . . the punctilio of an honor the most sensitive . . . ,' *but* in the case before us . . .";[75] or when another judge refers to another of Cardozo's decisions which extended the scope of a firm's liability for negligence by the judgment "Danger invites rescue,"[76] and yet concludes that in the present case before the court another factor prevails to modify the former ruling? Moreover, the community of discussion is held to be even more unlimited when courts, in the absence of specific repealing statute, hold that the common law in many respects still prevails even after the expression of some legislative intent to enact law modifying this same common law.

I do not know whether it is quite proper to speak of the moral substance of the religious traditions of a people, or the positive teachings of the living religious communities within our nation, as an actual functioning part of this general procedure of decision-making after the analogy of a "friend of the court," the court itself still giving the judgment as to the right or good in law. But it seems clear that there is strong analogy between the general procedure of arriving at legal decision and Protestant views of the natural law set within the context of the confidence that, to whatever (however limited) degree justice may be determined, it is most likely to be determined rightly through the unlimited discussion of free men. This is the only proper or possible meeting between moral theology and jurisprudence.

If not formally as a "friend of the court," the heritage of the community's religious teaching at least enters materially into forming the mind and the conscience of the judge. In disengaging himself from submission to that hydra-headed monster, the opinions prevalent in society at the time, a judge "will always—unless he loses his sanity—find himself agreeing with and supported by a significant strand of public opinion."[77] If this is allowed to be proper, then nothing hinders this strand from being the traditions of a given religious community. That this should be so is dangerous only when in rendering decision the authority of religious precedents is allowed to override factors in the concrete situation that otherwise by nature and reason would have led to another decision, or

in the unlikely event that a judge may suppose that *as judge* he belongs
more to his particular religious community of discussion than to the
discussion and decision enshrined in law. There is a danger, it must be
acknowledged, and one a democratic society simply has to find some way
of living with, where the religious community to which a judge or legislator may belong is not itself a community of discussion and decision-
making in which all may share but one that enlists his submission to
authoritative ecclesiastical positivism. In this instance, a self-denying
ordinance on the part of such persons is the only hope for social peace and
consensus as to civil righteousness, by which they clearly affirm that the
natural law made known to them by supernatural positive republication
is *therefore* not a fit subject for legislation or for determining judicial
decision.[78] In general, however, and but for this special case, it is through
the interstitial spaces in what the law allows the judge to do in his
official capacity, and by illuminating the imponderable human relations
and indeterminate freedoms that still remain after steady attention to the
prism of the case, that a profound religious apprehension of human
existence may serve to transform natural justice and raise the good in law
to a higher power.

But this requires men who have made their Exodus from the Egypt of
the natural and the positive law. To what this may mean we turn in the
next chapter. Here, in conclusion, it is sufficient to say that the symbolism
in speaking of "Egypt" and the "Exodus" in connection with the natural
law means that there was more in Egypt than fleshpots to which the
people of God yearned to return in their times of distress over not knowing to what land God was leading them. There was the security and
integration of the whole of life which came from living wholly within a
knowable order of natural justice. On the night before the Exodus, the
people robbed more than the houses of the Egyptians; they despoiled
themselves of the moral security of an organic legal system resting upon
only one source of right. More than the first-born of the Egyptians died
that night: the covenant people and their own sons died to the natural
order of immanent-divine principles and were made to live toward a
transcendent source of justice unthinkable apart from the God who
revealed himself and set them on pilgrimage.

This is the glory, and the agony, of Western systems of morals and
philosophies of law, since men came to believe they were citizens of "two
cities" and not just of one Pharaonic order or one Greek *polis*. Of course,
the people of God continue to live within the natural order and within
some legal system, whether this be the law of Pharaoh or of Hammurabi—
of the Medes and the Persians, the Roman law, or the Anglo-Saxon legal
heritage. "Egypt" may, therefore, be used as a symbol for the security
provided by any "one world" view of morality or any closed system of
natural justice. The "Exodus," then, is a symbol for the invasion of the

natural or human order by more than immanent requirements. Biblical ethics may be summarized as the molding of human action into the form of God's action. The whole duty of man shifts toward the standard and measure of God's steadfast faithfulness. More than justice, righteousness is required, and of the whole nation. This poses the question, "What is the relation between distinctively Biblical ethics and the justice contained in legal systems? between natural and supernatural or revealed morality?" In the following chapter we shall attempt to distinguish in our Western moral heritage and in ethical judgments between the good-in-law and this good-beyond-law. For certainly the outstanding problem of Christian social ethics is to clarify the relationship between the morality of the Exodus and the natural justice within the law or social institutions of whatever Egypt may be the present abode of the people of God.

Nine

Jacques Maritain and Edmond Cahn:
Man's Exodus from the Natural Law

I

In a book entitled *Israel and Revelation*,[1] the first in a projected six-volume philosophy of history, Eric Voegelin describes the uniqueness of Israel under the symbol of her Exodus from the cosmological principle of social order into historical existence in the immediate presence of God. The God of Israel was world- and nature-transcending; and in answer to His call Israel was disengaged from the natural order of cosmological civilizations, from any understanding of man as simply inserted in and integrated with cosmic-divine order. There and then occurred "a leap in being," [2] a "leap toward more perfect attunement with transcendent being." [3] There occurred an entering into the historical action of God through the entering of divine reality into historical confrontation of men. The leap in being was "the entering of the soul into divine reality through the entering of divine reality into the soul." [4] For a moment it did not extend beyond the soul of Abram, this ordering of man which originated "through the inrush of divine reality into his soul and from this point of origin expands into a social body in history." [5] Yet social events and institutions, which formerly might be regarded as world-immanent, were now placed under "perpetual mortgage" [6] to the transcendent God. There took place a "molding of human action into the action known by God." [7] A beachhead was established amid the pressures of mundane existence, and into the natural order there entered the requirement of living toward the Transcendent in every historical present. This, says Voegelin, was the meaning of the conflict between Moses and the principle of Pharaonic order, and the significance of Israel's Exodus from cosmological civilizations. "History as the present under God was the inner form of Israel's existence." [8]

Hereafter, "society in cosmological form becomes Sheol, the realm of death"; and whoever undertakes the Exodus discovers the immanent order of the natural world to be, as it were, a Desert this side of Jordan.[9] Israel's temptation will be to return to the Sheol of civilizations from which Moses has led his people into the freedom of history in the presence of God.[10] Their proper punishment will be for them to have to wander in the desert of the natural-divine order which cannot, except by a miracle, preserve their clothing. Because of frequent backslidings into the Sheol of cosmological civilization[11] (or its equivalent), prophets were to arise who "judged conduct in terms of its compatibility not with a fundamental law but with the right order of the soul" [12] and the ordering of the nation to God.

All this needs explaining; and we must then apply the ethical significance of biblical revelation to the question of the good-in-law. The significance of acknowledging the fact of revelation in one's past and out of which one lives may be succinctly expressed by quoting, and paraphrasing, a statement of Martin Buber: He who does not himself say "A Wandering Aramean was my father . . . and the Lord brought us forth out of Egypt with a mighty hand" (Deut. 26:5, 8) ceases to be a Jew. "He who does not himself remember that God led him out of Egypt . . . is no longer a true Jew." [13] He who does not himself remember that God redeemed him from sin and death by the life and passion of Jesus of Nazareth ceases to be a Christian. This expresses the self-understanding characteristic of Judaism and Christianity.

The ethical consequence of such self-understanding may also be succinctly expressed: The righteousness of God was shown not to be merely corrective or proportionally distributive (as Aristotle supposed were the chief forms of Justice) but delivering, redemptive justice. "It was not because you were more in number than any other people that the Lord set his love upon you and chose you; but it is because the Lord loves you, and is keeping the oath which he swore to your fathers. . . ." (Deut. 7:7, 8). From the righteousness which God manifests, the righteousness that should prevail among men takes its direction, quality, and goal. "You shall not oppress a stranger; you know the heart of a stranger, for you were strangers in the land of Egypt" (Exodus 23:9). Hence a homily for godly rulers and judges enjoins them to:

> Give justice to the weak and the orphan;
> Do right by the afflicted and wretched;
> Set free the weak and needy,
> Rescue them from the hands of the wicked (Ps. 82:3-4).

Similarly, the New Testament views righteousness among men in the light of God's righteousness disclosed in Jesus Christ. "While we were yet helpless, at the right time Christ died for the ungodly. Why, one will hardly die for a righteous man—though perhaps for a good man one will dare even to die. But God shows his love for us in that while we were yet sinners Christ died for us" (Romans 5:6-9). When Jesus said to his disciples, "A new commandment I give to you, that you love one another," so far that was no new commandment; and it only became a new word when he went on to explain the love wherewith they were to love one another: "Even as I have loved you, that you also love one another" (John 13:34). Hence we may summarize biblical religion as faith in the *faithfulness* of God; and we may summarize biblical ethics as the molding of human action into the action of God's faithfulness. Thus, the love-commandments really mean, You shall be faithful to the Lord your God with all your soul, mind and strength, and You shall be faithful to your neighbor's being and well-being as to your own—or rather, as God has proved himself faithful to you in these events of deliverance upon which your faith rests.*

Man's Exodus from cosmological civilization with its ordered meaning was re-enacted many times. Out of whatever any generation imagined to be the immanent natural order of things, people heard the call into present historical existence in the presence of God. Thus, the Baal-worship of the Canaanite order required that right human action be located wholly within the immanent-divine forces of fertility. This was the meaning of sacred prostitution: that by engaging ritually in the act of sexual intercourse men might so identify themselves with and so locate and attune their lives to the divine energy that makes for productivity of flocks and vineyards that the favor of the gods of nature would be guaranteed them. But Israel had in principle already undertaken Exodus from this and every other immanent order; she was enabled to stand upright and attune behavior to the transcendent God met in the ancient covenant. Therefore, "the relationship between Israel and Yahweh did not begin to be moral in the eighth century [with the writing prophets]; it began to be moral when it began to exist." [14] Israel started where a respectable society has difficulty ever ending[15]—attuned to a genuinely nature-transcending Purpose. Here was room for the progressive addition of all the moral insights for which mankind has the capacity; but these were only added onto the essential core of covenant-relationship whose standard of righteousness was already known through the revealing and saving action of God. This followed from the fact that the harmonious integration of society into nature was broken, and from the fact that the quite reasonable expectation of all the securities that flow from such harmonious integration of social institutions with mundane conditions was denied to biblical men.

This same relationship between the ethics of revelation and the

---

* Thus, by interpreting scripture by scripture, would I now correct the statement that, in the twofold love commandment, "one has to go in heavily for analogy, or even commute back and forth from one meaning to another, ever to suppose that 'love,' *or any other single term*, can adequately convey the meaning of a Christian's response to God and also his love for neighbor" (Paul Ramsey: *Basic Christian Ethics*. New York: Charles Scribner's Sons, 1950, p. 129). Faithful, faithfulness, *hesed*, is the single, univocal biblical concept in terms of which the meaning of "love" in Jesus' twofold commandment has to be understood.

Pharaonic or the Baalistic order repeated itself when a single verse out of St. Paul became the bridge across which the entire arsenal of Stoic natural law theory crossed over into Christianity. St. Augustine's view of the two cities—the history of the *civitas Dei* and the *civitas terrena*—in both of which man has citizenship was the immediate result; together with all the discussion of the tension between grace and nature, revelation and reason, in medieval theology; and the conflict between justification and justice, and the two realms, spoken of in Protestant theology. This is what we must now examine systematically under the symbol of man's Exodus from the natural law.

II

It has to be said at once that only confusion can be the result of the *codification* of the revealed law of God (in Orthodox Judaism, fundamentalistic Protestantism and the canon law of the "teaching church" in Catholicism), or for that matter the codification of any republished natural law, so long as the endeavor is made to bring these positive religious laws into *direct* relation to law-making in the modern age. This happens when Roman Catholics do not make a distinction between what they believe right in the matter of contraception and what should be legislated, or between permissive legislation for people generally in society and the practice they may want to make mandatory by the use of "spiritual" sanctions for their own membership. Confusion of the purposes of legislation, and a good deal of waste in moral energy on trivial matters, also takes place when Protestants do not make a similar distinction with regard to bingo or Sunday laws. Communicants of any religion may still believe that such matters were settled for them by revelation, or by the fixed and formal republication of natural law by the authority of the church; and they may even *believe* that there is here an objective obligation in the ethics of nature which is valid for all men. Still, so long as such wide diversity of sincere opinion on these matters exists in our society, the distinction between mandatory and permissive legislation, or between state-action and the voluntary acceptance of certain standards by any religious group and their imposition upon its membership by "spiritual" sanctions, must plainly be made.

More important for basic legal or political philosophy than the foregoing illustrations, an ominous relic of another view of the relation between civil law and canon law is still endorsed in the Catholic "liberalism" of Jacques Maritain and John Courtney Murray. Unlike conservative Roman Catholics, these men, of course, do not mean by freedom of religion simply the freedom of private conscience from repressive measures used by the state to foster the "true" religion. Theirs is no program for a "Christian state." Rather, the "freedom of the church" in any ideal

Christendom of the future would be sufficiently insured by a "pluralistic" society in which the right of religious assembly and freedom of propaganda is extended equally to "heretical" religions and "erroneous" opinion. Still there remains, for both these thinkers, a significant point at which it is quite proper for the force at the command of civil law to be placed behind the canon law, just so long as similar enforcement is at the same time given to the positive traditions or to the surrogate "canon laws" of other religions than the Roman Catholic. Thus, Maritain writes, "In a pluralistic society it is but normal that the particular regulations of an autonomous body may be sanctioned by civil law, from the civil society's own viewpoint, when the interests of the common good are concerned." [16] What this may mean is spelled out in another footnote in praise of the constitution of Portugal for, in a predominantly Catholic society, "disestablishing" the Church in the sense that no tithes are collected for it by the state and the rites of the unfaithful are tolerated, yet where religious rules as to marriage are enforced by the state upon all who enter this estate as Catholics. Just as "the Portuguese Concordat forbids divorce only to those who have contracted Catholic marriage," so in the ideal pluralistic society of the future " 'civil legislation might coincide or concur with Canon Law for the Catholics,' while for other spiritual lineages it might be different. . . ." And Murray is quoted as writing, "This provision illustrates what I mean by saying that the State organizes what is 'there' in society." [17]

Thus it is envisaged that the civil law of marriage would be pulverized and would consist of any number of canon laws given civil status, as well as "secular" marriage for all others. Not only this, but the law for Catholic marriage could not be enforced by the civil power without grave violation of natural justice as this is understood in a liberal society with its voluntary principles of religious association, because of the Catholic teaching that baptism as an infant makes a person in some sort a permanent member of the corporate society of the Church. There are at the present moment Protestant clergymen who cannot obtain permission to marry in Spain (even though this is permitted under the civil law) because they happen to have been born and baptized Roman Catholics. There is now a growing pressure in the United States toward making prenuptial contracts between Catholics and non-Catholics regarding the religious training of children *enforceable* in the courts—for the common good, of course, and from the civil society's own viewpoint. This is what may come from the state's assuming responsibility for enforcing what is 'there' in a society. Nothing in what I have seen written by these liberal Catholics rules this out as a possible and legitimate application of the civil enforcement they propose for the canon law of various spiritual lineages in a pluralistic society. This cannot be said to be compatible with the liberal societies achieved in the modern period.

Perhaps it is unrealistic to expect religious folk, or anybody else, to have the wisdom and restraint not to want to legislate everything they sincerely regard as objectively right and proper for mankind generally. But legislators and judges should resist this propensity—in themselves and on the part of others. At the same time, religious communities which are the bearers of our biblical heritage should realize that the relation between God, or their obedience to God, and the civil law never was in its essence a matter of the codification of the law of God. It is rather a question of the bearing, if any, of the *righteousness* of God upon the ongoing work of the law. Man's Exodus from the natural order was not into existence in the present under a Book of Laws.* That would be existence in the past under God, and it would, in fact, break the liberating tension which exists between attunement with transcendent righteousness and the order of natural and positive laws. If *codified* religious teachings, of church or synagogue, cannot without confusion compounded be brought into *direct* connection with the law, is there not possibly some direct relation between the law and man's living toward the goal of responding faithfully to the faithfulness of God, or between the law and the measuring of human justice in terms of the redemptive justice of God? This is the question which arises after the Exodus.

III

Let us raise, first, the question of why man should be regarded in law (and beyond the law) as a bearer of any rights which should be taken notice of and cared for in the conduct of public affairs. Is this due to divine justice or natural justice? Is this a part of natural law known by reason through inclination and the sense of injustice? Or does this conviction arise from that in man which has as its goal the attunement of himself to the God who meets him in personal history, the God who turns and draws man out of entire accord with the natural and rational ordering of life, and who has by this act spoken to us the living word that a man does not belong wholly, or essentially, to his life in society however good this may be? In short, do the rights of man derive from ethical and legal reasoning about the nature of man or of man-in-society, or from the Exodus out of the Egypt of viewing man within these limits?

Now, it is the great glory of the Western tradition of morals and law that these questions cannot be answered conclusively. In the web of life our religion, our morality and our law are too closely interwoven for these strands to be separated and one examined apart from the others.

---

* Eric Voegelin, "The fundamental fact that the Bible was never the book of Israel lies so deeply below the historians' consciousness that today it is practically forgotten" (*Israel and Revelation*. Baton Rouge: Louisiana State University Press, 1956, pp. 372-73. Cf. pp. 364-65).

Fortunately, we as yet have been spared the decisive historical experiment which would enable us to say categorically—if demonstration is demanded—that without biblical religion even our so-called natural morality would be quite different from what it is, or that without this particular religious tradition of morals the good in law would never have taken the shape it has. We know as a living experience no law entirely apart from this morality, and no concrete morality apart from the molding of human action into the action of this righteous God. But blessed be he who can without sentimentality believe great and worthy things of man on the basis of reason and nature! We ought not—on behalf of religious faith—bludgeon him into remembering that his reason may have been acculturated by twenty centuries of teachings about the higher law or twenty centuries of preaching the righteousness of God. Yet there is enough breaking-up of our heritage in the modern period to pose the urgent question whether the "post-Christian" era may not in fact prove to be a post-humanistic and even a post-humane age. It is important today for us to reflect soberly about the source and ground of the human rights acknowledged and protected in our law, even if actually no experimental isolation of the various grounds for belief in them is either possible or desirable.

Consider what Jacques Maritain says about the person and the common good as an example of the question I have raised. The person, he writes, asks to be treated as a *whole* within society, not as a *part* only. "To say, then, that society is a whole composed of persons is to say that society is a whole composed of wholes." [18] The common good, therefore, is common to the whole *and* to each member. The common good "flows back" upon each and every person.[19]

Now, why should this be so? What is the justification for including all? Why not increase the "greatest happiness altogether" or the greatest common good altogether *regardless of numbers* and without reference to distribution or inclusion? This was in fact the immanent logic of John Stuart Mill's utilitarianism with which he was happily inconsistent, both in his practical concern for liberal social reform and when he wrote "greatest number." The latter involves a reference to some other ground of moral judgment than "greatest happiness altogether"; and, like the flowing back of the common good upon every member (wholes, not parts) of society, this requires justification in political theory.

Maritain offers a justification; and at first glance it looks as if he regards this as simply an aspect of the natural law for man, limiting what should be said about man-in-society. Man is indeed a part of society; but he is not a part of society to the *whole extent of his being*. He is in fact engaged in historical, worthwhile causes and wholly included within the pressures and responsibilities of mundane, social existence; but not every dimension of his person is devoted to these goals. There is an "extra-territoriality" of the person relating him to supertemporal ends. He ought not, therefore, to be reduced to and absorbed wholly by collective goals.[20] Now we arrive at the crux of the matter: How do we know that this is true?

One answer is that right reasoning draws this conclusion. Maritain illustrates what he means by pointing to how the social involvement of the mathematician with its corresponding duties does not extend to the whole extent of a man who belongs also to the realm of society-transcending mathematical truth. The mathematician has learned all he knows about his subject "thanks to the educational institutions which social life alone has made possible." In a sense, all that he is he owes to others; and in return society may require of him that he teach mathematics if, as at present, some crisis facing the common good demands that no one hide his light under a bushel. Yet in another sense and at the same time the mathematician

> transcends the political community by reason of the things which, in him and of him, deriving from the ordering of the personality as such to the absolute, depend as to their very essence on something higher than the political community and properly have to do with the supratemporal fulfillment of the person as a person. Thus mathematical truths do not depend upon the social community; they relate to the order of absolute goods belonging to the person as such. And the community never has the right to require the mathematician *to hold as true* one mathematical system in preference to another, and to teach such mathematics as may be judged more suitable to the law of the social group. . . .[21]

Now, who wants absolutely to deny this? Yet is it not the case that in our day, when the life of the mind has been separated from its religious roots, mathematicians themselves have come to regard their enterprise as a matter of playing games—skillful game-systems, no doubt, but hardly a matter of that in them and of them which makes sun-clear man's purchase upon a realm of supertemporal and ultimate ends.

Hegel in the early nineteenth century could still point to art, philosophy and religion as manifestations of "universal spirit" which transcend the limits of the concrete spirit realized in history and in the political order. Again, who wants to hear this utterly denied? Yet recently paintings by two gorillas were exhibited in London. And, marvelous to behold, they started where a respectable human artist has difficulty ever ending: art as the imitation of nature was not for them, the paintings were abstract ones, thus revealing a subtle artistic temperament with its vision of a more real order beyond the appearances of things. Does such art or *art as such* really convince us that man has his spiritual fatherland in an entire order of super-societal meaning and value; and that this is what, in man and of man, demonstrates that no human being should ever be wholly, or to the entire extent of his person, submitted to the ends of a collectivity?

What of philosophy? No doubt there was a time not so long ago when the quest for wisdom was believed to relate the mind of man directly, if dimly, to an order of eternal truth. But "truth" has now come to be regarded as only a property of propositions; philosophy, a matter of logical analysis; the metaphysical bent of the mind is refused, and they gather at Oxford to discuss the puzzle involved when anyone makes the statement, "The concept 'horse' is not a concept." Yet we moderns heap scorn on those supposedly futile and intricate medieval debates over how many angels could congregate on the point of a pin! It ought to be remembered that such a controversy could not even arise unless men had, like St. Augustine, first learned from Plato *how to conceive, how even to think,* of "spiritual substance"; and unless in truth they know the real and incommensurable difference between the nature of any spirit and the point of even the smallest pin which is of "material substance."

The foregoing has been said not in order to denigrate reason, but in order to suggest how close reason has come to denying itself in this, the only known period of human history in which a human culture and social institutions have been based on mass atheism and not on some religious foundation.

In any case, even if man's exodus into the truth and the attunement of his mind toward ultimate meaning in mathematics, art and philosophy were sufficient to show that there is something about the comparatively few men who actually transcend to these realms which escapes inclusion in collective goals, this would be too aristocratic a viewpoint ever to serve as the basis for the rights of man and the good in just law. Supposing *such* a mind were not engaged in society to the whole extent of its being, how does this serve to warrant the rights of the kind of fellow who usually appears in law court? What is man with his murder, rapine and pillage?

In order that every individual—no matter how close to clod or blubber he may seem to be—still may not be denied his proper claims in the dispensation of justice, political and legal theory may have recourse instead to some principle capable of including everyone without distinction. Thus Rousseau and Kant attribute to reason a formal (and empty) principle of equality and generality of application. So also, Henry Sidgwick corrects and props up the utilitarian norm of the "greatest happiness altogether" by reference to certain supposed rational "intuitions" without which, he admits, there would be insufficient grounds for justice: these are the intuitions of "rational benevolence" ("Each one is morally bound to regard the good of any other individual as much as his own, except when he judges it to be less, when impartially viewed, or less certainly knowable or attainable by him") and of justice or equity ("Similar cases ought to be treated similarly").[22] Under this head falls also Edmond Cahn's analysis of the sense of injustice consisting in an "imaginative interchange" by which the self is known to stand in the jeopardy that befalls any man.

Again, no one will want to deny this. Yet he may wonder whether, without some more fundamental doctrine of man, some more material principles of morality and justice, a merely formal justice is likely to prove sufficient. In a day when the march of events and movements of thought have conspired systematically to darken the human sky and to pull in its horizons, it has become extraordinarily easy to live by the "golden rule," which may require only an interchange of a modicum of the respect which manhood formerly was held to be worth, or even only a reciprocal exchange of *dis*respect: "I'm no good, but neither is my neighbor." [23] I'm no longer a child of God but only an earth-bound animal, a creature of impulse caught in a complex of more or less reason-able—in any case, unavoidable—societal purposes; and so also is my neighbor. This may be the formal meaning left in "You shall love your neighbor *as yourself*" when its material meaning and theological rootage is forgotten. What jeopardizes either me or my neighbor, or what in us and of us is placed in jeopardy by injustice, may not be regarded as very significant. It is not evident that human beings have much worth if the Transcendent does not value them.

With some reluctance (because he too has taken a few nips out of the flask of the Enlightenment) a contemporary man will be driven to the conclusion that the *chief* pillar of the Western idea of justice rests in man's Exodus from the natural law. It was not because you were more in number that the Lord set his love upon you; but it is because the Lord loves you, and is keeping his oath. This is the reason you know the heart of the stranger and the wretched who need redemption. Or it is because through Christ you know the heart of the ungodly, who strive in the toils of hostility and alienation, that you do not derive from man himself the norms of morality, but from the righteousness of God which has shown forth from the faithfulness of God to the faith of men.

Therefore we may find it necessary to look again at the reasons Mari-tain believes the common good should flow back upon every member, or that man in society is not engaged therein to the entire extent of his being. This is not actually established in his thought by reason, the natural law or by human inclination alone. It is true he affirms that "the transcendence of the person . . . *first* asserts itself in the philosophical perspective and relates *first and foremost* to the order of nature"; and he considers it "important to stress the fact that even in the natural order itself the human person transcends the State, to the extent that man has a destiny superior to time. . . ." [24] Yet where he says this he had just written about another matter that is first and foremost: "it was *first* in the religious order and through the sudden pouring forth of the evangelical message that the transcendent dignity of the human person was made manifest. But from that moment on, the consciousness of this dignity little by little won over the sphere of the natural order itself, by penetrating and renewing our consciousness of the law of nature." [25] Thus, "the tap root of human personality is not society, but God." [26]

Now, how are we to understand this apparent commuting back and forth between two things both of which are said to be first and foremost? It is in Maritain's thought the synthesis of the time before and the time after the Exodus from natural law, or the synthesis of revelation with reason, of grace with nature. We do not grasp Catholic political theory correctly if we think that revelation or grace are simply added on to reason or nature which are supposed to be fully intact and sufficiently strong and clear by themselves to furnish us with the ordered structure of just political institutions. This is the side of the matter that is always shown most prominently to the secular humanist or slightly unnerved liberal who needs, it is supposed, first to be convinced of the greater reasonableness of the Roman Catholic view of man and society in contrast to the irrational fideism of Protestantism. But revelation not only *presupposes* reason or grace *presuppose* nature. It must be stressed even more that grace *perfects* nature as revelation *illumines* and *perfects* reason. Under this rubric, Roman Catholic thought can range from a great deal of confidence in the power of natural reason by itself to provide the grounds for justice all the way to an emphasis upon the necessity of revelation for strengthening and fulfilling the tentative suggestions of nature.

Protestant thought, with its more radical understanding of sin and grace, places its emphasis at this end of the scale. But this does not mean that natural law must necessarily be rejected. It may mean rather that reason is simply freed to come to whatever conclusions seem to it valid. In making the Exodus into existence in the immediate presence of the divine righteousness, Protestant thought is not bound in advance to accept and defend only those philosophies of mathematics, law, art, metaphysics and morals which hold these to be evident supertemporal ventures of the human spirit manifesting man's transcendence of society and culture. If a kind of positivism seemed required to interpret rightly these human activities, the morality of the Exodus would still be asserted, resulting in a theological positivism combined with positivisms within the sphere of reason. On the other hand, the theory of natural law, if it seems acceptable within Protestant thought, is saved from the suspicion that by affirming these *other* supertemporal ventures of the human spirit the way was simply being prepared for a defense of the credibility of believing that God actually called us out of Egypt and holds us to our destiny beyond the Desert of civilizations.

In either case, the principal point is that the "knowledge of good and evil" which Adam found it impossible to gain possession of, and which God proposed to keep to his own charge and to hold between Himself and mankind, was the knowledge made manifest in the story of his self-revealing acts and his righteous purpose in making us migrants. This was not the knowledge of good and evil for which man's natural capacities may be competent. Like tilling the ground, keeping sheep, building cities, learning to play on the lyre and the pipe or to forge instruments of bronze and iron—said to be among the capacities of man even after the Fall—the laws of reason and a morality within legal rules can be whatever they in fact are. It simply must be said that while man has the conceptual power to name the animals and thus manifests a human mastery over and penetration of their essence and the mystery of their very being (which is the significance of all naming in the Bible), man cannot name the name of God nor inherently possess the concept of his righteous will. Nor can he name Eve, or himself; for the ultimate meaning of a man's life—whatever may be his knowledge through inclination—lies in the divine naming of him.*

One need not go so far in this direction, however, as to deny the basic meaning of natural law theory as this may be manifest in congeniality or connaturality. For that simply means that Uncreated Reason is "at play not only in *establishing* Natural Law (by the very fact that it creates human nature), but in *making Natural Law known*, through the inclinations of this very nature, to which human reason listens when it knows Natural Law." [27] If man is created for Exodus, it should not be surprising if there is present among the utterances of his created nature an echo of his call into covenant, or that he will sometimes suppose this in him to be the first and only originating voice of the moral law of his very essential being. As Karl Barth might put the point that has to be made: natural justice or the requirements made known to us through fundamental inclination or disinclination are the external or natural basis, the precondition, and the possibility of Exodus into covenant; while covenant-righteousness is the internal basis, the true meaning and the final purpose of whatever utterances of essential human nature may be produced in man's intellect as he seeks to know the good.[28] The question to be raised is whether the morality of Exodus into covenant is not needed as the *explicit* theological premise *actively at work* in the moral life of men in every Egypt of the natural order in order to sustain any proper ethics, to comprehend and interpret it adequately, or even to restore it in this hour of moral and political disorder.

---

* For a fuller development of the theme of the foregoing section, see Chapter One.

IV

So far we have dealt only with the importance for man's life within reason, and within rules of law, of the *fact* that he is ordered to existence in the presence of a transcendent God. However, it is only after we also take into account what sort of righteous God He was and is that we will see the full scope and feel the full force of the problematic relationship between living within reason and nature and living beyond them, between natural justice and redemptive justice.

This relationship may be clarified by some reflections upon the case *United States v. Holmes* and Professor Edmond Cahn's discussion of it.[29] Holmes was one of nine seamen who in an overloaded and leaky lifeboat, in obedience to the orders of the mate and because all members of the crew were deemed necessary for rowing in the storm, threw overboard fourteen male passengers to lighten the boat. The judge, in charging the jury as to the law, said that if no seaman could possibly be dispensed with, then the victims should have been chosen from among the passengers by casting lots, provided—as in this case—there was time enough to do so. Acting under these instructions the jury found Holmes guilty of manslaughter, but he was given a light sentence because of the jury's recommendation of mercy.

Now it seems to me that in his very penetrating and sensitive discussion of this case Professor Cahn does not sufficiently distinguish between the good in law and the good beyond law. He wants rather to "judge Holmes' judge than Holmes" [30]—for his ruling that lots should have been cast. In drawing this conclusion Cahn imports the good beyond law directly and unrefracted into the arena of legal decision and established societal expectation. The dimensions of that crucial moral situation seem to him utterly incommensurate with the arrangement the judge suggested: "the crisis involves stakes too high for gambling and responsibilities too deep for destiny." From what Cahn understands to be the absolute requirements of righteousness when men face such options, he is driven to conclude that none can "be saved separately from the others" and that "if none sacrifice themselves of free will to spare the others," "they must all wait and die together." I cannot myself believe that any such thing can be the meaning of that natural justice which the law ought to endeavor to exact. Instead of fixing our attention upon "gambling" as the solution—with all the frivolous and often corrupt associations the word raises in our minds—we should think rather of *equality* of opportunity as the ethical substance of the relations of these individuals to one another that might have been guarded and expressed by casting lots. Then we will see that the judge spoke for the good in law. In many other matters, what the courts undertake to impose of social control and corrective justice often seems incommensurate with the human relations involved, e.g., when they assess money damage for loss of life or limb.

On the other hand, Cahn speaks admirably of the good beyond law; yet at this level also question may be raised whether his analysis of it is quite right. Cahn's reflections on this case actually show much of the imprint of biblical righteousness, although he mistakenly insists that his is an "anthropocentric" view of the law. The lifeboat situation, he writes, brings into full force the "morals of the last days." This means that all the established relationships in which an individual usually stands are stripped away; all his distinguishing features and all the special bonds of responsibility that pertain to normal human existence in its fixed orders and institutional framework are now gone. This leaves him "a generic creature only," responsible only but fully to the *genus* in every man in the boat and not to their specific particularities which are defined by continuing social relationships. ". . . Every person in the boat embodies the entire genus. Whoever saves one, saves the whole human race; whoever kills one, kills mankind." "For where all have become congeners, pure and simple, no one can save himself by killing another. . . . He has no moral individuality left to save. Under the terms of the moral constitution, it will be *wholly* his self that he kills in his vain effort to preserve himself."

It should be pointed out in passing, so far as the good in social procedures is concerned, that these people in their desperate plight were not wholly stripped to congeneric relationships. Two married men and a little boy were spared; and two women—sisters of one of the victims— voluntarily leaped to join their brother in his death. And the mate selected the males only, and not women or children, for inclusion among those to be forcibly ejected. If this was not entirely right, should he perhaps have thrown overboard a 300-pound woman, if she had been aboard, for the sake of saving two 150-pound men? It is, of course, to forestall such dilemmas arising (in which any solution which suggests itself is so obviously incommensurate with what is at stake in the collision of life with life) that Cahn attempts to abstract from every specific particularity of the situation.

It is more important to indicate, however, that in his reflection upon this situation Cahn transgresses the limits of his own "anthropocentric" view of the good in law and of the moral good beyond the law. He speaks, of course, of people becoming "mere congeners" under circumstances in which the "morals of the last days" prevail. In spite of this terminology, however, it seems clear to me that no interpretation of merely generic responsibility provides adequate basis for, or is the actual source of, the conclusions he draws (apart from whether the judgments he feels driven to make define the justice possible in law or only the meaning of a righteousness that goes beyond possible legal enactment). I think it is clear that these are the requirements not of the "moral constitution" but of human life-in-community constituted by the Exodus or by the covenant-righteous-ness of God.

It is noteworthy that thinkers in the past who have put forward theories fundamentally like that of Cahn have not ordinarily drawn such extreme conclusions merely from a morality of generic responsibility. Kant's categorical imperative was: "Act so that in your person as well as in the person of every other you are treating mankind also as an end, never merely as a means"; [31] but it is doubtful whether he would suppose that fidelity to "mankind" as an end would itself go the length of all waiting and dying together. For John Locke, men in a state of nature—where all are congeners—suffer the inconvenience of having to judge in their own case; yet as such they have the right and the duty to preserve man-kind in general. But in saying that it is the law of nature and of reason for man also to preserve the rights of others as his own, Locke inserts this qualification: *"when his own preservation comes not in competition,* ought he, *as much as he can,* to preserve the rest of mankind." [32] Surely this is the extent of obligation that can be "anthropocentrically" based on nature and reason or on the "moral constitution"; and this was enacted in the judge's ruling that lots should have been drawn. Generic duty gives equal primacy to self-preservation while setting it in the context of any arrangement which makes this most compatible with the preservation of mankind generally. Who knows, perhaps if the male passengers had not been thrown violently overboard at what must have seemed to them the arbitrary command of the mate, if instead they had been called upon to share in lots as the means of securing general and equal application of what had to be done to and upon all alike, they might not have resisted so wretchedly—they might have evidenced their agreement with the general will arising *from all* and not only from the mate's command. To such height "conscience's generic commands" [33] and rules of law may rise. But hardly to the level of *requiring* that men should all wait and die together rather than that the lives of some be saved.

Cahn is actually voicing a moral judgment that roots in the biblical tradition which measures fidelity in terms of a higher righteousness. It is not without significance that he writes: "The crisis in the longboat was apocalyptic in character, the kind of crisis in which, as Jesus saw, family ties, earthly possessions, and distinctions of every conceivable kind become null and void." It is only the immediate presence of the claims of the righteousness of God between man and man, and not any sense of generic injustice, which asks of men that on occasion they be unwilling to save their lives at the unavoidable cost of another, and which enables them on occasion to have such faith that their own lives are securely in God's hands as to be able actually to make the sacrifice.

This was indeed the burden of Jesus' teaching as an expression of man's Exodus from the natural order into existence in the immediate presence of God and of his redemptive purpose. His ethics is not understandable apart from the presence of God's kingdom. It was not, as Schweitzer supposed, the imminent *coming* of the kingdom which produced Jesus' teachings as an "interim ethic." It was rather the *presence* of the kingdom which produced his unlimited estimate of what one man owes another in prompt and radical service;* and at the same time it was his living in the presence of God which rendered negligible the fixed relationships among men in this present age. His message does not stand or fall with his conception about the quick end of the world. It would be better to reverse this proposition and say that this expectation about the future sprang rather from Jesus' conviction about God and from Jesus' existence in his presence. Jesus and the prophets were so overwhelmed by their sense of the sovereign majesty and utter faithfulness of God and the absolute character of his covenant-will that the kingdoms, the legal systems and the customary or natural moralities of this world were already liquidated before their eyes, and consequently they foreshortened the coming divine act of judgment. Contrasted with God and his righteous will, the world seemed such a trivial place that it was already, as it were, at an end. Natural self-preservation was suspended, as also were the rules about Sabbath observance, if they stood in the way of manifesting the concrete response of serving the slightest need or self-sacrificially saving the life of the neighbor. Jesus was so convinced of God's will and determination that he felt himself to be standing on the frontiers of time, on the frontiers also of any natural justice. He viewed the world exclusively *sub specie Dei*. In the situation of direct encounter with God and neighbor, the future was taken out of man's hands.[34] The frontiers of the righteousness of God expanded to establish everyone within its territory even if the sun has not yet gone down on a Sabbath, or even if we apparently still live within the natural and within the present social order.

Jesus' teaching was not based on insight into the natural law. In the story of the Good Samaritan he did not simply depict "the workings of the moral constitution with sublime accuracy and realism." It is true he begins by saying "a certain man" and not by calling the man's proper name. But this does not restrict us to the conclusion Cahn draws, namely, that "the person in need of succor is to be conceived in purely generic terms. He stands for mankind in its prototypical predicament." Instead, this is true in the sense that he epitomizes the predicament of the man whom the whole righteousness of God is bent on helping. To step within the divine purpose means to act out of the thought that the person in need stands for the whole human species *in God's eyes*. Therefore Cahn is

---

* The above paragraph significantly changes the emphasis, but not the substance, of my interpretation of the relation between eschatology and ethics in Jesus' teachings in *Basic Christian Ethics*, ch. 1.

on safer ground when he writes, "The duty is so high because by execut-ing it one most closely emulates God's functional relation toward man, i.e., one acts toward the species as He is conceived to act." [35] Moreover, not only the person in need but the ungodly, the unjust, the enemy and the aggressor are included within the scope of this righteousness. Be-cause Cahn undertakes to interpret much of this in anthropocentric terms only, and because he intends it for an account of the good in law, he of course cannot go quite as far as this out of regard for the genus alone. While no one should suffer himself to be saved at the expense of another who might lose the casting of the dice, still Cahn is of the opinion that if a man is set upon by an unjust aggressor no generic demands or the morality of the "last days" requires that self-defense be omitted. St. Augustine, in accepting with greater ease than Cahn all manner of crude devices for public or common defense and while still viewing private self-defense as outside the pale of the righteousness God wants extended toward any member of the needy, sinful race, saw somewhat more clearly the meaning of the good beyond law and consequently at the same time he found bringing it into relation with the law somewhat more problematic.[36]

Yet Cahn shows extraordinary perception of the ways in which our common religious heritage is effective within decisions of the courts. For example, in whittling down the irresponsibility of a passer-by for the "stranger" in need of rescue, do we not have an echo of the reminder that "you know the heart of a stranger," and at least some dim recollec-tion of God's right relation to him? . . . "No matter how careful one may be in exercising control over a piece of machinery, if a 'stranger' happens to become entangled in it, there arises an affirmative duty to halt the machine." Here I fail to discern the consistency between the discus-sion in the case of the lifeboat and Cahn's description, with evident ap-proval, of the further rule of law: "But if halting the machine would require the operator to incur a grievous injury to himself, that is beyond the limits of his legal duty. In other words, the law's tendency is to com-pel men to act like good neighbors and leave heroism to individual option." [37] The law does not enact that they must run the risk of dying together. Not that this is incorrect, but that if it is correct then "judging Holmes' judge" was not—so far as concerns the law or "conscience's generic commands"; [38] and apart now from the moral responsibility that may be incurred, from some other source beyond the legal limits and beyond an ethic that takes its measure for human behavior from man himself.

We need to examine with extraordinary care the relationship between this redemptive righteousness beyond the law and the good in law itself. I have already pointed out that no codification of God's law can be brought directly into connection with the civil code. No legal system can tolerate within its own sphere a rival code of law, whether it be revealed law, or republished natural law, or even a codified and inflexible natural law. And it was for this reason that we looked behind the biblical codes and specific religious teachings to the divine measure of righteousness or faithfulness. It now has to be pointed out that, while this redemptive righteousness may exert a transforming pressure upon men in the process of lawmaking and decision-making, it cannot (any more than a revealed code) be taken as the direct aim or goal of the legal system. No earthly society can be based simply on divine charity; only the kingdom of God has that as its constitution and fundamental rule of law. Whatever may be the significance of the Exodus for the actual conduct of affairs, and however much openness our system of legal rules and procedures should have to such an understanding of the ultimate meaning of righteousness among men, it seems plain that love cannot be regarded as the direct and exclusive purpose of the law.

On the other hand, God places the requirement of righteousness in some sense upon the whole nation as well as upon individuals in their private affairs. The "morals of the last days" always impinge upon the administration of justice; and "this planet we live on is not entirely unlike the longboat of the *William Brown*." It is not enough to say that this is only a metaphor. It is not enough to say that an awareness of the "morals of the last days" or of the righteousness of God between every man in the longboat of the social order provides us "only a moral attitude or an answer, not a moral decision." [39] For at every moment we are making *decisions* as men ultimately before the righteousness of God, either to throw our lives away or to keep them for a possible better accounting, even if only for a better opportunity for meaningful sacrifice. As men whose actual generic situation has been revealed *under God* to contain possibilities and duties we would never have suspected, we must decide whether to preserve the genus in ourselves, or the genus in others, or else we settle for some feasible arrangement for doing both with natural equity and justice. In at least some of these decisions, the righteousness of the God who has known us in times past will have something to do with our perception of a possible justice, and it may enlarge and make more sensitive the justice we discern.*

---

* It was necessary for Cahn to strip his analysis of "congeneric" morality of much of the extremism it derives from covenant-faithfulness in order, in his latest book, to make this the possible substance of moral and juridical decisions. See the quotation on pp. 225-26 above. There "identification" with the victim in the dock as a "specimen of the genus" means to judge and to care as if "we already stand there." This means equality, regard for another *"as thyself"* with emphasis. I suggest that, in this passage from his latest book, the "morality of the last days" (from *The Moral Decision*) has transformed and elevated Cahn's more naturalistic views in *The Sense of Injustice;* but that at the same time, by becoming more than an attitude and upon becoming the material principle of actual decisions, "generic morality" has necessarily lost a

I have said that Cahn grasps with penetrating understanding the meaning of the righteousness that ultimately judges the actions of men, but
that he does not exercise due caution in importing this directly into the
legal system as a rule of law in the case we have discussed. His suggested
ruling that in "the morality of the last days" all must wait and die together may be regarded as the introjection of the self-sacrificial spirit of
charity into the structures of natural justice, which then as a rule of
law (of the fundamental law, no less) is impervious to the creative possibility of saving some by means of any fair arrangement which a wise
charity might devise. The same is true of some aspects of the Roman
Catholic ethics of natural law. Some of the authoritative teachings of the
church manifest an *extremity* which is doubtless to be accounted for as a
result of the impact of divine charity upon the republication of natural
law by the teaching church, and at the same time an *inflexibility* which
(because this is then said to be *natural* law) is quite impervious to any
renewed determination of what is good even by charity itself. Again, due
caution is not exercised and righteousness of a sort becomes impacted in
an ethical rule. This is then believed to be the natural law which absolutely determines the *means* that may be used and those which may
never be employed even for the sake of the ends of charity. Before introducing this analogy to Cahn's conclusions in the Holmes case, let me say
that he would himself vigorously deny the comparison. He would draw
a sharp distinction between the ethics of the birth room, where all normal
social and scientific instrumentalities are available and no useful ones
should be refused, and the ethics of the lifeboat situation, which means
that our normal choices have been suspended and generic obligation
alone should prevail. I have said enough about the universal relevance
of the "morals of the last days" to every decision which confronts us in
this frail craft in which we all dwell to indicate that I do not see any
significant distinction to be drawn between the two cases. Cahn will
either have to revise his opinion and say that the lifeboat situation was
a crisis utterly beyond the competence of law to rule, or agree that some
of the extreme conclusions drawn in moral theology are comparable to his.

Suppose the case of a pregnant woman suffering from a severe kidney
disease. Because her weakened kidneys cannot function for herself and
also for her child, medical prognosis is that her life will end before the
fetus becomes viable. Both will die together. It is, of course, totally wrong
to say that the church's teaching, in this and similar cases, is that the
child's life, or its chance of life, should be *preferred* to that of the mother.
Rather, both have *equal* right to life; and since neither is an unjust aggressor, no *direct* action may be taken against the life of one for the sake

---

good deal of its prophetic and eschatological vitality. This is a nice illustration of
how alone covenant-righteousness interpenetrates the morality or the structures of
any actual juridical order.

of saving the other. Both are congeners, and (if direct action to save both without direct action against either should fail) both must wait and die together. If the child were an adolescent delinquent and threatened his mother's life with a gun, she could repel his unjust aggression by any means, e.g., by taking his life. But since, in the supposed case, there is to be found no violation of natural justice on the part of the child whose growth imperils the life of its mother, the generic justice which declares that "whoever kills one, kills mankind" determines the right action in the case. Both are congeners, with an equal right to life which should not be denied. To kill one by direct action would be murder. Of course, whether the woman aborts or whether she does not, the child dies; but to induce abortion would mean to choose to do positive wrong in order that some good may come of it, i.e., that at least one of the two lives may be saved. Not even divine charity can make it right ever to do something inherently wrong simply because it may be a means to some good consequence.

Now, one may object against this line of reasoning that the fetus is not a congener, and he may say that it does not become a full member of the genus with rights equal to those of the mother until there is motion felt in the womb, or until birth, or until the child is two years of age, and so on. But granting that decision has been made on these presuppositions, it may rightly be claimed (in the words of a recent Roman Catholic book which discusses this case) that while the Church appears merciless, she is not: "It is her logic which is merciless." [40] Indeed, it is true that one cannot grant the premises and then refuse to draw the conclusion of this natural-law argument. Someone may wish to join issue with the Roman Catholic understanding of the natural law in this and in similar cases. However, it is more important to call attention to the fact that the more moral theology in this tradition lays claim to clear and certain knowledge of the natural law, the more charity is ruled out of any influence upon moral decisions.

On the one hand, this natural-law theory seems quite certain that natural self-defense against an unjust aggressor is quite all right. To the contrary, so long as divine charity directed moral decision to what was primarily required of it, private self-defense against even an unjust aggressor was the last thing to be found among the permissions of love; and it was not until the triumph of Aristotelian naturalism and the founding of ethics more emphatically upon the basis of natural law that Christian ethics grew accustomed to this assumption. On the other hand, this natural-law theory seems quite certain that on no occasion may direct action be taken against the life of another. To the contrary, and at the same time private self-defense was ruled out, charity was flexibly wise in being able to accept the good that might be gained (or the greater harm that might be prevented) by participation in warfare for a just cause.[41] In fighting a *justum bellum* a Christian soldier takes *direct* (if unavoidable) action against the life of the enemy as a means to some good consequence which cannot be obtained in any other way; and, unless one wants to split the longitudinal quarter-sections of hairs, he has to admit that the ethical dilemmas confronting charity in its work of saving life in the birth room are of the same order.

In the case of a woman with a growing fetus in her Fallopian tube, a natural-law decision about means again is given the supremacy in Roman Catholic teachings, while, of course, in this case as in the other, maximum use is made of the distinction between direct and indirect effects. If there is honest doubt whether the swelling is a fetus or a malignant growth, the growth may be removed. If the tube has burst, the hemorrhage may be stopped, in attempting to save the mother's life, even if the unavoidable indirect result of this is the death of the fetus. But, since both mother and child are congeners, whoever kills one directly, kills mankind. As for the morality of removing an intact Fallopian tube which contains a fetus unable to live separately from the mother, the moralists are in disagreement; and on this point Catholic moral theology may be in process of changing its conclusions about the natural law of such cases. Some say, both must wait and die together; or at least the doctor must restrain his mercy until the tube has burst, and then action to save the mother's life will have its predicted double effect. A few moralists say that the tube itself is in a pathological condition else the fetus would not have been implanted there. An increasing number of Roman Catholic moralists, however, are saying that in any case the tube is showing such an abnormal reaction and has already suffered grave damage from the extraordinary event taking place within it that it may be regarded as a "diseased" organ and removed.* In other words, the solution is to preserve the natural-law reasoning quite intact and supreme; but in this case to discover that the natural-law rule which actually applies is "the principle of the whole." This is to say, the case should be analyzed in terms of the relation of a diseased part to the whole organism, rather than as primarily a matter of the relation of one human life to another.[42] In all this, again, charity has no role in determining the means, but must always wait for reason to supply it with distinctions of right from wrong drawn from nature.†

* When the authorities disagree, and the church has not spoken, the matter remains "uncertain." A merely "probable" opinion leaves decision no ground for *theoretical* certainty; but it may be resolved *practically* into sufficient certainty for action, even though the "probable" but "grave" opinion is held only by a minority, or one or two, of the moral theologians.

† A more complete discussion of the relation of charity (or the morality of the Exodus) to an ethics of natural law means (and to the morality of ectopic operations) will be found in Paul Ramsey: *War and the Christian Conscience*, Durham, N.C.: Duke University Press, 1961, ch. 8.

What has gone wrong in this scheme is that the relation between the good in natural law and the good beyond law, or the morality of the natural order and the morality of Exodus into the sphere of the redemptive righteousness of God, has been misconceived. The result is that here there is at once too much mercy made a matter of legal requirement and too little mercy transcending and still able to transform the legal or natural requirements. There is too much supernatural righteousness made immanent to the legal order and petrified into static limits upon moral action: what conscience generically demands, or what "knowledge through inclination" or the sense of injustice, in short what "nature herself teaches," shows pervasively the influence of the religious conception of each individual soul's unique relation to God. Each is an immortal soul—both child and mother—and only God who keeps unto himself the divine significance of their names has the dominion over each life. Moreover, the full force and flavor of this call to obey the law of nature participates in a redemptive righteousness which ventures to regard the life of another as choiceworthy in preference to one's own when decision must be made between them. In short, the good in law has been invaded by the meaning of the good beyond law. For it ought not to be denied that it may be a noble thing for a mother, when choice can be made, to sacrifice her life that her child may live; or even that, in the case of ectopic pregnancy, it may be a noble thing—at least an allowable manifestation of free human choice—for the mother to join her child in death, as the sisters did who followed their brother out of the longboat. But we need to exercise extraordinary care how we say that grace perfects nature in order not hastily and rigidly to make this a rule of canon law, or of hospital practice.

To regard such actions as morality to be legally *enacted*—either in the civil or canon law or in hospital practice—would be altogether different from openness to graceful possibilities which may be freely chosen. To enforce this requirement would be truly a merciless ethic, limiting in advance by a so-called natural law (even by grace-perfected nature) the skillful arrangements which a creative, redemptive justice may have the wisdom to devise for the saving of life. Here it must be said bluntly that it would be a sentimental view of charity and its work of enlightening specific decision to rule out the possibility that someone in the position of the mate vis-à-vis such crucial alternatives (e.g., the doctor or the husband) may even conclude that casting lots on behalf of the two congeners (however incommensurate this devise may be with what is at stake) is a feasible and choiceworthy way of insuring them equal opportunity for life. Short of this, of course, charity if it is flexibly wise may discern that in the actual situation life has not yet been utterly stripped of all particular relationships: there may be the mother's responsibility to older children to consider. This will be the direction given to attitude and action if our understanding of the moral dilemma is not reduced to static legal demands but rather kept open to the "morality of the last days" and to a possible new and concrete meaning of extending redemptive righteousness to those in need of succor. In no case would indecision be called for, or both be allowed to wait and die together.

In another of its teachings the Roman Catholic Church has shown an inflexibility in natural law definitions of means; but in this instance an opening was made for decision in terms of charity. Yet the same issues we have been discussing are revealed in the reluctance or hesitancy which Catholic moral theology has had in arriving at the conclusion that sometimes it is a rightful act of charity for an individual to donate a healthy part of his body, e.g., an eye, to be grafted into the body of another person who needs one. This would seem obviously permissible; although anyone should sit down first and count the cost to see whether in fact he has a vocation for it, because, unlike undertaking the celibate life, he cannot go back on it once the gift is made. But, according to sound and ancient teaching, the ethics of operating on a single physical body should conform to "the principle of the whole" (i.e., a part of the human body may be sacrificed for the health of the whole).

An individual person, however, does *not* stand in relation to the whole society or to his fellow man as part to whole. It is a natural injustice forcibly to use him for medical experiment, no matter what good may come of it for the whole of humanity. In our day we have learned the importance of having such barricades in our ethical heritage; and the same is true for the conservation of our sense of the value of life by the unchanging teachings of the Catholic Church against the views sometimes voiced that infanticide, after all, should be made a matter of private morality and not of the legal order.[43] Still charity relates life with life in covenant closer than can be imaged by part-whole or whole-whole distinctions. It ought not to have debated so long about whether the sacrifice of a part of one body, not for its own wholeness but for the sight of another, is immoral, because the means used is never permitted by the natural law no matter what the goal. Just so, the ethics of the birth room, and of every other longboat situation, must be kept open to the requirements of a saving justice beyond the law. It is true that, in the abstract, the end never justifies the means. Even the supposition that an absolutely imperative end justifies the absolutely necessary means contains dangers of tyranny so long as the relation of utility is regarded as operating wholly within the natural or societal order.

The doctrine that it is better for one man to die than for a whole people to perish is a safe doctrine only in the decisions of someone like Jesus who applied it to himself and not on the lips of a Caiaphas who made this good beyond law into a definition of the good within legal rules and forthwith applied them to another man. Still, when the forces of physical nature are already fast at work choosing their own inexorable means for producing an undesirable result and narrowing the range of human choice, to draw the conclusion that the boat must be allowed to be engulfed by the waves unless some rescue ship appears on the horizon or that mother and child both must die unless medical progress (or some more refined verdict from the natural lawyers) comes in time would mean to regard the complicity of indecision in two or more wrongs as less heinous than a decisive and direct, if otherwise unavoidable, action against one to save the life of the other. At this point one might think of appealing to John Dewey's doctrine of the interpenetration of means and ends in all that we do. It is sufficient also—and it indicates a greater sensitivity to every dimension of the moral problem—to say that restricting choice to only one of these options, on the ground that we already clearly know which means are moral and which forbidden, is likely to occur only to a type of ethical reasoning which erects too closed a system of natural law and does not venture upon the Exodus, and consequently does not view right and wrong with that freedom which the righteousness of God both gives to prevail and demands as far as may be possible among men.

The conclusion of this and the previous chapter, then, is this: We have arrived at least at the borders of the only possible relationship between theological ethics and the philosophy and practice of law. If the former is not codified into a rival legal system and the latter is based on an unstructured, nondeductive "natural law" known in the context of the case through "the sense of injustice" or through "inclination," then both divine "righteousness" and natural "justice" may play a part creatively together in decisions, and may exert a converging pressure toward the growth and reform of law as a proper ordering of human reality.

Notes

Introduction

Something about Christian Social Ethics

1. *Christengemeinde und Buergergemeinde* (1946), in *Against the Stream*, p. 28.
2. New York: Charles Scribner's Sons, 1950.

One

Fyodor Dostoevski
On Living Atheism: No Morality without Immortality

1. See *The Point of View* (London: Oxford University Press, 1939), p. 70, and *Papirer*, X' A50.
2. *Crime and Punishment* (Modern Library edition. New York: Random House), Part V, chap. iv.
3. *Ibid.*, Part I, chap. vi.
4. *Ibid.*, Epilogue (italics mine).
5. *The Possessed* (Modern Library edition. New York: Random House), Part II, chap. v.
6. *Ibid.*, Part III, chap. vi, §ii.
7. *Ibid.*, Part I, chap. iii, §viii.
8. *Ibid.*, Part III, chap. vi, §ii.
9. *True Humanism* (New York: Charles Scribner's Sons, 1954), p. 53.
10. Gabriel Marcel, *Man against Mass Society* (Chicago: Henry Regnery Co., 1952), pp. 55-56.
11. *The Possessed*, Part II, chap. vii, §ii.
12. *Ibid.*, Part I, chap. iii, §iv.
13. *Ibid.*, Part III, chap. i, §iv.
14. *Ibid.*, Conclusion.
15. Emil Brunner, *Justice and the Social Order* (New York: Harper & Brothers, 1945), p. 213.
16. Marcel, *op. cit.*, p. 14.
17. *Ibid.*, p. 34.
18. *Ibid.*, p. 176.
19. *Ibid.*, p. 165.
20. *A Raw Youth*, Part III, chap. vii.
21. Quoted by Nicolas Berdyaev, *Dostoevsky* (New York: Sheed & Ward, 1934), p. 105.

22. Dostoevski, *Letters from the Underworld* (Everyman edition. New York: E. P. Dutton & Co.), Part I, chaps. vii and viii.

23. *The Brothers Karamazov* (Modern Library edition. New York: Random House), Book V, chap. iv.

24. *Darkness at Noon* ("Penguin Signet" ed.), pp. 116-17.

25. Marcel, *op. cit.*, p. 16.

26. "Second Thoughts about Humanism," *Selected Essays* (New York: Harcourt, Brace & World, Inc., 1932), p. 397.

27. Albert Camus, *The Rebel* (New York: Alfred A. Knopf, 1954), p. 204.

28. *Ibid.*, pp. 222-45.

29. *Ibid.*, p. 273.

30. *The Brothers Karamazov*, Book V, chap. iii (italics mine).

31. *Ibid.*, chap. iv.

32. *Ibid.*, chap. iii.

33. *Ibid.*, Book XI, chap. x.

Two

Fyodor Dostoevski

God's Grace and Man's Guilt

1. *Distinctive Ideas of the Old Testament* (London: Epworth Press, 1944), pp. 164, 165, 171.

2. See my *Basic Christian Ethics* (New York: Charles Scribner's Sons, 1950), pp. 288-92.

3. *Laws of Ecclesiastical Polity*, Book I, chap. viii, §§5-7 (Everyman ed., New York: E. P. Dutton & Co.), I, 177-80 (italics mine).

4. Karl Barth, *Dogmatics in Outline* (New York: Philosophical Library, 1949), p. 119.

5. Rudolph Otto, *Naturalism and Religion* (New York: G. P. Putnam's Sons, 1907), p. 155.

6. *Pensées*, §347.

7. Quotations from Dostoevski are taken from the Modern Library editions of *The Brothers Karamazov, Crime and Punishment,* and *The Possessed* (New York: Random House) and from the Everyman edition of the *Letters from the Underworld* (New York: E. P. Dutton & Co.).

8. Marjorie Grene, *Dreadful Freedom* (Chicago: University of Chicago Press, 1948), pp. 78-81.

9. *The Sickness unto Death* (Princeton: Princeton University Press, 1948), pp. 78-81.

10. *Ibid.*, p. 182.

11. *Works* (Philadelphia: Muhlenberg Press), I, 87.

12. Kierkegaard, *op. cit.*, p. 205.

13. *Ibid.*, p. 186.

14. *Ibid.*, p. 187.

15. *Ibid.*

16. *Ibid.*, p. 186.

17. *Ibid.*, p. 180.

18. Barth, *op. cit.*, p. 116.

19. Augustine, *On Nature and Grace*, chap. 21 (*Basic Writings of St. Augustine*, ed. Whitney J. Oates. New York: Random House, 1948, I, 533).

20. *Ibid.*, chap. 22 (*Basic Writings*, I, 534).

21. *Dostoevsky* (New York: Sheed & Ward, 1934), p. 71.

22. *Ibid.*

23. *On the Trinity* viii. 5 (*Basic Writings*, II, 778).

Three

Religious Aspects of Marxism

1. Alexander Miller, *The Christian Significance of Karl Marx* (New York: The Macmillan Company, 1952), p. 88.

2. *Ibid.*, p. 28.

3. John Macmurray, *Creative Society.*

Four

Jean-Paul Sartre
Sex in Being

1. New York: The Devin-Adair Co., 1955.

2. "Existentialism is a Humanism," in *Existentialism from Dostoevsky to Sartre* (ed. Walter Kaufmann). Meridian Books, 1956, p. 309.

3. *The Reprieve*, vol. II of *Roads to Freedom*. New York: Knopf, 1947, p. 407.

4. *Thus Spake Zarathustra*, IV, lxvii (The Philosophy of Nietzsche, Modern Library Giant, Random House, pp. 264, 267).

5. James Collins: *The Existentialists: A Critical Study*. Chicago: Henry Regnery Co., 1952, pp. 172, 179, 180, 181.

6. *Being and Nothingness*. New York: Philosophical Library, 1956, p. 545.

7. *Ibid.*, p. 537.

8. *Ibid.*, p. 540.

9. *Ibid.*, p. 545 and cf. 564.

10. *Ibid.*, p. 540.

11. *Ibid.*, p. 547.

12. *Ibid.*, p. 542.

13. *No Exit and Three Other Plays*. New York: Vintage Books, Inc.

14. *Being and Nothingness*, p. 185.

15. *Ibid.*, p. liv.

16. *Ibid.*, p. 78.

17. *Ibid.*, p. 173.

18. *Ibid.*, pp. 254-8.

19. *Ibid.*, p. 363.

20. *Ibid.*, p. 266.

21. *Ibid.*, p. 264, cf. 271.

22. *Ibid.*, p. 269.

23. *Ibid.*, p. 275.

24. *Ibid.*, pp. 259-62.

25. *Ibid.*, p. 263.

26. *Ibid.*, p. 578.

27. *Ibid.*, p. 263.

28. *Ibid.*, p. 222.

29. *Ibid.*, p. 268.

30. *Ibid.*, p. 288.

31. *Ibid.*, p. 410.

32. *Ibid.*, cf. 555.

33. *Ibid.*, p. 408.

34. *Ibid.*, p. 223.

35. *Ibid.*, p. 228.

36. *Ibid.*, p. 228.

37. *Ibid.*, p. 363.
38. *Ibid.*, p. 364.
39. *Ibid.*, p. 297.
40. *Ibid.*, p. 363.
41. *Ibid.*, cf. p. 286.
42. *Ibid.*, p. 408.
43. *Ibid.*, p. 297.
44. *Ibid.*, p. 367.
45. *Ibid.*, p. 367.
46. *Ibid.*, p. 316.
47. *Ibid.*, pp. 309, 323-6.
48. *Ibid.*, p. 303.
49. *Ibid.*, p. 289.
50. *Ibid.*, p. 346.
51. *Ibid.*, p. 352.
52. *Ibid.*, p. 353.
53. *Ibid.*, p. 371.
54. *Ibid.*, p. 374.
55. *Ibid.*, p. 375.
56. *Ibid.*, p. 376.
57. *Ibid.*, pp. 371-2.
58. *Ibid.*, p. 378.
59. *Ibid.*, p. 378.
60. *Ibid.*, pp. 379-80.
61. *Ibid.*, p. 382.
62. *Ibid.*, p. 383.
63. *Ibid.*, p. 406.

64. *Ibid.*, p. 387.
65. *Ibid.*, p. 393.
66. *Ibid.*, p. 384.
67. *Ibid.*, pp. 384-5.
68. *Ibid.*, p. 386.
69. *Ibid.*, p. 388.
70. *Ibid.*, p. 389.
71. *Ibid.*, p. 390.
72. *Ibid.*, p. 391.
73. *Ibid.*, p. 394.
74. *Ibid.*, p. 395.
75. *Ibid.*, p. 396.
76. *Ibid.*, p. 394.
77. *Ibid.*, p. 396.
78. *Ibid.*, p. 397.
79. *Ibid.*, p. 398.
80. *Ibid.*, p. 397.
81. *Ibid.*, p. 404.
82. *Ibid.*, p. 399.
83. *Ibid.*, p. 403.
84. *Ibid.*, p. 399.
85. *Ibid.*, p. 405.
86. *Ibid.*, p. 411.
87. *Ibid.*, p. 412.
88. *Ibid.*, p. 571.
89. *Ibid.*, p. 579.
90. *Ibid.*, p. 234.

91. *The Art of Loving: An Enquiry into the Nature of Love* (World Perspectives, vol. 9, ed. Ruth Anshen). New York: Harper and Brothers, 1956.
92. *Love, Power and Justice*. Chicago: University of Chicago Press, 1954.
93. *Being and Nothingness*, p. 566.
94. *Ibid.*, pp. 575-6.
95. *Ibid.*, p. 90.
96. *Ibid.*, p. 93.
97. *Ibid.*, p. 599.
98. *Ibid.*, p. 620.
99. *Ibid.*, p. 623.
100. *Ibid.*, p. 615.
101. *Summa Theologica*, I, p. 2, art. 1.
102. *Being and Nothingness*, p. 87.
103. *Ibid.*, p. 101.
104. *Ibid.*, p. 203.
105. *Institutes*, I, xv, 6.
106. "Existentialism is a Humanism," p. 307.
107. *Being and Nothingness*, pp. 67, 69, *passim*.
108. *Ibid.*, p. 70, n. 9.
109. "Existentialism is a Humanism," pp. 307-8.
110. *Ibid.*, pp. 291-2.
111. *Ibid.*, p. 295.
112. *Ibid.*, pp. 292-9.
113. *Being and Nothingness*, p. 408.
114. *Ibid.*, pp. 408, 409, 410.
115. *Ibid.*, p. 423.
116. *Ibid.*, p. 423.

117. *Op. cit.*, p. 58-9.

118. *Being and Nothingness*, p. 594.

119. "Existentialism is a Humanism," p. 294.

120. *Being and Nothingness*, p. 429.

121. See above, p. 77.

122. *Being and Nothingness*, p. 427-8.

123. *Ibid.*, p. 424.

124. *Ibid.*, p. 425.

125. *Ibid.*, p. 425.

126. *Ibid.*, p. 425.

127. *Ibid.*, p. 413.

128. *Ibid.*, p. 515.

129. *Ibid.*, p. 376.

130. "Rules for Married Persons, or Matrimonial Chastity," *The Rules and Exercises of Holy Living.*

131. *Sex Relation in Christian Thought.* New York: Harper and Brothers, 1959, p. 208.

132. *Sex in Christianity and Psychoanalysis.* New York: Oxford University Press, 1955.

Five

Reinhold Niebuhr
Christian Love and Natural Law

1. *Christian Realism and Political Problems* (New York: Charles Scribner's Sons, 1953), Chap. 10.

2. *Existentialism* (New York: Philosophical Library, 1947), p. 15.

3. *Ibid.*, p. 18.

4. *Ibid.*, p. 18.

5. *Ibid.*, p. 27.

6. *Ibid.*, p. 51.

7. *Ibid.*, p. 53.

8. *Ibid.*, pp. 54-55.

9. *Christian Realism and Political Problems*, pp. 129-130.

10. *Faith and History* (New York: Charles Scribner's Sons, 1949), p. 174.

11. Ibsen, *Peer Gynt.*

12. *Faith and History*, p. 175.

13. Nathaniel Micklem, *Law and the Laws* (Edinburgh: W. Green & Sons, Ltd., 1952), pp. 108-109.

14. *The Nature and Destiny of Man: A Christian Interpretation*, Vol. I, *Human Nature* (New York: Charles Scribner's Sons, 1941), 287. Cf. also his use of the analogy with health at the beginning of the section "The Locus of Original Righteousness," *ibid.*, pp. 276-277.

15. *Christianity and Society*, Spring, 1948, p. 27.

16. *Loc. cit.*

17. *An Interpretation of Christian Ethics* (New York: Harper and Brothers, 1935), pp. 209-210.

18. *Ibid.*, pp. 155, 159, 162, 165, 168 (italics mine).

19. *Loc. cit.*, p. 158.

20. *The Nature and Destiny of Man*, I, 280-281 *et passim*

21. *Loc. cit.*, pp. 154-155 (italics mine).

22. *Ibid.*, p. 172 (italics mine).

23. *Ibid.*, *pp.* 172, 173 (italics mine).

24. *An Interpretation of Christian Ethics*, p. 144.

25. *Ibid.*, p. 83.

26. *Ibid.*, p. 203

27. Jacques Maritain, *The Rights of Man and Natural Law* (New York: Charles Scribner's Sons, 1943), p. 70.

28. *Faith and History*, p. 180.

29. *Ibid.*, p. 174.

30. *Ibid.*, p. 181.

31. "Kinsey and the Moral Problem of Man's Sexual Life," *An Analysis of the Kinsey Reports . . .* , ed. Donald P. Geddes (New York: E. P. Dutton & Co., 1954), Chap. IV.

32. *Faith and History*, p. 183.

33. *Ibid.*, p. 182.

34. *Ibid.*, p. 183.

35. See, e.g., *An Interpretation of Christian Ethics*, pp. 105, 110, 111.

36. *Ibid.*, p. 106 (italics mine).

37. *Ibid.*, pp. 105, 107, 140 (italics mine.)

38. *The Nature and Destiny of Man: A Christian Interpretation*, Vol. II, *Human Destiny* (New York: Charles Scribner's Sons, 1943), Secs. II and III.

39. *Ibid.*, II, 254.

40. *Ibid.*, II, 248.

41. *An Interpretation of Christian Ethics*, p. 205.

42. *Ibid.*, p. 110.

43. *Ibid.*, p. 147.

44. *Ibid.*, p. 204.

45. Jacques Maritain, *Man and the State* (Chicago: The University of Chicago Press, 1951), pp. 91, 94, *et passim*.

46. *Ibid.*, Footnote 13, p. 98 (italics in the original).

47. *An Interpretation of Christian Ethics*, p. 112.

48. *Op. cit.*, Footnote 13, p. 98 (italics in the original).

49. "Love and Law in Protestantism and Catholicism," *loc. cit.*, p. 152.

50. *An Interpretation of Christian Ethics*, pp. 108, 149, 150, 196.

51. Cf. Maritain, *The Rights of Man and Natural Law*, p. 20 (italics in the original).

52. *An Interpretation of Christian Ethics*, p. 109.

53. *Ibid.*, p. 149.

54. *Ibid.*, pp. 149, 150.

55. *Ibid.*, p. 196.

56. *Op. cit.*, p. 70 (italics in the original).

57. *An Interpretation of Christian Ethics*, pp. 144, 146.

58. *Ibid.*, p. 147 (italics mine).

59. "Love and Law in Protestantism and Catholicism," *loc. cit.*, p. 173.

60. *The Children of Light and the Children of Darkness* (New York: Charles Scribner's Sons, 1944), pp. 77-78, n. 8.

61. *Ibid.*, pp. 68, 74.

62. *Ibid.*, p. 71.

63. *Ibid.*, p. 77 (italics mine).

64. P. 131.

65. Pp. 188-190.

66. *Christian Realism and Political Problems*, p. 135.

67. "Love and Law in Protestantism and Catholicism," *loc. cit.*, pp. 160-161.

68. *Op. cit.* (New York: Harper & Brothers, 1949).

69. *Ibid.*, pp. 133ff.

70. *Ibid.*, pp. 151, 152.

71. *Ibid.*, p. 168.

72. *Ibid.*, p. 71 (italics mine).

73. *Ibid.*, pp. 75, 76.

74. *Faith and History*, p. 178 (italics mine).

75. *The Nature and Destiny of Man*, Vol. II, Chap. III, p. 82.

76. *Ibid.*, Vol. II, Chap. IX, p. 247 (italics mine), where he is summarizing his earlier discussion (Vol. II, Chap. III, pp. 81-90) of the relations between the two loves.

77. *Ibid.*, Vol. II, Chap. III, p. 82 (italics mine). Cf. also *Faith and History*, p. 185.

78. *An Interpretation of Christian Ethics*, pp. 128-129.

79. *The Nature and Destiny of Man*, Vol. II, Chap. III, p. 88 (italics mine).

80. *Ibid.*, Vol. II, Chap. IX, p. 246.

81. Jacques Maritain, *The Rights of Man and Natural Law*, p. 63 (italics mine), and especially the interpretation of Maritain's revision of this treatise in his *Man and the State* given below, ch. 8.

82. *The Nature and Destiny of Man*, I, 277.

83. *Faith and History*, p. 193.

84. Review of Fromm, *Man for Himself*. *Christianity and Society*, Spring, 1948, p. 27.

85. *Inter alia*, p. 290 of Vol. I of *The Nature and Destiny of Man*, where he considers and partially rejects (or rather only partially accepts) the view that not by natural endowment does man learn that faith, trust, and love are the requirement of human freedom.

86. *Christianity and Society*, Spring, 1948, pp. 27-28.

87. *Faith and History*, p. 177.

88. Cf. Charles N. Cochraine's tribute to St. Augustine in his *Christianity and Classical Culture* (Oxford: Clarendon Press, 1940), p. 360.

89. *The Nature and Destiny of Man*, Vol. II, Chap. III, p. 81 (italics mine).

90. *Ibid.*, p. 84, Note 16.

91. *Ibid.*, p. 255-266, Note 8.

92. Herbert Butterfield, *Christianity, Diplomacy, and War* (New York: Abingdon-Cokesbury Press, 1938), p. 8.

Six

H. Richard Niebuhr
Christ Transforming Relativism

1. "Evangelical and Protestant Ethics" in *The Heritage of the Reformation* (New York: R. R. Smith, 1950), p. 222.

2. "The Center of Value" in *Radical Monotheism and Western Culture* (New York: Harper & Brothers, 1960), pp. 100, 103, 107.

3. *Ibid.*, pp. 108-109.

4. *Ibid.*, pp. 109, 110 (first italics mine).

5. *Ibid.*, p. 110.

6. "Value-Theory and Theology" in *The Nature of Religious Experience* (sym-

posium in honor of D. C. Macintosh) (New York: Harper & Brothers, 1937), pp. 105-106.

7. "The Center of Value," p. 113.

8. *Ibid.*, p. 112.

9. "Value-Theory and Theology," p. 109.

10. *Ibid.*, pp. 115-116.

11. "The Responsibility of the Church for Society" in *The Gospel, the Church and the World*, ed. by Kenneth Scott Latourette (The Interseminary Series, vol. 3; New York: Harper & Brothers, 1946), p. 114.

12. *Ibid.*, pp. 115-116.

13. *Ibid.*, pp. 116, 117.

14. *Ibid.*, pp. 119-120.

15. "The Hidden Church and the Churches in Sight," *Religion in Life*, XV, No. 1 (Winter, 1945-46), pp. 115-116 (first italics mine).

16. *Christ and Culture* (New York: Harper & Brothers, 1951), pp. 18-19.

17. *Ibid.*, p. 28.

18. *The Meaning of Revelation* (New York: The Macmillan Company, 1946), p. 165 (italics mine).

19. *Ibid.*, pp. 166-167 (italics mine).

20. *Ibid.*, p. 168 (italics mine).

21. *Loc. cit.*

22. *Ibid.*, p. 169.

23. Cf. *ibid.*, pp. 170-171.

24. *Ibid.*, p. 172.

25. Pp. 11-29.

26. "Reflections on Faith, Hope and Love" (an unpublished paper).

27. *Loc. cit.*

28. *Christ and Culture*, p. 15 and n. 13.

29. *Ibid.*, p. 24.

30. *Ibid.*, pp. 16, 19, 21-22, 23, 25.

31. *Ibid.*, p. 27.

32. "Value-Theory and Theology," p. 113.

33. *Ibid.*, p. 106.

34. *Loc. cit.*

35. *Op. cit.*, p. 38.

36. *Ibid.*, p. 37.

37. *Ibid.*, pp. 7-8 (italics mine).

38. *Ibid.*, pp. 9-10.

39. *Ibid.*, p. 13.

40. *Ibid.*, p. 16.

41. *Ibid.*, p. 17.

42. *Ibid.*, p. vii.

43. *Ibid.*, p. 18-19.

44. *Ibid.*, p. 58.

45. *Ibid.*, p. 21.

46. *Ibid.*, p. 79.

47. *Ibid.*, pp. 19-20.

48. *Ibid.*, pp. 10-11 (italics mine).

49. *Ibid.*, p. 11 (italics mine).

50. *Ibid.*, p. 84-85.

51. *Ibid.*, p. 88.

52. *Ibid.*, p. 48.

53. "Life is Worth Living," *Intercollegian and Far Horizons*, LVII, No. 1 (October, 1939), p. 4.

54. *Culture and Faith* (Chicago: University of Chicago Press, 1951), p. 269.

55. P. viii.

56. "The Nature and Existence of God," *Motive*, IV (December, 1943), p. 46.

57. *Op. cit.*, pp. 112-3.

58. *Op. cit.*, pp. 107-108.

59. *Ibid.*, p. 114.

60. *Ibid.*, pp. 115, 116.

61. *Op. cit.*, pp. 152-153.

62. "Value-Theory and Theology," p. 114.

63. *The Meaning of Revelation*, p. 188.

64. "The Nature and Existence of God," p. 3 (italics mine).

65. *The Meaning of Revelation*, p. 151 (italics mine).

66. *Ibid.*, p. 175.

67. *Christ and Culture*, p. x.

68. *Ibid.*, p. 11.

69. *Ibid.*, p. 33.

70. *Ibid.*, p. 14.

71. *Ibid.*, p. 2.

72. *Ibid.*, p. 232.

73. Emil Brunner, *Justice and the Social Order* (New York: Harper & Brothers, 1945), pp. 60-61.

74. "Toward a New Other-Worldliness, *Theology Today*, I, No. 1 (April, 1944), p. 79.

75. *Ibid.*, p. 84.

76. New York: Harper & Brothers, 1938.

77. London: Oxford University Press, 1940.

78. London: The Lutterworth Press, 1937, and Philadelphia: The Westminster Press.

79. New York: Harper & Brothers, 1945.

80. *Dogmatics* (Philadelphia: The Westminster Press, 1952), vol. II.

81. *Justice and the Social Order*, chap. 9.

82. *Christ and Culture*, p. 145.

83. *Ibid.*, p. 146.

84. Cf. *ibid.*, p. 102.

85. *Loc. cit.*

86. Appendix I in Otto Gierke's *Natural Law and the Theory of Society 1500-1800* (trans. by Earnest Barker; Cambridge University Press, 1934), vol. I, pp. 201ff.

87. Cf. *Christ and Culture*, p. 145.

88. *Ibid.*, p. 192.

89. *Ibid.*, p. 193.

90. *Ibid.*, p. 194 (italics mine).

91. *Ibid.*, pp. 208-209 (italics mine).

92. *Ibid.*, p. 209.

93. Charles N. Cochrane: *Christianity and Classical Culture* (Oxford: Clarendon Press, 1940), p. 360. Cf. Herbert Butterfield: *Christianity in European History* (New York: The Macmillan Company, 1953), pp. 13-14.

Seven

Paul Tillich and Emil Brunner
Christ Transforming Natural Justice

1. *The City of God*, Book XIX, ch. xxiv.
2. *Utilitarianism*, ch. 2 (*The English Philosophers from Bacon to Mill*, ed. E. A. Burtt. Modern Library editions. New York: Random House, 1939, p. 903).
3. *Ethics*. New York: Macmillan, 1955.
4. Subtitle: *Ontological Analyses and Ethical Applications*, New York: Oxford University Press, 1954.
5. *Ibid.*, p. 48-9.
6. *Ibid.*, p. 8.
7. *Ibid.*, p. 110.
8. *Ibid.*, p. 25 (italics mine).
9. *Ibid.*, p. 22.
10. *Ibid.*, p. 109.
11. *Ibid.*, p. 107.
12. *Ibid.*, p. 116.
13. Repeated several times, *ibid.*, pp. 6, 33-4, 51-3, 69-70.
14. *Ibid.*, pp. 51-2.
15. *Ibid.*, p. 116.
16. *Ibid.*, p. 30.
17. *Ibid.*, pp. 27-8.
18. *Ibid.*, p. 77 (italics mine).
19. *Ibid.*, p. 41.
20. *Ibid.*, p. 48.
21. *Ibid.*, p. 56.
22. *Ibid.*, p. 16.
23. *Ibid.*, p. 42.
24. *Ibid.*, p. 56.
25. *Ibid.*, p. 57.
26. *Ibid.*, p. 63.
27. *Ibid.*, p. 60.
28. *Ibid.*, p. 63.
29. *Ibid.*, p. 64.
30. *Ibid.*, p. 64.
31. *Ibid.*, pp. 81-2.
32. *Ibid.*, p. 80.
33. *Ibid.*, p. 10 (italics mine).
34. *Ibid.*, pp. 82-83.
35. *Ibid.*, p. 71.
36. *Ibid.*, p. 15. Cf. pp. 13-15.
37. *Ibid.*, p. 83.
38. *Ibid.*, p. 15.
39. *Ibid.*, p. 88.
40. *Ibid.*, p. 82.
41. *Ibid.*, p. 113. The word *un*necessary is a misprint.
42. *Ibid.*, p. 13.

43. *Ibid.*, p. 14 (italics mine).
44. *Ibid.*, p. 64.
45. *Ibid.*, p. 65.
46. *Ibid.*, p. 66.
47. *Ibid.*, p. 84-6.
48. *Ibid.*, p. 83.
49. *Ibid.*, pp. 116-119.
50. *Ibid.*, p. 86.
51. *Ibid.*, p. 120.
52. *Ibid.*, p. 108 (italics mine).
53. *Ibid.*, p. 110 (italics mine).
54. *Ibid.*, p. 111 (italics mine).
55. Edmond Cahn: *The Sense of Injustice.* New York: New York University Press, 1949; and *The Moral Decision.* Bloomington, Indiana: Indiana University Press, 1955.
56. *Justice and the Social Order.* New York: Harper & Brothers, 1945, p. 121.
57. *Ibid.*, pp. 126-7.
58. *Ibid.*, p. 125.
59. *Ibid.*, p. 128.
60. *Ibid.*, pp. 128-9 (italics mine).
61. *Ibid.*, p. 129.
62. *Ibid.*, p. 130.
63. *Ibid.*, p. 130.
64. *Ibid.*, ch. 13, pp. 96-109.
65. *Ibid.*, p. 129.
66. *Ibid.*, p. 117.
67. *Ibid.*, p. 129.
68. *Ibid.*, p. 29.
69. *Ibid.*, p. 129.
70. *Ibid.*, p. 27.
71. *Ibid.*, pp. 25-6.
72. *Ibid.*, p. 39.
73. *Ibid.*, p. 20.
74. *The Divine Imperative.* London: The Lutterworth Press, 1937, p. 210.
75. *Ibid.*, p. 212.
76. *Ibid.*, p. 214-5.
77. *Ibid.*, p. 223.
78. *Ibid.*, pp. 217-8.
79. *Ibid.*, p. 225.
80. *Ibid.*, p. 225 (last italics the author's).
81. *Ibid.*, p. 228.
82. *Ibid.*, p. 229.
83. *Ibid.*, Proposition to ch. XXI, p. 208.
84. *Ibid.*, p. 221.
85. *Ibid.*, p. 223.
86. *Ibid.*, p. 224.
87. *Ibid.*, pp. 398-9.
88. *Ibid.*, Proposition to ch. XXI, p. 208.
89. *Ibid.*, p. 214.
90. *Ibid.*, p. 215.
91. *Ibid.*, p. 217.
92. *Ibid.*, p. 218.
93. *Loc. cit.*
94. *Ibid.*, p. 230.
95. *Ibid.*, p. 231 (italics mine).

96. *Ibid.*, p. 228.
97. *Ibid.*, p. 233 (italics mine).
98. *Ibid.*, p. 227 (italics mine).
99. *Ibid.*, p. 223.
100. *Ibid.*, pp. 209, 220, 232 (italics mine).
101. *Ibid.*, p. 85 (italics mine).
102. *The Christian Doctrine of Creation and Redemption. Dogmatics,* vol. II. Philadelphia, Penn.: The Westminster Press, 1952, p. 317.
103. *Ibid.*, p. 321.
104. *Ibid.*, p. 320.

Eight

Jacques Maritain and Edmond Cahn
The Egypt of the Natural Law

1. Jacques Maritain, *Man and the State.* Chicago, Illinois: University of Chicago Press, 1951, pp. 88-9.
2. Cf. Emil Brunner, *Justice and the Social Order.* New York: Harper & Brothers, 1945, pp. 60-61.
3. Cf. the section entitled "The Right to Be Young" in Edmond Cahn's *The Moral Decision: Right and Wrong in the Light of American Law.* Bloomington, Indiana: Indiana University Press, 1955, pp. 72-7.
4. J.-J. Rousseau, *The Social Contract,* Bk. I, ch. vi (Everyman), p. 15.
5. *Naim v. Naim,* 197 Va. 80, 87 S.E. 2d 749, remanded 350 U.S. 891 (1955), motion to recall denied 350 U.S. 985, reheard in the state court 197 Va. 734, 90 S.E. 2d 849 (1956).
6. Until *Perez v. Sharp* the constitutionality of miscegenation statutes was generally conceded. In this case, the state court declared that, while marriage is subject to regulation by the state, if its laws are discriminatory and irrational they unconstitutionally restrict "not only religious liberty, but the liberty of marriage as well" [32 Cal. 2d. 711, 198 P. 2d 17, 18 (1948), and cf. "The Constitutionality of Miscegenation Statutes," *Howard Law Journal,* vol. 1, no. 1 (Jan., 1955), pp. 87-100].
7. Gooch, George Peabody: *English Democratic Thought in the Seventeenth Century,* Cambridge University Press, 1927, p. 156.
8. Gen. 9: 6,7 and Deut. 30: 11-14 were also cited as scriptural endorsements of the natural law.
9. New York: Charles Scribner's Sons, 1943, p. 62.
10. *Ibid.*, p. 62-3.
11. *Ibid.*, p. 63 (italics mine).
12. *Ibid.*, pp. 60, 61.
13. *Ibid.*, p. 62.
14. *Ibid.*, p. 69.
15. *Ibid.*, p. 63.
16. *Ibid.*, p. 70.
17. *Ibid.*, p. 69.
18. *Ibid.*, p. 70.
19. *Ibid.*, p. 7 (italics mine).
20. Chicago, Illinois: The University of Chicago Press, 1951.
21. *Ibid.*, p. 98, note 13.

22. *Ibid.*, p. 82-3.

23. *Ibid.*, p. 89.

24. *Ibid.*, p. 91.

25. *Ibid.*, pp. 91-2.

26. *Ibid.*, p. 96.

27. *Ibid.*, p. 98.

28. *Ibid.*, p. 98, note 13.

29. *Ibid.*, p. 91, note 11 (middle italics mine).

30. Italics mine.

31. *Ibid.*, p. 98, note 13.

32. *Ibid.*, pp. 90, 97-8.

33. *Ibid.*, p. 92.

34. *Ibid.*, p. 94.

35. *Ibid.*, p. 94.

36. *Ibid.*, p. 98-9.

37. *Ibid.*, p. 98, note 13.

38. Read to the *Society of Metaphysics*, February 24, 1951, and published in *The Range of Reason* (New York: Charles Scribner's Sons, 1952), ch. 3, pp. 22-29.

39. *Ibid.*, p. 26.

40. *Ibid.*, p. 24.

41. *Ibid.*, p. 28.

42. *Ibid.*, p. 22.

43. *Ibid.*, p. 28.

44. *Ibid.*, p. 28.

45. *Ibid.*, p. 27.

46. *Ibid.*, p. 26.

47. *Ibid.*, p. 27.

48. *Ibid.*, p. 27 (italics mine).

49. *Ibid.*, p. 27.

50. *Ibid.*, pp. 22, 26.

51. *Ibid.*, p. 23 (italics mine).

52. Subtitle: *Right and Wrong in the Light of American Law*. Bloomington, Indiana: Indiana University Press, 1955.

53. New York: New York University Press, 1949.

54. *Op. cit.*, p. 244.

55. *Ibid.*, p. 10.

56. *Ibid.*, p. 4 *et passim*.

57. *Ibid.*, p. 17.

58. *Ibid.*, p. 3.

59. *Ibid.*, pp. 11, 34.

60. *Ibid.*, p. 176.

61. *Ibid.*, p. 149 (italics mine).

62. *Ibid.*, p. 14.

63. *Ibid.*, p. 24.

64. *Ibid.*, p. 42.

05. *Ibid.*, p. 24.

66. *Ibid.*, pp. 24, 26, 102.

67. *The Moral Decision*, pp. 243, 254 (italics mine).

68. Edmond Cahn: *The Predicament of Democratic Man* (New York: The Macmillan Co., 1961), p. 14.

69. *The Sense of Injustice*, p. 11.

70. *Ibid.*, p. 6.

71. *Ibid.*, pp. 26, 175.

72. William Graham Cole, *Sex in Christianity and Psychoanalysis.* New York: Oxford University Press, 1955, p. 296.

73. *Justice and the Social Order.* New York: Harper & Brothers, 1954, p. 1.

74. Edmond Cahn, "Authority and Responsibility," *Columbia Law Review,* vol. 51, p. 838-51; *The Moral Decision,* p. 300-312.

75. Cf. *Meinhard v. Salmon,* 249 N.Y. 458, 164 N.E. 545 (1928).

76. *Wagner v. International Railway Co.,* 232 N.Y. 176 (1921).

77. Edmond Cahn, *The Moral Decision,* p. 308.

78. Cf. above, note on p. 227.

Nine

Jacques Maritain and Edmond Cahn
Man's Exodus from the Natural Law

1. Louisiana State University Press, 1956.

2. *Op. cit.,* p. 123, 130, 235, *et passim.*

3. *Ibid.,* p. 116.

4. *Ibid.,* p. 130.

5. *Ibid.,* p. 194.

6. *Ibid.,* p. 180.

7. *Ibid.,* p. 417.

8. *Ibid.,* p. 355.

9. *Ibid.,* p. 113.

10. *Ibid.,* p. 130.

11. *Ibid.,* p. 247.

12. *Ibid.,* p. 439.

13. Martin Buber, "Der Preis," *Der Jude,* October 1917, quoted by Will Herberg, ed., *The Writings of Martin Buber,* p. 31.

14. Robertson, *Religious Ideas of the Old Testament,* ch. III.

15. Cf. Eric Voegelin, *op. cit.,* pp. 315-6.

16. *Man and the State,* p. 161, note 17.

17. *Ibid.,* p. 169, note 25 (continued on p. 170). Perhaps it is not insignificant that these opinions are hidden away as minor modifications in footnotes.

18. *The Person and the Common Good,* quoted in *The Social and Political Philosophy of Jacques Maritain* (ed. Joseph W. Evans and Leo R. Ward), New York: Scribner's, 1955, p. 35. Cf. p. 86.

19. *Ibid.,* pp. 82, 86.

20. Cf. *The Rights of Man and Natural Law.* New York: Charles Scribner's Sons, 1943, pp. 11-17, *et passim.*

21. *Ibid.,* p. 17. Cf. pp. 76-7.

22. *The Methods of Ethics.* 7th Ed. London: Macmillan and Co., Ltd., 1913, ch. XIII.

23. Gabriel Marcel, *Man Against Mass Society* (Chicago: Henry Regnery Co., 1952), p. 165.

24. *Man and the State,* p. 74 (italics mine).

25. *Ibid.,* p. 73 (italics mine).

26. *Ibid.,* p. 18.

27. Jacques Maritain, *The Range of Reason.* New York: Charles Scribner's Sons, 1952, p. 28.

28. *Church Dogmatics* (Edinburgh: T. & T. Clark, 1958), III, 1, sec. 41, 2, 3.

29. 26 Fed. Cas. 360 (C.C.E.D. Pa. 1842); *The Moral Decision*, pp. 61-71.

30. This and subsequent quotations concerning this case are taken from *The Moral Decision*, pp. 70-71.

31. *The Fundamental Principles of the Metaphysic of Ethics.* New York: Appleton-Century-Crofts Co,. 1938, p. 47.

32. *Concerning Civil Government*, ch. 2.

33. *Ibid.*, p. 243.

34. Summary of Rudolf Bultmann, *Primitive Christianity.* Living Age Books. New York: Meridian Books, 1956, pp. 74, 78, 92.

35. *The Moral Decision*, p. 195.

36. *Ibid.*, p. 240.

37. *Ibid.*, p. 191.

38. *Ibid.*, p. 243.

39. *Ibid.*, p. 71.

40. Alan Keenan and John Ryan: Marriage: *A Medical and Sacramental Study.* New York: Sheed and Ward, 1955, p. 53.

41. Cf. Paul Ramsey, *Basic Christian Ethics.* New York: Charles Scribner's Sons, 1950, pp. 171-84; and *War and the Christian Conscience: How Shall Modern War be Conducted Justly?* Durham, North Carolina: Duke University Press, 1961, ch. 3.

42. Cf. Keenan and Ryan, *op. cit.*, pp. 108-110, and Davis, *Moral and Pastoral Theology*, vol. II, p. 171f.

43. "Infanticide should be dealt with as a psychiatric and social problem and not as a problem for the criminal law." John Dollard, Review of *The Sanctity of Life and the Criminal Law*, by Glanville Williams. *New York Times Book Review*, July 14, 1957, p. 20.